Terminate Terrorism

International Studies Intensives
Mark A. Boyer, Series Editor

International Studies Intensives (ISI) is a book series that springs from the desire to keep students engaged in the world around them. Books in the series address a wide array of topics in the international studies field, all devoted to getting students involved in the ways in which international events affect their daily lives. ISI books focus on innovative topics and approaches to study that cover popular and scholarly debates and employ new methods for presenting theories and concepts to students and scholars alike. ISI books pack a lot of information into a small space—they are meant to offer an intensive introduction to subjects often left out of the curriculum. ISI books are relatively short, visually attractive, and affordably priced.

Editorial Board

Titles in the Series

Forthcoming in the Series

Terminate Terrorism

Framing, Gaming, and Negotiating Conflicts

Karen A. Feste

Paradigm Publishers

Boulder • London

Copyright © 2010 Paradigm Publishers

Published in the United States by Paradigm Publishers, 3360 Mitchell Lane Suite E, Boulder, CO 80301 USA.

Paradigm Publishers is the trade name of Birkenkamp & Company, LLC, Dean Birkenkamp, President and Publisher.

Cataloging-in-Publication Data is available at the Library of Congress.
ISBN 978-1-59451-821-8 (hardcover : alk. paper)
ISBN 978-1-59451-822-5 (paperback : alk. paper)

Printed and bound in the United States of America on acid-free paper that meets the standards of the American National Standard for Permanence of Paper for Printed Library Materials.

Designed by Straight Creek Bookmakers.
Typeset by Raese Design.
Editorial production by the Book Factory.

14 13 12 11 10 1 2 3 4 5

To Serge

Contents

List of Tables

Terminating Terrorism

The Problem

On September 11, 1990, President George H. W. Bush, father of his namesake-successor George W., delivered a major address to Congress that unveiled ambitious plans for a "New World Order." Less than a year earlier, the Cold War had come to an end—not with a bang, but a ripple—through a series of fast-moving events that transformed the bipolar international system anchored in U.S.–USSR ideological confrontation and balance of power conflict, into a unipolar, American-dominated world. The challenge for U.S. leadership at the start of the post–Cold War period was to grasp how the world had changed and whether American foreign policy should focus on maintaining stability or adopting new visions. Bush's landmark speech, broadcast on national television by all major networks, outlined a future of global peace based on spreading democracy, free trade expansion, and governance through rule of law. Nations would share responsibility for freedom and justice—the strong respecting rights of the weak. It was a speech of victory: a proud moment in the life of America, timed perfectly to reflect new political dynamics. In the fall of 1990, U.S. Secretary of State James Baker had begun to assemble an international coalition of military forces drawn from both sides of the previous East-West divide in the campaign to liberate Kuwait from Iraqi occupation following the August 2 invasion by Saddam Hussein's forces; thousands of troops from more than thirty countries would shortly be dispatched to the Middle East, poised to fight a common enemy. Not all states were eager to join; the American promise of economic aid or debt forgiveness persuaded them. Within a few months, more than 500,000 U.S. forces alone would be deployed in the vicinity, mostly in neighboring Saudi Arabia, a solid American ally. In the brief January–February 1991 Persian Gulf War that followed, victory over Iraq came quickly and easily. Allied casualties were light. Moreover, in managing the first major international conflict of the new global era, the world had passed a milestone: the United Nations, freed from Cold War stalemate, could fulfill the vision of its founders, activating its role to punish aggressors and secure global peace. The United States, sole standing superpower, would lead the way.

Was the American president promising a structure of international relations based on a revitalized set of rules—respect for international law? Or, did the phrase "New World Order" merely signify a bid for supporting American intervention policy and traditional power politics? Interpretations vary. Ten years after the 1991 Gulf War ended, several thousand American troops still remained in oil-rich Saudi Arabia—a military situation that began to assume the shape of a permanent presence. The occupation policy linked two objectives: U.S. interests to protect and secure energy resources for the West, and Saudi Arabian officials' interest in maintaining power and regime stability in its closed political system. Designed to uphold the status quo, the dovetailed plan was not welcomed by everyone. Opposition from Saudi Arabian citizens who lived inside the country and beyond, voiced concerns over a policy that restricted possibilities for government reform and societal independence; long-standing and newly sprouting Islamic-based political groups in neighboring Middle East countries expressed resentment over the continued, commanding American influence in the region. Throughout the 1990s, American military presence in the Middle East and the tight U.S.–Saudi Arabian relationship, combined with ongoing, generous foreign aid the United States gave each year to Egypt and Israel (conditioned by the Camp David Accords of the late 1970s to help resolve the chronic Arab-Israeli dispute—the two countries were usually the top recipients of U.S. financial assistance distributed worldwide), produced a strong-winded, lethal current of anti-American "blowback," unintended policy consequences. Blowback manifested most vividly in a series of terrorist attacks directed against the United States.

Terrorism was designated as "the enemy of our generation," by President Bill Clinton in 1996. During his years in office, the number of Americans killed each year by international terrorists averaged fewer than fourteen (Bacevich 2002, 119), yet a small number of notable incidents—the 1993 World Trade Center bombing in New York; the Oklahoma City federal building bombing in 1995; the Khobar Towers bombing at the U.S. military compound in Saudi Arabia in 1996; the U.S. embassy bombings in Kenya and Tanzania in 1998; the bombing of the USS *Cole*, a Navy ship docked in Yemen, in 2000—provided evidence that terrorism was on the rise and becoming more ominous.

On September 11, 2001, the eleventh anniversary of Bush's "New World Order" speech, nineteen Arab Muslim hijackers commandeered four commercial aircraft in the United States and in suicide terrorist acts crashed them into the World Trade Center in New York and the Pentagon in Washington, DC. Another jet was downed in a Pennsylvania field. The worst international terrorist attack ever, nearly three thousand people died. Citizens of more than fifty countries perished at the World Trade Center site. American officials declared that Osama bin Laden—a wealthy Saudi Arabian exile with former close ties to Saudi royalty—as founder and leader of al Qaeda, an opposition terrorist group operating out of Afghanistan, was responsible for the tragedy. Shortly afterward, President George W. Bush (firstborn son of the elder President Bush), who had assumed the top American national executive post following U.S. elections in 2000, was delivering *his* landmark speech to Congress, crafting the Global War on Terrorism. Some of the concepts resembled those stressed by his father a decade earlier, notably the importance of freedom and American values. But the tone of younger President Bush's message was somber, impatient, and resolute. It was not a victory speech, but a call to arms: "Our war on terror begins with al Qaeda, but it does not end there. It will not end until every terrorist group of global reach has been found, stopped, and defeated. . . . Every nation in every region now has a decision to make. From this day forward, any nation that continues to harbor or support terrorism will be regarded by the United States as a hostile regime." Virtually every country condemned the terrorist attacks; many joined another American-led coalition, this time with terrorism as the common enemy. A strategy was designed to fight it on several fronts by using a variety of power instruments, including diplomatic, economic, intelligence, law enforcement, and military tools.

Operation Enduring Freedom launched a U.S. combat mission into war in Afghanistan on October 7, 2001. The first targets were al Qaeda training camps as Islamic extremists from North America, Europe, Africa, the Middle East, and Central, South, and Southeast Asia had used Afghanistan as a training ground and base of operations for worldwide terrorist activities, and military installations of the Islamic fundamentalist Taliban regime. Within months, the Taliban government was driven from power. Several thousand al Qaeda operatives were arrested or detained in more than one hundred countries, their organization weakened. But key terrorist leaders—Osama bin Laden and Ayman Zawahiri among them—escaped. Terrorism threats did not disappear.

In March 2003, the United States invaded Iraq. Part of its mission objective was dedicated to continue fighting the war on terrorism. Military intervention brought early success: American-led coalition forces took control of the entire country within a few months; numerous members of the ousted Baathist regime, including its leader Saddam Hussein were killed or captured within the next two years; and a new U.S.-friendly, democratic-oriented government was brought into office. But victory was short lived. Insurgency spread as al Qaeda forces and their sympathizers launched a series of mass casualty terrorist attacks inside Iraq. Although an important mastermind strategist, Abu Musab Zarqawi, the al Qaeda leader in Iraq, was killed in June 2006, fighting did not end. And in countries around the world, along with a string of uncovered violent plots, terrorist cells seemed to proliferate.

The first decade of the twenty-first century has not brought global peace. Seen through U.S. eyes and the eyes of others, world conflict dominates the international landscape: the war in Afghanistan, the war in Iraq, and the "Global War on Terror" have figured prominently. Faded and dated, the "New World Order" concept envisioned by the elder President Bush is a fleeting memory. The Global War on Terror (GWOT), a popularized phrase characterizing policies developed by the administration of the younger President Bush in the wake of the September 11 attacks, was abandoned within months after President Barack Obama assumed office in 2009. In late March 2009, the Defense Department replaced GWOT with "Overseas

Contingency Operations." On August 6, 2009, John Brennan, the president's top counterterrorism advisor, delivered a speech, stating that while the United States is at war with al Qaeda, portraying it in global terms reinforces precisely the image this group is seeking to project of a highly organized worldwide entity capable of overtaking sovereign nations. The conflict should not be called a global war. Whether these differences in terminology are real, heralding a new American approach to deal with the issue, or cosmetic in nature, preserving a perception of change in the Democratic administration while continuing George W. Bush's counterterrorism strategies, remains an open question. In any case, the enemy is elusive, and terrorist threats loom large in the current U.S. security framework.

What is the relationship between America's superpower position in the international system and the international terrorism leveled against it? Are threats inevitable? In 1997, a U.S. government report, "The Defense Science Board 1997 Summer Study Task Force on DOD Responses to Transnational Threats," concluded that a strong correlation exists between greater American involvement in international situations and increased terrorist attacks directed at United States' targets. Only a year before the 9/11 attacks, Chalmers Johnson in his book *Blowback* (2000, 29) underscored this connection when he predicted the United States would be a prime target of terrorist attacks against Americans. Examining terrorism incidents against American interests between 1968 and 1996, Sobek and Braithwaite (2005) found a consistent, positive relationship between American preeminence—measured in various forms—and the number of terrorist attacks. They hypothesized that as American security against other states increases, security against terrorist groups decreases, explaining that United States' dominance restricts opportunities for revisionist views within the system to be heard, which, in turn, encourages such actors to employ unconventional methods, including tactics of terrorism. Supporting this argument, Cortright and Lopez (2007, 249) assert that extensive American presence in the Middle East arouses intense feelings of resentment, sparking a surge in anti-Americanism that fuels political radicalization and creates ripe conditions for terrorism to take root.

American global dominance will probably last until year 2040, according to one carefully considered estimate (Fry 2007), implying terrorism threats to American interests are not likely to disappear soon. The problem requires vigilant attention. President George W. Bush in his final State of the Union address to Congress and the nation in January 2008 tried to reassure the public, promising that "We will stay on the offense, we will keep up the pressure, and we will deliver justice to our enemies." In a major speech to the Republican National Convention in 2004, Arnold Schwarzenegger, governor of California, put it more bluntly when he urged everyone to "be fierce and relentless and terminate terrorism."

What does it mean to terminate terrorism? In this book, it refers to dissolving a terrorist conflict whereby the immediate threat to the citizens of the targeted country vanishes: hostages are freed unharmed, a skyjacking campaign comes to a halt, a pattern of suicide bombings ends. To terminate a terrorism problem does not imply that its root causes have been contained, destroyed, or smashed forever across the planet. Nor does it mean that in a given situation the disputing parties—a terrorist group, its state sponsor(s) and the targeted government—reconcile their differences overall, establish a long-term friendship, and become international allies, their big issues blown away or decimated. Rather, termination means the attacks of illegal violence against unsuspecting citizens framed around a particular contextual situation of issues and demands and carried out by politically motivated groups come to an end. How does a terrorism conflict reach this point?

Terrorism termination may result from a fight between players until a one-sided victory is determined and the opponent surrenders (either the target government or the terrorists win), although this outcome is relatively rare or short-lived. Usually the pathway to ending a terrorism problem or campaign is more complex and unfolds slowly in stages. The first step for the target society is to confront the problem—recognizing the magnitude and severity of the direct threat of terrorism and formulating strategies of response. In the early phase, target governments typically set up defensive and offensive counterterrorism plans in an effort to deter potential attacks and simultaneously fight it out with the enemy. But if these resistance policies fail to eliminate the threat, the sustained, costly, stalemated terrorism conflict scenario may eventually lead a government to consider other policy alternatives that they rejected in the past to end the problem. This process involves a fundamental shift in decision-makers' thinking: moving from cognitive framing (who are these evil perpetrators of violence, and why do they hate us?) to strategic gaming (how do we cut our losses and resolve this problem?). A gaming perspective sets up possibilities for parties to consider negotiating with their opponent and bargaining a nonviolent settlement. The first chapters deal with each of these stages separately, followed by an examination of several recent cases of anti-American terrorism conflict and their endings, and a chapter on the dynamics and trajectory of al Qaeda terrorism. In conclusion, insights drawn from the case studies along general theoretic guidelines provide the basis for assessing terrorism termination.

CHAPTER ONE

Confronting Terrorism
Anti-American Violence

Terrorism has emerged as the world's "most salient and worrisome form of combat" and will likely remain so indefinitely, according to Smelser (2007, 3). Nash (1998), in his expansive, narrative encyclopedia of twentieth-century terrorism, predicted this development a decade earlier. Even before the international system transitioned into its post–Cold War power constellation, Clutterbuck (1977, 3) had declared terrorism to be the conflict for our time. A number of analysts view terrorism not as an abnormality, but as part of politics with its own logic and dynamics: a rational strategy used by the weak to air their grievances and confront the strong. It constitutes a form of war—mass violence attacks designed to achieve political goals through the greatest public exposure, drawing attention to their cause (Crenshaw 1990; Pape 2003, 2005; Neumann and Smith 2005, 2008). A twenty-year update of *The U.S. Army and Marine Corps Counterinsurgency Field Manual* (2007, 109) adopts this perspective in describing the reasons why groups employ these combative techniques: "They do not use terrorist and guerrilla tactics because they are cowards afraid of a 'fair fight'; insurgents use these tactics because they are the best means available to achieve the insurgency's goals." Essentially, terrorists seek to bargain with their enemies by committing acts of unconventional violence, for war is a form of bargaining—an interactive process of power moves intended to readjust a party's position of strength in order to enable domination over its opponent and forge settlement in its favor.

Political terrorism acts—skyjacking, hostage barricade, kidnaps, bombings, shootouts, suicide attacks—are complicated attempts by violent individuals to communicate messages deeply important to them. Terrorists, states Corsi (1981, 49), "are involved in a drastic crossing of majority norms. This crossing implies the judgment that a given cause is sufficiently 'right' to justify extreme behavior . . . in which terrorists intend to create a dangerous and emotionally charged situation for themselves and others." They engage in strategic, not senseless, violence to threaten others through extortion and blackmail and to create a bargaining situation to achieve their goals.

A campaign of terror, while it may appear as random, senseless violence, aims at a specific target for a specific purpose. Terrorist strategy is designed to weaken the other, substantially more powerful, side striking at its vulnerabilities in order to rearrange particular power balancing in a way that gives terrorists some significant, coercive capacity to impel the absolutely stronger (but weakening) party to give in to its demands. If capitulation is beyond the realm of possibility, a more modest goal, namely forcing the opponent into concession-making compromises, takes hold. An overarching purpose of terrorism is to force a power dependency relationship in order to ensure a conflict settlement in line with its perpetrator's demands. The stronger party, cognizant of the instrumentalism behind terrorists' acts—aggression designed to anger and engage a sparring reaction from its intended target, hoping its victim will actually overreact to give terrorists a sense of justified victimhood that may widen public support and expand the recruitment of members to their cause—tries to prevent any political pressure of this nature. For this reason, response to early attacks may be met with quiet but intense resistance approaches (clandestine operations away from the public eye) to apprehend perpetrators and put them in custody, or even a conflict avoidance approach, choosing not to react by open confrontation, but to seek ways to halt operations through intelligence and surveillance methods, a deliberate policy reaction by the target to ignore terrorists' probes. If terrorists are persistent—filled with resolve, gaining confidence, and backed by growing political support achieved by a series of successful attacks designed to intimidate its target—the targeted opponent is likely to assume a defensive pose, erecting barriers to prevent further attacks, and installing deterrence mechanisms to reduce violence and enhance security. When defensive measures are deemed inadequate to meet the challenge, the government may take on an offensive posture, seeking actively to destroy the terrorist threat (through various forms of punishment, ranging from sanctions to direct military attack). At that point, the conflict transforms into a terrorism versus counterterrorism bargaining situation. Each side fights to achieve its desired objectives.

An act of political terrorism—violence designed exclusively to cause physical harm to unsuspecting persons and/or to destroy property, often of symbolic value in a society, carried out by individuals or small cadres as a mechanism for expressing grievances against the policies or actions of a government—involves a complicated communication and bargaining strategy by the perpetrators. Terrorism is intended to generate massive fear among citizens of a state. The fear is supposed to threaten the public and rattle their political awakening. Terrorism is also intended to threaten a government by creating blackmail-like pressure on decision makers to change their policies. Its purpose is securing government attention through coercive power techniques as a way to enter political discourse and affect policy choices. Attention-grabbing violence is a strategy for building awareness and reducing the perceived omniscient power of some despised political authority. As a security threat, it is the opposite of the nuclear one: little nuisance shots instead of a big bang. These acts are meant to affect a large audience in a given population, in essence, revealing the "theatrical" nature of terrorism. The Hollywood effect and the importance of the media in this communication process cannot be overemphasized. Individuals or groups that engage in such violent acts make a judgment that a given cause is sufficient to justify extreme behavior, including the willingness of perpetrators to be placed in physical jeopardy, creating a dangerous, emotionally charged situation for themselves and others.

Solving the problem of global terrorism is a complex policy issue that requires a variety of initiatives to bring it under control. Among these are the following: *strategies of resistance*—the defensive and offensive tactics that set up barriers against vulnerabilities (enacting antiterrorism laws and arresting perpetrators, engaging in combat against terrorist forces, or passively reacting by trying to avoid conflict engagement); *strategies of reform*—policies addressing root causes presumed to precipitate and explain violence such as poverty, a stagnant economy, and corrupt political rule (promoting foreign aid packages for economic growth and democracy training programs in countries at risk); and *strategies of revitalization*—international law and global security initiatives (creating multilateral treaties designed to curb terrorism, structuring international communication-information exchange mechanisms, and building strong counterterrorism alliances).

The U.S. Global War on Terror was designed to incorporate these features. "The National Strategy for Combating Terrorism" (September 2006), updated from the original February 2003 statement, outlines a program to prevent attacks by terrorist networks, deny weapons of mass destruction to terrorists, advance democracy as an antidote to terrorism ideology, and create structures to help ensure long-term success. But the policy (modified by the Obama administration) continues to face serious challenges: terrorism remains a central security problem that demands attention— siphoning significant levels of financial resources and technical talent—amid an atmosphere of public fear and political uncertainty. Neither the war in Afghanistan nor the war in Iraq has stopped terrorist violence, slowed the development of terrorist recruitment, or seriously dented the popular appeal of al Qaeda's ideological message. Attacks outside the American homeland directed against U.S. (or, more generally, Western) interests continue. Political violence in countries where regimes have close ties with the United States—Egypt, Pakistan, and the Philippines—has been commonplace.

Directed *strategies of resistance*—fighting against terrorist groups to defeat them— rarely achieve intended objectives, according to a major research study by Pape (2005), whose comprehensive work on worldwide suicide bomber campaigns between 1980–2003 shows that targeted governments tend to concede to terrorists' demands. Groups find it advantageous to use terrorism tactics because they succeed in bringing about political objectives, most often the goal is forcing an outsider to withdraw from territory it had claimed and ruled, often for generations. Such violence has also produced favorable results for terrorists in another way: Palestinians got a voice and a place at the settlement table only after engaging in a spate of terrorist activities against Israelis, who always choose to respond combatively in the manner of violent resistance. In this case, terrorist violence led to negotiations between the disputing parties; a powerful military response by the target failed to stop the drive toward this end.

Alternative *strategies of resistance*—setting up barriers to protect targets from attacks—fare better at one level, stopping or slowing terrorist attacks originating from special, identifiable sites, but produce other unexpected, negative consequences. Installation of metal detectors in airports and embassy fortifications, have not halted violence but merely moved it elsewhere where targets are more vulnerable, according to Sandler and Enders (2007). The introduction of metal screening of air travelers in the United States in January 1973 had an immediate, enduring effect of decreasing the number of U.S. hijack incidents, but this innovative technology intervention was also associated with an increase in hostage-taking incidents as terrorists reacted to barriers by switching their mode of attack to softer targets. Attacks against protected persons (diplomats accorded immunity by international law) fell as screening mechanisms were placed in embassies (after their introduction in airports), but more assassinations and attacks against embassy officials occurred in nonsecure venues.

Another *resistance strategy*, the passive approach of conflict avoidance—seeking to stop violence by ignoring the opportunity to engage perpetrators in combat, hoping the nuisance will go away—has also led to a dead end. The policy seemed to be in effect during the Clinton administration throughout the 1990s. During this period, violence was not halted; it escalated. President Clinton, in speeches and talks with journalists that followed various incidents, was careful neither to accuse particular political groups nor to incite public opinion about the growing terrorism problem. For example, at a press conference the day after the first World Trade Center bombing in February 1993 (six people dead and nearly one thousand injured), he was asked whether this was a terrorist incident, and he replied, "I'm not in a position to say that now. . . . I cannot answer your question yet." A few days later, when queried once more about the event, he said, "I don't want the American people to overreact to this at this time." In March 1993, prompted again about terrorism after arrests were made, Clinton said, "I don't think that you should assume anything until you hear the statement today . . . [we're] trying to get as much information together as possible to give you later. . . . " And, in an exchange with reporters, he said, "I think it is very important not to rush to judgment here, not to reach ahead of the facts." In April and June 1993, his response was consistent, and similarly evasive. Clinton's remarks after the Oklahoma bombing on April 19, 1995, adopted exactly the same line in remarks to reporters. Following the attack against Americans in Saudi Arabia in November 1995, an event that killed five and injured sixty people, the familiar script was repeated. His approach changed a little after the June 1996 Saudi Arabian attack against U.S. soldiers in Khobar Towers that killed nineteen and wounded five hundred, when he remarked, after stating "let's wait until we see what the facts are," that the United States needed to figure out how to enhance prevention and what could be done to detect explosives. Still, there was no hint of retaliation or conflict engagement.

After the August 1998 attacks on two American embassies in Africa, in Kenya and Tanzania, resulting in more than two hundred deaths with more than five thousand people injured, most of them non-U.S. citizens (a total of twelve Americans lost their life in these acts of violence), Clinton adopted a more militant tone, emphasizing terrorist pursuit and bringing the perpetrators to justice for their crimes. He ordered retaliation strikes in Afghanistan and Sudan aimed at facilities held by al Qaeda, which was identified as source of the attacks. But the retaliation policy was short lived. Fourteen months later, on October 12, 2000, the USS *Cole*, an American navy destroyer docked in a Yemen port, was hit in a terrorist explosion (killing seventeen sailors and wounding thirty-nine). Despite verbally expressed outrage over the incident, Clinton ordered no military response or other punitive actions. The president was a lame duck by this time; after eight years in office and the early November election that resulted in leadership turnover from Democratic to Republican Party control, Clinton may have been reluctant to embark on a conflict adventure that would influence policies of the incoming administration in the mid-January 2001 turnover. Once the new Bush administration assumed power, there was no further reaction to the terrorist event. A conflict avoidance strategy followed by the United States throughout the decade of the 1990s failed to achieve desired ends: the terrorism problem did not disappear.

Attacking terrorism under the rubric of *strategies of reform* by paying attention to its root causes—based on the ever-popular frustration-aggression thesis that terrorists act out of their own miserable circumstances in less-developed societies—has not been productive either. President George W. Bush's plan, announced in 2002 at the UN International Conference on Financing for Development, to channel billions of dollars in aid to countries committed to ruling justly, investing in their people, and encouraging economic freedom, was based on research by Burnside and Dollar (2000) who concluded that foreign aid promoted economic growth so long as the recipient government had solid fiscal, monetary, and trade policies in place. Easterly, Levine, and Roodman (2004) challenged this finding in their research, showing that aid may not promote growth in good policy environments. Further, U.S. foreign aid patterns actually confounded evaluation of the policy. Massive financial support packages to Pakistan, Jordan, and Turkey, for example, are designed to support the global war on terrorism, not necessarily to contribute to the domestic economic development within these states, putting a different emphasis on how funding is distributed. In addition, some of the largest U.S. recipients of foreign aid—Egypt, Pakistan, and the Philippines—have been frequent sites of terrorist activity. American largess has failed to tackle terrorism's roots. Political tensions run high, suggesting the reform strategy notion, at least in current manifestation, is not effective. Piazza (2006), analyzing various types of terrorism events across countries over the 1986–2002 period, concluded that social and economic poverty are not causal agents of unconventional violence; terrorists may be angry and discontent, but their state of mind stems from a particular desire for political power and control, not just a comfortable life.

Finally, with respect to *revitalized* global security initiatives, international laws against terrorism and collective engagement in combating it directly have not produced the expected results. Analyzing historical data from 1968 through 1988 on the relationship between terrorism incidents and UN resolutions and conventions against skyjacking, hostage-taking, and diplomatic immunity violations, Enders, Sandler, and Cauley (1990) discovered that none of the international conventions, UN Security Council or General Assembly Resolutions, had a significant impact (in either the short run or the long run) in reducing terrorism. They explain this puzzling outcome by suggesting that collective action may on occasion carry burdening private costs for individual state signatories who, consequently, may choose not to abide by the stated provisions. The United Nations Security Council counterterrorism resolutions against Libya, Sudan, and Afghanistan in the 1990s helped apply pressure on regimes that lent support for terrorist operations, though, as Cortright and Lopez (2007, 9) state, their role in mobilizing world public opinion against state-sponsored terrorism was not significant.

Since September 2001, the Security Council's mandated global campaign by all UN members to deny financing, travel, or other assistance to terrorists or those supporting them, has led to considerable expansion of UN committees and professional staffing devoted to fighting terrorism. But inefficiencies and contradictions of UN counterterrorism efforts have reduced their measure of effectiveness, conclude Cortright and Lopez (2007, 10–11), who admit as well that a global counterterrorism strategy will be a difficult, long-term process for "preventive strategies pose enormous challenges for multilateral organizations." Drawing a sharper conclusion, Sandler and Enders (2007, 294), updating their original twenty-year (1968–1988) study to include data of terrorist acts and UN countermeasures through 2005, found that international conventions and resolutions to outlaw attacks against diplomats, hostage taking, and bombings had no impact.

In sum, policies designed to curb terrorism through strategies of resistance, strategies of reform, or strategies of revitalized international cooperation have not been able to achieve the primary objective to reduce the international threats of terrorism to the United States and its Western allies.

Are there other ways to resolve the problem? Miller (2007) examined thirty-four terrorist organizations across the ideological spectrum (national-separatist, left-wing, right-wing, and religious-motivated groups), and compared five policy options for governments dealing with them: do nothing (conflict avoidance), make conciliatory moves (including negotiations), institute legal reform (expand police powers, create terrorism-specific laws), impose restrictions to limit terrorist acts (harden targets, increase intelligence gathering powers), and direct violence (use force to injure or kill perpetrators). He concluded that policy success, in most instances, partially depended on implementing restrictions and instituting legal reforms. But restrictions and legal reform were *also* present in the majority of failed policies! Conflict avoidance was not effective in stopping terrorism. Conciliation was successful only in national-separatist terrorist conflicts, though it was applied by states confronting all types of terrorism.

In conflict resolution theory, there are basically four ways to bring disputes to an end (Pruitt and Kim 2004, 5–6): (1) contending: the parties may fight until a victor is determined; (2) conflict avoidance: one side may choose to avoid entanglement or engagement, refusing to be drawn into a competitive, adversarial setting; (3) yielding: one side may concede to the other's demands, thus determining a winning party; or (4) problem-solving: the parties may work out their differences in ways that are intended to end in mutual gains. Thus far, U.S. reaction to the terrorism problem has utilized the first two of these options: contending and conflict avoidance. Neither has succeeded in defeating terrorism to the point where it is no longer regarded as a central threat, although standing alone, each of these approaches, often used in different situations, is considered a respectable, viable way to achieve objectives. The contending approach—strategies of resistance—may eventually bring about desired results, although whether they will last is hard to tell. The conflict avoidance approach of the Clinton administration was not effective. The option of yielding to terrorists' demands by giving up in a surrender scenario is rarely considered seriously; it would be perceived as a victory for terrorism. Its overtones connote weakness, powerlessness, and humiliation as well as the moral objection implied by giving in to a political player who prevails through illegitimate means of violence.

The fourth alternative, problem-solving, has yet to be tried. It differs from other options in requiring full commitment and joint participation by all major conflict participants. The strategy is impossible to implement unilaterally. All parties engaged in terrorism conflict are fearful of moving in this direction. Negotiations may require costly concessions, jeopardize individual visions of future security, and affect one's political identity. Smelser (2007, 80–87) portrays obstacles to problem-solving as the confrontation between terrorist and antiterrorist ideologies: each side engages in demonization, vilification, opposition of absolutes, and stigmatizing symbols in characterizing the other party. Combined with standard emotional features, namely resentment, anger, and revenge, nonviolent conflict resolving potential seems limited and remote.

Conflict narratives reinforce strategies of "contending" over strategies of "problem-solving" in the decisional repertoire of terrorists and their targets. Despite these barriers, negotiated settlement in terrorism conflicts is not uncommon. Dolnik and Fitzgerald (2008, 154), analyzing recent cases of hostage-taking, conclude that "even the 'new terrorists' prioritize a negotiated agreement over martyrdom." Around the world, negotiating political solutions to end international disputes and civil wars—conflicts that often include a strong insurgency component—is becoming far more popular (Mason 2007). In the United States, negotiation has also been key to ending conflicts of terrorism but only in those situations that involve *international* actors; it does not apply to ending *domestic*-based terrorist movements. Conflict resolution in American domestic based terrorism situations is handled through law enforcement procedures under the authority of the state—accused terrorists are encouraged to surrender to authorities (often through negotiated efforts) and once apprehended, are treated as criminals for committing illegal acts of violence. But this procedure is not easily applied to the international arena, a context where those accused of terrorism are beyond jurisdiction of American law, who may reside in unstable places or hostile countries without extradition agreements with the United States. Moreover, sometimes acts of terrorism are regarded by another state as political activity rather than criminal behavior, a factor presenting formidable obstacles to law enforcement application. Dynamics of foreign policy between the United States and particular states override legal considerations in these cases and complicate government effort to deal with terrorism threats. Political negotiation becomes a last ditch effort, a necessary tool to bring the terrorism problem under control. But since the American government routinely reiterates its official policy—No Negotiations with Terrorists—in part to discourage demands for bargaining or opportunity for blackmail, an intriguing question is under what conditions the policy is stretched and violated.

Anti-American Terrorism Episodes

Since the end of World War II, the United States has been the target of several episodes of sustained terrorism. Domestic terrorist groups of recent vintage—the Weather Underground and the Symbionese Liberation Army (representing left-wing ideology), and The Order and Aryan Nation (representing a right-wing perspective)—are examples of organizations that posed significant, but not massive, threats to the American political system through violent, but in retrospect, small scale, limited operations. Four major distinct international terrorism periods developed: (1) the skyjacking epidemic with Cuba in the 1960s and 1970s; (2) the Teheran hostage crisis with Iran from November 1979 through mid-January 1981; (3) the Beirut kidnappings in Lebanon during the 1980s; and (4) the suicide bombings by al Qaeda, commencing with attacks overseas in the 1990s, to the dramatic events of 9/11, and continued threats into present day. These episodes—domestic and international, carried out through attacks based on strategic plans and objectives, were loosely organized efforts designed to achieve specific political goals.

The Weathermen, founded in 1969 by disaffected members from the popular nationwide, nonviolent campus political organization Students for a Democratic Society, issued a "Declaration of a State of War" against the U.S. government in 1970. Seeking destruction of American imperialism and its capitalist base, the group, whose members came from privileged backgrounds, carried out more than twenty-five bombing attacks across the nation for five years, ending in June 1975 (Braungart and Braungart 1992). They hit government buildings—police stations in Chicago and New York; the U.S. Army base at the Presidio in San Francisco; the National Guard Association building, the U.S. Capitol, and the State Department in

Washington; the Marin County Courthouse; and the Office of California Prisons—and corporate centers—the ITT headquarters and Anaconda in New York; Gulf Oil in Pittsburgh; and the Kennecott Corporation. Their attacks, accompanied by communiqués to explain a rationale for them, often reflected criticism of American foreign policy, especially the Vietnam War (Berger, 2006). For whatever reason, no one was harmed in their extensive bombing campaign of vandalism (advanced warnings were routinely issued to ensure evacuation prior to the explosions), except three Weathermen who died when accidentally detonating a bomb they had been preparing for later use at a U.S. Army base. Members of the group were able to evade capture for years, even though some of its members were on the FBI's Ten Most Wanted Fugatives list. Significant resources were devoted to finding Weathermen accused of terrorism; eventually, some individuals turned themselves in to authorities as a result of a complex court-based outcome that resulted from improper FBI surveillance measures and amnesty offers. They received minor sentences. (Years later, a few others, caught engaging in a bank heist, got lengthy prison sentences.) Weathermen terrorism terminated for several reasons: they never recruited more than four hundred members, and mostly they worried about hideouts, survival logistics, and group solidarity rather than advancing the revolution (Sprinzak 1990, 77). Law enforcement efforts forced their operations to go underground. U.S. peace accords and final American troop withdrawal from Vietnam in April 1975 must also be considered an important development in closing down this terrorism campaign and marking the end of an era. When the government changed it policy course, Weathermen Underground group passions deflated. The ending of terrorism came about partially through law enforcement surveillance efforts and partially through government policy turnaround that diffused the organization's reason for existence.

Other small groups such as the Symbionese Liberation Army, a left-wing terrorist-designated group active between 1973 and 1975, seeking to lift oppression and enhance the rights of Afro-Americans, and The Order, a right-wing terrorist-designated group active in 1983–1984, seeking to spark a race war and enhance white Christian supremacy, whose director also issued a "Declaration of War" against the U.S. government, engaged in crimes of violence against the public, including bombings, shootings, and armed robbery in the western part of the United States to advance their respective political causes. Their targeted aims at government and corporate centers were different from the Weathermen: their objectives were directed at fundamental aspects of American life, not specific government policies. In these conflicts, terrorism terminated with dramatic federal government shootout confrontation events at organization safe houses that resulted in killing the group leaders. Criminal convictions and prison sentences were levied on other members. Law enforcement was critical in bringing about terrorism termination.

International terrorism threats against the United States have played a far larger role in sustaining public attention, dominating media focus, and mobilizing government effort to resolve them. As exemplars of "propaganda by deed," these episodes of spectacular violence not only spread mass fear but jostled the images of America as an invincible world power, posing onerous threats in the eyes of citizens and policymakers. Each of these anti-American terrorist episodes formed a crisis, challenging American government power and American citizens. Other states in the global system were united in sensing the danger these terrorism event patterns presented, as they, too, sometimes became victims of copycat capers and its diffused effects. In the midst of the U.S.-Cuba skyjacking epidemic, aircraft hijacking techniques were adopted by a Palestinian group whose actions escalated and intensified Middle East conflict. During the Lebanese civil war, citizens of many nations—France, Germany, Egypt, and the Soviet Union, among them—were abducted in Beirut kidnaps as part of extortion and blackmail operations designed to bring enormous cash sums in ransom payout. Suicide terrorism, while a mainstay threat in Israel prior to the 9/11 attacks on U.S. soil, has affected numerous cities worldwide since then, including London, Madrid, and Riyadh.

The anti-American terrorism episodes appeared under the guise of prevailing global ideological tension, not as specific bilateral conflict with the United States. Politics of the Cold War, the East-West divide of communism versus capitalism, fueled the Cuba skyjacking problem; the clash of civilization values separating Islamic Fundamentalism from Western culture frame the others. Over the last fifty years, the primary tool of violence in international terrorism changed from skyjacking to kidnaps to suicide bombing; the duration period of concentrated violence events episodes has grown longer; and ransom demands have expanded into bigger, broader political aims. In the earlier period, short-term hijack incidents began with limited, often individually based, personal objectives. Later, long-term hostage captivity became barter for groups that demanded specific changes in American government policy. The mass killing sprees of recent times are linked to calls for fundamental overhaul of the entire global sociopolitical system. Over time, terrorism threats to human life have escalated; immunity from harm wrought by terrorist acts has been reduced. While global jihad terrorism seems similar to the historical Weathermen Underground movement in some ways—shared grievances, common bombing strategies directed at symbolic targets, and sweeping, vague demands—jihadis aim for mass casualties: their priority is to destroy people over property.

Today, three of the four international anti-American terrorism episodes have ended. By examining their progression and points of closure, perhaps some insights might be gleaned in how the current terrorist threat facing the United States could be terminated. Notably, and in spite of expensive and expansive U.S. resistance strategies, all of them came to a halt when the conflict dynamics were reframed into party choices that led to nonviolent, negotiated settlement. In no case was the trajectory negotiation inevitable. None of the parties intended to make concessions to the other; all of them operated with fixed demands. The problem for the United States was this: terrorism activity was having a major effect on American life. In the Cuban skyjacking crisis, air travelers in the United States were afraid they would be abducted as hijacked hostages. In the Iran hostage crisis, established laws of diplomatic immunity and protection seemed to be disregarded, setting off widespread fear and uncertainty about human safety. The fate of ordinary American citizens kidnapped by thugs in Lebanon was a constant thorn to the Reagan administration: why was the greatest country on earth unable to free them? U.S. law enforcement mechanisms were unable to resolve these issues; their reach did not extend to these environments. Politicians worried about their future electoral careers as their ability to govern effectively was brought to test over the lack of control in halting these highly publicized conflicts.

In the end, the terrorism stopped because of negotiation outcomes that resulted from political expediency. Skyjack terrorism ended in a bilateral accord with Cuba in 1973. The hostage-taking incident in Teheran ended with negotiated agreement between the parties, Iran and the United States, in 1981, as did the Beirut kidnaps, a multiple-player problem resolved in late 1991 through UN mediation. None of these "spectacular terrorism" incidents began as state-sponsored terrorism programs. By different routes, activities of the terrorists eventually merged with national-level interests, making international discussion and agreement possible. Terminating terrorism did not resolve broader, intense conflict issues, dividing the belligerents. Enmity continued. The United States has never restored diplomatic relations with Cuba or Iran; both remain on the U.S. state-sponsored terrorism list, and Hezbollah, a prominent player in Beirut kidnaps is marked as a foreign terrorist organization. What these cases showed was that terrorism episodes could be isolated from a larger conflict domain and brought to a halt through peaceful means.

The four cases of anti-American terrorism episodes fit into a twofold general strategic typology. The first type, a mass terror approach, is designed to strike fear in the public at large through a series of dramatic, continuous, criminal acts of violence—seemingly random aircraft hijackings, unpredictable targeted bombings—intended as media-grabbing stories that give swift and full attention to an ideologically based cause embraced by the terrorists who are motivated by a victim mentality of powerlessness in a David-meets-Goliath scenario. Like a protest movement of general grievances, their efforts are meant as advertisements and requests for political voice in a system that has ignored them. They are seeking a groundswell of popular support to create a climate open to changing the status quo or revealing its dark side. Loosely affiliated individuals or groups, through copycat schemes, may add to the campaign's intensity. In situations of mass terror strategy, the United States is being attacked for what it represents, or "what it is." The second type, a direct target terror approach, is intended to set up particular conditions of exchange through a type of blackmail or extortion system—kidnappings and hostage-taking incidents involving abduction of specific individuals by terrorists to be exchanged for some designated objective, fit into this scheme—to force a government to give in to the outlined demands of barter; to settle a score. Like an international crisis with an ultimatum, policymakers are faced with an imminent choice of unsavory options. Here, the United States is being attacked for its behavior and actions, or "what it does."

The Cuban skyjacking epidemic and al Qaeda suicide bombing episodes are more in line with the first type of terrorism—mass based, ideological protesting with copycat features (broadening affiliated groups and individuals who are only loosely linked to the overall campaign organizers and their objectives), suggesting large, publicized defensive protection measures are needed immediately for deterrence. The Teheran and Beirut hostage campaigns fit into a crisis model with concrete demands, setting the parameters for bargaining—in both cases, the Iranian government, ultimately in charge, sought a particular form of reciprocity with the United States: barricaded American citizens would be freed in exchange for something it wanted desperately (their deposed leader returned, weapons supplied, or cash back for items purchased but never delivered) but believed it could not acquire if the request was processed through normal channels.

Mass-based terror campaigns seek political opening in the victim's universe; their goals diffuse, these orchestrated efforts are future-directed, looking to expand perspectives on legitimate political life that include the terrorists' views. It is unclear what zone of resolution would be satisfactory to the parties involved, as the United States regards the terrorists' goals outlook strictly through a negative lens—beyond acceptable boundaries of discourse. Direct target terror campaigns, in contrast, seek real, contractual settlement deals; their objectives, pointed and concrete, are backward looking in that they aim to redress what is perceived as a wrongful act through a justified ransom reward. Here, too, the zone of resolution is unknown, as terms of "fair exchange" may shift. This type of episode also points to the importance of large, publicized defensive protection measures, deterrence aimed to ward off possible future attacks that could place the United States in a compromising position.

In both kinds of terrorist campaigns, perpetrators chose symbolically significant targets (bombing a government building, taking diplomats as hostages); a strategic approach designed to produce greater media coverage and pressure on a regime. The target resisted the implied concession-making resolution formulae as unattractive options for terminating violence. In the government's mind, a bargaining setup required consideration of terrorist's demands, however outrageous, radical, unreasonable, and unfair they seemed. Yet, at some point, political dynamics moved these conflicts of terrorism into negotiation range. How did it happen?

Investigating Terrorism Termination

The world today confronts vexing questions about terrorism. Why do groups turn to violence to express political opposition? What do terrorists want? How are these problems resolved? How do conflicts of terrorism terminate? Most terrorist conflict around the world consists of a set of belligerents positioned in one of two patterns: physically adjacent parties struggling to find ways to live together in power sharing or separatist arrangements (Sri Lanka and the Tamils; Basque separatists and Spain; Northern Ireland Protestants and Catholics; Israelis and Palestinians);

or mother country–colony situations (the British in Kenya; the French in Algeria), self-determination conflicts where the outside, intervening party eventually decides to withdraw from the indigenous territory.

Targeting the United States is different. First, apart from small, shortlived, internally driven efforts to build antiregime, opposition political movements (the Weathermen Underground and Symbionese Liberation Army in the 1970s are two prime examples of groups attempting to do so), major terrorism attacks on America have originated outside the nation's borders, though not in countries next door. Living together in power-sharing arrangements under a single governance structure is not the goal in anti-American terrorism campaigns. Second, although one might argue American intervention behavior is similar to colonization practice, the two are not one and the same: in most colonial situations, the ruler had total control over all facets of life (from education to business to community life, government laws and administration governed everything), unlike U.S. intervention, which has aimed to influence particular economic and military sectors. These differences have profound implications. Although power sharing, separatism, and territorial withdrawal may be essential to resolving some terrorism conflicts, to implement these features in the context of far-reaching dimensions of superpower politics and international system structure may demand more nuanced, creative, and deconstructed procedures.

Investigating the specifics of previous anti-American terrorist campaigns, how various policies influenced progress toward resolution, and what conditions brought these episodes to a successful end, may help bring into view scenarios of cessation for current terrorism problems. It is the difference of interests and how that difference is handled that forms the intriguing issue in understanding solutions to social conflict, says Carnevale (2007). A reasonable question in this context is whether and how incidents of the past might be compared to the present. Would insight from these cases have any relevance for resolving twenty-first century terrorism, or is the new paradigm of terrorism, one based on religious fanaticism and nihilism, so unlike its ancestral remnants founded in nationalism and self-determination, that what we thought we knew and understood about terrorism activity is rendered irrelevant? There are logical and empirical reasons for rejecting the notion that everything is new and different, for as Copeland (2003) and Cronin (2007) point out, terrorist groups still operate in terms of objectives, motivation, and organization, in the traditional mold within their historical roots. Still, a rationale is needed to compare cases along some of the main features of terrorism—actors, issues, and motives—in the context of operating environmental circumstances. Important differences exist between the past and the present. Each of the previous anti-American terrorist episodes had clearly defined parameters: the conflicts were essentially bilateral confrontations; the issues were bounded by specific demands or grievances; the motives of terrorists were limited and nonmysterious. Massive killing sprees did not occur. The skyjacking episode concerned U.S.-Cuban relations. Episodes in Teheran and in Beirut focused on U.S.-Iran relations. All of these conflicts were resolved through official state-to-state relations. Features surrounding the U.S.–al Qaeda conflict are more complicated.

Does the Global War on Terror concept, reflected in complex, interacting connections across all states, rule out any bilateral perspectives or assessments between individual states in imagining or creating potential solutions to the problem? The term global terrorism actually has a narrower, more distinctive reference than one might expect. Its terminology origins come from U.S. policy crafting. Its punitive effects are seen in the U.S. international alliance system: America and states friendly to it are the targets of violence. Like the World Series in baseball, "global terrorism" is primarily (though not exclusively) about the United States. Global terrorism concerns America's role in the world, specifically its leadership and support of particular regimes in a small group of countries, for that is the lens through which terrorist groups express their grievances. In this context, the anti-American campaign of violence is confined to a few important one-to-one relationships in U.S. foreign policy: the United States and Saudi Arabia; the United States and Egypt; the United States and Pakistan; and a few others. Absent these very close links and a substantial part of the current terrorism conflict domain falls aside. The top al Qaeda leaders, for example, have long expressed their goal to create revolutionary political change in these regions. Osama bin Laden seeks regime overthrow in his homeland, Saudi Arabia, and Ayman al Zawahiri was imprisoned for his links to the group that was responsible for Sadat's assassination in his native Egypt. The motivation behind Benazir Bhutto's assassination on the eve of the 2008 Pakistani elections has been attributed to her strong American connections. Combining all belligerencies, these particular ones and others, into a single pool to create a global effect where terrorism is seen as a worldwide problem to be tackled in a global level integrated formula, puts blinders on partitioning that may be essential in developing manageable resolution formats. As Judt (2008) put it, a serious mistake of the war on terrorism consists of lumping together all extremist groups under a generic problem of political violence and mixing international conflict and national level disputes. Braithwaite and Li (2007) conclude on the basis of their geographic spatial analysis of the distribution of terrorist attacks, that policymakers should limit their attention to "hot spot" countries, rather than worry about global terrorism.

Whether the current strain of al Qaeda terrorism actually operates from a global, rather than a national, base in its political aims is also at issue. One central tenet of insurgent groups—however small they may be—is to employ tactics that create an impression of a large, well-organized machine in order to appear more powerful and ominous than their capabilities suggest. The obvious al Qaeda strategy is to stress cross-national links and unity of purpose, using a special brand of Islamic identity and religious ideology among its followers. This offers a way for disparate groups operating within a country to claim affiliation with the larger entity in order to bolster their reputation, draw resources, and presumably enhance their chance for bringing about political change. It offers, too, prestige and attention for the original organizers of al Qaeda itself. Within each society, however, the threat posed by the terrorist group may be less than it seems to be when all links tie together. By pulling back some of the attenuated parts ascribed to "global" terrorism features, it seems the current anti-American terrorist campaign can be understood to share some features with the different conflict episodes preceding it.

Is U.S. policy directly responsible for—and in a position to—alleviating terrorists' grievances in a manner similar to meeting demands in previous cases? Politics and related violence are best understood by analyzing particular situations. In this context, the doctrinal development of Islamic jihadists sheds light on the specifics of a "global" approach in terrorism tactics. The terms "near enemy" and "far enemy" (referring respectively to Muslim governments and the powerful, intervening forces that controlled them, namely the government of the United States), coined by Mohammed Abd al Salem, who was executed for his role in the 1981 assassination of Egyptian President Sadat, appeared in a jihadi document written in the late 1970s. His manual "The Absent Duty," serving as operational doctrine for the jihadist movement throughout the 1980s and first half of the 1990s strongly stressed local, not international, politics. The shift from localism to globalism happened after pro-Western Muslim rulers suppressed uprisings launched by Islamic fundamentalists who, Gerges (2005, 65) says, had to choose to surrender or find a new mission. The terrorists' focus on defeating the "near enemy" was failing. Government security forces brought heavy losses on jihadis, killing and arresting thousands. Schisms within the movement developed, and in the later half of the 1990s, the conflict breathed new life as al Qaeda, then regarded as a fringe group (and perceived by some as a franchising organization putting nationalist groups under a single umbrella), decided to focus on the "far enemy." But the agenda of terrorists was not revised—the basic aims to topple impious rulers who had abandoned religion and fight Muslim communities that desert Islam, remained. Applying coercive pressure in another way, hitting the outside supporter who provided largess that kept these governments afloat, would be the way to achieve their localized objectives, and essentially rendered the problem a bilateral one between the United States and its ally.

Does the current anti-American violence campaign fit with the series of prior episodes, or is it set apart entirely as a new phenomenon by virtue of its mass killings? With respect to its dimensions of significantly higher casualty rates, the current episode of terrorism is neither discrete nor fundamentally different from other periods (thus rendering it in a comparable class with other cases). Clauset, Young, and Gleditsch (2007) demonstrate: the distribution of large and small terrorism events, where frequency is inversely related to severity (lots of little incidents occur; large events are extremely rare) shows that *all* terrorism occurrences can be placed within a single, continuing series, conforming to a scale invariance.

One final, important difference sets the current terrorist campaign against America apart from the others. Al Qaeda terrorism violence is not officially state-supported but comes from nonstate actors, small cells of political opposition groups with different, yet overlapping agenda united only through a loosely organized front. Rather than aligning with a government, they stand as outsiders, as nonrecognized opponents. In prior cases, the Cuban and Iranian governments lent their support to the terrorism initiatives and eventually took control over terrorists' actions. In the current situation, any existing government support for terrorism or terrorist sympathies within the major states of interests is not at the front lines of decision making but hidden away or denied. Negotiation possibilities between a superpower and such groups lacking any legitimacy status in the international community seem farfetched. Yet, it is important to mention that *all* previous anti-American terrorist campaigns started with nonstate actors who initiated the violent events. Only later did government officials enter as major conflict players, though there is some dispute, in each of the cases, about the role of individual officials within the respective governments of Cuba and Iran at the onset of terrorism. The point is that a state-to-state relationship dealing with the terrorist conflict was not immediate; it evolved. Critical to this process was consolidation of terrorism perpetrators' roles and goals, and host government capacity to control these forces that congealed into an entity that could serve as a responsible negotiating partner in deliberations with the United States.

How do anti-American campaigns of terrorism progress and come to an end? Benchmarks of U.S. experience show that previous domestic episodes were stopped with government violence and legal indictments; international campaigns ended with political problem solving, leading to negotiated settlements. What process moved parties from a contending strategy to one based in nonviolent discussion and resolution? How effective were these settlement outcomes in stopping terrorism? Knowledge about what works and what does not work in conflict resolution derived from the empirical record of regularities and causal mechanisms can provide useful lessons in resolution practice, proclaimed Zartman (1997). In this spirit, a framework of terminating tough cases of terrorism is applied to the three concluded anti-American episodes, and examined for fit on the fourth one, the al Qaeda campaign.

Can terrorism be defeated? No, says Simon (2001, 9), for terrorism grows out of political, economic, and social problems that can never be fully resolved, just as it is impossible to wipe out poverty, solve the drug problem, or cure all diseases. Religious fanaticism, nationalist causes, revolutionary ideologies, criminal greed, risks and thrills, identity, and group solidarity, are among the factors that have always propelled individuals into terrorist activity and will continue to do so. *Inside the Jihad: My Life with Al Qaeda, a Spy's Story* by Omar Nasiri (a pseudonym) offers a riveting, personal account of these various motivations that back terrorist acts (2006). The roots of terrorism are deep and not easily changed. Yet the evidence of global terrorist activity shows clear patterns that rise and fall—some countries are more affected than others in different periods, the timing of violence seemingly linked to contextual political issues—in nonrandom sequence (Braithwaite and Li 2007). Terrorism appears in waves, each period, lasting several decades, distinguished by tactics, targets, and the effectiveness of state responses (Rapoport 2004; Rasler and Thompson 2009). Hence, from the perspective of governments affected by these directed campaigns of violence, it is possible to manage, reduce, and resolve particular conflicts of terrorism.

The Framework

Conflicts of terrorism operate outside the bans of conventional warfare. Terrorist combatants are not ordinary soldiers—visible military troops organized by rank and responsibility. Battle plans are not designed for direct confrontation with the opponent. Instead, these fighters are nimble and shadowy; they employ criminal tactics for political purpose—to avenge a wrong, to exert power, perhaps to bring social change. Their violent actions entail neither codified rules of engagement nor specified procedures for terminating a fight. Terrorist campaigns are designed to threaten others through strategic acts of violence: skyjackings, assassinations, hostage barricades, kidnaps, bombings, shootouts, suicide attacks, representing complicated attempts of "power by the weak" to draw attention to a cause and communicate a political message to a target government, "forces of the strong," to coerce the powerful to open lines to political change. By this argument, the terrorists try to coerce their opponent and pressure them into a negotiation, since outright victory is largely impossible. In response, a target government will strongly resist this ploy, choosing to ignore the message or dismiss it and avoid bargaining with their perpetrators, whom they view as illegitimate, unreasonable, dangerous extremists. Targets commonly employ strategies of resistance by setting up defensive counterterrorism measures (target hardening, law enforcement, intelligence gathering) and engaging in offensive combative actions against their opponent when necessary in order to reduce the threat, solve the problem, and close off conflict. If government policy succeeds, the terrorism problem is brought under control and terrorist violence ends. This is the goal.

However, if this goal is not achieved: continued lethal attacks against the targeted government, extended hostage holdouts, and long-term serious threats—revealed through the scope and magnitude of thwarted plots—are indications of policy failure; it means terrorists continue to pose a serious problem in disrupting national security. This intensifies challenges for the government to restore it. If military means are not working effectively and further escalation is not a realistic option, alternative methods for halting violence—intermediate ceasefire agreements, a truce, withdrawal plans, or long-term peace treaty—might be considered. But these traditional approaches for halting violence do not readily apply to conflicts of terrorism, nor are their terms easy to implement. At the start, a fundamental transformation of the perception of the conflict dynamics in the mind of government policymakers needs to change before nonviolent resolution possibilities are contemplated.

The framework here provides a detailed sequencing of the termination process for "stuck situations" in drawn-out conflicts of terrorism. It is not a prescription for action but merely describes what works or not, operating as a kind of monitoring device. For this purpose, theoretical concepts advanced by leading conflict resolution scholars coupled with empirical evidence backing their claims are used to show how the process toward terminating might work. A template combines the key ideas into a composite framework for application. It has four elements that operate cumulatively in the order presented. First, when a terrorism conflict has reached a *hurting stalemate* (Zartman 1985, 1989) the target government may alter its thinking about the enemy, changing the foundation of its decision-making logic. Second, conflict strategy could shift if stalemate is accompanied by *turning point events* (structural, strategic or tactical changes directing the course of the conflict toward disaster or entrenched intractability), an idea advanced by Druckman (1986, 2001), and previous policies (resistance, reform) have failed to bring desired outcomes. Third, *negotiation readiness* (Pruitt 1997, 2005) to deal with the enemy emerges as parameters of the dispute are reduced from abstract "battle of ideas" to narrow, concrete factors and expectations about the opponent's commitment to implementing a solution rise. Fourth, conversion into *interest-based bargaining,* reciprocal exchange for mutual gains (Fisher and Ury 1981; Fisher, Ury, and Patton 1991) will be essential for settlement to succeed.

Negotiated solutions are interactive affairs and require full acceptance and participation by all sides. Although terrorist perpetrators may seek to negotiate, their reluctance to start the process delays settlement, for this side must weigh its power resources in the asymmetric balance and believe not only that it can advance no further by continued fighting, but also would stand to gain some concessions *at this point* by negotiating with its adversary. As the chief negotiator for the release of the Beirut hostages, Giandomenico Picco (2005, 12) puts it this way: "It would appear that contrary to public declarations by government leaders, institutions have dealt with terrorist groups almost consistently as long as the groups were prepared to deal with them. In other words, the crucial decision to enter into negotiation was not made by the governments but by the groups themselves. If they are ready, then the governments would find a way to communicate and engage. But if they were not, then no negotiations were to be had." So for both sides, the necessary changes in conditioning factors leading from stalemate to settlement include:

1. *Decision-Making Logic:* the evolution of thinking about the adversary from a framing (cognitive image) to gaming (instrumental) perspective, the result of a hurting stalemate.
2. *Conflict Strategy:* the evolution of reaction to violence from conflict avoidance to fighting to negotiating, the result of a hurting stalemate plus the anticipated effects of turning points.
3. *Conflict Scope:* the evolution of conceptualizing disputed issues from broad to narrow in breadth and meaning, the result of a hurting stalemate, turning points impact, plus negotiation readiness.
4. *Negotiation Preconditions:* the evolution of conflict dynamics from parties' tolerance to intolerance of continued violence and willingness to negotiate a solution, the result of a hurting stalemate, turning points impact, negotiation readiness, and reciprocal exchange terms for mutual gains.
5. *Bargaining Strategy:* the evolution of negotiating demands from a power-based or rights-based perspective to an interest-based orientation designed to craft a mutually acceptable agreement.

Decision-Making Logic

In terrorism conflict, each side—the target government and the terrorists—operates under three progressive decision-making narrative frames to move toward the end point. The frames do not appear simultaneously, nor do parties shift from one frame to the next at the same pace. Initially, each party will frame the conflict from its individualized point of view, seeing itself as a *victim,* targeted by a perpetrator who is regarded as a bully. This frame, first designed and developed over time within groups contemplating terrorist acts to build a rationale for their harmful behavior, instantly appears to their opponent—the target government—once their strategy of violence is unleashed. At the moment of outbreak, the conflict is framed around constructed self images of weakness and blamelessness. The victimization theme dominates: the government sees itself as a victim of terror; the terrorist group sees itself as a victim of the government's overall policies of control. A "framing" orientation gives meaning and emotional content to the conflict, but it does not set up strategic plans for pursuing ultimate goals or terminating the dispute.

As conflict progresses, once both parties have created a sufficient framework around their victimization, their conflict frames shift. Each side begins to see itself as a *fighter,* a "gaming" frame. The terrorist side unilaterally moves into a second narrative structure with this construct, imagining the conflict as an interactive power game at the moment the target government adopts the first frame image as victim. The terrorist side has adopted a bargaining orientation and pursues strategies seeking to create power dependency over its opponent in order to coerce the government to yield to its demands, or alternatively, to prepare a sufficient bargaining base for eventual negotiation with the other side. At this stage however, the government remains in a self image frame orientation and moves ahead on a unilateral plan of a series of defensive and deterrent measures to protect against the terrorist's assault and to break down coercive pressures and power dependency. The government prefers not to interact with the terrorist side—who it regards as unreasonable and perhaps irrational—in any bargaining capacity. This phase, consisting of a combination of framing and gaming orientations to the conflict, comes to an end in one of two ways: either the government prevails and overcomes the terrorist's threat, or conflict continues and a serious stalemate develops that moves the government into gaming orientation.

Finally, at the endpoint of a stalemated terrorism conflict, the adversaries transition into a third narrative framework where they turn into *negotiators;* the center of action moves into interest-based bargaining. In a conflict termination phase, both parties are positioned in a gaming perspective: the terrorist side fighting to retain or expand its power dependency against the target; the government side fighting to end that dependency of coercion. Actions and interpretations of actions by both sides are reflective and deliberate. When both sides have reached a gaming mode in a conflict, conditions are set up for negotiated settlement attempts. The goal of the terrorist side is to move across three framing narratives of conflict: from victim to competitive fighter to negotiator. The goal of the government side, however, is to move from victim to victorious fighter, at which point the conflict stops. The disputants' preferred end states are incompatible.

Terrorists move quickly into a gaming mentality—seeking bargained gains from their coercive strategy—yet they may not be ready to seriously consider negotiating with the more powerful adversary. Their reluctance comes from a self-perception of weakness, a problem to be overcome with continued successful terrorist attacks. Thus, the gaming has two phases—the first, "prenegotiation" where the terrorist side seeks to enhance its coercive influence over the target government to rebalance relative power; the second, "negotiation" where the terrorist side works with its adversary to construct a mutual gains agreement formula to end conflict. The government side, by contract, continues to hold a framing orientation focused on questions of perpetrator identity and wants, and what the conflict means, putting off a gaming, i.e., interactive, perspective as long as possible so as to avoid any bargaining occasion that may force its losses through undesirable concessions. Although government may be advocating settlement early in the conflict process (this occurred in both the Cuban skyjacking episode and the Teheran hostage problem), it is doing so from a high strength position and basing its argument strictly around power and rights, methods quite unlikely to bring the opponent into deliberations for agreement: the process will be seen strictly as favoring one side. But in order to reach settlement, both parties need to be operating in a gaming orientation so the question is, when will the government adopt this perspective?

When government moves from a framing to a gaming view of the conflict depends on key moments that signal changing dynamics: specifically when the weaker side realizes it has maximized its likely gains. While the weaker, terrorist side rushes into a gaming perspective eagerly seeking interaction with its adversary, it does not rush into a negotiation, but awaits ripe conditions. Conversely, the sufficiently stronger target government slowly moves into strategic interaction decision making, but if a conflict has reached a stalemate, is more likely to accept the negotiation option first. The resolution moment comes when the parties are willing or driven to try something new or to do something to deflect or transform the relationship in ways that produce more satisfying or efficient results for them. It includes two prerequisites essential to terminate violence through a settlement format: outcome reassessment—what ending is desirable and possible; and conflict reframing—what is this conflict about and what does the adversary want. Table 1.1 summarizes the progression of phases.

Conflict Strategy

What strategies are most appropriate for resolving terrorism conflict? Fighting to win is appropriate when a party places high value on the issue in dispute, it is necessary to overcome assertive weaker parties, and unfavorable decisions by the other side may be costly. Thus, a fighting strategy is most common so long as terrorism is conceptualized as a pervasive problem of global sweep; an ideology based on hatred

**Table 1.1 Decision-Making Logic:
Framing and Gaming in Terrorism Conflict Phases**

Phase	Party	Self-Image	Orientation
Conflict Onset	Terrorists	Victim of U.S. Oppression	Frame
	Government	Victim of anti-Americanism	Frame
Conflict Mid-Point	Terrorists	Fighter seeks power over government	Game
	Government	Victim of anti-Americanism defends power	Frame
Conflict Late Stage	Terrorists	Fighter seeks to maintain power	Game
	Government	Fighter seeks to end power dependency	Game
Conflict Termination	Terrorists	Negotiator for mutual interest solution	Game
	Government	Negotiator for mutual interest solution	Game

and a clash of civilizations over irreconcilable values pursued by nihilists who love violence. Negotiating a settlement with mutual gains is appropriate when issues are complex, commitment requires other parties for successful implementation, no single party can solve the problem, parties are equally powerful, and a contending style is not successful (Lewicki et al. 2006). Consideration of a negotiated settlement is more likely when the terrorist problem is stripped of its ideological overtones and seen as an attempt at political bargaining, where treating an immediate, rather than long-term, complicated set of issues, is possible. The choice of strategy in the minds of the adversaries is determined mainly by subjective assessments of a conflict. All sides examine the power calculus—who has how much power, and how much and what type of power is each side willing to wield in an effort to settle the dispute. Parties assume it is preferable to bargain from strength; hence, the impetus of a terrorism campaign is to create a new balance between absolutely strong and absolutely weak sides with a critical, relative power dependency, significantly enhancing the leverage of the smaller side to determine an outcome in its favor. Stalemate occurs because neither party in the conflict believes it can push ahead any further or force its opponent to back down. A problem solving strategy becomes a default position, chosen when it is difficult to yield, contentious tactics seem infeasible or unwise, and delays are costly (Pruitt and Kim 2004). Higher levels of contending occur early in the process; problem solving comes afterwards and will be more effective in creating integrative agreements when preceded by contending behavior (De Dreu et al. 2007, 614).

In conflicts of terrorism, the top preferences for each side are incompatible: both want to achieve their objectives at the expense of opponent losses, a zero-sum condition. The next-to-worst option, a non-zero-sum condition, to negotiate (yielding would be at the bottom of desired choices) only takes place after both sides realize higher order, preferred outcomes are unattainable. Table 1.2 shows the desired end points for the terrorist side and for the target government. For the

Table 1.2 Conflict Strategy:
Party Outcome Preferences in Terrorism Conflict

Terrorists	
First preference	Fight to Victory: government yields to its demands
Second preference	Fight to Gain Power: set up coercive dependency over government
Third preference	Negotiate: if power gains threatened, achieving some government concessions
Government	
First preference	Fight to Victory: terrorist threat minimized or eliminated
Second preference	Fight to Maintain Power: prevent a bargaining situation with terrorists
Third preference	Negotiate: if power losses threatened, granting some government concessions

terrorist side, achieving victory is quite unlikely—it rarely happens; negotiation is a far more realistic goal. For the government side, maintaining the status quo or achieving victory over terrorists more commonly occurs, but, as shown in research results, negotiation happens in a number of instances. Conflicts of terrorism do not move into a problem-solving, negotiation mode until expectations about achieving higher preferences change.

Strategic choices between fighting and problem-solving need not be mutually exclusive. For example, Caruso (2007) showed that once involved in violent interactions, a party may choose a second instrument of conflict management (e.g., communication, negotiation signaling) in order to improve the outcome of a dispute in its favor. But to be effective, the use of dual, simultaneously employed instruments must show both to be serious, committed costly investments in order to have a direct impact on both sides' payoff. Conflict situations foster mutual distrust, minimizing possibilities for honest communication or reasonable discussion between disputants, and encourages the dominance of resolution by force—a fighting strategy. Parties engaged in terrorism conflict are fearful of moving in the direction of negotiated settlement. Negotiations may require costly concessions, jeopardize individual visions of future security, and affect one's political identity. But fighting and negotiating are not independent in time or in structure; the conflict outcome may actually depend on the mixed effect of these two elements. Table 1.2 summarizes parties' preference orderings.

Conflict Scope

The problem of terrorism has been approached as a global issue, an ideology based on hatred, a clash of civilization over irreconcilable values, where frustrated individuals, dissatisfied with their political, economic, and social position, engage in aggressive behavior to vent their discontent. This perspective suggests understanding and rectifying root causes of the conflict, recognizing that any policy implementation may

Table 1.3 Conflict Scope:
The Meaning of Terrorism and Resolution Difficulty

Broad Scope difficult to resolve	Narrow Scope easier to resolve
Terrorism is:	
a pervasive problem of global sweep	confined actions in limited settings
an ideology based on hatred and violence	a political directed strategy
Terrorist Conflict represents:	
a clash of civilization over irreconcilable values	political bargaining over differences
nihilists punishing innocent victims	asymmetric warfare
Terrorism Conflict Resolution requires:	
rectifying root causes of terrorism	stopping immediate problem of violence
fighting the enemy until achieving victory	negotiating with the enemy if fighting fails

take generations to correct—weeding out the malcontents, minimizing frustration levels, and creating fundamental change in mindsets. In this way, terrorism reflects a social movement. Differences of ideology are central; the essence of the dispute is regarded as a war of ideas. From this vantage point, terrorism conflicts are difficult to resolve. By contrast, if terrorism is seen as a particular problem of criminal behavior, a matter of specific differences between radical groups and government authority over concrete objectives rather than a division of abstract notions and world views, reducible to minimize flash points of contention essentially breaking down the whole matter into several smaller parts—managing a solution through bilateral country-to-country arrangements on short-term issues with more immediate solutions, conflict resolution becomes easier. Narrowing the conflict scope is one way to move a solution-thinking environment forward.

The meaning of the conflict and hence, settlement parameters, need to change into narrower, less contentious terms in order for any agreement to end a dispute. The value of continuing to fight must be less than the value for settlement, but no agreement will occur between extremely hostile parties if the objective of a negotiation is to determine who is right or whose principles should prevail or who can wield more power or about persuading one side to adopt the other's position. Fisher (1964, 107) proposes fractionating big issues into smaller ones to overcome these problems, but points out that hardliners are against breaking up the issues and thereby inhibit action that might bring about the changes they desire. Moving toward resolution in conflicts of terrorism means all parties need to readjust their perceptions of the issues and the stakes defining their dispute in order to reduce the level of resolution difficulty. Conflicts difficult to solve are perceived in zero-sum terms for winners and losers; ethics clash and values divide disputants into ideologically distinct groups. These conditions hinder the task of finding common ground or mutual interest overlaps essential to establish discussion on viable reciprocal exchange. By contrast, conflicts

Table 1.4 Negotiation Preconditions:
Terminating Terrorism Conflict

Mutual Hurting Stalemate—Conflict Ripeness

Definition:	Each party realizes escalation is no longer an option and that deadlock is too costly
Objective measure:	Terrorist campaign longevity + target defense expansion
Indicator:	Decline in attack frequency (Pre-agreement observation)

Turning Points

Definition:	Each party experiences events moving them toward accepting negotiating
Objective measure:	Structural, strategic, or tactical changes in the political environment
Indicator:	Events or deadlines denoting negative change of future conflict trajectory

Negotiation Readiness

Definition:	Each party accepts the opponent as a negotiation partner
Objective measure:	Acceptable mediators and host-state control over terrorists
Indicator:	Party verbal indication that negotiation is acceptable*

Interest-Based Bargaining

Definition:	Parties propose reciprocal exchange terms for mutual gain solutions
Objective measure:	Specific exchange formulae floated
Indicator:	Commodities of barter exchange noted*

*Usually some parts are conveyed in secret communication.

are easier to resolve if issues are divided into smaller parts, and ideas of reciprocal exchanges can be imagined and realized through negotiated arrangements. Table 1.3 shows levels of conflict resolution difficulty.

Negotiation Preconditions

Four elements bring parties into a negotiated setting to terminate a terrorism conflict: a mutual hurting stalemate, turning points, negotiation readiness, and interest-based mutual gains bargaining (see Table 1.4). The transition into problem solving negotiations in terrorist conflicts is facilitated by the existence of a power stalemate where neither party is able to prevail under its current, contentious, adopted strategies; and negotiation readiness—the capacity (a physical and political reality) and willingness (a psychological mindset) by both sides to talk to the other—which is facilitated by different turning points (often outside, threatening events) that influence each side leading them to favor quick, nonviolent settlement, and coupled with that, a sense of what the final barter of reciprocal exchange benefits might be (e.g., returning hostages in exchange of military withdrawal from specified territory; outlawing any form of international hijack operations by treating terrorism as strictly criminal behavior and establishing an extradition treaty for enforcement). This point occurs at a moment when the adversaries are closest to a power balance equilibrium (given the extreme asymmetry of their overall power), when each side is dependent on the other for granting or withholding some important rewards in spite of their mutual efforts to eliminate such reliance. Although the absolutely stronger party still holds a far greater amount of power, the weaker side has been able to create coercive conditions that directly weaken and hence, threaten it.

Any developmental features toward preconditions defining negotiation, shows the impact of a mutual hurting stalemate, growing effectiveness of defensive measures, the existence of turning points moving adversaries into accepting the negotiation option as a way to terminate conflict between them transforming the conflict issues into fractionated, concrete parts eligible for settlement, and floating reciprocal exchange formula for doing so.

Table 1.4 lists the four negotiation preconditions for terminating international terrorism campaigns, along with a brief definition and an observable measure for determining whether it exists in any campaign episode.

As a final noted factor, leadership change in the target government may be of significance. In the three terrorism campaigns concluded, each began when one governing administration was in power but was either ended or ending as that group moved on. Cuban skyjacking started under President Lyndon Johnson; the U.S.–Cuba hijack accord happened under President Richard Nixon. The Teheran hostage crisis was the nemeses of President Jimmy Carter; agreement formed with the Reagan administration. Beirut kidnapping victims were abducted during President Ronald Reagan's term, but freed during the first Bush presidency in the final moments when the highest UN official was stepping down from office. Agreements seemed to come with new administrations, perhaps a face-saving feature for all sides, and were formed when a high point of public concern hype had passed and after the U.S. had deployed an elaborate set of defensive measures to prevent future terrorist incidents. Notably, agreement happened only when the conflict trajectory had moved into a de-escalation mode.

The recipe for estimating the likelihood of negotiating an end to a terrorism campaign is indicated when "signal strength" is high on all the preconditions. Their level of strength influences the conflict termination process. When these factors are in place, conflict strategy opens to a consideration of negotiation; the conflict phases move on to gaming and termination decision-making thinking; the scope of conflict loses its ideology content and shifts to solve immediate, concrete problems. Yet this process is not unidirectional; conflict reframing and outcome reassessment affect strategic choices. Caruso (2007) advocates opening a second front in conflict management, that is, to engage in negotiation while continuing to fight the adversary.

Bargaining Strategy

Once parties are ready to negotiate, there is no guarantee they will be successful in reaching an agreement. Progress will depend partially on the strategies of bargaining employed on each side. Fisher and Ury (1981) outline positional bargaining—each side takes a position, argues for it, and makes concessions to reach a compromise—identifying two styles: hard and soft. A hard bargainer will view negotiation as a competitive process where what one wins the other loses. Opponents are viewed as adversaries, who accordingly do not trust one another. The strategy involves demanding concessions from the other side, holding fast to a stated position, and trying to win in a contest of wills by applying pressure. Power-based thinking is a hard-bargaining perspective, demanding compliance from others due to coercive dominance—the threat of punishments and rewards. A rights-based conflict resolution approach is also a form of hard bargaining; the essential message is to persuade another party to accept one's views by reference to explicit rules, procedures and regulations, implied standards and norms operating in the environment. Positional bargaining agreements are not easily reached in terrorism conflicts. As an alternative, Fisher and Ury advocate principled bargaining, an interest-based approach focused on parties' needs and concerns. This normally includes efforts to understand the interests of the other side, and apply some standard of reasonableness and justice within the contextual case setting. The heart of the approach is not to assert what a party needs nor argue on rights through an established rule, but to assert a value, as the premise for deciding how to resolve conflict. As Mayer (2000, 40) states, conflict participants blend and mix different negotiation approaches, but at any time, a single approach seems to define the essence of a party's engagement in conflict. Neither power-based nor rights-based approaches are likely to bring parties closer to a settlement, though they dominate because of the victimization perspective each side has framed of itself in the terrorism conflict environment. Only when principled bargaining, anchored in an interest-based orientation of party needs, concerns, and exchanges takes hold, will serious negotiations be more likely to advance.

A closer look at the preconditions, specifically how they were satisfied in previous anti-American campaigns, and their role in contemporary conflict, provides information to help project terrorism termination. But first, a more detailed description of decision logic and settlement preconditions is in order.

CHAPTER TWO

Framing and Gaming

Decision Logic

Two approaches in policymaking are relevant to analyzing terrorism termination processes: framing and gaming. The framing approach is based on cognitive judgment designed for understanding the meaning of the conflict and labeling the actions of one's opponent; the gaming approach is based on calculating instrumental moves against an opponent to maximize one's gains. The two approaches derive from different assumptions and premises. Payne (1982) calls them the perceptual and cost-benefit frameworks. Kahneman and Tversky (1983) note the tension between the two in the study of judgment and choice. The first emphasizes problem construction and formulation. The second emphasizes the use of strategies to acquire and evaluate information. Gonos (1977) views the frame approach as fixed pictures of understandings to provide working principles for action. Cognitive framing emphasizes perceptions arising from norms, expectations, or operating rules of practical discourse (March and Olson 1998; Risse 2000; Wendt 1999). Strategic bargaining is a rational choice perspective focused on parties' interests and preferences in the process of interaction.

Theories of decision making usually assume humans rely on reasoning to make choices, that is, that people consciously analyze alternatives and carefully weigh costs and benefits in a deliberate, logical manner. But this is a relatively new function of the brain, argues Jonah Lehrer (2009, 24–25). From an evolutionary perspective, the more developed system of processing information is based on emotional impulses that require very little information to influence judgment. Emotional influences represent the wisdom of experience: capturing a multitude of data points that translate into practical feelings. The function of emotions is to provide information summaries of everything the mind contains but does not consciously perceive. Expert opinion, says Lehrer (2009, 61, 248), depends naturally on emotions that have been translated into "useful knowledge" in order to think through a situation, breaking down puzzles and complexities into simplified understanding. But the system is not without flaws.

Intuitive judgments may get out of control and run wild, leading to poor outcomes. Making good choices requires activating both parts of mental processing—the system of feelings and the system of reasoning. Yet, as Lehrer (2009, xv) cautions, "we weren't designed to be rational creatures. Instead, the mind is composed of a messy network of different areas, many of which are involved with the production of emotion. Whenever someone makes a decision, the brain is awash in feeling, driven by inexplicable passions. Even when a person tries to be reasonable and restrained, these emotional impulses secretly influence judgment." This suggests that mental operations of cognitive framing precede the mental operations of rational gaming in decision-making formula of both terrorists and the target government.

Framing, a cognitive orientation based in belief systems, norms, aggression motivations, and dogma, helps to define the enemy and circumscribe ways of thinking through policy formation. It constitutes the starting point for each side. For terrorists, it motivates their original plans of violence by envisioning the opponent, the target government, as an unreasonable, evil, powerful giant who must be confronted. For governments, it motivates policy assessments and configuration of the terrorist opponent as irrational, mad, and evil. Gaming, a bargaining framework with its attendant cost and benefit assessments, determines the movement in conflict progression. Both sides engage in strategic operations, both sides are affected by cognitive influences, and both reflect forms of communication, carried out with different operating tools. The bargaining model—gaming—is focused on power jockeying, and because weaker players always seek to enhance their power, terrorists are foremost identified with this strategy over the duration of a conflict of terrorism. The cognitive understanding model—framing—seeks to interpret what a situation means, since the violence and its perpetrators are beyond the expected norms of operation; terrorists lack status and respect and are not regarded as legitimate players in international politics. For this reason, it is more closely allied with the perspective of the target government that maintains a frame model orientation in conflicts of terrorism as long as possible. Eventually, the government may move into a gaming orientation when it becomes necessary to redefine its strategic situation. Finally, once both parties reach their limits in purely strategic behavior, they realize the range for their actions will contain alternatives oriented toward common understandings, a kind of switch from a self-based rational actor, fighting model to a relational-based mutuality of choice-making characteristics of the problem-solving perspective.

Conflict originates with enemy "frames" and ends with converging "games." Both target governments and terrorists initially focus on framing features. Once the terrorists have launched a serious campaign, they move into a "gaming" model. Government, however, retains a "frame" orientation and only reluctantly, after restructuring a problem and evaluating outcome probabilities, may move into a "game" model. When both sides are focused on "gaming," it is possible for them to consider interwoven resolutions—a perspective government resists for it most likely means making some concessions, symbolically or real.

The conflict scheme developed by Rapoport (1960) in *Fights, Games and Debates,* provides a further description to differentiate cognitive judgment from a strategic orientation perspective. In a "fight," the objective is to sidetrack the opponent rather than take up an opportunity to engage in conflict. The belligerent in a fight is regarded as "mainly a nuisance. He should not be there, but somehow he is. He must be eliminated, made to disappear, or cut down in size or importance" (Rapoport 1960, 9). It represents the cognitive aspect of evaluating an enemy, applied by the target government in conflicts of terrorism. A "game," is entirely different; here, the opponent is absolutely essential and all moves—behavioral acts—are designed to elicit counter acts from the other party. It represents the strategic bargaining aspect, and terrorists apply it.

Those conflicts perceived as "fights" reach resolution when one side is destroyed or driven away. Conflicts perceived as "games" are resolved when the eventual outcome becomes perfectly clear to both players. In conflicts of terrorism, terrorists adopt a "game" perspective. They are challenging the status quo. They see themselves as protesters seeking to enter the political arena. In order to do so, they are required to engage their opponent—the opponent's participation is necessary for them to be heard and to achieve credibility as an action, goal-oriented, committed group. The target government has an entirely different perspective: they adopt a "fight" orientation. As a defender of extant conditions, preferring not to enlarge the setting of legitimate political participants, they aim to maintain the power structure and eliminate the challenger.

A third conflict resolution strategy, "debate," is a situation in which belligerents reach a negotiation point (Walker 2004, 281). The convergence from fighting to gaming to debating requires that terrorists and target governments move into a different decision-making framework where they essentially abandoned the premises of their original view of the conflict, which thereby opens opportunity for dispute termination and settlement through negotiation mechanisms.

The overall process of ending a conflict consists of four parts, according to Mitchell (1991, 35): a complex decision, which brings adversaries separately to the conclusion that a possible range of compromise solutions has become preferable to the continuation of fighting; communication where adversaries initially signal to each other their willingness to engage in talks and the terms upon which they will finally agree to meet and attempt to reach a negotiated settlement; negotiation bargaining to obtain the best of acceptable compromise solutions or settlements; and implementing the agreement. A key to this process is that judgments of benefits and estimates of achieving desired outcomes may change over time. Parties may reach an entrapment stage where sunken resources exceed possible benefits that cause them to reconsider reward pursuit and cost justification. Negotiation comes into consciousness, involving a major turnaround in the minds of the belligerents, moving from strict strategic calculations into changed cognitive views of the conflict process. To negotiate is to overcome obstacles and reach agreement.

Table 2.1 Player Orientation in Terrorism Conflict: Framing and Gaming*

	FRAMING	GAMING
Conflict Perspective	Cognitive judgment Constructivism Referent images	Instrumental strategy Rational choice Bargaining
Conflict Dynamics	Understanding and meaning Interpreting conflict onset	Cost-Benefit analysis Projecting conflict ending
Settlement Pathway	Problem interpretation Pictures and metaphors Self and opponent identity	Strategic plans Interactive effects Power and interest moves

*Distinctions between these orientations draw out the two tracks identified by Gonos (1977); Payne (1982); Payne, Bettman, and Johnson (1993); March and Olson (1998); Risse (2000) and Wendt (1999). But framing theory in broadest form incorporates gaming as a subset. A prime example is prospect theory developed by Kahneman and Tversky (1979; 1995; 2000).

Negotiations aim to end conflict. The end may be a suspension of the conflict by stopping violence; a management of the conflict, moving it from violent to nonviolent political debate; resolution of the conflict by settlement of the issues; or transformation of the conflict by creating a process to build strong positive relations between parties (Zartman and Kremenyuk 2005, 1). It is easier to suspend violence than settle all conflict issues or construct a framework between adversaries, outlining future positive relations. Progress along the conflict termination scale is a function of how parties approach the purpose of the negotiation.

What determines the choice of a particular decision strategy? Payne, Bettman, and Johnson (1993, 70–73) assume that individual goals, constraints, and capabilities are important factors. Any change in decision strategy requires a belief that the current approach is not sufficient to bring about expected results, that a better strategy is available, and that one is capable of executing the alternative approach (111–112). This process—the initial selection of a framing perspective and the shift to a gaming one, and changes that may occur as result of terrorist conflict progression—helps to explain the confluence of decision-making terrorist logic and target government logic that may lead to negotiation possibilities. Table 2.1 summarizes key features of framing and gaming.

Terrorist Dominant Decision Logic

Gaming

Conflict Perspective. The operating proposition is that terrorism is a legitimate form of political protest for groups that wish to bargain but lack the resources to do so.

According to Wilson (1961, 292), certain groups may select a strategy of protest based on threats that require mass action or response, putting the target party in jeopardy. The response to protest can be conceived as a cost–benefit analysis, weighing of the probable costs of enduring the protest against the expected costs of making concessions. The protesters' task is creating possibility for meaningful bargaining on a range of issues by being able to offer other parties compensation for ending a protest campaign (Wilson 1961, 298). A group enters into a bargaining relationship, a situation where two or more parties seek conflicting ends through the exchange of tangible and intangible compensation out of hopes of gain. But if that group has nothing to offer to the other—it has no resources the other party (the opponent) needs or wants—it is difficult to place itself in a position in which the first party must bargain. This is the problem of the powerless. Relatively powerless groups lack conventional political resources, and are characterized by a minimal sense of political efficacy, states Lipsky (1968, 1144–1145), who sees protest activity as a mode of goal-oriented political action carried out through "showmanship or display of an unconventional nature, and undertaken to obtain rewards from political or economic systems while working within the system." The problem of the powerless in protest activity is to activate their target authorities or opponents to enter the implicit or explicit bargaining arena in ways favorable to the protesters. Once groups have sufficient resources as bargaining chips, they may engage in direct confrontation.

Conflict Dynamics. Terrorism is bargaining: a dynamic model of war that envisions the initiation and termination of conflict as part of a single process (Reiter 2003, 27). Conflicts of terrorism are about power leverage. Weak parties sometimes attack stronger ones, even when it is clear they have no chance at victory. If the weaker side succeeds in challenging the stronger it can benefit from fighting and settling, says Slantchev (2003, 622). The position of relative power achieved immediately prior to negotiating has a strong effect on the bargaining outcome. Differences in power make a difference in the way negotiations proceed and the outcomes that result: more powerful parties are better able to control the negotiation process and obtain outcomes they desire. But a weak party is able to gain more if the stronger side fails to examine its power in a rational, systematic way and, hence, may act unwisely (Salacuse 2000, 256–257). Issue-specific power matters in a given situation. The weaker party is not at the mercy of the stronger party since an overarching goal links both parties together (Pfetch and Landau 2000, 22). But the stronger player will attempt to dominate the exchange and to reach favorable outcomes at the expense of the weaker party by manipulation.

Settlement Pathway. Negotiations usually take place within a bounded range of power asymmetry. As Nicolaïdis (1999, 103) says, the very act of negotiation signals a certain degree of power symmetry: absolutely weak parties do not negotiate, they surrender; and absolutely strong parties do not negotiate, they conquer. In deciding whether to negotiate or not, the weaker side must determine beforehand whether it has sufficient bargaining power to achieve an outcome through this process that would be more desirable than the status quo. This means specifically assessing its structural power capacity to use bargaining tactics in crafting an outcome preferred over continued fighting. The most important feature of power perception is dependency—"the backbone of bargaining relationships" (Bacharach and Lawler 1981, 79). The perception of a party's bargaining power is determined by the opponent's dependence. If one party has few alternatives to secure a given outcome, and high commitment to the outcomes at issue, while the other side has many alternatives and a low commitment to the outcomes at issue, the dependency of one enhances the bargaining power of the other (Bacharach and Lawler 1981, 59–60, 69, 77). Power is the crux of conflict and negotiation, but it is not the actual distribution or balance of power that matters so much as how leaders perceive their relative strengths and weaknesses. In summary, terrorists aim to reach a point where they can negotiate a solution of their conflict with the target government on most favorable terms. This emerges after the government has experienced sufficient suffering, setting fatigue—costs of continued fighting become too high or its benefits minimized; the level of fear is significant—uncertainty of the terrorists' resolve and future actions create discomfort; and when operating force balance between the terrorist and target government is no longer changing—the display of power dynamics have reached a steady state, a stalemate.

Target Government Dominant Decision Logic

Framing

Conflict Perspective. The primary assumption is that terrorism is illegitimate political violence. In terrorism, random violent activity is used to spread fear. Ordinary citizens are not immune from political harming, though in most norms of political code they are innocent politically, as civilians are innocent militarily. But it is precisely those people that contemporary terrorists try to kill because it breaks political norms across moral limits.

Legitimate discourse consists of interaction between groups focused on working together to achieve reasoned decisions derived from reasoned arguments with critical analysis of opposing positions in an environment of respect for advocates of opposing positions (Johnson and Johnson 2000). Illegitimate discourse is focused around rejection and disparagement of opposing positions, personal attacks on opponents, rigid adherence to own point of view regardless of logic, and a short-term focus on self interest regardless of negative consequences. Political discussion becomes destructive rather than illuminating, which is the goal of terrorism.

Conflict Dynamics. Terrorists are strategic bullies (Ferris et al. 2007, 197). They engage in conflict in ways designed to hurt, frighten, threaten, and tyrannize others. Their selected tactics of influence are designed to convey a particular image and place targets in submissive, power-down positions whereby they are more easily influenced and controlled, in order to achieve organizational objectives. In bullying, regardless of its form, the intention and desired consequences are the same: to influence the target to act in some preconceived direction or manner that subordinates the target to a position of weakness or helplessness to reinforce and strengthen the terrorists' own power and, therefore, increase the probability of accomplishment (Olweus 1993). Bullying is tyranny; undue interference to harm others. It violates norms or rules of customary moral. When applied, the level of resentment in the target increases, particularly when the intention to harm is seen as excessive and unnecessary. Bullying, like terrorism, goes beyond self-defense. Bullying is terrorism: it is blatant aggression seen by the victim as unjustified behavior. It is not an appropriate response to a political problem.

The best response to bullying behavior is to ignore it, by avoiding conflict engagement. Extensive study on school bullying reported in McGrath (2007) says bullies' desires for power is stronger than their empathetic sense, so they are willing to hurt others in order to feel powerful; in fact, they enjoy the power they have over their victims and focus on behavior that will hurt or embarrass their targets. Thus, conflict resolution and mediation are not fit responses to bullying behavior; rather the message should be that this behavior is inappropriate and it must stop now. Bullying is not about grievance expression or political interaction; it's just mean and threatening behavior without legitimate cause. A target does not "reason" with anyone displaying this behavior. By this analogy, an initial response of the terrorist targets is choosing to ignore the aggression by refusing to engage: the conflict avoidance strategy. Alternatively, the bully image calls forth another reaction from the target: a direct, harsh demand that perpetrators stop it, unconditionally, without discussion and without negotiation. Through this frame, a government's policy of no negotiations with terrorists is the strategic response.

An editorial in the *Asian Wall Street Journal* linked bullying and terrorism by describing how the Philippines President Gloria Macapagal Arroyo allowed Iraqi militants to determine the staying power of her nation's military commitments through the negotiated deal to free an abducted truck driver in exchange for Filipino troop withdrawal. Calling the agreement an "irresponsible capitulation to terrorists," the article described inconsistencies in President Arroyo's policy, stressing no negotiation with terrorists that had been applied to recent incidents where American hostages were held by extremist groups in her country, concluding that a mutual agreement was in order: "No negotiations with terrorists, no deals with bullies" (Dillion 2004). The link between terrorism and extortion is also evident in this argument. Extortion, a criminal offense, occurs when someone acquires money, property, or services from another through coercive means of intimidation or threats, or requires a payment for protection to halt future violence. "Terrorism is extortion in the service of politics" (The Belmont Club 2006).

Settlement Pathway. Continuous acts of violence, increasingly threatening, in a sequence of growing event frequency, suggests another strategy response as the "bully" image of a terrorist gradually transforms into a "fighter" image, when the target abandons the notion that terrorism is nothing more than random acts of violence and begins to see a concerted terrorist campaign against it. Now the conflict is more than mere nuisance; it has transitioned into a near crisis, or may even be regarded as a war. Here, changing "frames" of the enemy lead to changing the "frame" of the conflict, as the perspective of crisis and war elicits a "fight" response by the target government. If target "fighting" responses are not successful in stopping terrorist attacks, the conflict eventually moves into a hurting stalemate. At this point, the cognitive impression of terrorists in the mind of the government changes again. The terrorist fighter becomes a terrorist protester who becomes part of a negotiation group when stalemate lingers and the target government is eager to resolve the problem.

Convergence Toward Settlement

Individuals facing decisions might have different preferences in different framing of the same problem. This does not imply that preference reversals are necessarily irrational, since "the practice of acting on the most readily available frame can sometimes be justified by reference to the mental effort require to explore alternative frame and avoid potential inconsistencies," and "framing of acts and outcomes can also reflect the acceptance or rejection of responsibility for particular consequences, and the deliberate manipulation of framing is commonly used as an instrument of self-control" (Tversky and Kahneman 1981, 458). James Druckman (2004, 671) defines a framing effect as "different, but logically equivalent, words or phrases causing individuals to alter their preferences," and shows in further experiments that contextual forces shape psychological reactions. The perspective on an issue matters; a reformulated frame provides alternative ways of seeing a problem, and initial frames may push individuals in one direction while reformulations move in the other direction.

Terrorists seek bargained gains from their coercive strategy but may be hesitant to enter negotiations to set terms of conflict termination with their much more powerful adversary. The government side holds a framing orientation, putting off a gaming perspective as long as possible to avoid a bargaining occasion. In order to reach settlement in a stalemate situation, both parties will need to be operating in a gaming orientation, so the question is when will the government adopt this perspective? This depends on key moments that signal changing dynamics: specifically when the weaker side realizes it has maximized its likely gains. To determine the causes of peace, it is always necessary to take the vanquished's point of view, states Calahan (1944, 252–254), for "when an aggressor belligerent knows it cannot win, it wants to make peace while there is a chance to negotiate it. When all resistance fails, it must accept a dictated peace—not a negotiated peace. The stronger it is at the time of the negotiations, the better the terms it can obtain."

Each side makes an evaluation on two levels before indicating a willingness to terminate violence through a settlement format: (1) outcome reassessment (what ending is desirable and possible?); and (2) conflict reframing (what is this conflict about and what does the adversary want?). The first feature is most important for the terrorists, and the second is critical for the government side and essentially represents a model of political negotiation originally described by Iklé and Leites (1962) as a process of modifying utilities.

"War is coercive bargaining and ends because opponents succeed in coordinating their expectations about what each is prepared to concede," states Slantchev (2003, 621). How do parties coordinate these expectations? By fighting to convince the opponent to accept a settlement, which happens after the opponents learn enough about their prospects in war to decide that continuation is unprofitable. The principle of convergence states that once expectations converge sufficiently, war loses its informational content, and hostilities can terminate with a negotiated settlement. Grieg (2001) shows that negotiated solution becomes possible not when underlying issues are resolved but when sufficient traumatic losses force all sides to change their perceptions of the dispute. Various factors influence prospects for agreement success: costs and pain throughout the lifetime of the conflict, perceptions that parties are unlikely to unilaterally alter the status quo in their favor, the level of threat perceived by each disputant, and a belief that a settlement provides a way to escape the conflict.

The metaphors of terrorism signal shifts in conflict frames that structure strategic response by a target government. The metaphors refer to the images of the terrorists, and images of the conflict itself. The terrorist may be regarded at the onset as a "bully," an irritating interrupter of the social order whose harmful taunts are completely unacceptable and inappropriate, in which case the target decides to ignore the taunt, under the assumption that when bullies are not accorded attention for their acts, they will eventually stop their behavior. Later, the terrorist may be seen as a "fighter," a battling, angry contender, and if the conflict reaches a point of mutual hurting stalemate, the terrorist image may slide into a new form as a kind of "protester" a political opponent characterization where the enemy has been transformed into a party with realistic demands who seeks concessions. At that point, negotiation becomes an acceptable alternative to resolving the conflict.

The three frames brought into the target's cognitive understanding reflect ways the government will choose to manage the threat it faces. Each image is attached to particular motivations or intentions attributed to the enemy. For the bully image, the perceived intention is deliberate harm but without clear or tenable political purpose; for the fighter image, the attributed intention is deliberate harm without legitimate political purpose though the objectives may be clear and tenable; and for the protester image, the accompanying set of intentions consists of deliberate harm with clear, tenable political objectives (containing a set of grievances and demands to satisfy them) that may have some legitimacy, in which case creating an opening for serious thinking about reciprocal exchanges and deal-making concessions.

Terrorism—images of the terrorist and accompanying intentions behind the acts of violence—evokes three associated strategic responses: conflict avoidance as a reaction to the "bully" frame; fighting as a reaction to the "fighter" frame; and problem-solving as a reaction to the "protester" frame. Strategic reactions impact the cognitive model, altering or sustaining it, depending on the success of strategic choice moves in running down the terrorist threat. Only when strategic moves fail to achieve their intended objective, that is, continuing a conflict avoidance strategy that does not deter terrorist attacks, will an alteration in enemy image occur. Transitioning from the "bully" to "fighter" image, or from "fighter" to "protester" calls forth new reference points. The causal linkage posits that the image of the enemy precedes the strategic choice that a target selects as a response to terrorism.

These images cannot be observed directly but only inferred. Thus, if an enemy image (perception) is deduced from the strategic response (action) the relationship becomes tautological: knowing the perception after the fact is not analytically useful if it has no independent verification or validation. But as Levy (1994) argues, why an actor frames a choice in a particular way is important for making causal inferences about framing around a reference point, shifting the value of strategic preferences and choice. Is it possible to observe the operating frame of terrorism in the minds of the target government in advance of the behavioral reaction? From a strictly scientific perspective, it is not. The data are limited to observations—response to the violence documented via verbal and written expression and associated actions—but memoirs, speeches, and other polity material may help develop interpretations about perceptions.

Terrorism usually emanates from nonlegitimate sources in the political arena, that is, individuals or groups having no nation-state grounding or support who operate independently without cover of legitimacy or sovereignty. It is assumed at the start that their acts of violence will be interpreted as bully behavior: harassment or blackmail attempts against an unapproachable, overpowering giant—the target government. The weak status of terrorists and their coercive techniques determine the image created in the minds of their opponent. But if a terrorism *campaign* (a pattern of repeated attacks) is carried out successfully, the image of those terrorists will shift. It is assumed that a set of concerted attacks implies not only commitment to political intention and specific goals behind a strategy of violence but growing popular support for a cause. Terrorists become fighters and then political protesters. Evidence of a conflict stalemate—a condition where the threat of terrorism has not been eliminated and the parties have not solved their problem—can be drawn from terrorism event frequency patterns. It is further assumed that only sharp or clearly identifiable downturns in these events would indicate counterterrorism programs have succeeded; the absence of a trend in this direction can be interpreted as a stalemate condition. Recognizing a mutual hurting stalemate in a conflict is not sufficient to

Table 2.2 Terrorism Meaning and Metaphors

Terrorism is	the calculated use of violence	
	aimed at	physically and psychologically harming the opponent for political ends
	directed at	selected individuals (leaders) or anonymous civilians: innocent bystanders
	designed to	advertise a cause and generate wide-spread psychological fear among citizenry
	intended to	coerce or intimidate government or society to meet political demands
	tactics include	physical violence: destroying property, harassment, and extortion (through assassination, hostage-taking, kidnapping, hijacking, piracy, bombing)
Bullying is	the calculated use of violence or threat of violence	
	aimed at	psychologically harming the opponent for political or personal ends
	directed at	selected individuals (leaders or others) *not* anonymous civilians or innocent bystanders
	designed to	generate psychological fear for selected individuals
	intended to	coerce or intimidate individuals to meet political, financial, or personal goals
	tactics include	physical or verbal violence: destroying property, harassment, extortion
	substituted as	first-order image of terrorism by victim governments
Protesting is	the calculated use of violence or threat of violence or nonviolent coercion	
	aimed at	psychologically harming the opponent for political ends
	directed at	selected individuals (usually leaders), *not* anonymous civilians or innocent bystanders
	designed to	advertise a cause and generate wide-spread support
	intended to	coerce or intimidate government or society to meet political demands
	tactics include	physical or verbal violence: destroying property, harassment
	substituted as	late-order image of terrorism by victim governments

bring parties to a negotiating table; a cognitive shift in enemy and conflict frames are necessary prerequisites.

Tables 2.2 and 2.3 show how these elements connect. The classification of framing is not based strictly on gains and losses perceptions; it is based rather on interpreting terrorism through the target government's lens, a process that evolves due to the broad, vague meaning of the term itself, and its associated referents: bullying and protesting are somehow linked to the idea. The images associated with terrorism compared to features of the bully and the protester show an extended overlap of key ideas across the concepts with subtle differences between them. The overlap between terrorism, bullying, and protesting in Table 2.2 shows all three coercive tactics are

Table 2.3 Terrorists vs. Government:
Cognitive Framing and Strategic Gaming in Conflict Phases

Conflict Party	Conflict Phase	Enemy Frame	Conflict Frame	Conflict Game	Desired Enemy Response
Terrorists The initiator	onset mid-point end	bully fighter negotiator	war war politics	initial attack continuous attacks forced stalemate	fight yield* problem solve
Government The target	onset mid-point end	bully fighter protester	harassment (near) crisis politics	avoidance defend and attack problem solve	yield* yield* problem solve

*If compliance, conflict ends

calculated attempts intended to harm the opponent in order to achieve political ends. Terrorism and bullying desire to create fear among the targeted individuals; protesters seek greater support for their views. In Table 2.3, the relationship between cognitive frames and strategic response is displayed. The cognitive frames of the terrorist enemy as perceived by the government dictate the response. Only in the final stage, when terrorists have forced a stalemate situation, will problem-solving negotiation come into view.

How do conflicts of terrorism fit into this scheme? Conflicts may end in the "bully" frame if governments successfully defeat them. Alternatively, conflicts may end when terrorists have "advanced" into the fighter frame and are successfully put down by the government. Neither resolution includes negotiations. Lastly, conflicts may end with terrorists seen as legitimate opponent protestors with whom government is working out a settlement. Only if the progression of interactions leads to a mutual hurting stalemate will this be possible.

Interpreting the information arrayed in Table 2.3, an initial terrorist attack against a target government is intended to bring about a "fight" conflict behavior response. Instead, the target may just portray the perpetrator as a bully and see the situation framed as harassment, selecting a strategic response of conflict avoidance or issuing an ultimatum. Target responses also intend opponent reactions as noted. Only when conflicts of terrorism reach their final stages, close to a forced stalemate in line with terrorists' desires, does a problem-solving perspective enter into the respective response sets of policy options. The persistence of a terrorist campaign creates changes in the government's operating metaphor. At the point of a mutual stalemate, the image of the terrorist has shifted from bully to protester. This implies problem solving negotiations are possible, although they may not occur for a while.

Perceptions of terrorist campaigns are influenced by the nature and degree of violence projected. Within a conflict structure, terrorist moves of sabotage designed to cause minor, temporary disruption of property and to reduce social functioning efficiency (transportation, communication, or utility network damage) constitute one type of threat. Terrorist moves to capture and hold large groups of people against their will in a type of blackmail scheme (through kidnapping, hostage-taking, hijacking, and piracy) constitute another. Terrorist moves explicitly designed to kill and destroy individuals: assassinations, bombings, including suicide bombing, arson, chemical, biological, and nuclear attacks constitute the greatest threat. Severity of perceived threat points to likely responses to terrorism events. While target hardening, emergency response preparedness, intelligence gathering and surveillance, cutting networks of communications and finance, enacting new laws and creating treaties may be a part of overall strategic reaction to any serious threat, the option of using military force to combat terrorism activity is most likely when the threat is most severe. This corresponds to the target government decision makers' cognitive enemy frame of the terrorist as fighter—not a bully, and not a protester. Although all terrorist campaigns evoke the fighter image of the terrorist, military force is not necessarily used in responding, and even when it is, some campaigns escalate only to a crisis, or a near crisis before the belligerent parties enter the nonviolent resolution stage. For campaigns of terrorism conflict escalating to war, transition into peaceful resolution may take longer or it may be more abrupt. In either case, parties will usually come to an ending point that incorporates at least some features of negotiated solutions.

The metaphors of terrorism (viewing terrorists as bullies, viewing terrorists' demands as extortion, interpreting a terrorist campaign as a political crisis, or imagining terrorists are protesters) interact with the conflict game—costs and benefits affiliated with various options, including wins and losses that may accrues—under given decisional strategies and other features of conflict transformation processes altering party interactive moves from contending to problem-solving. The conflict is not exclusively a cognitively perceived issue, nor merely a strategic interaction game model. These features connect with the power balance dynamics of conflict. Signals of metaphors of terrorism suggest they are critical in understanding how the conflict moves from a "bullying" to a "crisis" perceived stage, and then from a "crisis" perception, into regarding terrorism as linked to a kind of protest movement seeking political change. The metaphor change comes out of a cognitive understanding of the conflict process, not a bargaining, strategic calculation but as a result of strategic interaction effects in fighting terrorism.

The "weakest of the weak" groups who seek political change through violent acts are usually labeled "terrorists." As they grow in strength, whether through active membership, greater popular support for their grievances, and stepped-up levels of successful activity against their targets, within a clearly delineated confined, conflict-ridden space, their label may change to reflect size and scope of activity. Groups developing a formidable power relative to its targets may transform into "insurgents" or "guerrilla fighters." Palestinian political groups including the Palestine Liberation Organization (PLO) have been designated as terrorists and guerrilla fighters by Israel and the West, though the guerrilla label disappeared from media reporting in the 1970s. Operations carried out by al Qaeda are usually seen as acts of terrorism except for their campaign in the Iraq war, which is often recognized as insurgency. Part of the definitional confusion is a function of the overlap in tactics employed by oppositional forces. Bombing (including suicide bombing), random shootings, hostage-taking, and kidnapping are among the common tools used by terrorists, insurgents, and guerrillas to assert their power. Part of the distinction between the labels may be due to the immediate political objectives of such groups: those seeking violent overthrow of a regime engaged in civil war are more likely to be deemed insurgents or guerrillas than labeled terrorists; acts by global jihad, however, which recognizes no territorial boundaries and fights outside conflict-ridden settings, are called terrorism. Of what consequence is this labeling for understanding how a conflict ends? In situations of a mutual hurting stalemate, a target government may be unlikely to entertain the idea of talking to leaders of terrorist groups but may be more likely to consider doing so with the leaders of guerrilla fighters, although this may only apply to ongoing civil war settings involving nationalist, separate causes. When acts of illegal violence are directed at an enemy across state borders, they will be seen as acts of terrorism. Still, there are times when governments agree to talk to terrorists and reach a negotiated agreement and the transformational metaphors, regarding terrorists as bullies, fighters, or protesters from the perspective of the target government become important to understand this process.

How important is it to examine people's ideas and thought processes in explaining their political choices? Lepgold and Lamborn (2001, 4–6) assert that both reference points, cognitive and strategic understanding, play important roles in this process. The first one consists of comprehension through cognitive channels: how and when people construct and maintain coping mechanisms; simplified views of the world through belief systems, images, and schemas; and when a phenomenon "makes sense" to someone in a direct, intuitive way in which conclusions are drawn from prior knowledge through information processing, the use of analogies, and receptivity to argument. Strategic preferences and outcomes are ultimately informed and shaped by expectations and perceptions that come from cognitive processes. Bazerman and Neale (1991, 120) say the frame in which negotiators view a problem can have a dramatic effect on negotiating behavior. Attribute framing influences the content of peoples' thought, though less is known about how it affects the processes assumed to precede those thoughts, and negative framing stimulates more effortful and thorough information with more analytical thinking processes than positive framing (Kuvaas and Selart 2004).

Reframing refers to the transformation of a problem or the way each party develops a different field of vision for understanding it, unfreezing past definitions of issues and reformulating new ones, challenging the way a party conceives of an issue through demonstrating that a current frame is ineffectual (Putnam and Holmer 1992, 129). It also occurs through employing new metaphors or analogies to represent a qualitatively different approach in analyzing the problem. Policy makers confronted with a set of choices will adopt cognitive shortcuts to rational decision making, including cognitive predispositions and affect-driven biases that influence choice, according to Mintz (2003). Leaders approach problems in two stages: first, from a cognitive perspective to deal with complexity and uncertainty, and then strategically, using expected utility logic, report Mintz, Geva, Redd, and Carnes (1997). Wierzbicki (2007) developed a "strategic intuitive decision process," stressing that intuition and analytical thinking result from training. By this argument, terrorists and target governments will think differently about the conflict between them and use abbreviated tools to select a decision strategy. Policymaking becomes dialectic, reflective practice, a process not fully understood or observed in detail by its participants (Schön and Rein 1994).

Framing and gaming are rhetorical devices. They function to organize, interpret, and justify one's understanding of a political process and are useful means for constructing problem views in specific policy situations. Frames that shape policies are tacit; they are built from metaphors to give legitimacy for a course of action inspired by intention. Practical difficulties in constructing frames or games can be overcome by carefully nuanced observations and analyses of the process by which policy and actions evolve over time and at different levels of the policymaking process. People do change their minds, even in fundamental ways, where positions have been reorganized—reframed—in a way that opens up accommodation controversies that had at first seemed hopelessly intractable.

Examining three cases—reunification of the two Germanys, the Israel and Egypt Peace Treaty, and China and the United States normalized diplomatic relations—Armstrong's 1993 analysis showed that: initiatives to improve relations with an adversary succeed when (1) costs of maintaining hostile policies are growing or threatening to grow; (2) major issues are fractionated; (3) negotiations are conducted at a high level (senior government officials with direct access to heads of government), are nonpublic, and involve the fewest possible participants; (4) the negotiating strategy includes offers of concessions on a reciprocal basis; and, finally, (5) parties agree to disagree or seek ambiguous formulations on matters of central principle. Incentive structures for each of the parties to the conflict are critical to reach settlement of differences, and incentive shifts in the need to settle causes each party to reframe its image of the other side, opening the way for resolution.

For decades, Israel and the Palestine Liberation Organization (PLO) adamantly refused to negotiate with one another. Israel vowed it would never "negotiate with terrorists"; and the Palestinians refused to recognize its adversary as a legitimate political entity. Yet, despite many delays, the party leaders eventually talked together and bargained a solution plan. The meetings, first held in secret sessions, involved approval and decision making from the highest levels on each side and led to several agreements between the parties. The conflict has not disappeared—it was not transformed; the ultimate goals of each party have not changed substantially over time. Yet participant willingness to pursue diplomatic mechanisms to achieve their aims did change. What accounts for this shift in strategies? The argument presented suggests that gaming and framing and turning points allowing for openings were key features to this process.

Summary

Negotiation is conceivable with respected enemies but is not appropriate to conduct with bullies. Throughout the conflict process, terrorists, the strategic players, aim for power, hoping to create a stalemate condition through violence engagement acts that allow them a voice for change. Their strategy is clear, simple, and direct. The target government, focused on cognitive framing, thinks differently about the conflict, choosing to characterize the enemy in a way that makes negotiating impossible ("terrorists are bullies"). They seek conflict avoidance, and by not recognizing the other side, they intend to deny terrorists power. Yet, persistence by terrorists may force the parties into a stalemate. When both sides agree that its hurt is intolerable, they seek to break it through problem solving, a point where strategic interaction and cognitive framing decision-making strategies shift.

The critical question is determining which conditions influence strategy shift to open avenues for negotiated settlement. Because strategic interaction models are more sophisticated, it is easier to extract predictable changes. Cognitive framing is looser and less precise. It takes its cues from strategic interaction observations of the other side and readjusts the frames accordingly. Thus, cognitive framing requires a strategic bargaining assessment in order to proceed, for in conflicts of terrorism it lacks an independent structure for reaching resolution. Understanding conflicts of terrorism and prospects for resolution require different decision-making models for assessing how each side—terrorists and governments—evaluates its position from its own perspective and moves toward de-escalation.

Decision-making strategies employed by the two sides in the context of conflict dynamics explain how the parties separately come to this point to engage in conflict resolution. As frameworks for analysis, they project how each side moves toward or away from negotiated settlement. Overall, these developments might be expressed as an application of the constructive controversy model developed by Johnson and Johnson (2000, 29). Central points paraphrased below illustrate the way that disputes such as anti-American terrorist campaigns can move toward settlement. They set the stage for specifying the preconditions of negotiation:

1. When groups confront a problem, they make a judgment based on categorizing and organizing incomplete information, their limited experiences, and their specific perspective, placing a high degree of confidence in their judgment conclusions that freezes the epistemic process.

Terrorists seek change of their political marginality and attempt to attract political attention to their protest by using violence strategically as a bargaining game, engaging authorities in order to reset power balance conditions leading to negotiated settlement in their favor. Target governments prefer the status quo and conflict avoidance by using cognitive framing to view terrorists as bullies rather than legitimate political actors.

2. *When groups present their judgments and its rationale to others using higher-level reasoning strategies, they deepen their understanding of their own position.*

Terrorists intensify their self-view as legitimate protesters, advertising their cause to a wide audience by stressing the negative traits of the adversary, naming and blaming the opponent for their problem, continuing attacks. Target governments intensify their self-view as victims of bullying, advertising their situation to a wide audience by stressing the negative traits of the adversary and blaming the opponent for their problem.

3. *When groups are confronted with different information drawn from new observations, experiences, and perspectives, they become uncertain about their judgments, and conceptual readjustment or disequilibrium is aroused. They unfreeze their epistemic process.*

Terrorists confronted by events generated by forces beyond their control that influence the value of their newly acquired bargaining pressure may shift their strategy. Target governments, as a result of changed conditions in the opponent's calculation of its power, may modify their enemy image into a legitimate political opponent.

4. *When groups face uncertainty, conceptual conflict, or disequilibrium, they are motivated to search for more information and a more adequate, appropriate, cognitive perspective and reasoning process to resolve their uncertainty.*

Terrorists seek out possible strategies that will bring the conflict into range of a negotiated settlement by putting forth tentative proposals or becoming more acceptant to proposals already presented, signaling their opponent. Target governments seek out possible strategies that will bring the conflict into range of a negotiated settlement by putting forth tentative proposals or becoming more acceptant to proposals already presented, signaling their opponent.

5. *When groups adapt their cognitive perspective and reasoning through understanding and accommodating the perspective and reasoning of others, they derive a new, reorganized judgment that opens possibilities for solutions to problems, competencies in managing conflicts constructively, and conflict termination.*

Terrorists signal a willingness to participate in negotiations to end conflict through settlement procedures. Target governments signal a willingness to participate in negotiations to end conflict through settlement procedures.

CHAPTER THREE

Negotiating

Conflict Settlement Preconditions

When are parties prepared to negotiate an end to terrorism? The point when adversaries come together, after independently reaching the decision to negotiate and signaling their intention to the other side, emerges late in a conflict timeline. Theoretically, both terrorists and the target government will have moved to a "gaming" conflict orientation and converged in their thinking to consider negotiating: the terrorist side by reassessing outcomes; the government side by reframing the dispute.

Ample reasons exist for resisting negotiations, among them, whether the opponent can be trusted as a reliable party committed to forming a solution that satisfies needs and meets demands for all sides. Devious objectives of disputants (individual empowerment, face-saving moves, and delaying tactics) may be operating (Richmond 1998).Yet, negotiations happen.Why? The most prominent factor is the commitment of actors to settle—a function of issue salience, fighting fatigue, mutual perceptions of a moment of opportunity to move ahead, the power balance dynamic, and projected benefits associated with pursuing this course of action—determined via convergence of two tracks of decision-making logic, cognitive framing and strategic thinking, that have informed each side's conflict-bargaining orientation. Another factor is optimism, a belief that it is possible to create a mutually satisfying, reciprocal exchange agreement with the adversary. A third element is conferring status and credibility on the opponent as a viable negotiating partner capable of implementing decisions for mutual advantage. These components indicate adversaries have moved into a principled bargaining format where interests can intersect in a mutual agreement of reciprocal exchange.

What causes a party in conflict to conclude a situation is hurting its interests so badly that it cannot be allowed to continue? Why and how do the adversaries come to the conclusion that joint effort is necessary to resolve their differences? These questions emerge in a prenegotiation period; they refer to starting a political process aimed to alter a relationship that will lead to the end of violence. Prenegotiation begins, according to Zartman (1989) when one of the parties considers negotiation as a policy option and communicates its intention to others. It ends when the parties agree to begin formal negotiations. Phase one in a prenegotiation period means defining the problem and deciding to engage (Saunders 1996, 426). Parties recognize they cannot get what they want by unilateral action and explore whether negotiation—a process consisting of an effort with the other side to find a joint solution—might be possible. Their exploration often has to be conducted in secret through back channels because the symbolism of talking with an enemy may render direct and open talks taboo. Decision makers on the threshold of taking this step are often reluctant or fearful to reach out to the other side because of the mutual hatred, lack of trust, and risk of uncertain results. Some estimates of an outcome of success have to be made before serious discussion with the other side. When leaders decide to commit themselves to attempt a negotiated settlement, they have to consider whether this type of solution would be better than continuing the present situation, whether a politically manageable fair settlement can be created, and whether leaders on the other side will be able to accept the settlement and survive politically.

Settling conflict with terrorist groups through a negotiation process does not enjoy wide resonance among members of a victimized public, a targeted state government, or even the leadership of the perpetrators of violence. Whether to take this step at all is a contentious issue. Further, a hard-line approach projecting a standard of toughness against negotiating is common among policymakers on both sides. Thus, to explore negotiation preconditions, as a first step it is essential to survey perspectives on its appropriateness. Is negotiating an acceptable way to end this type of conflict? If acceptable, is it feasible? Feasibility can be evaluated along four dimensions: (1) Does a mutual hurting stalemate develop to a point that the conflict is "ripe" for resolution? (2) Have "turning points" occurred that move parties toward settlement? (3) Are all parties willing and ready to carry out negotiations? and (4) Do parties believe they will discover a suitable reciprocal exchange agreement? These considerations shape the context of a potential bargaining environment. They differ from the unilateral demands a party may issue as prerequisites to negotiating with its enemy such as establishing a truce before talks can begin, or forcing a party to relinquish a particular policy goal prior to scheduling a meeting with its adversary. Negotiation preconditions reflect the sum of subjective assessments of all the parties in conflict. In conflicts of terrorism, once these conditions are met, negotiation may result. Short of satisfying all four dimensions, negotiations for settlement to end terrorism are unlikely.

Is Negotiating Acceptable?

Is negotiating a wise strategy for governments to consider? Hughes (1990, 79–80) argues that governments should recognize terrorist's legitimacy, thus enabling them to abandon and leave behind the methods of terror; the means to do so is through discussion because "negotiation is a search for legitimacy in the other side." This argument is not widely accepted. Although various counterterrorism models and policies have their critics, resistance strategies, and reform programs command far greater acceptance among political decision makers, informed elites, and public opinion than reframing terrorist conflict into problem-solving negotiation. The reasons are clear. As Neumann (2007, 128) states, "the argument against negotiating with terrorists is simple: Democracies must never give in to violence, and terrorists must never be rewarded for using it. Negotiations give legitimacy to terrorists and their methods and undermine actors who have pursued political change through peaceful means." Negotiations should be resisted. They give terrorists respectability approximately equal to that of the government, or legitimacy by admitting that they have real grievances that are negotiable. Target governments may refuse to negotiate with terrorists, seeing them as common criminals, bandits, or thugs. In addition, demands of terrorist groups are usually expressed in extreme and nonnegotiable rhetoric, so negotiations can never have a positive or productive outcome. Proponents of a "no concessions" policy to terrorists offer two reasons for refusing to negotiate: it rewards terrorists for violent behavior—if groups believe they can reach their goals through violence, terrorists will continue to use such tactics in the future; and if target governments hold firm to their position that nothing will be conceded, then terrorists will have no incentive to attack. Yet historically, governments have conducted such negotiations—irrespective of their aversion and declared official positions not to do so—though usually as a last resort rather than as first response. Fisher and Ury (1991, 161) argue that a government should negotiate with terrorists because "in the sense that you are trying to influence their decisions—and they are trying to influence yours—you are negotiating with them, even if you are not talking with them." Negotiation does not mean giving in or compromising one's principles, but finding a solution and working out an arrangement "that is arguable consistent with each side's principles" (164). But in deciding to pursue this strategy, governments must ask themselves whether a better alternative to negotiating an agreement actually exists and if they are willing to carry it out to achieve desired ends. Governments often overestimate this prospect, state Fisher and Ury (165), who advise that, in general, parties victimized by terrorism should be willing to invest in negotiation to discover if something satisfactory can be developed; nonviolent means should always be considered seriously.

Is negotiation a smart move for the terrorists to consider? Manifestos of terrorist groups think otherwise. Terrorists employ armed struggle to secure political objectives that cannot be achieved in any other way. As political players, they are seen as relatively weak partisans in an intensely felt conflict against an insurmountably stronger opponent. They seek three objectives: to be noticed, to be understood (as people with political aims; not common criminals), and to alter the existing political situation, states Clark (1990, 7). The usual strategy for a terrorist group is to continue the pursuit of political objectives through armed struggle, as shown clearly, for example, in the Palestine Liberation Organization (PLO) charter. The

1968 PLO statement was known for "the three no's" in defining its relationship with Israel: no negotiations, no concessions, no recognition. The position was designed to instill fear and produce a strong sense of national insecurity for Israelis to lead them to believe their future rested on violent probes from Palestinians. But years later, the two parties agreed to meet and negotiate a solution to their differences, which led to the Oslo Accords in 1993. Although the negotiation did not bring political stability to resolve the Israeli–Palestinian dispute, it illustrates a shifting position by a terrorist-labeled group. Similarly, the 1985 Hezbollah manifesto declares "no treaty, no ceasefire, no peace agreements" with Israel. Yet, a negotiated swap between the parties—five militant Lebanese prisoners exchanged for the remains of two Israeli soldiers—occurred in July 2008.

The logic against negotiating with the enemy in conflicts of terrorism, apart from how that enemy is defined, is powerful and persuasive. Governments may regard negotiating as a weakness, for it implies giving in to unreasonable demands of an illegitimate group who have formed their influence through unacceptable political channels. Terrorists, too, may regard negotiating as a weakness, since a transition from violent to nonviolent bargaining will severely restrict their effective pressure on the target regime and consequently limit the range of potential concessions. Both sides are reluctant to start the process; both sides desire their respective strategies of confrontation will succeed in wearing down their opponent. Both hope their traditional aims—in vision, directed at conquering the other side; in reality, directed at deterring negative acts against it and strengthening their own power—will work. Conflict continues because cessation of violence is not the most important thing on the political agenda. Everyone wants it to end, but they want it to end on their terms. As long as this condition exists, there is not much to offer to the parties in conflict. Negotiating would be a mistake. Furthermore, if negotiations are successful and result in a temporary cessation of hostilities, the consequence is simply giving the adversaries time to regroup and gather strength for a new round of violence later.

Another obstacle to opening negotiations between a government and terrorists is the perceived absence of credible negotiating capability within the militant community. Governments do not expect those they call terrorists, including countries on a designated state-sponsored terrorism list, to hold firm to their promises. Thus, if terrorists (or states sponsoring terrorism) desire a negotiated settlement, they have to find ways to convince a targeted government that they will not defect; if a government opts for negotiation as a way to end conflict, they must find a legitimate negotiating partner that represents terrorists' interests and committed to implementing agreements. A capability to negotiate combined with willingness by both sides to do so signal "negotiation readiness" (Pruitt 1997). Host state ties are important to terrorists for conducting operations and safe havens, says Bapat (2006, 21–218). In negotiations, the host can become the guarantor of terrorist behavior by enforcing the terrorists' compliance with an agreement (Bapat 2006, 218). To induce negotiations, the host must devote resources to policing terrorists.

There are some benefits to be gained from a negotiated settlement. Face-to-face discussion between the sides (either direct representatives or intermediary parties) on matters ranging from cessation of violence and other issues related to law and order, to political negotiations involving fundamental objectives of the terrorist group, may help parties discover points of agreement that would cause terrorists to end their violent attacks or alter their behavior in some other way (Clark 1990). Though negotiation leading to a truce might represent only a temporary lull in fighting the broader dispute, it may help reduce the level of emotion and anger common in terrorist conflict situations, so that other steps may be taken to terminate the struggle over the longer term. A successfully negotiated agreement, whatever its limited scope, may play some role that helps build mutual trust and confidence, qualities usually in short supply in these situations. The process may help move the system toward the eventual conclusion of hostility. Or negotiation may be the best solution, not because it is such a good option, but simply that others are bad or impossible to implement. Pakistani authorities, following their new approach to end extremism through negotiations, struck a deal with tribal elders of the Kyber Pass in mid-2008 to reduce insurgency in the region.

A terrorist act in isolation is not linked to any message about negotiating with the other side. But a patterned sequence of events that culminates in a clear terrorist campaign may be communicating just that. Thus, these events of violence and the target's reaction to them together may be conceptualized as a "prenegotiation" time, that is, a bargaining period of the steps taken prior to, and in preparation for, eventual formal talks between antagonists. The process constitutes attempts by each side to improve their positioned balance of power ratio against the opponent because a key factor that affects negotiated outcomes is the power distribution structure in operation at negotiation onset. It is assumed that greater power means an agent has greater leverage and more coercive influence over its opponent in crafting a final contract; greater influence enhances one's probability of reaping greater benefits in any agreement. Reduced power implies the opposite. Understanding what motivates parties in conflict and the factors altering those conditions provides clues to any eventual resolution process.

Addressing the issue whether to negotiate with terrorists, former U.S. diplomat Marc Nicholson (2003) asks under what conditions terrorists' means justify their ends, stating that America must distinguish between movements that may be addressed by negotiation and those that must be annihilated: genuine political movements, albeit groups using terrorist means, "may be dealt with more cheaply (if holding our noses) by negotiation." But "terrorists who lash out from hatred but without concrete and achievable political goals, including those whose political goals are so sweeping as to be delusional—such as al Qaeda members 'acting out' the multiple failures of Middle Eastern societies—are practically, if not philosophically, nihilists with nowhere to go. Their acts are pointless. They are a psychotic, not a political, phenomenon and the only reasonable answer is the use of force to kill or incarcerate them, while seeking in the longer term to address the social pathologies which produce new recruits." Oxford historian David Selbourne in *The Losing Battle with Islam* (2005, 486) states that the values of Islam and the ideas of democracy, human rights, and free markets are diametrically opposed, classifying the divide, as Muslims do, as a clash of civilization between the two worlds. "To declare 'terrorism' rather than Islamism to be the true foe of the non-Muslim world, and especially of 'the West' and its ways, is therefore an error of judgment." And while admitting that coexistence is a necessary ideal, he says that "Islamism is on its guard against 'infidel' attempts to deflect its energies by negotiation, bribery, or cooptation," quoting Khomeini who asserted that the committed clergy had never been in a state of conciliation and never will be. Former U.S. Secretary of State Madeleine Albright (2007, 74) has written that

> In any conflict, reconciliation becomes possible when the antagonists cease dehumanizing each other and begin instead to see a bit of themselves in their enemy. . . . When people are pursuing the same goal, each side should be able to understand what motivates the other. To settle their differences, they need only find a formula for sharing what both want—a tricky task, but one that can at least be addressed through an appeal to reason. Not all conflicts of this sort lend themselves to this sort of negotiation. . . . Today, al Qaeda's lust for a war of vengeance fought with the tools of terror cannot be accommodated. Some differences are too great to be reconciled. In most situations however, reconciliation will be eminently preferable to continued stalemate or war.

Challenging the assumption that terrorists' demands are so extreme as to be nonnegotiable, Louise Richardson (2006, 212–213) asserts that "it would be worth finding out if that is, in fact, the case. Yet suggestions that their demands might be negotiable are treated with deep suspicion, and suggestions that we actually talk to the terrorists are considered tantamount to treason." While admitting governments always resist talking to terrorists for fear it will be seen to confer legitimacy on them and to admit their violent, illegal acts of attention-getting succeeded, Richardson (2006) believes talking is an invaluable opportunity for gaining information about the opponent. By knowing your enemies, you can learn what they want and thus decide whether to deny or grant their wishes, or to negotiate a resolution of the conflict that brings about an end to their terrorist campaign. Other states have followed this course in the past. Talks need be neither open nor direct, but conducted through intermediaries.

U.S. Policy and Practice

The American approach to deter terrorism has long centered on a policy of "no concessions" in dealing with hijackings, kidnappings, and hostage-barricade situations.[1] Policies toward shootings and bombings that do not involve abducting individuals have emphasized multilateral conventions against terrorism (Evans 1979,

9, 78). In February 1971, the Nixon administration issued a report to Congress—
"U.S. Foreign Policy for the 1970s: Building for Peace"—stating that "we need an
agreement between the nations of the world that will guarantee the punishment
of those who commit such crimes [hostage situations and skyjacking] wherever
they go and whatever motives they profess . . . we need to make certain that there
is no profit in such a crime, and no sanctuary for those who commit it" (Nixon,
Department of State Bulletin 1971, 426). The official policy of the United States against
negotiating with terrorists was tested in the wake of a hostage-taking incident at the
Saudi Arabian embassy in Khartoum, Sudan, in March 1973. The Palestinian group,
Black September, abducted ten members of the diplomatic community, including
three Westerners (two Americans, the U.S. chief and deputy chief of Mission to
Sudan, and the Belgian Chargé d'affaires) who were assassinated during the ordeal.
The terrorists sought freedom for several hundred prisoners, primarily Palestinians
held in Israeli jails, and Sirhan Sirhan, incarcerated in the United States for killing
presidential candidate Robert Kennedy during the 1968 campaign. President Nixon
made it clear that America would not yield to the terrorists' demands to trade hostages
for prisoners. During a news conference, he said that the United States "would not
play blackmail. We cannot do so and we will not do so" (*Christian Science Monitor*,
March 3, 1973, 2). The policy has been publicly reaffirmed over the years. But Patrick
Buchanan (www.townhall.com, August 4, 2006) points out that the United States has
dealt with numerous individuals and groups it labeled terrorists. President Franklin
Roosevelt conceded Eastern Europe to the Soviet Premier Joseph Stalin, the "Great
Terrorist," following World War II; Viet Cong atrocities in South Vietnam did not
impede negotiations in Paris with U.S. Ambassador Averell Harriman; and other world
leaders accused of terrorism in their political careers, Menachem Begin, Mummar
Khadafi, Josef Tito, among them, have been honored guests at the White House.

U.S. Secretary of State Colin Powell reiterated the pledge never to negotiate with
terrorists in September 2004, following the beheading of two American hostages in
Iraq, in light of recent deals the Philippines government had made with Iraqi terrorists.
After militants kidnapped a Filipino truck driver in the war zone, President Gloria
Arroyo agreed to withdraw her country's military troop contingent in the coalition
force in exchange for his release. But the United States secretly agreed to demands
set by a group that kidnapped two Fox News journalists in Gaza in August 2006.
Two sets of demands—one was publicly issued, another managed through secret
channels—were involved in the event. Publicly, the terrorists were demanding the
release of all Muslims held in American prisons in exchange for the two abducted
reporters. When they were released, without any freeing of prisoners, it was stated
that both had converted to Islam as a reason for their freedom. However, in private,
the terrorists really wanted the United States to pressure Israel to reopen the Rafah
border crossing between Egypt and Gaza and to cease shelling Palestinian residences in
the area. It appeared the United States participated in negotiations and complied with
the request, as the terrorist's wishes were fulfilled. A State Department spokesperson
refused to comment when confronted with the story.

Tom Casey, a Department of State deputy spokesman, responded to a question during a daily press briefing in July 2007, concerning South Koreans taken hostage by the Taliban in Afghanistan and negotiated efforts to release them, saying, "It remains U.S. policy not to make concessions to terrorists." Queried about whether to *negotiate* with them, he repeated, "Again, the policy as written over the past twenty years or so is to not make concessions to terrorists and that remains our view." Buchanan (www.antiwar.com, August 5, 2006) argues in an online news journal that nations often declare adversaries "terrorists" in order to delegitimize them and to remove any obligation to negotiate with them, falling back on the declared policy, "We do not negotiate with terrorists," in a veiled reference to America's refusal to negotiate with Iran, a country accused of state-sponsored terrorism. Pipes (*New York Sun,* July 26, 2005) turns the issue around, stating that most anti-Western terrorist attacks these days are perpetrated without any expression of demands, raising questions about whether negotiation would ever work: "Bombs go off, planes get hijacked and crashed into buildings, hotels collapse. The dead are counted. Detectives trace back the perpetrators' identities. Shadowy Web sites make posthoc, unauthenticated claims. But the reasons for the violence go unexplained." Because it is up to analysts to speculate about motives behind the violence—from personal grievances to an intention to alter U.S. policy or an effort to change the world—and up to the terrorist groups to articulate their goals, in the end, says Pipes (2005), militants construct a never-ending mountain of grievances to build their cause that renders negotiation unlikely, for without realistic, viable demands, negotiation is worthless.

Negotiation appropriateness may depend on how terrorism strategy is perceived. Lapan and Sandler (1988) argue that beliefs and resolve of the terrorists are crucial in identifying when a nonnegotiation strategy is useful. If governmental declarations are not completely credible and the government's costs of not negotiating are uncertain, then never negotiating will not be seen as plausible policy. Governments minimize costs by negotiating only if this strategy costs less than continuing conflict; sometimes, a nonnegotiation policy may be more costly than talking to the enemy. Negotiation appropriateness also depends on how the terrorists themselves are perceived. Has a new type of terrorism evolved that sharply differentiates it from the goals and practices of previous groups? Experts disagree. Hoffman (1998) and Laqueur (1999) say today's terrorists represent a very different and more lethal threat than terrorist groups of the past. Hayes (2003) concurs, stating that an "absolute" form of terrorism (marked by radical, impossible demands) more dangerous that previous ethnic groups, has emerged. But other scholars (Copeland 2001; Duyvesteyn 2004; Tucker 2004) argue that the new paradigm of motives, tactics, and goals of terrorists differs little from the old model. Duyvesteyn (448) asks whether the increase in the number of deaths that result from terrorism forms a conscious choice of terrorists, as stressed by the "new terrorism" school, or is a result of technology progress and increased effectiveness of the instruments and also a necessity to strike harder to achieve the same effects achieved by groups before. Terrorists seek publicity for their cause and need the media's attention to do so. Global media attention will be directed to report dramatic events of terrorism but not "routine" or lesser events. Hence, reduced-scale terrorist activity will not be an effective way for power-seeking terrorists to be heard, and as a result, they will be unable to threaten their targets. Increased lethality does not indicate terrorists today are different from previous generations. Despite their opposing views, Copeland (2001) and Hoffman (1999) agree on a major point, namely that "old" terrorists and "new" operate with common goals—seeking attention, recognition, and power. What they hope to achieve and what methods of coercion they use in their pursuit may be different.

Is Negotiation Feasible?

What are the preconditions for the terrorists and target government to move out of a deadlock situation? For terrorists, it means changing their expectation based on their demands that would alter the payoff structure in their game of strategy by visualizing their status or fate in the future. For governments, it means changing the frame of the conflict—what is the conflict about—changing the frame of the opponent from an illegitimate to legitimate political participant, and imagining proposals where mutual gains outcomes are conceivable. In each case, the shift required is psychological, though these changes are determined by the presumed impact of outside events, new perceptions of interactions, and fresh calculations of risk and reward. In a study of the U.S.-Vietnam conflict and negotiations, the Paris peace talks of 1969–1973, Zartman (1976, 390–393) characterized the dispute as a mix of different military strategies in which standards of winning and losing vary: the guerrilla wins by not losing, but the conventional side loses by not winning. This implies that it takes less for the weaker side to claim victory and far more for the stronger power to do so—a dynamic important to power balancing perceptions. Zartman (1976) concluded that three conditions are necessary for negotiations to take place: clear problem identification, a stalemate condition, and willing parties that negotiate to break the deadlock and form a solution. From theses roots, negotiation feasibility, which are preconditions for settlement, have evolved along different theoretic lines.

First, the notion of "conflict ripeness," pioneered by Zartman (1985, 1989), is centered on objective and subjective factors of the dispute context, especially a mutual hurting stalemate. Tipping point theory—a popular idea developed by Gladwell (2002), which illustrates that when a small amount of weight is added to a balanced object it causes it to suddenly and completely topple—provides an explanation for breakdown in mutually hurting stalemate tolerance among disputants that moves them to consider conflict settlement.

Second, "turning points" in negotiation, a concept finetuned by Daniel Druckman (2001), emphasizes the important moments, including outside events, that influence party decisions to move a negotiation process forward (or backward). Catastrophe theory (Zeeman 1977), stating sudden shifts in behavior that arise from small changes in circumstances may lead to dramatic change, provides an explanation for the influence of turning points in negotiation.

Third, "negotiation readiness," an idea put forth by Pruitt (1997, 2005), expresses a psychological element of player willingness and capacity to participate in the bargaining process. Chaos theory (Kiel and Elliott 1997) says in chaos there is order where infinitesimally small changes at the start can lead to bigger changes later, providing an explanation for the effects of readiness—party willingness and capacity to negotiate.

Finally, the idea of "interest-based bargaining," a negotiation strategy advanced by Fisher and Ury (1981) and Fisher, Ury, and Patton (1991), in which reciprocal exchange of mutual gains intersect in win-win solutions making agreement possible. Game theory (e.g., Harsani 1965; Schelling 1960) determines how rational players attempt to maximize gains and minimize losses under interdependent choices provides an explanation for the effects of principled bargaining based on minimax strategy.

A mutually hurting stalemate condition is closely associated with "conflict ripeness." Parties' uncertainty about their opponent's power and resolve connects to the "turning points" feature. Negotiating partner credibility and guaranteed security for the adversary is linked to "negotiation readiness." The value of settlement, clarity of demands, and rewards divisibility and party separation are tied to "interest-based bargaining."

Conflict Ripeness

What Is It? The notion of "conflict ripeness" (Zartman 1985, 1989, 2000) specifies two primary conditions that must exist between the disputing parties prior to negotiation onset: a mutually hurting stalemate or impending catastrophe that leads all players to conclude escalation is no longer an option and continued deadlock is too costly; and a perception that there is a way out of the conflict that will not sacrifice parties' basic interests—not a specific solution but a shared sense that settlement is possible and everyone is willing to search for that end. Zartman (1985, 231, 237) identifies dimensions determining the suitability for conflict resolution—conflict escalation processes, policy tracks, and power relations—noting the point of "ripeness" for resolution is a realization that neither side is able to reach its aims to resolve the problem, and a realization by both sides that matters will get worse if they do not take joint action to mitigate impending disaster. The ripe moment is not a literal idea but emerges from feel and instinct and is imperfectly configured. Parties have to convince each other of their good faith, credibility, and reliability—developments that occur only when alternative, usually unilateral, means of achieving a satisfactory result are blocked and the parties find themselves in an uncomfortable and costly predicament. The key to successful conflict resolution lies in the timing of efforts to move in this direction. Zartman (2000, 225–227) sees ripeness is a necessary but not sufficient condition for the initiation of negotiations; it is not self-fulfilling or self-implementing, nor identical to its results and, therefore, not tautological.[2] It represents the perid prior to a search for an agreed outcome.

A mutual hurting stalemate contains both objective and subjective elements, although only the latter really matter. Since mutual hurting stalemate is a subjective estimation, it can be perceived at any point in the conflict, early or late. But the greater the objective evidence, the greater the subjective perception of a stalemate and its pain is likely to be, and this is more likely to develop after all other courses of action and possibilities of escalation have been exhausted. Conflicts not treated early appear to require a high level of intensity for a mutual hurting stalemate perception to kick in and negotiations toward a solution to begin (Zartman 2000, 229). The other component of a ripe moment—a perception by both parties of a way out—is easier to identify since leaders often indicate whether they believe that a deal could be formulated with the other side, particularly when they change their minds. In sum, an expression of the parties' subjective sense of pain, impasse, and inability to bear the costs of further escalation, related to objective evidence of stalemate (data on numbers and nature of casualties and material costs) along with decision-makers' assessments and indications of a way out, constitute the existence of conflict ripeness.

Analytically, ripeness might be considered as a confluence dynamic where perceptions of terrorist power may be increasing relative to perceptions of a government's power that may be decreasing. When these trajectories have come to a stopping point and neither side is willing or able to bring about a major change in the situation, the convergence creates a mutual hurting stalemate. For less intense conflicts, ripeness may consist of an opportunity for settlement that grows more attractive because issues defining the dispute are becoming less salient in the political discourse. Zartman (2000, 241) suggests that such openings might be termed mutually enticing opportunities, another necessary but not sufficient condition for the onset of negotiations. Hancock (2001) examines different conceptions of ripeness to evaluate their usefulness to war termination theory and practice, concluding that it can be enhanced through a systematic combination of its objective and subjective elements within a framework of policy options, including prerequisites listed by Haass (1990): a shared desire to come to agreement, ability of leaders to come to agreement, room in negotiations so parties can claim they protected their interests, and a negotiation process acceptable to both parties. What is critical is that actors must believe they can no longer achieve their preferred goals before they are able to perceive conflict ripeness. Occasionally, changes in leadership during the conflict process may lead to a settlement if it is in the practical political interests of the new leader.

How Does It Apply? Grieg (2001) searched for conflict ripeness in a study of enduring rivalries, defined as dispute dyads that persisted at least twenty years with at least six conflicts, using international data covering the period 1946–1992. Moving toward settlement was positively affected when mediation efforts were initiated by at least one of the rivals and fundamental changes in regime structure increased prospects for improvement in rivalry relations. The existence of threats to the rivals that emanated from outside the immediate conflict had a mixed effect as disputes involving fatalities did not increase likelihood of an agreement, and the effect of rivalry power distribution indicated that power disparity made use of force less likely than a parity balance. Mooradian and Druckman (1999) found a mutually hurting stalemate was a condition for negotiating a ceasefire in Nagorna-Karabakh. Schrodt, Yilmaz, and Gerner (2003), using data from several conflicts (Israel-Lebanon, Israel-Palestine, former Yugoslavia, civil wars in Liberia and in Sierra Leone), found that ripeness measured as a hurting stalemate over long-term change in the amount of conflict (frequency measured across a number of months) is a better predictor than the levels of conflict (based on absolute levels of violence) correlating with the onset of negotiation and declines significantly after negotiation. Mahieu (2007), drawing on various cases of civil wars (Northern Ireland, Liberia, Cyprus, Niger, Bosnia, Mozambique), concluded that the ripe moment to suspend hostilities is when belligerents have reached a broad consensus on the political issues underlying their conflict, and when they have arrived at a general formula for the negotiations. Once they come to this point, they realize a negotiated solution to their dispute is within reach. Conflict can be allowed to follow its course while negotiations are underway in the hope of accelerating the finding of an agreement. But this will work only if the problem is not too complex and allows for a relatively quick settlement.

In Sum The conceptual features identifying conflict ripeness—a mutually hurting stalemate, and a perceived way out of the conflict—can be translated into observable markers shown to have positive empirical effects in evaluating conflict ripeness. These factors include the duration of a dispute, and the frequency and severity of violent events.

Turning Points

What Are They? The concept of "turning points" (Druckman 1986, 2001) is based on the idea that external, dramatic events beyond the control of the prenegotiation process may affect parties individually, moving them toward or away from consideration of agreement indicated by changes that occur. Turning points with positive impact on negotiated settlements contribute significantly to uncertainty, feeding fears and insecurity with respect to the perceived future, striking urgency for a party to reach a solution, usually due to unexpected actual or perceived costs. Susskind (2004, 339) says there are critical moments, important turning points in most negotiations, though they are not easy to identify either in a general way or on a case-specific basis as they are occurring but are clearly recognizable retrospectively. These critical moments in negotiation consist of the point where one of the parties is willing or driven to try something new or to do something to deflect or transform the relationships in ways that produce more satisfying or efficient results. Central to this explanation is the idea of turning points or events that move the process on a trajectory toward or away from the agreement. The concept is considered along with stages, defined by Druckman (2001, 519), as "events or processes that mark passage from one stage to the next, signaling progress from earlier to later phases." In form, turning points constitute key events that may help resolve an impasse, lead to developing formulas for the bargaining process, or change evaluations of the terms for talking. These events are viewed as instrumental in moving the negotiations from one stage to the next.

Turning points are different from ripeness: they are part of a negotiation or prenegotiation process rather than only a condition for negotiation onset; they are indicated by changes that occur during the process rather than by conditions that lead to the change, and they are indicative of downturns or escalations as well as upturns or de-escalations in the process, states Druckman (2005, 187). Although both refer to changes in the course of a process or relationship, and occur often as a result of an impasse, turning points are indicated by departures from the process, which have consequences for the way the process unfolds toward or away from agreement.

How Does It Apply? Druckman (2001) discovered that a relationship between types of negotiation and factors that precipitate the occurrence of turning points exists. While trade and environment negotiations might be affected by internal shifts and new substantive information received by the parties, in security issues, negotiations are often antagonistic, conducted in an atmosphere of mutual distrust with slow, incremental adjustments. Governments are risk adverse when dealing with their security and reluctant to alter the status quo or take bold initiatives and for this reason, progress depends on external events. Thus, turning points are driven primarily by external events; activity outside or more distant from the immediate, confined negotiation setting. Druckman (2001, 537) says that security negotiations turning points are affected by external events, that security negotiators make few concessions and offer few proposals for agreement and are sensitive to possible losses rather than potential gains, making them less likely to take risks or to depend less on their own initiatives than external intervention or outside events to move forward. Druckman (2005) examined turning points in thirty-four cases of negotiations categorized by issue area: security, political, and trade-economic. Security cases included defense, strategic policy making, arms control, and war termination. Results showed that most of the precipitants in security negotiations cases were external with a typical path: an external precipitant led to abrupt departures in the existing negotiation process, which led to de-escalations. Rasler (2000) investigated shocks, expectancy revisions, and de-escalation of protracted conflict. Shocks, a concept akin to turning points, play a critical role in transforming intractable conflicts if they influence the adversaries to reevaluate their prior expectations but their impacts are highly contingent on timing, context, and changes in leader expectation. Shocks include external threats, changes in domestic political leadership, and decreases in economic resources, all catalytic events that cause adversaries to reconsider assumptions about their rivals or their ability to compete with them. Rasler (2000) examines the Israeli-Palestinian conflict from 1979–1998, discovering three shocks: the Israeli invasion of Lebanon in 1982, the Intifada in 1987, and the Gulf War in 1991, on the Palestinian side and two shocks—the Intifada and Gulf War—on the Israeli side strongly affected agreements between the parties. These shocks changed expectations and strategies of key decision makers and opened opportunities for decision makers to change their institutional structures in ways enabling them to pursue conflict de-escalation; as turning points, they delineated moments when parties reassessed their strategies and policies.

In Sum The conceptual features identifying turning points toward negotiation are shown to have positive empirical effects in moving a conflict process toward negotiation. These factors include major political movement within the international system that alters the perceived significance of the direct issues facing the disputants, and other demonstrations of force or violence affecting one of the parties that alters their calculation of power leverage.

Negotiation Readiness

What Is It? The concept of "negotiation readiness" (Pruitt 1997, 2005, 2007) is a combination of willingness, and a motivation to escape the conflict; optimism, the sense that mutually acceptable agreement is possible; and leader capability—skills and resources for all parties to adequately represent themselves in bargaining to decide it is in their best interest to negotiate an agreement rather than continue in conflict. Motivational ripeness (willingness to give up a lot now in exchange for substantial concessions from the other rather than waiting until later in the hope that the other can be persuaded to make these concessions unilaterally) plus mutual dependence in achieving the goal, states Pruitt (1997) point to negotiation readiness. Spector (1998) writes of readiness, referring to negotiators' capacity to negotiate. The overall emphasis is placed on the motives and perceptions of each party separately to explain the asymmetric patterns that are often found, that is, one side may be more motivated to settle a conflict than the other. Optimism about the other party's reciprocity is a variable that determines the extent to which a goal of mutual cooperation will affect behavior: the stronger a party's optimism, the more fully it will act on its goal, and without optimism, no conciliatory action will be taken (Pruitt 1997, 239). Readiness asserts that a party moves toward resolution if it is motivated to achieve de-escalation and is optimistic about finding a mutually acceptable agreement that will be binding on the other side. Unlike ripeness, which theorizes about the conflict dynamics, readiness theorizes about dynamics of the parties in the conflict. Negotiation readiness for conflict resolution occurs when both parties are motivated and both are optimistic. These results fit the analysis of Forde (2004) who described Thucydides' views on ripeness and conflict resolution as a matter of combatant passions, specifically their psychological state and intensity of their motivations to settle.

Antecedents of optimism about finding a mutually acceptable agreement include whether a party trusts its adversary, believes that the other party is ready to make concessions in the interests of settlement, perceives a common ground for resolving the conflict exists among all parties within a substantive formula that satisfies everyone's minimal aspirations, and has found a valid spokesman, someone who can commit the other side (Pruitt 1997, 242). Negotiation readiness is about the perceptions each side has toward the other. As Spector (1998, 43–48) states, nonnegotiation is the guiding principle in some conflicts where the other side is elevated to the role of villain, demon, rogue, or pariah. If an enemy is the incarnation of evil, symbolizing the antithesis of a country's core values and beliefs, acting opposite to the manner of accepted norms of specific societies, then consideration of negotiation and peaceful dispute resolution are closed. Negotiation is viable only if leaders are able to shift away from rigid policies of nonnegotiation with their villains in a manner that allows them to ward off accusations of appeasement; the decision to negotiate with villains requires some modification of the "villainization process" (a major reason for stalemate) but does not imply that any ideological divide is compromised. One approach suggests that enemy evilness is not the critical factor on the assumption that all parties understand and seek to maximize their self-interests and will be motivated by interests, not ideology, in choosing to negotiate. Spector (1998, 56–57) advises that any decision to negotiate with villains can be seen as a principled choice, morally neutral, but managed in businesslike communications, putting aside taboos of contact with the adversary and focusing on interests. Abba Eban (1998, 40, 82) stated that peacemaking demands an attitude that favors compromise, the taking of long views, and working for distant ends; by contrast, moralizing attitudes about evil and virtue based on immovable principles of a clash in values inhibit flexible responses and compromise, concluding that it is easier and more preferable to deal with competing interests.

How Does It Apply? Spector (1998) describes four cases that illustrate shifts away from villainization where negotiations took place: Israel's decision to negotiate with the PLO in 1993; the U.S. decision to negotiate with North Korea in 1994; the U.S. decision to negotiate with military leaders of Haiti in 1994; and Great Britain's decision to negotiate with Sinn Fein of Northern Ireland in 1994. Sometimes, the villain was forced to change before the government acceded to direct negotiations (Sinn Fein); sometimes, the government played a strategy of brinkmanship (Haiti). When deciding to negotiate with villains, additional factors came into play: the sense of the drama of time and opportunity and leaders who were risk takers and willing to break the established conflict process.

Armstrong (1993), examining three cases of Cold War animosity, concluded that only when the principle of genuine mutual advantage in their bilateral relations took hold (replacing earlier insistence by one or the other of a unilateral advantage), was there any possibility to improve relations. The acceptance of mutual advantage with respect to interests constituted the essence of a strategy for achieving cooperation between adversaries. In Pruitt (2005) readiness theory was applied to three cases: Oslo Israel-Palestine negotiations, Northern Ireland, and civil war in Zimbabwe. In the first two, readiness existed: parties were ready for agreement and highly motivated for settlement in part due to hurting stalemates and changed circumstances that allowed the parties to open with informal bargaining talks that eventually move on their own into official negotiated agreement. In the last case, progress toward agreement was dependent on heavy, directive tactics from outside mediators. Pruitt (2007) examines the Northern Ireland conflict in detail, extending readiness theory to include a central coalition of groups participating in a peace negotiation all of whom must be above the readiness threshold. This includes armed groups and implies that it may be necessary to negotiate with terrorists.

In Sum The conceptual features identifying negotiation readiness—party willingness, party optimism, and leader capacity to bargain—can be translated into observable markers shown to have positive, empirical effects in evaluating the readiness factor. These include a decline in villianizing the adversary, abandonment of unilateral advantages, and acceptance of the principle of mutual advantage of interests—identifying leaders who are supportive and committed to a resolution process and circulating reciprocal exchange formula for a solution.

Interest-Based Bargaining

What Is It? The concept of principled bargaining is a process in which parties seek to meet their needs and accomplish their goals by focusing on interests and mutual gains: a reciprocal exchange. Interest-based approaches focus on mutual party needs, concerns, and fairness as the premise for deciding how to resolve conflict and thus locate convergence on a reciprocal exchange arrangement (Fisher, Ury, and Patton 1991). Terrorists tend to focus on their original terms of trade—release of hostages in exchange for fulfillment of demands—and are not open to looking for alternative options or creative solutions. "It is not the matter of negotiations as such that encourages instrumental terrorism but rather the degree of their demands that they are able to achieve by negotiation," asserts Zartman (2003, 448).

Settlements vary in how benefits are distributed among the parties engaged in the fight, the balance of vested interests to sustain or to undermine the settlements, and the degree to which the agreements are regarded as one in a series or as final and irrevocable (Kriseberg 2003, 323). Interest-based terms of settlement in terrorism negotiations are based on two ideas: the notion of equality matching—each party provides the other as much as they can, based on what they receive; and the notion of market pricing—parties in dispute exchange unlike commodities in proportion to their market value (Fiske 1991, 16). In market pricing negotiations, a barter situation prevails: parties seek to determine what constitutes a reciprocal exchange reached through haggling over exchange comparisons. In market pricing, parties seek a fair deal in proportion to costs and benefits. Buying and selling in the diplomatic market is close to barter, resembling an ancient bazaar where traders have no accepted medium of exchange, states Blainey 1973, 115–116). In diplomacy, each nation has the rough equivalent of a selling price—a price that it accepts when it sells—and concession, the equivalent of a buying price. Under bargaining principles, equality matching and market pricing negotiation complexity can be handled in different ways, states Fiske (1991): through logrolling—trading high and low value issues; bridging interests—devising alternatives that give all the disputants what they want in terms of interests (the reasons, concerns, and values that generate their demands); and nonspecific compensation, where each side agrees to an opponent's demands because it receives something of value in exchange.

How Does It Apply? Some studies (Rubin and Brown 1975; Spector 1977) conclude bargaining effectiveness is increased by converting intangible issues (saving face, enhancing reputation, conveying the appearance of strength) into tangible ones (e.g., real, material payoffs), although the results draw on experiments where college students form the subject base. Working with real data, that is, groups of live, actual disputants, Doob (1974) and Cohen et al. (1977) discovered difficulties in transforming negotiation parameters to a win–win, needs–centered outlook. Weiss-Wik (1983) notes a heavy emphasis on adopting a win–win outlook within a structure concentrated on negotiator's needs, sources of power, communication abilities, and skill in finalizing agreement, although empirical evidence demonstrating successful outcomes is lacking. But Sederberg (1995) concludes that, historically, regimes have repeatedly engaged in conciliation with challenger groups that use terrorism. Concessions range from ransom payments for the release of hostages to formal political accommodations with their antagonists to bring a cessation of hostilities.

In Sum The conceptual features identifying interest-based bargaining refer to whatever one player receives with respect to what constitutes appropriate compensation in equality matching or market pricing barter. In logrolling one side's concessions on its low priority issue is compensation for the other sides' concession on the other's low priority issue. Parties stay within the set of issues, specifically what is exchanged to eliminate the terrorist threat, rather than reach out for new issues or dimensions of values.

Negotiation Preconditions

A composite framework of negotiation preconditions includes several phased elements as precursors to negotiation onset, in effect bringing the prenegotiation process to conclusion. The starting point is stalemate creation that arises out of power interdependencies between the parties; neither is able to advance its goals in the current environment, including extracting concessions from the opponent.

Initially, parties have to reach a *mutually hurting stalemate* point and be motivated to do something about their joint plight based on perceived current and future ratios of conflict pain against diplomacy promise. Second, individually, each side must be perceived by the other as a *willing and capable negotiating partner*, not only committed, but skilled, to conduct and implement a negotiated settlement responsibly and sincerely believe agreement is likely. Third, the goals for each side in the conflict must be important enough to force parties to work intensely to achieve them through some agreed *reciprocal exchange formula*—measured in commodities or promises. Fourth, both sides will be pressured to negotiate a settlement when *turning point* events happen, or they perceive events that expand their fear of escalated conflict, and imagine an escalation that may lower their power base and the disputant power differential position of their relationship. Event pattern recognition on each side will be a critical factor for understanding series' discontinuity that may advance the process to begin negotiations more quickly or set it back. Above all, subjective, shared perceptions of the desirability to reach an accord must exist—a willingness by everyone to search for a peaceful settlement, a factor that incorporates some level of relationship trust, and acceptance of the opponent as a rational and viable negotiating partner, believing that they will be worse off in the future if no deal is struck; and political leaders on all sides need enough power and leverage to do so in a way that persuades their constituencies that interests have been protected. Although willingness is a minimal requirement for a settlement to come about, Klieboer (1994, 115) stresses that even when all parties are willing, it does not guarantee a problem-solving negotiation phase will begin.

A mutually hurting stalemate is not sufficient to bring parties to the negotiating table. Other conditions must hold: each side must have experienced a turning point that directs them to serious consideration of a negotiated solution, events originating within or beyond the immediate conflict environment that contribute significantly to uncertainty, feeding fears and insecurity with respect to the perceived future, that escalation of the conflict may develop beyond their control, shifting a power balance and hence affecting the conflict outcome.

Turning points for parties of the conflict combined with a mutually hurting stalemate will not be sufficient to bring them together to resolve their differences peacefully. There must be solidly based evidence and a perception that official appropriate leadership capacity exists on each side to conduct and carry through any negotiated agreement, to control the flow of terrorist activity. The capacity to negotiate implies official involvement in the terrorism problem at the highest levels. Terrorism problems often begin at the nonstate level; no negotiations will occur until the issue advances openly into official circles.

Elevating the terrorist problem into an official international issue, coupled with negative effects brought about by turning points and a mutually hurting stalemate, establishes a setup for negotiation but will not guarantee it occurs. Both sides must be willing to engage, having some confidence that the other side will not back away. This point is reached once exchange parameters (promises on future policy as well as material resource bartering) are tested and future negotiating parties understand the range—though not the specifics—of the bargaining space.

Examining conflict ripeness and negotiating readiness in the South African and Israel-Palestine conflicts, Lieberfeld (1999) found several factors important to conflict de-escalation: a mutually hurting stalemate, perceptions of possibilities to negotiate with the adversary, and leadership changes that brought pragmatism focused on interest solutions. But Grieg and Diehl (2006), in a cross-national study combining features of ripeness and readiness into their concept, "softening up" to test conditions of de-escalation processes for 226 different pairs of rival states in the period 1946–1995, concluded that neither a hurting stalemate, nor leadership changes were significantly linked to the onset of a conflict resolution process, but prior attempts by parties to negotiate their differences did matter. Among their findings were the following: that the costs of conflict push parties toward settlement, but in periods where the pain and danger of conflict are most apparent to adversaries, they are less likely to turn to conflict management. Their results, based on a complex quantitative methodology, suggest that we may lack a complete understanding of the conflict resolution process with respect to the role of conflict ripeness, turning points in negotiation, and negotiation readiness.

Addressing the question when to negotiate with terrorists, Pruitt (2007) believes talking makes sense when other confrontational strategies, including combating— the most popular government strategy to punish illegal violence that requires no concessions, aims to defeat terrorists' demands, and isolating them—or a policy of marginalizing terrorist groups by making concessions that provide sufficient benefits to turn moderates against terrorists, have become too costly, too risky, unsuccessful, or simply impractical. Willingness to negotiate is a confession of mutual need. When a hurting stalemate develops, the only way to deal with the conflict is by dealing with the adversary. Readiness to enter negotiation depends on optimism about success—a belief that negotiation offers a way out of the conflict, which depends on a perception of the other side's flexibility in reciprocating concessions sufficiently to make agreement possible. It is reasonable to assume that most parties in a negotiation, including terrorists and governments, begin with extreme demands that cannot easily be met by the other side. Many of them become more flexible as a result of circumstances. Flexibility derives from the same forces that push parties into negotiation: a sense that the conflict is counterproductive coupled with a perception that the other party is ready to make concessions.

Addressing the question how to signal willingness to negotiate with terrorists, Daniel Byman (2006) says that opening a dialogue with terrorists, however difficult, is often a necessary first step on the way toward political settlement and a cessation of the violence. To start the process, terrorists and government decision makers may require gestures of good will from one another beforehand since both sides are accustomed to viewing the adversary as an evil enemy. Among the methods for initiating talks, governments may issue formal open statements that offer a promise or hint of talks subject to certain concessions by the terrorist group, deliver the

Table 3.1 Terrorism Conflict Bargaining and Negotiation Phases

Phase	Activity	Description
Stage 1: Bargaining to Negotiate		
Prenegotiation Startup	terrorist campaign onset	balance of power challenged
Prenegotiation Endpoint	mutually hurting stalemate	new balance of power proposed
Prenegotiation Closure	turning points	new balance of power created
Stage 2: Engaging in Negotiation		
Negotiation Startup	negotiation readiness	new balance of power fixed
Negotiation Endpoint	reciprocal exchange bids	new balance of power reflected
Negotiation Closure	agreement	new balance of power norm

message through intermediaries (foreign governments, dependable community members, media), or discreetly work through intelligence agents in back channels. Choosing whether or not to negotiate carries risks: refusing to engage in talks may strengthen extremists by showing that nonviolent means offer no hope for airing grievances while participating in them demonstrates that terrorists' tactics succeed. In either case, the policy may have negative consequences, yet the opportunity for engagement should not be overlooked.

Tracing how parties come to the table rests on prenegotiation power dynamics, specifically how the smaller party successfully challenges its dominant foe. Table 3.1 summarizes the ordered sequence of these elements matched with stages in balance of power shifts that account for the onset of negotiation.

Prenegotiation is defined in this scheme as the conflict phase, setting it apart from problem-solving activities. It consists of an issue-framing process, mechanisms for focusing on particular problems, and targeting selected parties. Results from international case studies (Stein 1989) suggest that leaders decide to consider negotiation when they see a need for a strategy of crisis avoidance or postcrisis management or when they see a conjunction of threat and opportunity; and when they anticipate benefits from the process that are largely independent of whether or not it culminates in agreement. The period defined by prenegotiation bargaining provides the framing for problem-solving negotiations by setting boundaries for the talks to follow, determining what issues will be included and excluded and also what terms of exchange will be entertained.

The process of moving from bargaining to negotiate to one of engaging in negotiation begins when both of the parties feel that the costs of an agreement are less than the costs of further contentious tactics to strengthen tactical bargaining positions. Determining the nature of the power balance at the commencement of negotiations will reveal each sides' strength and weaknesses, suggest tactics each side may find effective, and indicate which side must work harder to achieve its desired outcome. Both sides want to negotiate from a position of strength; neither wants to be seen as seeking conflict resolution from a position of weakness. What terrorists have to offer at the bargaining table is their ability to turn off the violence—if they have played that card before the game begins, why should the government negotiate? But as long as the terrorist group exists, the threat of violence will always loom over the bargaining discussion no matter what kinds of verbal commitments exist between the two sides.

Negotiating parties "face and manage fuzzy, ambiguous, and messy situations" conclude De Dreu et al. (2007, 611). Parties lack full and accurate insight into the structure of the negotiation. They lack information about their partner—not knowing what is and what is not important to the other side, nor the amount of gain or loss their partner faces on specific issues, or what goals their partner strives for. Most conciliatory initiatives follow or anticipate some major form of change, or are undertaken after some drawn-out deadlock that produced frustration. Mitchell (2000, 63–67) states that the decision to engage in negotiations involves a major reversal of strategy. It's a comprehensive reconsideration. Various levels of external or internal changes offer leaders the chance to initiate negotiation plans: structural change in the conflict system; strategic changes in the relationship between disputants; or tactical changes in the patterns of interaction between adversaries. The following examples show how the terrorist side in anti-American cases reversed its strategy and agreed to negotiate a conflict ending.

Structural change refers to shifts in the global constellation of players and power distribution in the world system that impact the conflict players and their power. The Beirut kidnapping campaign started in the 1980s during the U.S.-USSR bipolar rivalry of the Cold War. A negotiated setting came into focus only after the world had changed into the new American, unipolar-dominant, post–Cold War environment, and notably after the Gulf War to free occupied Kuwait ended, which structurally affected U.S.–Middle East relations.

Strategic change refers to lulls in the existing conflict behavior pattern, or anticipation of some central, highly undesired event that will alter that pattern. The Teheran hostage-taking terrorism case reflects strategic change effects as serious negotiation consideration in Iran started only *after* the U.S. rescue mission attempt in the Iranian desert, marking a sharp shift in American policy toward a willingness to undertake aggressive actions.

Tactical changes concern triggers and symbols that introduce a shock or new leaders coming to power who may have different orientations toward settlement. The Cuba skyjacking terrorism was resolved when Castro realized that perpetrators shooting and killing those who tried to foil their plans to hijack planes to fly to Havana were not necessarily politically motivated individuals but common criminals seeking to avoid arrest.

In order to move from conflict bargaining into problem-solving negotiations in terrorist conflict, transition is facilitated by the existence of a power stalemate where neither party can prevail under current contentious strategies that lead to conflict ripeness; and negotiation readiness—a capacity and willingness by both sides to talk to the other, which is facilitated by different turning points that influence each side, leading them to favor quick, nonviolent settlement coupled with a sense of

Table 3.2 Terminating Terrorism Conflicts

Conflict Characteristics	Negotiation Preconditions	Conflict Settlement
Mutual Hurting Stalemate—Conflict Ripeness		
Frequent terrorist attacks		
Counterterrorism measures	*mutual hurting stalemate*	stalemate resolved
Turning Points		
Stable conflict dynamics	*conflict dynamics change**	
	turning points toward negotiation	negotiation accepted
Negotiation Readiness		
State vs. non-state terrorists	*terrorist host-state partnership*	state-to-state interactions
Terrorists are evil, irrational	*terrorists are instrumental, rational*	
Interest-Based Bargaining		
Fight-to-win orientation	*problem-solving orientation*	negotiating starts
Broad, abstract issues	*concrete, fractionated issues*	fractionated issues settled
Unilateral demands	*reciprocal exchange floated*	mutual gains agreement

*Change may be structural (shifts of power distribution in the international system) strategic (shifts of conflict behavior of parties), or tactical (triggers or symbols that introduce a shock and/or new leaders).

what the final reciprocal exchange of benefits might be (e.g., returning hostages in exchange of withdrawal from specified territory; ceasing any form of international hijack operations by establishing an extradition treaty). This point occurs when the adversaries are closest to a particular power balance equilibrium, when each side is dependent on the other for granting or withholding some important rewards in spite of their mutual efforts to eliminate such reliance.

Table 3.2 pulls together the four strands of conflict profiling to assess whether a negotiation process is feasible. The far left column lists characteristics of a conflict of terrorism. The center column—negotiation preconditions—shows these factors transformed to open the possibilities for parties in conflict to entertain the idea of negotiating with their enemy. Some of these factors are objective events—turning points, and a terrorist host state taking over negotiating authority, for example; others are grounded in party perceptions—stalemate intolerance, images of terrorists as irrational or rational actors. The column on the right side, the conflict resolution piece, indicates the basic outline of a settlement. In this instance, settlement is equated with resolution in that the terrorism of the conflict stops, "resolved" through agreement.

With respect to information arrayed in Table 3.2, terrorism conflict is characterized by a win-lose outcome orientation, and terrorists are gaining relative power through their coercive acts, forcing a target government to expand its defensive, protective measures against such violence. Under these conditions, terrorists are seen as fanatical villains; a strategy to negotiate with them is unacceptable. Under preconditions defining negotiation, the center column of the table shows the impact of a mutual hurting stalemate, the existence of turning points moving adversaries into accepting the negotiation option as a way to terminate conflict between them, or other factors that transform the conflict issues into fractionated pieces eligible for settlement, and reciprocal exchange formula for making an agreement.

How do these features apply to anti-American terrorism conflict termination? In the skyjacking terrorism campaign, Castro's turning point—when Cuba decided to negotiate with the United States to resolve the crisis—occurred after a few American criminals, in the final leg of their prison escape plan, fatally shot ticket agents during their attempted plane hijack to Havana. No longer was the situation bounded in political propaganda; outright murder was happening. The onset of negotiations began within days after the event—the turning point leading to final agreement. In the case of the U.S. hostages in Teheran, Iran decided to enter into serious negotiations shortly after the U.S. rescue mission attempt to free the hostages. At that point, their negotiating style turned from one based on rights and justice to an interest-based approach. Solution followed shortly thereafter. Individuals held in the Beirut kidnapping gained their freedom in a more complicated form—Iran needed to settle before the United Nations secretary-general issued his report on the Iran-Iraq War and left office. In this case, the impending deadline led to agreement and involved principally the matter of setting fair reciprocal exchanges and financial pricing levels that were tied closely to U.S-Iran contracts established during the time of the Shah. In the three terrorism campaigns concluded, each began when one governing administration was in power but was either ended or ending as that group moved on. Cuban skyjacking started under President Johnson; the U.S.-Cuba hijack accord happened under President Nixon. The Teheran hostage crisis was the nemeses of President Carter; agreement formed with the Reagan administration. Beirut kidnapping victims were abducted during President Reagan's term but freed during the first Bush presidency in the final moments when the highest UN official was stepping down from office. Agreements seemed to come with new administrations, perhaps a face-saving feature for all sides, and were formed when a high point of public concern hype had passed and after the United States had deployed an elaborate set of defensive measures to prevent future terrorist incidents. Agreement happened only when the conflict trajectory had moved into a de-escalation mode.

Summary

Terrorists operate strategically—their acts are purposeful. They have political goals: to change government policy. They seek coercive power—through threats and violence of their acts—in order to build a power dependency over their adversary. They initiate conflict to engage government in conflict escalation. They are resolute—they do not give in or give up. Governments, too, operate as resolute, powerful, strategical actors with political goals, and use their coercive power to threaten and punish terrorists. Both sides prefer unilateral victory; neither prefers bilateral, negotiated settlement. If either wins (by implication, the other concedes), the conflict process ends; if neither wins, conflict continues. Due to *absolute* power weakness, terrorists may seek to establish a stalemate by forcing government into a power dependency relationship. Due to *contextual* power dependency, government may be backed into a stalemate where only options are: "take it or trade it." Both parties are aware that a stalemate opens opportunities for negotiation, but that mutual recognition of a stalemate cannot guarantee negotiations, and that negotiated settlement means some concessions. For these reasons, serious negotiation with terrorists are likely to start very late in a conflict process—at a point where parties are desperate and aiming for agreement to end immediate problems rather than discuss wide-ranging differences.

If negotiations are acceptable and feasible, they will succeed only if the bargaining style on each side is interest-based, rather than a power, or rights-based strategy. Further, the onset of serious negotiations implies that parties *a priori* understand and accept the bargaining range of fair reciprocal exchange. Four negotiation onset conditions are critical in this process:

Mutual Hurting Stalemate—Conflict Ripeness: Neither party is willing or able to pursue their goals any further and frustrated in their attempts to prevail. Government has built up defense security but still faces a power dependency threat with terrorists. Terrorists, largely thwarted from carrying out violent acts due to defense structure, see their power dwindling. Both sides value resolution. A stalemate can be identified by a postpeak slight downward trend in terrorist act frequency or a long-unchanged situation of coercion that parties are eager to resolve.

Turning Points: Each party has experienced independent, exogenous, threatening events that strongly influence their decision to move toward negotiating an outcome to the conflict. Turning points can be identified by outside events, beyond the immediate conflict setting, that affect each party separately and force new considerations in the choice to negotiate. They might be impending deadlines (that will change their power status in a negative way), or other moves that affect both sides' predictions of an outcome.

Negotiating Readiness: Each party accords some level of trust to the other side with respect to credibility and seriousness as a negotiating partner, expecting the other side to implement provisions in any agreement reached, and is optimistic about terminating their conflict. Readiness can be evaluated by the changed characterization of terrorists, reducing the frequency of describing the adversary as "evil" for example, or devillianizing the enemy and recognizing leaders on the other side.

Interest-Based Bargaining Formula: Each party understands the interests of the other side, and has imagined how various material and psychological needs might be traded off and combined into a composite package containing mutual gains. Reciprocal exchange arrangements are not easy to discover *a priori* for these terms due to political sensitivities may or may not be open to public scrutiny.

If these features are in place, parties will be willing to talk about settlement of their conflict. Only two of these elements—stalemate conditions and turning points—are observable prior to negotiation onset, though identifying turning points is a more complicated process and easier to apply retrospectively. Reciprocal exchanges might be known beforehand—depending on what terrorists demand, but formula and details will be held in secret. Negotiating capacity and negotiating willingness are assumed conditions ex post facto. With respect to the sequencing of these elements leading toward negotiation onset, stalemate conditions must exist before turning points, which necessarily operate as disturbances to status quo conditions. Reciprocal exchange solution proposals may develop at any point but circulate only after negotiating capability assessment, when government-to-government talks (going beyond any role for a nonstate terrorist actor in this process) become possible.

Only if these four variables unfold in a direction pointing toward a negotiated settlement, do parties become willing to negotiate. With respect to the time-series pattern within these elements, negotiation onset is most likely in a period well after the intensity of conflict has crested (terrorist attacks are diminishing, defensive barriers are well situated), when stalemate has become a fairly well-established norm, but immediately after a major perturbation in this unfolding conflict pattern. Turning point disruptions are critical in this process for they threaten the power balance perceptions assumed by each disputant pushing the parties toward settling their differences. Only if all sides have a good sense of the basic shape of a proposed agreement, the parameters of reciprocal exchange, are negotiations likely to proceed.

To understand the signaling and progression from terrorist conflict to negotiated outcomes in anti-America campaigns, the following chapters provide detail on selected cases.

CHAPTER FOUR

The U.S.-Cuba Skyjacking Crisis, 1968–1973

Tightened security measures at American airports assumed top priority in counterterrorism policies introduced after the 9/11 attacks. As a major international terrorist threat, skyjacking demanded the nation's attention. Decades earlier, hijackings had also caused dramatic public alarm. Between 1968 and 1972, a sharp upturn in aerial piracy incidence worldwide reached epidemic proportions: more than 325 events occurred—the highest ever recorded (U.S. Department of Transportation, 1986). The bulk of activity involved the United States and Cuba in a common scenario: armed hijackers boarded planes at U.S. airports and, with menacing abuse to passengers and crew, demanded flight diversion to Havana where a warm welcome and political asylum awaited them in Fidel Castro's Communist regime. The hijackers themselves were not undertaking acts of violence in an official capacity for their government; the general impression was that mostly they were acting alone, though on occasion, some may have been recruited by clandestine intelligence agents. American travelers and airline crew were increasingly apprehensive about flying. Hijack terrorism—unpredictable, disruptive, fearsome—had become a serious national security issue.

The hijacking of modern commercial jets into international airspace is a special form of theatre, says St. John (1999, 27). A spectacle of fear, excitement, and communication are concentrated inside the hull of a single aircraft. The plane may explode. Passengers might be taken hostage or killed. Hijack frequency patterns, while indicative of political problems and relaxed security protection, cannot convey the magnitude, drama, or impact of individual events. One notable 1985 hijacking, TWA flight 847, enroute from Athens to Rome and ultimately diverted by armed Shiites to Lebanon, commanded extensive, live television coverage for more than two weeks. Most passengers were released within the first days as the plane sat on the tarmac in Beirut, but one American—a U.S. serviceman—was killed, and the crew was held hostage until negotiations were settled at the end (Clutterbuck 1987, 21; Testrake 1987).

America and Cuba officially resolved their terrorist conflict on February 15, 1973, with a "Memorandum of Understanding on Hijacking of Aircraft and Vessels and Other Offenses." Following several negotiation efforts, these enemy states finally came to agreement—their first broad accord since Castro's rise to power some fourteen years earlier. The truce had immediate impact: combined with greater emphasis on aviation security (mandatory electronic metal detectors at U.S. airports were in place by early January 1973), hijacking rates declined significantly thereafter and despite Castro's public denunciation of the pact in October 1976, stayed at low levels.[1]

Conflict resolution required sufficient progress along two separate trajectories: (1) unilateral homeland defense measures: technology development and installations designed to prevent skyjack occurrence—a high-cost solution, according to Landes (1978, 29), who estimated the net increase in security due to the screening program at more than $3 million to deter a hijack attempt; and (2) bilateral disputant negotiation measures: a legal agreement designed to deter and punish hijack offenders—a solution without concrete price; its base derives from intangible elements related to security and policy. Henceforth, hijackings would be treated as criminal, not political, acts. To reach this point, the parties essentially applied policy premises that had been adopted in recent multilateral international conventions held at The Hague in 1970, and Montreal in September 1971. Although the United States had ratified the multilateral conventions, Cuba opposed them. Given the volatile relations between these states—extending to high profile propaganda extracted from hijacking events—the accord represented something of a breakthrough. How did the parties come to agree on this issue?

At the start of their antagonistic relationship during the Cuban Revolution (1958–1961), all hijacking activity consisted of Cubans flying to the United States, where the offenders were not condemned. The United States saw the hijackers as escaping to freedom—making a political statement. The Cubans saw thieves stealing planes from their national fleet of aircraft—hijacking was clearly criminal behavior. Attempts at resolution failed. Terrorism motivation perspectives will trump its criminal nature in cases where parties are seeking political asylum. As a general rule, the country of escape, the *hijacking-from* party, will see hijack terrorism it as a criminal act, but the country of destination, the *hijacking-to* party, will view it from the political frame. Between 1947 and 1958, aircraft hijackings were mostly committed by East Europeans seeking escape from communism and political asylum in the United States, and despite requests from Czechoslovakia, the USSR, Poland, and Yugoslavia to return hijack offenders of planes, trains, and ships, the United States refused to do so (Sofaer 1986, 909). Within the Cold War framework, America did not see these acts as terrorist or criminal behavior but part of politics. About a decade later, positions shifted: the United States tended to categorize hijacks as illegal events, criminal, terrorist activity, but the Cuban regime extracted political capital by regarding skyjacking as part of their ongoing ideological conflict with the United States. At the peak of the global hijacking era in 1970, The Hague Convention for the Unlawful Seizure of Aircraft, declaring hijacking as a criminal rather than a political act that required extradition or prosecution, was signed by fifty nations—including the United States. Cuba was not a signatory. Again, attempts at resolution failed. At the end of 1972, both parties came to view hijacking as a criminal event, but only after two particularly violent, deadly skyjacks occurred. By early 1973 the United States and Cuba had formulated an agreement to extradite or prosecute offenders that arrived from either direction. For a time thereafter, terrorism events between these countries, in all forms, showed significant reduction. Hijack incidence on a global scale fell.

Skyjack incidents involving Cuba happened in several distinct phases: the first wave started in 1958, during the Cuban revolution. These hijackings were primarily attempts by anti-Castro individuals to divert Cuban planes to land in the United States; after the U.S. Bay of Pigs invasion in 1961, the direction of hijacking reversed. American planes were diverted to Cuba, often by Cuban exiles. In September 1961, President Kennedy initiated the first U.S. sky marshal program as a deterrent to hijackings to and from Cuba and signed legislation prescribing twenty years imprisonment or the death penalty for air piracy. U.S.-Cuban hijacking attempts declined rapidly (U.S. Immigration and Customs Enforcement report on Commercial Aviation Terrorism and Air Marshals). Very few incidents occurred between 1962–1967.

The second phase emerged in 1968. The late 1960s experienced a growing number of airline skyjackings to Cuba, particularly among aircraft crossing the southern United States. The problem, beginning on February 21, 1968, when a fugitive (an escaped murderer) forced a DC-8 plane to fly to Havana, had become, by midsummer, "so epidemic that one airline servicing Miami and other southern cities in the United States has decided to equip pilots with approach charts for Havana's José Marti Airport and written instructions on dealing with hijackers to 'do as they say'" (*Time*, July 26, 1968). Various counterterrorist actions had been considered: permitting airline crews to be armed (action generally opposed by both airlines and pilots who argued that a side trip to Cuba was preferred over midair gun battles); locking the cockpit cabin during flight operations (seen as ineffective as terrorists could still take a flight attendant hostage and give orders to the crew through the intercom system); conducting individual passenger body searches (too time consuming and unsettling); and using metal detection devices (the technology was primitive and did not perform satisfactorily).

Understanding hijacker motives became important at this stage. Profile characterizations of these terrorists varied: they were alternatively, political asylum seekers, armed bandits seeking profit, political conflict fighters, or psychological misfits. Placing most U.S. to Cuba cases in the later category, McWhinney (1987, 12) stated "these were emotionally disturbed or mentally unbalanced people with very little political or social awareness, and drawn mainly by the contagion of past example, and the lure of the massive publicity given by the communications media (newspapers, television, and radio) to past successful hijacking attempts." Coleman's (2004) copycat theory, illustrating how media may trigger mayhem, supports this thinking. Holden (2003), analyzing 1968–1972 hijacking data, concluded contagion effects accounted for successful hijackings originating in the United States (unsuccessful attempts, however, had no effects, nor did successful or unsuccessful hijacking attempts outside the United States).

The third and last phase was jolted by a particularly violent hijacking. On October 29, 1972, an Eastern Airlines plane in Houston, Texas, was overtaken by four men, who after killing a ticket agent and wounding a ramp serviceman, forced their way onto the aircraft, demanding the plane fly to Havana, where it landed safely. This event resulted in a note from the Cuban government, indicating a willingness to reach agreement with the Americans to halt hijacking. Two weeks later, on November 10, three hijackers on a flight from Birmingham, Alabama, demanding $10 million, ten parachutes, and food supplies, ordered the pilot to fly to Havana, where the plane eventually landed. The passengers were released, the copilot shot and wounded. On November 19, Cuba accepted a U.S. proposal to begin formal negotiations on the issue leading to the antihijacking agreement of 1973 (U.S. Congress, *Hearings,* 1973, 1).

Background

The troubled relationship between the United States and the island of Cuba, some ninety miles off the coast of Florida, began with Fidel Castro's emergence as a strong national leader in 1959. Ever since, it has been a flash point of American foreign policy; aerial hijackings and other forms of terrorism, namely bombings and assassination attempts, frequently defined and dramatized the parties' high-profile conflict. Cuba turned to Communism under Castro's leadership, after ending a long stretch as a U.S. protectorate. Under Castro's first two years of leadership, the government enacted agrarian reform laws, expropriated land held by U.S. sugar companies, nationalized various industries (banking and telecommunications) previously under U.S. control— all without compensation to American companies—and embarked on other policy directions to cement close relations with the Soviet Union. In response, the United States cancelled the sugar quota and imposed a trade and economic embargo on Cuba, broke diplomatic relations, and, using anti-Castro CIA-trained exiles as soldiers, invaded the island at the Bay of Pigs in April 1961. The intervention was not successful; most of the twelve-hundred-strong Brigade members were captured, the rest were killed (Blum 2004, 186).

In May 1962, the USSR decided to place nuclear missiles on the island, an issue that brought the two superpowers to the brink of war in the Cuban Missile Crisis of October.[2] The crisis threatened world peace. Since then, and certainly in the climate throughout the 1960s and 1970s, the U.S. government never deviated from its goal of ousting Fidel Castro from power, marking him as an untrustworthy, dangerous leader.[3] Numerous CIA-supported operations were carried out to eliminate him, often by U.S.-based Cuban exiles, but none achieved their goal.

Air service between the United States and Cuba was terminated with the 1962 Missile Crisis. Afterward, the number of Cubans fleeing to the United States by small boats increased considerably, a fact played up by the American government:

Cubans wanted to escape. Castro's response, in September 1965, announced that participation in the Cuban Revolution was voluntary—anyone wishing to leave could do so if friends or family from the United States picked them up in small boats at the port of Camarioca. Within a few days, many people gathered, hundreds of boats converged, and several thousand Cubans left for the United States. During the month of sealift operations, at least a dozen boats went down, and a major maritime tragedy was predicted to occur in the near future. The United States proposed the idea of airlift, with several daily flights for Cubans wishing to leave home. The Freedom Flights Program by agreement of both governments, allowed 250,000 Cubans to come to the United States by 1971 (U.S. Department of State, *Chronology of Cuban Relations 1958–1998*, 2). The Cuban Adjustment Act adopted by the U.S. Congress in November 1966, changed the legal status of immigrants arriving from Cuba: they would be treated as refugees and granted political asylum.

Cuban refugees were coming to the United States; American hijackers were leaving the United States destined for Cuba. The pattern reflected political tension between the two countries. American hijackers were seen as lone operatives, not part of any organized political group though they may have held specific ideological convictions. Profile characterization of these terrorists varied: they were alternatively, psychologically disturbed nuts, fugitives from justice, copycat risk-takers, extreme escapist idealists, or simply homesick individuals seeking to return to their native land. Cuba, although granting asylum to those responsible for hijacking, reportedly "never let on whether they regard the hijackings as a welcome embarrassment for the United States or a simple nuisance for Cuba" (*Newsweek,* July 22, 1968, 13). Was the Castro government benefiting from Cold War propaganda that resulted when U.S. nationals sought to leave their (presumably comfortable) home for a future life in Cuba, conveying the message to the world that superpower citizens of the West were choosing to live in a Soviet-sponsored Communist state? And what did it cost for an airliner that is hijacked to Cuba? An invoice breaking down specific charges including the following: landing fees, handling, flight dispatch, aeronautical services, customs services, fuel, ground transportation, and catering to feed hijacked passengers and crew—the largest figure in each instance—was routinely submitted by the Cuban government to the U.S. State department. The United States also made the payment for servicing two unscheduled aircraft landings in Havana: a DC-9, arriving August 20, 1970, at $1,160.47; and a Boeing 727, arriving August 24, 1970, at $872.50. In reviewing these bills, hijacking was seen by at least one member of Congress as a profit-making operation for Castro (U.S. Congress, *Hearings*, 1970, 115–116).

How broadly did airline hijacks represent popular opposition to government policies? Was this form of expression likely to grow and become more dangerous? When an Israeli El Al aircraft flying from London to Tel Aviv in late July 1968 was hijacked by three Palestinians (members of the Popular Front for the Liberation of Palestine—PFLP) and flown to Algeria, the focus of demands shifted: no longer was destination the direct or symbolic goal; the hijackers were demanding the release of captured Palestinian fighters from Israel's control. The hijacking by the same group of an American carrier, TWA flight 840, in August 1969—scheduled to fly from Rome to Athens but diverted to Damascus—showed a similar trend in political demands, but in this case the target was U.S. foreign policy. The earlier flights to Cuba, "transportation hijackings," were viewed less ominously than the new intensified "extortion hijackings" phase. Neither the U.S. government nor the major airlines had a solution to either problem. Did the motivations of hijackers matter? While there may be different reasons why individuals decide to illegally seize an aircraft and demand changes in flight plans, William A. Gill, Jr., president of the Flight Engineers' International Association, stated in Congressional testimony that hijacker motives do not matter during the moment of the terrorist act for neither the crew nor the passengers can anticipate the level of danger presented.

In late 1968, the Airline Pilots Association, concerned by the sudden and continuous rash of airline hijackings, asked the U.S. government to take action to stop such offenses (Taillon 2002, 19). The tense political situation between Cuba and the United States complicated the use of diplomatic channels and made attempts to extradite these terrorists extremely difficult. Neither the U.S. government nor the major airlines had a solution to the problem of aerial hijacking.

In mid-January 1969, a federal court in Brooklyn issued an arrest order for the hijackers of an Eastern Airlines DC-8 that had been seized earlier that month. Although there was little hope of prosecution, the federal judicial system signaled that action would be taken against hijackers. This was predicated on a 1961 U.S. law that imposed prison sentences of up to twenty years, and in some cases the death sentence, for aircraft seizure. As one airline attorney argued, one arrest followed by full conviction might solve the whole problem. The reality was that the majority of hijackers at this time did find political asylum (Taillon 2002, 21). In the fall of 1969, six Americans who had been in Cuba six months or more voluntarily returned to stand trial for diverting aircraft to Cuba. As stated at the time, these individuals preferred to undergo trial in the United States rather than continue living in Cuba, so it was hoped the publicity message regarding the trials would deter those who might consider hijacking an aircraft as an easy means of leaving their personal troubles (Taillon 2002, 23). In September, Mike Mansfield, Democratic leader of the Senate, and George Aiken, dean of Senate Republicans, urged the Nixon administration to send representatives to meet with the Cuban regime to seek ways of stopping plane hijackings, as they believed a Cuban agreement to return hijackers to the United States for prosecution would solve the problem. Meanwhile, hijacking planes to Cuba continued.

On September 11, 1970, a date later to become infamous in skyjack history, President Nixon, addressing the problem of air hijacking, proposed a series of measures to counter the threat, including the presence of armed guards on both domestic and international flights susceptible to hijacking; wider use of electronic and other surveillance devices at airports; research into methods of weapons and explosive detection, installation of X-ray machines and metal detectors in airports; and boycotting nations that refused to punish or extradite hijackers. At the opening of Congressional Hearings on the problem of airplane hijacking, on September 17, 1970, Captain Charles Ruby, president of the Airline Pilots Association International, in his official statement stressed the importance of international agreements leading to the extradition of hijackers so they could be prosecuted in the country in which they boarded an airplane registered in that country. He pointed out that bilateral agreements could be made with some countries that would not be a party to a multilateral agreement, citing Cuba, which had a law that would permit that it work with other countries to solve the hijacking problem only on a reciprocal, bilateral basis (U.S. Congress, *Hearings*, 1970, 5–8). Representative Wayne Hays of Ohio said negotiating bilateral agreements seemed nonsensical, and with Cuba, impossible. "You can negotiate from now until kingdom come, and you are not going to get a bilateral agreement. We don't even recognize Cuba. How are we going to get a bilateral agreement with them? . . . If you could negotiate with the people we need to negotiate with, that is one thing, but you can't negotiate with these Palestinian guerrillas, and you can't negotiate with Castro . . . " (11–12). Others, too, raised the issue whether any effective international agreement with Cuba was possible. Hijacking planes to Cuba continued, unabated.

In his concluding 1970 testimony, Captain Ruby glimpsed the distant future of terrorism in sobering comments: "It is regrettable that aircraft hijacking has become, so to speak, a diplomatic tool. The situation was difficult enough when we had to contend with the escape hijacker, the casual hijacker, and the suicidal hijacker. We feel that if we learn to overcome the present problems involving hijackers using guns and knives, that the hijacker will become educated accordingly. In other words, we feel an escalation to the use of explosives or the pretended use of explosives to a much greater extent than they are now employed" (32).

By the end of 1971, major U.S. airports were using electronic magnetometers to screen passengers; around fifteen hundred sky marshals were riding aboard the nations' airliners at a cost of $37.7 million annually, but the system was not perfect (Taillon 2002, 29). In November, an American Airlines 747 leaving New York's Kennedy Airport bound for San Juan, Puerto Rico, was hijacked by a lone individual and ordered to go to Cuba. The 221 passengers and 16 crew members included 3 U.S. sky marshals plus a vacationing FBI agent, who conferred with the pilot, deciding no one should take any action to endanger those on board, as it was assumed the terrorist was armed and dangerous. The plane landed in Havana. It was then learned the hijacker was not actually carrying a weapon, an important fact that should have been discovered during preboard screening in New York. However, American Airlines, arguing these procedures were too time consuming and irritating for flight goers, had not turned on a metal detector (Taillon 2002, 29)! The one-sided technical solutions to deter aircraft terrorism—metal screening devices, posted ground and air security personnel, and passenger profiling—while helpful, did not put the hijacking problem to rest. The threat of unscheduled flights to Cuba still existed. Although more hijackings occurred in the United States than in any other country, this form of terrorism had become a worldwide concern. Peak years for transportation hijacking outside the United States were 1969 and 1970. Between 1968 and 1972, there were almost as many hijackings to Cuba from outside the United States as there were from within. Table A.1 (see page 90) lists bombing and kidnapping incidents along with hijacking events in the U.S.-Cuba relation between 1958 and 1980. It is readily apparent that 1968 and 1972 were decisive up and down turning points in the pattern of aerial hijack terrorism. Hijackings were rare between 1972 and 1979. Cuban exile bombing raids were not, but these campaigns were directed at specific Cuban targets, not the mass public.

Proposals for Agreement

Multilateral Efforts

The United Nations Security Council and General Assembly, from December 1969 through August 1973, had passed a series of resolutions directed at the aircraft hijacking problem, though one analyst (McWhinney 1987, 18–19), said they were not terribly effective because they were formulated on rather vague and general terms, "strong in moral precept, no doubt, but rather weak in terms of operationalism and the offering of any very concrete remedies."

The Tokyo Convention of 1963, "On Offences and Certain Other Acts Committed On Board Aircraft," constituted the first major attempt at aerial hijacking lawmaking by multilateral convention. More than six years after signing the agreement, it was ratified and entered into force in the United States on December 4, 1969. Cuba was not a signatory state. The treaty defined air hijacking as an unlawful act of interference of control of an aircraft in flight and provides that the state of first landing of a hijacked aircraft should restore control of the plane to its commander and take custody of the hijackers. Extradition was not mandatory. The Hague Convention, coming into force on October 14, 1971, declared that hijacking constituted an extraditable offense. The Montreal Convention, signed in September 1971, "On the Suppression of Unlawful Acts Against the Safety of Civil Aviation (Sabotage)" entered into force in the United States on January 26, 1973 (Alexander, Browne, and Nanes 1979, 63–70), contains further specification about unlawful acts against civil aviation safety, and reproduces—in the same language—parts of The Hague convention concerning punishment and extradition. Both The Hague and Montreal conventions require contracting states either to extradite the offender when the person is found within their territory, or punish the offender. If the offender is not extradited, the contracting state is required only to submit the case to its competent authorities for the purpose of prosecution; there is no provision that prosecution will necessarily follow.[4]

U.S.-Cuba Negotiations

In 1961 there were suggestions of a U.S.-Cuban accord on the hijacking problem after the first American civil passenger aircraft was seized and taken to Havana. On July 24, an Eastern Airline aircraft with thirty-two passengers and five crew members was taken over by a gunman during a flight from Miami to Tampa, New Orleans, and Dallas who demanded the plane fly to Havana. Upon the Cuban arrival, passengers and crew stayed overnight at the airport hotel and returned to Miami the next day on a Pan American flight. The original hijacked plane was detained by the Cuban government that proposed an exchange with the U.S. government of Cuban planes—specifically those hijacked by anti-Castro refugees—currently being held. At least twenty-five Cuban planes had been hijacked; eighteen by refugees. In the United States some were seized by judicial authorities and nine sold in response to court orders to satisfy property loss judgments, resulting from Cuban nationalization policies. On August 16, Cuba returned the Eastern Airlines plane to the United States after a deal was worked out: the U.S. government asserted the claim of sovereign immunity with respect to a Cuban naval vessel that had been recently seized and brought into U.S. territorial waters by anti-Castro Cuban refugees, and the patrol boat was returned to Cuba (McWhinney 1987, 68).

The difficulties in reaching formal agreement beyond the ad hoc quid pro quo stemmed from the hostile interchanges between the two countries—nationalization of American-owned property in Cuba, cancellation of the U.S.-Cuban sugar quota, mutual withdrawal of diplomatic missions—and also the flow of numerous anti-Castro refugees onto the United States mainland, who arrived by air and also by sea in small ships and boats between 1958–1960. The U.S. government viewed such events as acceptable forms of political escape in the hardening ideological contest between Communism and the West. Behind the hijackings was a legitimate political cause. The Cuban government saw things differently. Hijackers were criminals. They wanted full reciprocity in any agreement: in exchange for the extradition or forced return from Cuba to the United States of hijack offenders on American airplanes to Cuba, they insisted the U.S. government return any anti-Castro refugees who might have hijacked Cuban planes or vessels in escaping to America.

The hijacking problem, in spite of ideological overtones and disturbingly high frequency, never escalated to serious East-West confrontation. According to Raman (2000, 2–3), the CIA used hijacking as a psychological weapon to discredit the Castro regime (from 1958 onwards), which led to retaliatory hijackings inspired or instigated by Cuban intelligence, involving some U.S. aircraft carrying large numbers of American citizens. When the second Nixon administration came to office in January 1973, hijacking use as a CIA covert action weapon against the Castro regime was discontinued; Cuban intelligence followed suit.

Anti-hijacking negotiation efforts developed in three phases, each following an upsurge in skyjack events: (1) 1961 when Cuba proposed a settlement; (2) 1969 with U.S.-initiated talks; and (3) 1972 when Cuba opened the negotiation window leading to the 1973 agreement.

On August 17, 1961, a secret meeting was held between two high-level, official policy makers in Cuba and the United States: Che Guevara and Richard Goodwin, Assistant Special Counsel to President Kennedy. In their conversation, Guevara thanked the United States for the Bay of Pigs invasion—it had been a great political victory for Cuba that transformed them from an aggrieved little country to an equal—and stated that however difficult negotiations might be, it should be possible to open them by discussing subordinate matters such as the airplane issue as a cover for more serious conversation. Guevara reported later he felt the conversation was quite profitable. According to Goodwin (1961a),

> He touched on the matter of the plane thefts. He said he didn't know if I knew but they had not been responsible for any hijackings. The first plane was taken by a young fellow who was a good boy but a little wild and who is now in jail. They suspected that the last plane was taken by a provocateur (a CIA agent). He is afraid that if these thefts keep up it will be very dangerous.

Ten days later, the Cuban Task Force met at the White House and outlined a plan: the public posture toward Cuba was to be quiet as possible and ignore Castro; covert activities would focus on destroying economic targets carried out by Cuban revolutionary groups on the island; a psychological warfare group would assemble information on the Sovietization of Cuba; and the CIA was asked to create a precise, covert procedure for continuing the below-ground dialogue with the Cuban government to encourage a split in the hierarchy. It was agreed that Cuban exiles should be taken into U.S. confidence, for they would be needed to accomplish policy objectives (Goodwin 1961b). In short, the United States did not agree to negotiate.

Hijacking of aircraft had become a serious problem in the United States in the late 1960s. Seventeen U.S. planes were taken in 1968; by early February 1969, nine more U.S. commercial aircraft had been forced to fly to Havana. Some of these terrorists had found haven there. William Graham, indicted in the United States for murdering an airline ticket agent in a 1972 hijack to Cuba, was now a college student in Havana, staying in a hotel with room service (*Washington Post,* January 7, 1975). A memorandum from Henry Kissinger to newly elected President Nixon on aircraft hijacking (February 7, 1969) summarized the issues, stating the United States had proposed a bilateral solution to the Cubans for the return of hijack offenders. He mentioned one historical aspect that might be embarrassing: "In 1961, when there were several cases of ships and planes seized by Cubans escaping to the United States, we did not respond to a Cuban note proposing a mutual agreement to return the persons responsible for those actions to the country of registry. In effect, we refused to consider essentially the same proposal we have now made to the Cubans." No progress in reaching a formal agreement on hijacking occurred, however, in spite of extended exchange of notes. The United States blamed Cuba for its unresponsiveness.

The skyjack banditry incidents in late 1972 with shootouts, killings, and extortion—the Southern Airline hijackers extorted some $2 million in their escapade in November—prompted Cuba to reopen negotiations. To enter these discussions, the United States was in a dilemma. As a quid pro quo, Castro insisted on a promise that America curb the activities of Cuban exile groups in Florida, which he charged were attacking Cuban coastline villages and fishing vessels and helping people escape from his country. America would need to decide whether to turn back refugees and sacrifice its tradition of giving asylum. The issue took on urgency in December 1972. Cuban exiles hijacked a Cuban ship and forced the crew to take them to Florida's shore. For the first time, the refugees were arrested by U.S. authorities and ordered to return to their home country, prompting a State Department official to remark that "if the price of a skyjacking accord with Castro is the deportation of three trusting men, then the price is too great" (*Time*, January 15, 1973). Negotiated settlement would not come easily.

The bilateral hijacking accord between the United States and Cuba, "Memorandum of Understanding on Hijacking of Aircraft and Vessels and Other Offenses," successfully concluded through the respective surrogates of each country, the Swiss representing America, and Czechoslovakia representing Cuba, was signed by William Rogers, U.S. Secretary of State and the Minister of Foreign Affairs of Cuba on February 15, 1973, and went into effect immediately. There were no subsidiary provisions or understandings attached to the agreement; the text—open and complete—was meant to stand simply on its own (U.S. Congress, *Hearings,* 1973, 17).

Both countries agreed to either prosecute or extradite persons who either seize or otherwise take possession of aircraft or oceangoing vessels (the latter added at Cuba's insistence) and bring them illegally to the other country's legal territory. Hijacking an airline was considered a crime. Money taken illegally would also be returned to the original party (2). One provision, interestingly, addressed the political dimension of terrorism: someone in imminent danger of death with no alternate means of escaping other than hijacking and does not commit any serious crime in the process could be accorded political asylum (2). This construction favored U.S. policy, requiring conditions to be fulfilled before the other party would consider granting political asylum, over the broader concept prevalent in Latin America (2–3). Cuba signed a similar hijacking accord with Canada, on the same day the U.S. agreement went into effect, and one with Mexico shortly thereafter. The agreement would be in force five years, renewable by express decision of the parties. Either party could terminate it at any time by written denunciation submitted at least six months in advance (4, 15).

The year 1973 marked a turning point for suppressing hijack terrorism: airport screening devices, the U.S.-Cuba hijack accord, and public awareness of threats to air travel security, all contributed to reducing dimensions of the problem confronted during the five previous years. Aircraft hijacking as a terrorist tool did not disappear,

Table 4.1 Aircraft Hijacking Events, 1965–1980

Year	U.S. to Cuba	Other, to Cuba*	Total, Cuba Destination	Worldwide, Other Destinations	Total
1965	0	0	0	5	5
1966	2	2	4	0	4
1967	0	0	0	6	6
1968	19	10	29	6	35
1969	40	32	72	15	87
1970	14	25	39	44	83
1971	10	13	23	35	58
1972	6	4	10	52	62
1973	0	5	5	17	22
1974	0	2	2	24	26
1975	0	1	1	24	25
1976	0	0	0	18	18
1977	1	0	1	31	32
1978	2	0	2	29	31
1979	6	0	6	21	27
1980	16**	5	21	20	41

*Hijackings to Cuba from outside the United States

**Thirteen of the incidents occurred during August 10 to October 25, including three events on August 16. In most cases the hijackers, native Spanish speakers, used cigarette lighters and what they claimed to be flammable liquid as weapons, threatening explosions if the plane was not diverted to Havana. The Mariel boatlift, that transported 125,000 Cuban refugees to the United States, was in operation from April through September 1980. On September 11, an attaché of the Cuban Mission to the United Nations was assassinated by anti-Castro, U.S.-based exiles.

Source: U.S. Department of Transportation, Federal Aviation Administration, Office of Civil Aviation Security, "U.S. and Foreign Registered Aircraft Hijackings," 1981.

but significantly lower levels of incidents worldwide appeared thereafter. Data in Table 4.1 show the effects of measures introduced in early 1973, with hijack frequencies in years before and following. In 1976, the memorandum was denounced by Cuba who argued the United States had failed to control American-based Cuban exile anti-Castro terrorists who had planted a bomb on a Cuban civilian aircraft that killed seventy-three persons (*Washington Post,* October 19, 1976, A18).[5] In practice, however, Cuba continued to extradite or imprison hijackers.

Analysis

Among factors that influence participants to initiate negotiations, Jackson (2000) and Walter (2003) identify these: conflict duration—a longer period of time without resolution; conflict harm—higher but not exorbitant costs to continue fighting; party willingness—a mutual commitment to solve problems through nonviolent means; and stalemate—a countervailing power balance that prevents either party from outright victory. The conditions encouraging belligerents to reach agreement,

Table 4.2 Preconditions for Negotiating an End to Terrorism: U.S.-Cuba Skyjacking Problem

Conditions	1961	1969–1970	1972–1973
To initiate negotiations			
Conflict duration	short	medium	long
Conflict harm to U.S.	least	most	moderate
Conflict harm to Cuba	most	least	moderate
Party willing to negotiate			
Cuba	yes	no	yes
U.S.	no	yes	yes
To reach agreement			
Turning point for U.S.	none	public outcry	hijack fatalities
Turning point for Cuba	planes stolen	none	hijack fatalities
Terrorism concept for U.S.	politics	crime	crime
Terrorism concept for Cuba	crime	politics	crime

adapted from Druckman (2001) and Schmid (2004), include the following: turning points—external events affecting each of the parties adversely; and terrorism conceptualization—moving away from a political motive focus to one based on criminal behavior. Comparing these conditions for negotiating an end to the U.S.-Cuba hijacking problem in effect at three different periods—1961, 1969–1970, and 1972–1973, shown in Table 4.2—provide clear markers supporting the research results.

In the first two attempts at negotiation, only one of the parties was ready to do so. Cuba was prepared in 1961, but the United States was not; America was prepared to do so in 1969–1970, but Cuba was not. Both sides had to experience significant events that, from their individual perspectives, turned them toward seeking a negotiated solution to the conflict. A stalemate was not enough to move them in that direction Nor was the level of harm as perceived by each of the sides, for at the time of resolution, each was experiencing less damage than previously. The coming together in mutual thinking mattered, and one of the central turning points had to be the hijack fatalities that seemed to mark the problem as criminal, not political, behavior.

Would this agreement open the way for further discussion of issues of mutual concern between the United States and Cuba? No. Announcing the pact at a news conference shortly after signing, Secretary of State William Rogers said the accord did not foreshadow any improvement in America's relations with Castro's government. When asked if the agreement represented a significant symbol of change in Cuba's attitude, Rogers said it was a good sign but insufficient for changing American policy. Rogers went out of his way to mention that the truce should not be interpreted as move toward improving relations or easing the U.S. diplomatic and economic boycott of Cuba. In December 1972, Castro, too, had made it clear that discussions to solve hijack terrorism would not be expanded into other issues, when he stated in a radio address that the talks begun in November that year were just limited to hijacking; that Cuba had no interest in improving relations (U.S. Congress, *Hearings*, 1973, 8).

What was the role of negotiation in halting hijack terrorism? An answer to this question comes from three levels: How did the agreement affect international relations between the parties? How was the public affected? What were the effects on terrorists? Raman (2000, 3–4) states categorically that the discontinuance of hijacking by intelligence agencies in state-sponsored terrorism in 1973, plus security measures installed in airports, led to a 50 percent drop in global hijack frequency, noting, in this context, that both the American and Cuban agencies ceased this form of covert action around the time the two countries reached agreement for the prosecution or return of hijackers. Is it possible that negotiators privately reached tacit agreement to cease state-sponsored hijackings while producing the public statement on hijacker punishment? Did the talks take in both issues in some way, thereby rendering greater significance to the role played by negotiations in reducing the terrorism problem? If so, the negotiations were of considerable importance in stopping hijacking. The political pact was critical. If the real *quid pro quo* behind the agreement was essentially a trade-off truce across two types of terrorist activity used by the respective parties' intelligence agencies: hijackings from America to Havana encouraged or sponsored by the Cuban government, and bombings of Cuban properties or Cuban interest targets in America encouraged or sponsored by the U.S. government, using Cuban exiles residing in the United States, the negotiations were very significant in halting terrorism between the parties.

From at least two points of view, however, these negotiations were insignificant. U.S.-Cuba hijack incidents had followed a downward path after 1969. The trend, coupled with heightened precautions in airport screening and security well in advance of the start of the negotiations in late November 1972, suggest the problem was already under control. Moreover, if the argument of intelligence use of hijack terrorism is discounted for lack of tangible, transparent evidence, the negotiations seem to matter very little in resolving the hijack problem.

Negotiation Preconditions

How did the parties come to agree on the issue? The focus of attention that got the parties to the negotiating table moved away from their big conflict circle, framing their differences, namely the West versus Communism debate, and away from scoring points in the war of ideas towards a direct, shrunken look at their immediate problem and what could be done to alleviate it. Timing was an important factor. The hijackers involved in the autumn 1972 incidents that led Cuba to the negotiating table were violent, shootout sky bandits seeking escape and fortune. With these events, the conflict contours were changing in a dangerous direction—hijacking, rather than framed as political expression, was transformed and framed into a crime of banditry—armed robbery in the air. These three developments suggest a ripe moment for resolution: (1) conflict reframing from a general basic ideological dispute to a smaller concrete problem with needs and concerns of each side; (2) an interdependent, correlation relationship between party needs that could be satisfied through a mutual win solution; and (3) potential for serious escalation in the hijacking terrorism presented by the sky bandit cases. By the end of 1972, conflict fatigue had set in on both sides, making disputants more open to agreement. Moreover, the United States had also improved passenger screening devices and announced in December mandatory installation at all major airports (more than five hundred were included) by early January 1973. This feature would play a central role in preventing hijack occurrences and a U.S.-Cuban accord, while helpful, would only become important for offenders able to penetrate through the new defensive system. Neither the Cubans nor the Americans would be giving up much in the new environment as electronic metal detection devices would be able to ward off most potential hijack situations. Still, Castro might have timed his bilateral agreement with the United States—knowing the unilaterally installed security features would contribute the lion's share to substantially lower hijacking terrorism incidents—as a clever political move to advertise to the world that Cuba would no longer be hijacker haven, and also as a clever political move to advertise to the world that Cuba's participation in bilateral negotiations with the Americans made a huge difference in solving the hijack problem. After all, the occasion of the agreement was front page news. Once more, the Cuban leader would be deemed—in his own eyes—as an important and essential international politics player. To summarize, the inhibiting factors to earlier resolution include: (1) an unwillingness by either side to fractionate issues into smaller pieces; (2) a belief by one side (the United States) that negotiations were not essential to deal with the issue—unilateral moves would be sufficient; and (3) tolerance and energy by one side (Cuba) to maintain existing conflict levels until the other party was desperately fatigued.

The United States and Cuba remain enemies. Since February 1982, Cuba has been on the list of states sponsoring terrorism by the U.S. State Department (put into this category initially for its support of the M-19 movement in Colombia). Cuba, for its part, argues, in its United Nations report on terrorism submitted after September 11, 2001, that for more than four decades it has been the victim of ruthless state terrorism by the Americans, who have systematically and constantly financed terrorist acts against Cuba. In July 2003, a Cuban hijacker was found guilty and sentenced to twenty years in prison in the United States after he brandished two fake grenades and forced a passenger plane to fly to Key West under U.S. fighter jet escort. The same month, the Bush administration turned over a dozen Cubans who had commandeered a vessel and attempted to reach U.S. shores to Cuban authorities. As reported, it was a rare case of U.S. policy action where the Americans pleased the Cuban government rather than the American-Cuban exile community. In response, Cuba praised the valuable contribution by the American government

Table 4.3 Terminating Terrorism:
Factors in the U.S.-Cuba Skyjacking Case

Mutual Hurting Stalemate—Conflict Ripeness

The pattern of skyjacking from the United States to Cuba moved from a high of forty incidents in 1969, to fourteen in 1970, to ten in 1971, and to six in 1972. Still the problem of skyjacking remained. Castro was no longer reaping the propaganda benefits. The skyjacking events were a disturbing nuisance.

Turning Points

For the United States, the 1970 copycat skyjacking events that developed in a new environment, the Middle East, signaled a dangerous future in air transportation if the problem with Cuba was not solved soon. For Cuba, the turning point came later, in Autumn 1972, when common criminals took to skyjacking and in the process killed several people, signaling criminality, not politics, was defining the problem.

Negotiation Readiness

For the United States, after attempts to forge an agreement with Cuba at the height of the hijack epidemic in 1970, and by developing metal detection devices, installing them at selected airports during 1972 with a mandated plan to place them in all U.S. airports by January 1, 1973, American could depend more on its own defensive mechanisms rather than Cuban cooperation in efforts to halt terrorism. For the Cuban government, the pressure by the United States to halt skyjacking was felt less—since frequency of events was declining—and hijack-caused fatalities suggested worse events might occur. Cuba came to negotiations for its own reasons, seeking to avoid the impression of providing a safe haven for hardened criminals.

Interest-Based Bargaining

The United States was concerned about its hijacked aircraft bound for Havana. Cuba was concerned about its hijacked fishing ships bound for Miami. The net effect placed both forms of transportation within the stipulations of the agreement on the suppression of hijacking: both specified parties must extradite or punish perpetrators.

to fight against air and maritime hijacking for illegal immigration (*Lexington Institute Report*, July 24, 2003).

In various ways, the accord between the United States and Cuba was a success: hijacking was brought under control, pulled back from its epidemic dangers. The United States and Cuba were able to achieve a small agreement that would partially govern terrorism between them, but were unable or unwilling to leap into negotiations on bigger issues. For general problems, the parties remained (and continue to remain) stuck. Table 4.3 lists the factors in terminating this terrorist campaign.

Appendix

Table A.1 Terrorism Events in U.S.-Cuban Relations, 1958–1980*

Date	Hijackings, Bombings, Kidnapping Incidents

1958

Feb 19	**Bombing** of U.S. owned company by rebels
April 13	**Hijacking** of Cuban airplane, flown to Miami
	Outcome: passengers and plane return to Cuba
June 26–30	**Kidnapping:** 14 U.S. businessmen and 30 U.S. Marines by rebels
	Demands: U.S. cease arms shipments to government, U.S. Guantanamo Naval Base not used to supply arms, U.S. recognize rebel territory of Cuba
	Response: U.S. persuades government to cease bombing rebel positions while hostages are held, U.S.-rebel negotiations established
	Outcome: all hostages released by July 18
Oct 20	**Kidnapping:** 2 U.S. citizens
	Response: U.S. threatens to renew arms shipments to government if hostages not immediately released
	Outcome: all hostages released by October 23
Oct 22	**Hijacking** of Cuban airplane
	Outcome: aircraft disappeared
Nov 1	**Hijacking** of Cuban airplane leaving Miami
	Outcome: plane crashed, 17 dead
Nov 6	**Hijacking** attempt of Cuban airplane
	Outcome: passengers returned

1959

Jan 1	**Hijacking** of Cuban airplane to New York
Apr 16	**Hijacking** of Cuban airplane to Miami
Apr 25	**Hijacking** of Cuban airplane to Key West, Florida
Oct 2	**Hijacking** of Cuban airplane to Miami

1960

Apr 12	**Hijacking** of Cuban airplane to Miami
July 5	**Hijacking** of Cuban airplane to Miami
July 17	**Hijacking** of Cuban airplane to Miami
July 18	**Hijacking** of Cuban airplane to Fort Lauderdale
July 28	**Hijacking** of Cuban airplane to Miami
Oct 29	**Hijacking** of Cuban airplane to Miami
	Outcome: onboard gunfight, 1 dead; on landing, passengers granted asylum. Plane held for Cuban debt repayment to U.S.
Dec 8	**Hijacking** attempt of Cuban airplane
	Outcome: plane crashed; surviving hijackers executed

1961

Jan 1	**Hijacking** of Cuban airplane to New York
Apr 17	**Military Intervention:** Cuban Exiles trained and financed by U.S., invade Cuba in "The Bay of Pigs" event.
May 1	**Hijacking** of U.S. plane to Havana (First time)
	Outcome: Hijacker released in Cuba, later arrested and imprisoned in the U.S. (1975), other passengers and plane returned

Table A.1 (continued)

Date	Hijackings, Bombings, Kidnapping Incidents
July 3	**Hijacking** of Cuban airplane to Miami *Outcome:* political asylum
July 24	**Hijacking** of U.S. plane to Havana *Demands:* Plane held for exchange naval vessel, small boats and 6 Cuban planes held in U.S. Castro suggests U.S.-Cuba sign agreement to return each other's planes. *Outcome:* hijacker indicted. Still a fugitive Plane flown back to U.S., U.S. releases Patrol boat to Cuba
Aug 3	**Hijacking** attempt of U.S. plane to Havana *Outcome:* hijackers arrested and imprisoned in U.S.
Aug 8	**Hijacking** of Cuban freighter to Norfolk, Virginia *Outcome:* political asylum
Aug 9	**Hijacking** attempt of Cuban airplane to Miami *Outcome:* onboard gunfight, 3 killed
Aug 9	**Hijacking** of U.S. plane to Havana *Outcome:* hijacker arrested in Cuba, then deported to Mexico all passengers returned to the U.S. U.S. adopts laws: keep cockpit doors locked except during takeoffs and landings; unauthorized persons forbidden to carry concealed weapons in planes or to threaten or assault crew members

1962

Date	Hijackings, Bombings, Kidnapping Incidents
Apr 13	**Hijacking** of U.S. plane to Havana *Outcome:* hijackers deported to U.S., arrested and imprisoned. plane and passenger returned immediately
Sept 10	**Attack**: U.S. Cuban Exiles attack 3 Cuban ships in Cuban port *Outcome:* group escapes capture
Oct 8	**Attack**: U.S. Cuban Exiles raid Cuban port, 20 people killed
Oct 12–13	**Attack**: U.S. Cuban Exiles sink Cuban patrol boat

1963

Date	Hijackings, Bombings, Kidnapping Incidents
June 11	**Attack**: U.S. Cuban Exiles sink Cuban patrol boat *Outcome:* group escapes capture
July 18	**Hijacking** of U.S. plane to Cuba *Outcome:* neither plane nor hijacker return to U.S.

1964

Date	Hijackings, Bombings, Kidnapping Incidents
Feb 18	**Hijacking** of U.S. airplane to Havana *Outcome:* hijacker retained in Cuba, others returned
Mar 20	**Hijacking** of Cuban helicopter to Key West *Outcome:* onboard gunfight, 1 dead; hijacker and plane returned to Cuba
June 6	**Hijacking** attempt of Cuban airplane to Florida *Outcome:* 42 passengers removed on suspicion
Sept 13	**Attack**: U.S. Cuban Exiles fire on Spanish freighter, boats in Caribbean Sea, 3 killed
Dec 11	**Attack**: U.S. Cuban Exiles fire rocket against UN building in New York where Cuban Revolutionary Che Guevara was addressing General Assembly. *Outcome:* 3 attackers arrested

Table A.1 (continued)

Date	Hijackings, Bombings, Kidnapping Incidents
1965	
Oct 26	Hijacking attempt of U.S. flight to Havana *Outcome:* Cuban exile hijacker arrested and acquitted
Nov 17	Hijacking attempt of U.S. airline to Havana *Outcome:* hijacker arrested and imprisoned
1966	
Mar 27	Hijacking attempt of Cuban airplane to Miami *Outcome:* onboard fight 1 dead, in flight back to Cuba, hijacker escaped, later arrested in Cuba
July 7	Hijacking of Cuban airplane to Kingston, Jamaica *Outcome:* onboard gunfight, 1 dead. Plane returned to Cuba
1967	
Apr 3	Bombing of Cuban UN Acting Mission Chief
Oct 16	Bombing near Cuban, Yugoslav and Finnish UN missions in New York City
1968	
Jan 9	Bombing of parcel mailed by Cuban Exiles in New York in Havana post office
Jan 25	Bombings of parcels mailed by Cuban Exiles in Miami directed against people doing business with Cuba
Feb 8	Bombing of British consulate by Cuban Exiles in Miami
Feb 17	Hijacking of U.S. plane to Havana *Outcome:* hijacker returned to U.S. from Canada November, 1969 sentenced to prison
Feb 21	Hijacking of U.S. airplane to Havana *Outcome:* hijacker given asylum in Cuba, later surrendered in Spain, committed to mental institution, later imprisoned; plane and passengers returned to U.S.
Mar 12	Hijacking of U.S. airplane to Havana *Outcome:* hijackers indicted in Florida, they remain fugitives
Mar 19	Bombing attempt by Cuban Exiles in Miami of Spanish National Tourist Office
Apr 22	Bombing of Mexican consulate by Cuban Exiles in New York *Outcome:* 9 criminals arrested
May 24	Bombing of Mexican consul general residence by Cuban Exiles in Miami
Jun 21	Bombing of Spanish National Tourist Office by Cuban Exiles in New York
Jun 29	Hijacking of U.S. airplane to Havana *Outcome:* pilot imprisoned by Cuba, later released and sought asylum in U.S. Plane and passengers returned
Jul 1	Hijacking of U.S. airplane to Havana *Outcome:* hijacker remained in Cuba; plane and passengers return to U.S.
Jul 4	Bombing of Canadian consulate by Cuban Exiles in New York
Jul 4	Bombing of Australian National Tourist office by Cuban Exiles in New York
Jul 7	Bombing of Japanese National Tourist Office by Cuban Exiles in New York
Jul 9	Bombing of UN mission of Yugoslavia by Cuban Exiles in New York
Jul 9	Bombing of UN mission of Cuba by Cuban Exiles in New York
Jul 12	Hijacking of U.S. airplane to Havana *Outcome:* hijacker deported to the U.S., imprisoned. Plane and passengers return

Table A.1 (continued)

Date	Hijackings, Bombings, Kidnapping Incidents
Jul 12	**Hijacking** attempt of U.S. plane to Havana *Outcome:* hijacker committed to mental institution
Jul 14	**Bombing** of Mexican National Tourist Office by Cuban Exiles in Chicago
Jul 15	**Bombing** at residence of Cuban ambassador to the UN in New York
Jul 16	**Bombing** attempt of Mexican consulate and Mexican National Airline in Newark N.J.
Jul 17	**Hijacking** of U.S. plane to Havana *Outcome:* hijacker remained in Cuba, plane and passengers return to U.S.
Jul 19	**Bombing** of Mexican National Tourist Council, Mexican Travel Agency, Air France, Japan Airlines, Shell Oil Bldgs in Los Angeles by Cuban Exiles
Jul 30	**Bombing** of British consulate in Los Angeles by Cuban Exiles
Aug 3	**Bombing** of Bank of Tokyo Trust by Cuban Exiles in New York
Aug 4	**Hijacking** of U.S. airplane to Havana *Outcome:* hijacker imprisoned in U.S., plane and passengers returned
Aug 8	**Bombing** of British ship *Caribbean Venture* in Miami port by Cuban Exiles
Aug 17	**Bombing** of Mexican airline office in Miami by Cuban Exiles
Aug 22	**Hijacking** of U.S. airplane to Havana
Sept 16	**Shooting** of Polish freighter in the port of Miami by Cuban Exiles
Sept 20	**Hijacking** of U.S. airplane to Havana *Outcome:* hijacker remained a fugitive; plane and passengers returned
Oct 23	**Assassination** attempt against Cuban UN Ambassador in New York *Outcome:* terrorists arrested
Oct 23	**Hijacking** of U.S. plane to Havana *Outcome:* hijacker arrested in Cuba, later imprisoned in the U.S. Plane and passengers return
Nov 4	**Hijacking** of U.S. airplane to Havana *Outcome:* hijacker indicted in U.S., remained a fugitive
Nov 23	**Hijacking** of U.S. airplane to Havana *Outcome:* hijackers indicted in U.S., remained fugitives. Plane and passengers return.
Nov 24	**Hijacking** of U.S. airplane to Havana *Outcome:* hijackers arrested by Cubans, indicted in U.S. and imprisoned
Nov 30	**Hijacking** of U.S. plane to Havana *Outcome:* hijacker indicted, remained a fugitive. Plane and passengers returned.
Dec 3	**Hijacking** of U.S. plane to Havana *Outcome:* plane and passengers returned
Dec 11	**Hijacking** of U.S. airplane to Havana *Outcome:* hijackers indicted in U.S.
Dec 19	**Hijacking** of U.S. airplane to Havana *Outcome:* hijacker arrested in Cuba, imprisoned in U.S. Plane and passengers returned
1969	
Jan 2	**Hijacking** of U.S. airplane to Havana *Outcome:* hijacker back in U.S. to months later, shot while robbing a bank in New York. Plane and passengers returned

Table A.1 (continued)

Date	Hijackings, Bombings, Kidnapping Incidents
Jan 9	**Hijacking** of U.S. airplane to Havana *Outcome:* hijacker imprisoned in Cuba, later imprisoned in U.S.
Jan 11	**Hijacking** of U.S. airplane to Havana *Outcome:* hijacker charged and acquitted of air piracy
Jan 13	**Hijacking** attempt of U.S. airplane to Havana *Outcome:* hijackers apprehended, imprisoned
Jan 19	**Hijacking** of U.S. airplane to Havana *Outcome:* hijacker indicted by U.S.
Jan 24	**Hijacking** of U.S. airplane to Havana
Jan 28	**Hijacking** of U.S. airplane to Havana *Outcome:* hijackers apprehended, given suspended sentences
Jan 28	**Hijacking** of U.S. airplane to Havana *Outcome:* hijackers remain fugitives. Plane and passengers returned
Jan 31	**Hijacking** of U.S. airplane to Havana *Outcome:* hijacker indicted in the U.S., plane and passengers returned to U.S. Airlines pays $2,500 to Cuba
Feb 3	**Hijacking** of U.S. airplane to Havana
Feb 3	**Hijacking** attempt of U.S. airplane to Havana *Outcome:* crew talked hijackers out of their plan
Feb 10	**Hijacking** of U.S. airplane to Havana
Feb 11	**Hijacking** of U.S. airplane to Havana
Feb 25	**Hijacking** of U.S. airplane to Havana *Outcome:* hijacker imprisoned in U.S.
Mar 5	**Hijacking** of U.S. airplane to Havana *Outcome:* hijacker arrested in Cuba
Mar 17	**Hijacking** of U.S. airplane to Havana *Outcome:* hijacker imprisoned in Cuba, then released to mental institution
March 19	**Hijacking** attempt of U.S. airplane to Havana *Outcome:* hijacker arrested, charges dismissed due to insanity
Mar 25	**Hijacking** of U.S. airplane to Havana *Outcome:* hijacker indicted in U.S., lived in Cuba
Apr 13	**Hijacking** of U.S. airplane to Havana
May 5	**Hijacking** of U.S. airplane to Havana *Outcome:* hijacker returned to U.S. from Canada, imprisoned
May 11	**Hijacking** of U.S. airplane to Havana *Outcome:* hijackers indicted, remain fugitives
May 26	**Hijacking** of U.S. airplane to Havana *Outcome:* hijackers indicted, remain fugitives
May 30	**Hijacking** attempt of U.S. airplane to Havana *Outcome:* hijacker abducted in U.S., sent to mental institution
June 17	**Hijacking** of U.S. airplane to Havana *Outcome:* hijacker arrested in Cuba
June 22	**Hijacking** of U.S. airplane to Havana
June 25	**Hijacking** of U.S. airplane to Havana *Outcome:* hijacker indicted, remained a fugitive
June 28	**Hijacking** of U.S. airplane to Havana *Outcome:* hijacker returned to U.S., imprisoned

Table A.1 (continued)

Date	Hijackings, Bombings, Kidnapping Incidents
July 26	**Hijacking** of U.S. airplane to Havana
	Outcome: hijacker returned to U.S., imprisoned
July 31	**Hijacking** of U.S. airplane to Havana
Aug 5	**Hijacking** attempt of U.S. airplane to Havana
	Outcome: hijacker committed to mental institution
Aug 14	**Hijacking** of U.S. airplane to Havana
	Outcome: hijackers indicted, remained fugitives
Aug 29	**Hijacking** of U.S. airplane to Havana
Sept 7	**Hijacking** of U.S. airplane to Havana
Sept 10	**Hijacking** attempt of U.S. airplane to Havana
	Outcome: hijacker committed to mental institution
Sept 24	**Hijacking** of U.S. airplane to Havana
Oct 9	**Hijacking** of U.S. airplane to Havana
Oct 21	**Hijacking** of U.S. airplane to Havana
Dec 2	**Hijacking** of U.S. airplane to Havana
Dec 26	**Hijacking** of U.S. airplane to Havana
1970	
Feb 16	**Hijacking** of U.S. airplane to Havana
Mar 11	**Hijacking** of U.S. airplane to Havana
	Outcome: hijacker imprisoned in Cuba
Apr 22	**Hijacking** of U.S. airplane to Havana
	Outcome: hijacker declared mentally incompetent
May 25	**Hijacking** of U.S. airplane to Havana
	Outcome: hijacker remains a fugitive in Cuba
July 1	**Hijacking** of U.S. airplane to Havana
	Outcome: hijacker remains a fugitive in Cuba
Aug 2	**Hijacking** of U.S. 747 airplane to Havana
	Outcome: hijacker remains a fugitive
Aug 19	**Hijacking** of U.S. airplane to Havana
Aug 20	**Hijacking** of U.S. airplane to Havana
	Outcome: hijacker arrested in Cuba, later imprisoned in the U.S.
Aug 24	**Hijacking** of U.S. airplane to Havana
	Outcome: hijacker was returned to the U.S. by Cuba, committed to mental institution
Sept 19	**Hijacking** of U.S. airplane to Havana
	Outcome: hijacker returned to U.S., imprisoned
Oct 30	**Hijacking** of U.S. airplane to Havana
Nov 1	**Hijacking** of U.S. airplane to Havana
Nov 13	**Hijacking** of U.S. airplane to Havana
Dec 19	**Hijacking** attempt of U.S. airplane to Havana
	Outcome: hijacker imprisoned
1971	
Jan 3	**Hijacking** of U.S. airplane to Havana
	Outcome: hijacker imprisoned in U.S.
Jan 22	**Hijacking** of U.S. airplane to Havana
	Outcome: hijacker extradited to U.S., imprisoned

Table A.1 (continued)

Date	Hijackings, Bombings, Kidnapping Incidents
Feb 4	**Hijacking** of U.S. airplane to Havana
	Outcome: hijacker apprehended, imprisoned
Mar 31	**Hijacking** of U.S. airplane to Havana
	Outcome: hijacker in U.S., tried, put on probation
Apr 5	**Hijacking** of U.S. airplane to Havana
July 24	**Hijacking** of U.S. airplane to Havana
Sept 3	**Hijacking** attempt of U.S. airplane to Havana
	Outcome: hijacker overpowered, stabbed crew members later imprisoned
Oct 9	**Hijacking** of U.S. airplane to Havana
	Outcome: hijacker returned to U.S., imprisoned
Oct 25	**Hijacking** of U.S. airplane to Havana
Nov 27	**Hijacking** of U.S. airplane to Havana
	Outcome: hijacker drowned in Cuba, March 1973

1972

Jan 7	**Hijacking** of U.S. airplane to Havana
	Outcome: hijacker returned to U.S. December 1978; sentenced, conviction reversed
Mar 7	**Hijacking** of U.S. airplane to Havana
	Outcome: 1 hijacker killed in Jamaica December 1975; 1 hijacker imprisoned in Cuba
Mar 19	**Hijacking** of U.S. airplane to Havana
	Outcome: hijacker returned to U.S. December 1978, imprisoned
May 5	**Hijacking** of U.S. airplane to Havana
	Outcome: hijacker returned to U.S. June 1975, imprisoned
Oct 30	**Hijacking** of U.S. airplane to Havana
	Outcome: 3 hijackers apprehended by U.S. July 1975, imprisoned, 1 fugitive in Cuba
Nov 10	**Hijacking** of U.S. airplane to Havana
	Outcome: hijackers imprisoned in Cuba September 1973; returned to U.S. October 1980.

1973

Mar	**Bombing** of Center for Cuban Studies in New York City by Cuban Exiles
Dec	**Bombing** of Business in New York City by Cuban Exiles
Dec 30	**Bombing** of ship in Miami dock by Cuban Exiles

Aircraft Hijacking Incidents Only

1974	none
1975	none
1976	none

1977

Dec 25	**Hijacking** attempt of U.S. airplane to Havana
	Outcome: hijacker apprehended in U.S., imprisoned

Table A.1 (continued)

Date	Hijackings, Bombings, Kidnapping Incidents

1978

Mar 13   **Hijacking** attempt of U.S. airplane to Havana
Outcome: hijacker apprehended in U.S., committed to mental institution

Dec 14   **Hijacking** attempt of U.S. airplane to Havana
Outcome: hijacker apprehended in U.S., sentenced 5 years probation

1979

Mar 16   **Hijacking** attempt of U.S. airplane to Havana
Outcome: hijacker apprehended in U.S., committed to mental institution

Jun 11   **Hijacking** of U.S. airplane to Havana
Outcome: hijacker taken in to custody in Cuba

Jun 30   **Hijacking** attempt of U.S. airplane to Havana
Outcome: hijacker apprehended in U.S., commit to mental institution

Jul 20   **Hijacking** attempt of U.S. airplane to Havana
Outcome: hijacker apprehended in U.S., committed to mental institution

Aug 16   **Hijacking** attempt of U.S. airplane to Havana
Outcome: hijacker apprehended in U.S., committed to mental institution

Dec 12   **Hijacking** of U.S. airplane to Havana
Outcome: hijacker in Cuban custody, returned to U.S., committed to mental
     institution

1980

Jan 25   **Hijacking** attempt of U.S. airplane to Havana
Outcome: hijacker apprehended in U.S., imprisoned

Apr 9   **Hijacking** of U.S. airplane to Havana
Outcome: hijacker apprehended in Cuba, fate unknown

July 22   **Hijacking** of U.S. airplane to Havana
Outcome: hijacker apprehended in Cuba, fate unknown

Aug 10   **Hijacking** of U.S. airplane to Havana
Outcome: hijacker apprehended in Cuba, fate unknown

Aug 13   **Hijacking** of U.S. airplane to Havana
Outcome: hijacker apprehended in Cuba, fate unknown

Aug 14   **Hijacking** of U.S. airplane to Havana
Outcome: hijacker apprehended in Cuba, fate unknown

Aug 16   **Hijacking** of U.S. airplane to Havana
Outcome: hijacker apprehended in Cuba, fate unknown

Aug 16
(2nd incident)   **Hijacking** of U.S. airplane to Havana
Outcome: hijacker apprehended in Cuba, fate unknown

Aug 16
(3rd incident)   **Hijacking** of U.S. airplane to Havana
Outcome: hijacker apprehended in Cuba, fate unknown

Aug 26   **Hijacking** of U.S. airplane to Havana
Outcome: hijacker apprehended in Cuba, fate unknown

Sept 8   **Hijacking** of U.S. airplane to Havana
Outcome: hijacker apprehended in Cuba, fate unknown

Sept 12   **Hijacking** of U.S. airplane to Havana
Outcome: hijacker apprehended during flight, imprisoned in U.S.

Sept 13   **Hijacking** of U.S. airplane to Havana
Outcome: hijacker apprehended in Cuba, fate unknown

Table A.1 (continued)

Date	Hijackings, Bombings, Kidnapping Incidents
Sept 14	**Hijacking** attempt of U.S. airplane to Havana *Outcome:* hijacker apprehended in U.S., imprisoned
Sept 17	**Hijacking** of U.S. airplane to Havana *Outcome:* hijacker apprehended in Cuba, extradited to U.S., imprisoned
Oct 25	**Hijacking** attempt of U.S. airplane to Havana *Outcome:* hijacker apprehended in U.S., imprisoned

Sources: Mickolus (1980); U.S. Department of Transportation, Federal Aviation Administration, Office of Civil Aviation Security, "U.S. and Foreign Registered Aircraft Hijackings" 1981.

Chapter Five

The U.S.-Iran Hostage Crisis, 1979–1981

In the midst of the Islamic revolution in Iran, several hundred students marching in protest against the United States stormed the American Embassy in Teheran on November 4, 1979, taking sixty-six American officials as hostage. The seizure had been carefully planned by a recently organized group, the Imam's disciples, drawn from the leadership of Islamic associations at local universities who intended to occupy the U.S. quarters for a short time—several hours, maybe a few days, according to reports—but the event developed into a highly publicized international spectacle that lasted more than a year. Although some of those sequestered—African Americans and most of the women—were freed after two weeks, fifty-two U.S. citizens were held in captivity 444 days until their release on January 20, 1981. The hostages were often paraded in blindfolds, with hands tied, in front of local crowds and television cameras. The event riveted the U.S. government and the public; the act was an outrage. More than diplomatic insult, it defaced national honor. As Rosenthal (1981, 35) put it, all Americans and "our very government, had been taken captive and held in that embassy." The event dominated newspaper headlines and TV networks. ABC created a special program, "America Held Hostage," anchored by Ted Koppel, to provide daily updates on the hostages' fate, an airing that evolved into the long-running series, "Nightline." Warren Christopher (1985, vii) then U.S. Deputy Secretary of State, has asserted that

> Few events in recent decades have so consumed the attention of the nation and the energies of its leaders as the seizure of the United States Embassy in Teheran in 1979.... The shaping of the national agenda and the conduct of the 1980 presidential campaign were drastically altered. The world economy was triggered into a severe recession by a doubling of oil prices closely associated with the crisis. Perceptions here and abroad of American power and will to deal with crises in the world were sharply influenced.

When the Embassy in Teheran was attacked and its occupants barricaded, the incident was viewed as an aberration of international politics in spite of periodic kidnapping for extortion, or occasional abductions by bands of terrorists to shield themselves from possible police retaliation (Sick 1990, 231). The incarceration of diplomats or private citizens for political purposes was considered an unusual event then, but today it is far more common.

The United States passed the Hostage Act in 1868 that says when a citizen of the United States is unjustly deprived of liberty under the authority of a foreign government, the U.S. president shall demand the reason of such imprisonment, and if it appears "wrongful and in violation of the rights of American citizenship" shall demand the citizen be freed. If the release is unreasonably delayed or refused, the president shall use such means, "not amounting to acts of war," as deemed necessary and proper to effectuate the release. Since 1949, the Geneva Conventions strictly forbid hostage-taking as contrary to human rights (Faure 2003b). The International Convention Against the Taking of Hostages, adopted on December 17, 1979, defined hostage-taking as "the seizing or detaining or threatening to kill, injure, or continue to detain a person in order to compel a third party to do or abstain from doing any act as an explicit or implicit condition for the release of the seized or detained person." In March 1987, the United Nations passed a resolution categorically condemning all hostage-taking regardless of abductor motivations.

The practice of hostage-taking constitutes a form of instrumental terrorism. By abducting innocent individuals for the purpose of obtaining political advantage, terrorists seek to negotiate with authorities in order to exchange victims for something—publicity, ransom money, prisoner release, freedom. Hostages are bargaining chips. Many countries have firm policies against making deals with terrorists under the premise that negotiation—understood as a process of concession and compromise—will reward groups for bad behavior. Yet, in order to save lives, negotiation often proceeds. To secure freedom for the fifty-two hostages, outgoing U.S. President Jimmy Carter agreed to unleash $8 billion in frozen Iranian assets. How did the parties come to this bartered arrangement?

The chaotic situation in Iran at the end of the 1970s presents an opportunity to examine the evolutionary process in bargaining, including the negotiating style and competing demands of the target government and terrorist side. What bargaining strategies were used by each side to resolve the conflict? How did particular initiatives influence recipient response? Which negotiation strategies were more effective in achieving desired results? Basic strategies outlined by Ury, Brett, and Goldberg (1988), Fisher and Ury (1981), and Fisher, Ury, and Patton (1991) include negotiating by: (1) exerting power; (2) softly yielding; (3) expressing rights; (4) focusing on interests; or (5) appealing to fairness, a principle-based approach. Fisher and Ury (1981, 13) identify two styles of bargaining, *hard* and *soft*, corresponding to the first strategies. Parties following a soft strategy will make concessions to build a relationship with their adversary and to avoid conflict escalation. They change position quite easily and are willing to accept losses against the price of reaching an agreement. Softies yield to pressure. Hard bargainers view negotiation as a zero-sum situation: what one wins the other loses. They do not trust their opponent. They demand concessions. They dig into their stated position and apply pressure to get their way. In positional bargaining, hard bargaining dominates a soft one.

Power-based bargaining is the ability to get what you want from a dispute—to have your claim granted. If you have a range of good alternatives for doing so, your power is enhanced (Brett 2001, 98). Power may encourage people to resolve disputes: when disputants recognize their worst-case scenario is bad, they may be motivated to compromise principle and settle. In a *rights-based* approach, a party tries to persuade their adversary to adopt their position by virtue of legal reasoning and morality claims; invoking rules, procedures and regulations, and implied standards and norms operating in the environment. Both power-based and rights-based negotiation approaches are designed to yield solutions of triumph for one side. *Interest-based* approaches focus on party needs and concerns. This normally includes efforts to understand and emphasize with the interests of others. In this approach, disputants try to deal with the conflict by discussing various needs they have rather than imposing a solution through the application of power or assertion of rights. A *principle-based* approach appeals to fairness. While similar to the interest-based approach because principles are related to interests, it emphasizes instead what rightful action might be undertaken by invoking external criteria of fairness or justice. In appealing to an external set of standards, a principle-based approach is similar to a rights-based approach, but the nature of the standards in the two approaches are very different, and this leads to different ways of engaging in conflict. Rights-based arguments are likely to escalate the dispute rather than resolve it as will-power-based negotiation. Both strategies trigger reciprocal moves by the other side, leading to an impasse or a one-sided agreement (Brett 2001, 110). Interest-based bargaining—finding an integrative resolution to a dispute—preserves some of the values of each side and provides face-saving to disputants.

In the U.S.-Iran hostage-taking terrorism event, two negotiating strategies were employed by the parties at first: a rights-based approach and a power-based approach, attempts to force the other side to accede to its demands through coercive means. Neither approach brought the parties closer to a settlement. Only when principled bargaining, anchored in an interest-based orientation of party needs, concerns, and exchanges took hold, did serious negotiations advance.

Background

Iran contains huge amounts of proven oil reserves and the second-largest deposit of natural gas. Its population is among the largest of states in the region. During the Cold War, Iran's resources and geographic location in the Middle East made it a point of contention between the superpowers. The United States became directly involved in Iran in the early 1950s shortly after the Iranian parliament decided in April 1951 to nationalize the Anglo-Iranian Oil Company, a move its British commercial partner refused to accept. The U.K. eventually convinced their U.S. ally that covertly removing the central Iranian nationalist leader, Mohammed Mossadegh, from his role as prime minister, was necessary. President Eisenhower, inaugurated in

January 1953, believed Mossadegh was incapable of resisting a coup by the Iranian Communist party, Tudeh, were it backed by Soviet support. So in August, the CIA staged a coup, which resulted in the prime minister's departure and reinstatement of the Shah and monarchical control. The chief issue was Iran's right to nationalize a British oil giant that held exclusive rights to drilling and selling the country's petroleum, but Washington saw a possible Soviet takeover by the Iranian Communist Party. The regime upheaval reinstalled the power of the Shah, Mohammad Reza Pahlavi, who ruled with a strong hand for the next twenty-five years until his exile in January 1979. He relied extensively on the United States for military and political support. The special relationship with the United States allowed Iran to purchase any nonnuclear weapons system from the U.S. arsenal. In return, the Shah provided exemptions from Iranian laws to U.S. military personnel, permitted U.S. listening posts to spy on the Soviet Union, and provided support for American foreign policy. Iran's role in the Persian Gulf became especially important after British naval forces withdrew from east of the Suez in 1971.

The American intervention in 1953 was a momentous event, etched in the minds of Iranians: the decision to intervene in the internal affairs of Iran was not forgotten. A decade later, on October 13, 1964, the Iranian parliament approved a law that provided American military personnel and their dependents stationed in Iran with full diplomatic immunity, exempting Americans serving in the military advisory positions in Iran from local law: they could no longer be held accountable in Iranian courts for any crimes that they may have committed in the country. Known in the United States as the Status of Forces Agreement (SOFA), in Iran it was called the Capitulations agreement. Parliament barely passed the measure. Twelve days later, the parliament approved a bill, authorizing the government to accept a $200 million loan provided by private American banks and guaranteed by the U.S. government to purchase modern military equipment from the United States. Iranians viewed this money as payoff for accepting the new law, states Bill (1988, 156–160); both secular and religious intelligentsia of Iran bitterly opposed the immunity legislation. On October 26, Ayatollah Khomeini, a religious leader, delivered a fiery speech, attacking the Shah and America for attempting to destroy the dignity, integrity, and autonomy of Iran. Shortly thereafter, on November 4, 1964, Khomeini was exiled. He lived abroad until the Iranian Islamic Revolution was in full sway, ceremoniously returning in February 1979 to provide the new religious-based leadership for his country, a political shift that has endured into present day.

The Shah pursued westernization policies made possible by an enormous increase in Iran's wealth from oil income, and he engaged in a major military buildup encouraged by the United States. In July 1969, a new U.S. foreign policy, the Nixon doctrine was announced, stating that America would increasingly expect smaller countries threatened by foreign or foreign-assisted aggression to play a greater role in their own defense. The doctrine allowed the purchase of sophisticated military weapons to allied countries, and was designed in part, to keep U.S. defense contractors in business after the eventual wind-down of the Vietnam war. Iran took advantage of this opportunity. In 1971–1972 a major program was developed to modernize and equip its armed forces. U.S. private sector investment in Iran during the 1970s was relatively small; the major emphasis was on military expansion. The United States sold Iran equipment and training programs, installations, and communications, worth approximately $20 billion in military expenditures in a period of six years: fighter bombers, helicopters, transport aircraft, tanks, artillery and rocket launchers, frigates, destroyers, and associated parts inundated the Iranian army and air force. No country in the third world, except India, obtained more weapons. President Richard Nixon and National Security Advisor, Henry Kissinger, visited Tehran in 1972, promising the Shah he could purchase any conventional weapons he wanted from the American inventory, including extremely sophisticated F-14 and F-15 aircraft, creating a bonanza for U.S. weapons' manufacturers. By 1977, the military and security establishments in Iran were absorbing more than 40 percent of the Iranian state budget. A U.S. senate report criticized these huge arms transfers, raising the problem of anti-Americanism that might arise if there were a change in government in Iran leading to a crisis, for then "United States personnel in Iran could become, in a sense, hostages" (Bill 1988, 202).

A sizable group of leading American industrialists held a conference in Tehran in 1970 to pursue opportunities in Iran, whose increasing oil wealth made it a very attractive business center on the international scene. David Rockefeller of Chase Manhattan Bank was a leading organizer of the project. But middle-class nationalists and religious groups strongly condemned the conference. Political demonstrations broke out, including an attack on the Iran-American Society offices in Tehran (180–181). By 1974, the regime had five major prisons with heavy concentrations of political prisoners. Torture was systematically practiced. Between 1971 and 1975, Iran witnessed approximately 400 bombing incidents, 341 guerrillas and members of armed political groups lost their lives battling the Shah's regime (187–191). The Carter administration began pushing the Shah to grant more political freedoms for Iranian citizens in 1977, and the U.S. Congress became concerned about the large number of U.S. advisers and expatriate personnel working in Iran. In 1970, the number of Americans living in Iran was approximately 8,000; by 1978, the figure was nearly 50,000 (381). The Shah visited President Carter in Washington in November 1977, where thousands of shouting students—Iranians studying in the United States—were demonstrating against their monarch just outside Whitehouse gates. Police used tear gas to control them. Yet, around this time, the CIA had concluded the Shah would remain in power well into the 1980s and predicted no radical change in Iranian political behavior in the near future (258). Carter visited Iran on New Year's Eve, delivering a speech stating, "Iran under the great leadership of the Shah is an island of stability in one of the more troubled areas of the world. This is a great tribute to you, Your Majesty, and to your leadership, and to the respect, admiration and love which your people give to you" (quoted in Bill, 232–233).

The Islamic revolution in Iran developed from a combination of changes in the nature of the state, the position of the elites, and the conditions of popular groups; high inflation undermined middle-class living standards and hurt portions of the working class and urban poor, who mobilized to oppose the Shah in open demonstrations. The state responded with repressive measures. As Moshiri (1991, 118) describes it, the increased revenues led to reckless spending and a distorted economic policy that had overstretched the state's oil wealth. As the government came to rely increasingly on foreigners both for labor and for technical advice, political dependence on the United States and the aggressive economic policies of the state alienated nationalist elites and resulted in debt dependence and high inflation. The voice of the opposition became that of Islam, says Fischer (1980, 190). The causes of the revolution owed much to the tradition of religious protest. By 1978, the Iranian regime was lacking political legitimacy and relying essentially on the army and foreign support in the face of an organized and determined opposition. The Shah was increasingly isolated. "Shi'ite preaching had been honed into a highly effective technique for maintaining a high level of consciousness about the injustice of the Pahlavi regime and for coordinating demonstrations," states Fischer (1980, 183); a call for an Islamic ideological revolution and liberation for Muslims to seek social justice. The government was unresponsive to its citizenry, exacerbated by a military and police buildup intended to maintain the stability of oil production for the industrial world. Human rights abuses were widespread. During 1978, clerics and religious students staged demonstrations. Police opened fire. People were killed and many wounded, including religious leaders. These protest marches gained momentum with time until opposition forces covered the entire nation. Violent events in each month centered on major anti-regime demonstrations; throughout this period, an estimated 10,000 to 12,000 people were killed and another 45,000 to 50,000 were injured (Bill 1988, 236).

On January 16, 1979, the Shah was forced from the throne and the country. On February 1, Ayatollah Khomeini triumphantly returned to Iran after many years of exile, vowing to institute an Islamic republic. Recognition of the new government came from Pakistan and the Soviet Union, then from others, including the United States and Morocco. Iranian officials signed a memorandum of understanding with the United States, terminating military contracts under the condition that the network of contracts and deliveries in the absence of responsible authority in Tehran became impossible to manage (Sick 1991, 45). Shortly after Khomeini returned, the U.S. embassy was under siege: one hundred hostages were held in mid-February 1979, but abductors were forced a few hours later to release them and leave. It ended when the government of the new regime—just three days into office—intervened, and it resulted in an apology from a leading personality in the new Iranian regime (Sick 1990, 231).

Months later, pleading emergency medical treatment need, the Shah, suffering from lymphoma cancer, was admitted to the United States. He arrived on October 22, 1979. The deposed Shah was flown from his refuge in Mexico to New York City. Both the State Department and the Iranian government had repeatedly warned against allowing the Shah to enter the United States—it would give the appearance to Iranians that American policymakers were plotting another coup against their country.

Henry Kissinger and David Rockefeller (who was owner of Chase Manhattan Bank, in which the Iranian government was a very significant depositor and very important customer) argued the country should offer refuge to a man who had been a loyal friend; President Carter cited medical humanitarianism (Fischer, 1984, 232–233).

On November 4, 1979, which was "Students' Day" in Iran, several hundred Iranian demonstrators surged into the area just outside the American Embassy compound to voice their disapproval of President Carter's decision to allow the deposed Shah of Iran to enter the United States. A group of students implementing an organized plan, broke open the gates and seized the U.S. quarters. (The American Embassy stood as a symbol of twenty-five years of U.S. relations with the Shah; American policy was coterminous with the Persian monarchy. "Situated north of downtown on the edge of the wealthiest section of the city and within viewing distance of the Elburz Mountains, the embassy in Teheran reflected both the favor that the United States enjoyed in prerevolutionary Iran and the importance that it assigned to that country during the Cold War. Comprising roughly twenty-seven acres with twenty-five buildings set amid rows of shade trees and carefully cultivated lawns and gardens, states Buhite [1995, 161], "the compound radiated an aura of luxury unusual even for American diplomatic facilities.") They demanded the Shah be returned to stand trial. A huge crowd, thousands of angry protesters, gathered shouting "Death to America." U.S. Ambassador William Sullivan along with members of his staff and dependents had already left the country. The garrison group of embassy employees who remained barricaded themselves in the chancellery building; marine guards held the doors shut long enough for officials to destroy some secret documents. Then they surrendered to the militants. More than sixty Americans were sequestered. At the outset, it was not clear what the militants planned to do with the hostages. Should they be put on trial in Iran? Shot? Or simply barricaded until an acceptable exchange could be arranged? While Khomeini quietly disapproved the move—he made no comment on the occupation for several days, waiting to gauge American reaction—he later became a strong supporter when realizing the overwhelming popularity of the act among the Iranian masses (Bill 1988, 295).

What options were available to the United States to free the hostages? President Carter denounced the occupation as terrorism and flatly rejected extradition of the Shah. Military intervention was ruled out, as it might be a danger to the hostages. Their captors threatened executions at once if the United States made any military move to liberate them. To resolve the issue, Carter at first tried dealing with Iranian Prime Minister Mehdi Bazargan, who seemed sympathetic on the day after the seizure of the hostages. Bazargan had met with U.S. National Security Advisor Zbignew Brzezinski in Algiers on November 1, during Algerian independence celebrations, and at the time called for the Shah's return to Iran. But Bazargan resigned on November 6, once he learned Khomeini endorsed the embassy siege and in realizing his political views clashed with the ayatollah's vision of a theocracy.

The hostage incident occasioned major power struggles between political groups in Iran: extremists vs. moderates; theocrats vs. secularists; formal governmental authorities versus student militants. The latter were convinced the embassy was a center of American espionage—a nest of spies (297). They captured thousands of pages of diplomatic documents and correspondence to support their claim that the United States, "the Great Satan," was trying to destabilize the new regime. Various groups—from Islamists to leftists—saw the hostage terrorism as an attack on American imperialism, and in the heat of revolution, there was great political danger for anyone seen as accommodating the United States and working out a negotiated settlement to release hostages.

From November 1979 until mid-January 1981, the United States engaged in strategies with Iran designed to meet their primary goal: safe release for all Americans held hostage. Iranians, too, in revolutionary upheaval, had a set of objectives and pursued their own plans. For President Jimmy Carter, the fate of the hostages was on his mind every waking moment, as he states in his memoir (Carter 1982, 4): "The holding of the American hostages had cast a pall over my own life and over the American people since November 4, 1979. Although I was acting in an official capacity as president, I also had deep private feelings that were almost overwhelming. The hostages sometimes seemed like part of my own family. . . . More than anything else, I wanted those American prisoners to be free." Gary Sick (1990, 237) a member of the National Security Council at the time, stated that the hostages' lives "were present as a palpable reality in the minds of key decision makers at every stage of the crisis. Concern over their welfare affected every major policy decision." *Time* magazine (1979) reporting on the December 1979 Christmas season, stated that "[O]ver in the White House, the nation's official Christmas tree is dark except for one star at the top, because the hostages in Iran have yet to receive the Christmas gift of freedom from the unwise men of the East." A basic counterterrorism rule is that decision makers not meet with the victims' families because the emotional environment might result in unwise actions leading to greater problems in the future (Kraft 2008, 4). Zbigniew Brzezinski, National Security advisor, had advised that the greater responsibility for America was to protect the honor and dignity of the country and its foreign policy interests, which should take precedence over the safety of the diplomats (Sick 1990, 239; Jordan 1982, 44).

President Carter's inability to rescue the hostages marred his leadership and led to the end of his term of office. The hostages were not released until January 20, 1981, more than a year after their abduction, but less than an hour after Ronald Reagan was sworn in as the new U.S. president. The long duration of captivity for the American hostages has been blamed on internal Iranian politics—the attempts by various forces to consolidate their power and build a fresh ideological base of nationalism out of a chaotic situation took time to stabilize—and also on internal politics in the United States—the 1980 presidential campaign activities intensified solution-seeking for Republicans and Democrats, who came to see the hostage problem as a decisive event for ensuring victory. Similarly, the central features explaining conditions for negotiated settlement of the issue have emphasized, alternatively, changes in the political situation within Iran, and changes in U.S. domestic politics.

Proposals for Agreement

For fourteen months, throughout the period of hostage captivity, a number of proposals and backup actions to support them were prepared by officials on each side of the conflict to resolve the situation. A variety of independent efforts undertaken by private individuals and others in designated roles also tried to find ways to break the logjam and ensure the hostages safe release. In the first six months of the crisis following the November 1979 takeover, the terrorist campaign was characterized by positional bargaining—each side presented its own demands; neither compromise-based nor mutual gains–based agreement seemed possible.

America stipulated that all hostages must be released unconditionally—no blackmail, no extortion—for the abductions violated diplomatic immunity granted by international law. But this appeal had no effect. So, less than two weeks into the crisis, the United States froze billions of dollars of Iran's assets, a move that also forced a halt to military weapons' transactions. Iran insisted the Shah be returned to his native country—he had been their leader and had brought the country to ruins—the principle of sovereignty in international law meant the United States ought not interfere with Iranian internal affairs. Neither side was willing to budge from their principled positions; the parties were deadlocked. Serious negotiating never occurred during this period of power display and rights-based argument.

U.S. leaders, frustrated and impatient, attempted to free hostages through a dramatic military rescue in April 1980, but the effort was not successful. Secretly landing aircraft and troops along the desert in eastern Iran, two helicopters on the mission failed, and when the commander decided to end the mission, one helicopter and a C-130 transport plane crashed into each other. The collision resulted in the death of eight U.S. servicemen. The incident was tragic, humiliating, and a great embarrassment to President Carter; no effort, it seemed, could bring the hostages safely back to America. Further, Iran and the United States haggled over the return of the dead soldiers' bodies. (The failed rescue also had negative consequences for Iranian military officers, who, some political groups charged, had secretly assisted the United States aircraft to escape radar detection as they entered the country. Later, a number of them were accused with plotting a coup to overthrow the state and on orders from a military tribunal up to 140 officers were shot. Wider purges of the armed forces followed [Metz 1987]. The destructive fallout to both sides in the aftermath of the aborted military mission had a major impact on the atmosphere of the conflict that appeared to reduce options for a solution.) The environment within Iran, and also within the United States, hardly encouraged the parties to seek a relationship with their adversary to search for acceptable terms for reaching agreement. The setting was extremely hostile and polarizing. But rather than halting efforts of conflict resolution, serious attempts to find openings that might lead to eventual negotiations for settlement began.

During the next six months of the crisis, from May through October into the first days in November, through a variety of contacts and secret meetings, the parties moved away from their previous dominant strategies focused on conditioned demands that were unacceptable to the other side, toward earnest probing for possible, delicate ways to bring the terrorism episode to conclusion. Interest-based, principle bargaining techniques came into play as the parties in conflict were, in a sense, overtaken by events beyond their immediate control. Key turning points affected the dynamics of negotiation. The original terms for a bargained exchange that would free the hostages, indeed the cause of their abduction, was the return of the Shah to Iran. However, he had left the United States for Panama months earlier and headed for Egypt, where he died in late July 1980. In the same month, one hostage, Richard Queen, diagnosed with multiple sclerosis, was released and sent back to America for medical reasons; the hostage-takers had demanded nothing in exchange for his freedom. An isolated gesture, it conveyed a humanitarian message within the terrorism campaign. In Iran, the invasion by Iraq in late September, escalating border skirmishes ongoing since April, initiated a war that diverted attention away from the hostage problem and brought another crisis into focus: how would the supply of military weapons that until the revolution had relied completely on American products be maintained for fighting action? For America, the U.S. election campaign was in full pitch; the two contending parties strongly believed that major breakthroughs in the hostage crisis would surely determine the voting outcome. If Carter could secure the release of those held in captivity and bring them home before November, he'd win the election. If not, he'd lose. Stakes were high. What specific conditions would secure the hostages' release?

It was under this overall set of circumstances that the basic shape—the reciprocal exchange terms—of an eventual agreement were decided by the parties. Iran wanted two things: the United States to free up billions of dollars of Iranian financial assets that had been frozen in response to the abduction of the hostages, and to have the United States reinstate the flow of arms transfers to replenish and build up Iranian military supplies needed to fight Iraq. In the end, Iran got what it wanted. So did the United States-the hostages were freed. But since Carter could not secure their release by November, he lost the election. The Republicans prevailed.

Two major narratives have emerged to explain the process of negotiating a settlement to end the terrorism campaign during the critical six-month period beginning in May 1980. One version—the official open record—credits the Carter administration with steadily and painstakingly crafting the solution essentially based on bartering hostage freedom for unfrozen Iranian financial assets that led to agreement (e.g., Christopher *et.al.* 1985; Newman and Walker 1999); the other version, popularly known as the "October Surprise," highlights the role of Reagan's presidential campaign strategists in cleverly closing a deal with flourish to seal the election outcome (e.g., Bani-Sadr 1991; Sick 1991; Parry 2004). The second version, based on bartering hostages' freedom for military armaments, unofficial and secretive, has achieved a level of notoriety in addition to some level of factual accuracy; each explanation may shed some light to account for dynamics of haggling, promises, and rewards that unfolded. Although they point in opposite directions to indicate precisely who was responsible for solving the problem and what specific conditions for reciprocal exchange was agreed, these explanations share important commonalities. In particular, they lend support for settlement factors denoting serious negotiation intent: readiness to talk to the enemy; a focus on interests over rights-based arguments in structuring proposals for solution; trust and commitment by all sides to finding a way out of the conflict; and consideration for assigning a market value on commodities to be traded. Both explanations are rooted in the same bartering sketch, only the details (significant ethical issues pertaining to timing hostages' freedom, among them) vary.

A brief chronology of U.S.- and Iranian-initiated positions are displayed respectively in Tables B.1 and B.2. Numerous private initiatives and secret talks are part of the overall picture, but only major plans have been included. They were constructed from news reports published in *the New York Times, Los Angeles Times, Washington Post, Chicago Tribune, and Christian Science Monitor.* Two volumes of historical accounts, *American Hostages in Iran: The Conduct of a Crisis* (1985), and *Revolutionary Days: The Iran Hostage Crisis and the Hague Claims Tribunal a Look Back* (1999), containing articles by American officials deeply involved in the crisis (Warren Christopher, Harold Saunders, Robert Owen, Robert Carswell, and others) provide details on the proposals. The tabular listing references demands and conditions that appeared in written form and became part of the public record. Handshake promises and off-the-record side payments, part of informal negotiating within the documented agreement associated with the controversial, "October Surprise," activities are described, too. Though surrounded with secretiveness, never openly admitted by the parties allegedly involved, the extensive, compatible detail of these special negotiations provided by a number of sources: Bani-Sadr (1991); Ben-Menashe (1992); Hoffman and Silvers (1988); Honegger (1989); PBS *Frontline* (1992); Parry (1993; 1999; 2004; 2006); Roberts (1991); Sick (1991); Strong (2004); Tarpley and Chaitkin (2004); and Parsi (2008), but disputed as a conspiracy by Pipes (2003), suggest the second narrative account of negotiation processes merits some attention. U.S. Congressional Investigations in the Senate and House of Representatives in 1992 dismissed allegations of an October Surprise, a decision supported by Snepp (1992); *Newsweek* and *The New Republic;* but the evidence base for the committee's conclusion is regarded by some (Mughal 2005; Parry 2004; 2006; Sick 1993; and Steve Weinberg 1992) as either incomplete or incorrect.

The data show the main developments in negotiation positions and the evolution of negotiating strategies—drawn from publicly available primary sources, and secondary accounts and assessments of meetings and decisions that transpired— employed by the Iranians and the Americans, the parties in dispute. The chronology is not a comprehensive array of every substantive idea offered for solving this terrorism issue but reflects the general unfolding of a process leading to conflict settlement. Nor are the descriptions of negotiation phases intended to determine which of the two competing narratives explaining the negotiated outcome is totally correct.

The Iranians had initiated the terrorism game in order to set up negotiation possibilities for an exchange to bring the Shah back to their country for trial—

but their barter plans failed. Rejecting that arrangement, early in the conflict, the United States envisioned the hostages could be freed in exchange for freeing Iranian assets and listening to Iran air their grievances, but that plan did not work. At the midpoint of the conflict, after the U.S. military rescue attempt, when cascading events of domestic politics affected each side, the parties began to consider more alternatives in crafting conditions for an agreement that might be acceptable to the other. Iran and the Americans were pressing their respective demands and dealing with various proposals, a stage where all players had moved beyond power-based and rights-based negotiation approaches into interest-based bargaining. Whose ideas were most influential in moving negotiations forward and producing the settlement conditions? Published accounts of what actually happened to resolve this conflict differ; in fact, significant political controversy surrounds some of the analysis and speculations in the interpretations of who was responsible for structuring viable negotiation processes. However intriguing, the main focus in this study is not to decide *who* mattered, but rather to determine *how* demands and terms of conditions were offered. How did the recipient respond to the proposal? What was the outcome of the proposed solution? How did the early demands of each side relate to the terms of final agreement? In short, the driving analytical interest is on *strategies* of negotiation, because according to conflict resolution theorists, strategies are important in predicting a successful settlement.

Admittedly, there is a risk in drawing out the pattern of negotiation approaches applied in the conflict since the information on processes remains incomplete. The comprehensive record of all the negotiations leading to eventual agreement in resolving this terrorism problem may never be known. Full disclosure is unlikely; some of the deliberations among decision makers in the United States and within groups in Iran are not accessible, other accounts may be spotty, and particular negotiation encounters might lack documentation altogether. Moreover, available accounts by those involved, both Americans and Iranians, could be misleading, lacking in truthfulness, or, on occasion, even self-serving. However, the possibility that bargaining orientation practiced by the parties represented in the collected record of demands, conditions, and responses gathered from open reports would be categorized incorrectly is remote. The portrayal of negotiating strategies, a less politicized element in understanding what led to conflict resolution but central in seeking to discover how a terrorism campaign is ended by settlement, is probably accurate.

What strategies were used by each side to resolve the conflict? How did particular initiatives influence recipient response? Which strategies were more effective in achieving desired results? Tables B.1 and B.2 at the end of this chapter provide a description of individual "negotiation modules," initiated respectively by the United States and Iran, arranged by date, including specific demands and accompanying action—the form of communicating them; proposals of conditions for exchange (if offered); the reaction by the other side; initiator's bargaining approach: *soft* (willingness to consider concessions), *hard* (threatened negative action), *rights* ("what's due us"), *interests* (needs on both sides, mutual exchange), and *principled* (what is reasonable and fair); and the recipient's response (compliance, noncompliance, no response.

Analysis

What strategies were used by each side to resolve the conflict? The United States tried different approaches to negotiation: first, opening with a principled strategy on hostage return and, later, moving to a sequence of hard and soft strategies followed by a set of consistent tough stands in the spring of 1981. None of these efforts produced the desired effect, that is, hostage release. Iran tended to depend on rights-based negotiation for the most part, which did not have a positive impact to push negotiation settlement forward. The American strategy showed a progression from principled and soft to hard and firm, then to interest bargaining. The Iranian position largely stayed within a zone of rights-based thinking. Two gestures of Iranian "good will" negotiating strategy occurred during the crisis. A group of thirteen U.S. nationals (women and blacks) captured in the embassy takeover was freed just a few weeks later. As Saunders (1985, 79) states, their release was not negotiated. But the basic idea was planted in the very early stages of the crisis by American would-be negotiators (See Table B.1 under "U.S. Proposal, November 6, 1979, on page 118). Some months later, in July 1980, a hostage was released to the United States for medical treatment. However, neither act had a significant impact in altering the overall course of the negotiation process.

How did particular initiatives influence recipient responses? Neither principled bargaining nor rights-based demands and proposals led to engagement by the other side to move the dispute toward resolution. The initiation of a hard, power strategy by the United States in April 1980, however, probably convinced the Iranians to come to the table. Following the rescue attempt, Iran sought out channels for starting secret negotiations on the financial aspect of the crisis and, later, secret negotiations on all conditions for hostages to be released, and if true, the interest-based alleged negotiation sessions with the American Republican party began. Early United States' initiatives, following new negotiation guidelines to emphasize principles for a fair solution, did not work in this case. Perhaps that was due to cultural differences, or perhaps not. We can only speculate short of a detailed investigation on the impact of this variable. A key question must be why the Iranians decided (if in fact they did) to negotiate a deal with U.S. Republican strategists. What assurances did they foresee? How were calculations of their negotiation goals applied? Here, information is scattered and incomplete; the negotiations were conducted in secret. Not all participants have admitted their involvement, and, indeed, many of them are dead. But it seems that Iran, now threatened by the U.S. rescue attempt, had a turn of mind and began thinking about maximizing its interests in the context of larger U.S. concerns: how can we save face, place the United States in blackmail jeopardy, maximize our gains financially, and get assurance of U.S. noninterference in our domestic affairs? They occupied a powerful position in this negotiation (holding the hostage bargaining chip), knowing that America was deeply committed to securing safe release of these U.S. nationals. Iranian negotiators weighed the alternatives. All Americans wanted to find a deal. The Republican presidential campaign strategists wanted to find a deal—whatever it would take to resolve the crisis in the context of ensuring their election victory in November, backing their assurances with financial support and arms delivery. To Iranian negotiators, this group most likely presented a set of fresh faces that appeared less wrapped up in recent U.S. and Shah ties. It was a chance for a new beginning: the Carter-Shah connection could be replaced by the Reagan-Islamic Republic connection and establish a different foundation for Iran-American relations. The Carter administration, by contrast, not only carried the burden of responsibility for the troubled, violent anti-Americanism in Iran, but also had incorporated a principle for defining bargaining space to resolve the current crisis, namely no exchange of arms for hostages. Iranian interests were not aligned with Carter's ethical principles.

Which strategies were more effective in achieving desired results? Only two seemed to work: hard bargaining—power display by the Americans in April 1980, forcing Iran to think about solutions, and interest-based bargaining, either as a result of the meetings between the U.S. Republicans strategists, Iranian officials, and members of the Israeli intelligence and arms trade community; or the similar approach in the secret negotiations in Bonn in September 1980, when Christopher told his Iranian counterpart that time was short, and though "We both had probably a number of speeches that we might want to make to each other. . . . It would be more efficient if we focused on the conditions for the return of the hostages" (Gwertzman 1981, 2). Iran was the only party operating with full access to all channels and was in a position to select among the proposals for resolution, which reaffirms that the party with negotiating power (not necessarily absolute power) runs the game. U.S. efforts, both the Republican strategists and the official Carter group, struggled from operating in relatively weaker positions and consequently were forced to figure out concession arrangements to get the other side engaged in dealmaking. The Carter negotiating style was soft and principled at the start, almost apologetic, and willing to recognize Iran's grievances. At one point in the conflict, Khomeini denounced the U.S. approach as "diabolical trickery, [which] was an attempt to deceive us through flattery" (*Washington Post,* April 1, 1980, A1). Later, it turned tough, causing Khomeini to respond that "No power can impose its will, neither America nor the Soviet Union. . . . They [the Americans] said they intended, for example, to intervene militarily and obliterate everybody. These were words. Do not be afraid of words" (*Washington Post,* April 1, 1980, A14). Republican strategists, if the story is accurate, shifted the negotiating strategy into an interest-based approach. Now, emphasis addressed needs and concerns on both sides and from that point found an integrative solution to the problem. The rights-based approaches presented several times by Iran led to naught. Their strategy shifted, too, after the aborted rescue mission attempt.

The main points of the public hostage-release document, *The Algiers Accord Declaration*, included the following: *Nonintervention in Iranian Affairs:* the United States pledged not to intervene, directly or indirectly, politically or militarily, in Iran's internal affairs; *Return of Iranian Assets and Settlement of U.S. Claims:* the United States agreed to revoke all trade sanctions directed against Iran in the period November 4, 1979, to date and unfreeze Iran assets; and *Return of the Assets of the Family of the Former Shah:* the United States agreed to freeze and prohibit any transfer of property and assets in the United States within the control of the estate of the former Shah or his family. These were points that Iran had presented first in November 1979.

Several details of the negotiations process published online by the Harvard Negotiation Project in 2006 indicate that principled bargaining features and interest-based negotiation developed by Roger Fisher (Fisher and Ury 1981) are important to assessing conflict resolution in the Teheran hostage problem. On the day the embassy was overtaken by the militant students, Fisher estimated the crisis would last eleven months: the seizure would strengthen Khomeini's religious forces over secular ones in Iranian politics, and an impending deadline for reaching a solution would be the American elections in November 1980. In July 1980, the U.S. State Department contacted Fisher for negotiating assistance, who subsequently had a telephone conversation with Ayatollah Beheshti (head of the Islamic Revolutionary Council) in which they discussed justice and fairness in solving U.S.-Iranian issues. It was not an official negotiation. Their interchange continued until the end of August when Fisher drafted a text for consideration—not an offer, nor an official proposal—and sent it to Beheshti and Rafsanjani, speaker of the Majlis, with the objective, Fisher stated, "as something concrete to criticize." It contained these points: (1) The United States accepts the legitimacy of the Islamic government of Iran; (2) The United States will not interfere in Iranian internal affairs: (3) the United States will take no punitive action against Iran; (4) The United States will terminate all sanctions against Iran—after hostages are released no government restriction on sales to or purchase from Iran shall exist; (5) the United States will seek to locate funds belonging to the government of Iran wrongfully removed by the Shah and will support legal remedies to recover such funds; (6) the United States will be responsible for financial compensation with respect to the hostages; (7) the United States will actively promote just settlement of private financial and commercial claims with Iran through negotiation and an international claims commission, understanding that Iran wishes to pay its just debts; and (8) the United States will encourage its allies to continue full cooperation with Iran. (www.pon.harvard.edu/hnp/iran/onetext1.shtml). No official reply was received. About a week later, Iran requested, through West Germany, an urgent, secret meeting with U.S. officials. On September 11, in advance of the talks, Khomeini's statement of Iranian conditions for settlement was transmitted to Washington from the German foreign ministry: "On the return of the deposed Shah's wealth and the cancellation of all the United States claims against Iran, a guarantee of no United States military and political interventions in Iran and the freeing of all our investments, the hostages will be set free" (*New York Times*, January 28, 1981).

These points were part of Fisher's list. They structured the final agreement that began with a small, secret meeting on September 16 between Christopher and Tabatabai held in Bonn. The testimonial of Fisher is strong evidence that principles of interests, fairness, and justice helped conclude this terrorism episode, but upon hearing them on September 13, Iranian President Bani-Sadr (1991, 36), who by this time was not in the Khomeini-Beheshti inner circle, recounts that "[T]hese were not the conditions we had relayed to Jimmy Carter. They were prepared by the Americans themselves. . . . Khomeini as usual, was aiming at the two American presidential candidates, Ronald Reagan and Jimmy Carter, at the same time." Some time later, a formula for Iran and the United States to sign undertakings of Algerian intermediaries, as proposed by the American side, was accepted by all. Algeria had been acting for Iranian interests since April when the United States broke diplomatic relations.

On January 20, 1981, important features in the negotiated terms of agreement between Iran and the United States were fulfilled, bringing the terrorism campaign to an end: the amount of unfrozen assets deposited in an Algerian escrow account in the Bank of England reached $7.995 billion early in the morning (Eastern Standard Time); at noon (EST), the newly elected Republican President Ronald Reagan took the oath of office; and within the next hour, the United States received formal notification that all of the fifty-two hostages had been released, were flying out of the country, and had left Iranian air space bound for Algeria (Owen 1985, 322). The Algiers Accord consisted of a declaration by the Government of Algeria, reporting formal commitments of Iran and the United States within the framework of the four points stated in the resolution of November 2, 1980, of the Islamic Assembly of Iran. The agreement resulted in three documents, two made public at the time.

In the end, Iran received approximately $4 billion, or roughly one-third of the total originally sought as a loss, as a result of the hostage-taking. The cash loss to the Iranian treasure amounted to about $150 million for each of the hostages, more than $300,000 per day per hostage. The issue of returning the arms supplies Iran had previously paid for was never raised in the negotiations after Khomeini's declaration on October 21. Ten years later, in 1991, this material was still in storage in the United States; Iran had not received anything for compensation for the $300 million it had spent (Sick 1991, 190). Among party demands, the United States had insisted all fifty-two hostages be returned unharmed, in a peaceful dispute solution, a condition that was honored. Another demand, the sequencing of hostage releases and freeing Iran's financial assets (America advocated hostage release should be the first step, and Iran wanted control over its U.S.-held financial reserves before doing so) were handled by adding an intermediary step: initially, the agreed asset amount was deposited in a mutually accepted, neutral central bank. Soon after, the hostages departed Iran, and at that moment the funds were transferred to Iran. Three public demands were expressed by Iran throughout the crisis: (1) U.S. commitment to noninterference in Iranian affairs; (2) release of Iran's financial assets that had been held by the United States (first, $14 billion was demanded, and through negotiations the figure was reduced to $8 billion to ensure quick release of the funds); and (3) canceling of U.S. debts and claims against Iran were incorporated into the Algiers accord. Various other demands—the return of the Shah (who had died in July 1980), U.S. withdrawal of military forces from the Persian Gulf, American acknowledgement of some responsibility for the Shah's actions, and recognition of injustices of Iran under the Shah—were dropped.

Part of the negotiated, reciprocal exchange—American hostages would be freed and returned to the United States in exchange for freeing up frozen Iranian assets that would be returned—as a condition for ending the terrorism seems straightforward "market price" bargaining, and perhaps it was. The two factors appear as mutual threats in the acrimonious relationship between the countries; with conflict resolution, these threats disappeared. But this presumes the two elements were interrelated as foreign policy items. Were the hostages held captive in order to extort concessions from America? Were the Iranian assets frozen as a direct response to the embassy seizure? Some analysts (Bani-Sadr 1991; Moin 2000; Fayazmaneseh 2003) argue that completely unrelated domestic conditions within Iran and the United States, respectively, were really the causal mechanisms explaining these actions. The American hostages were actually seized in Teheran in order to strengthen certain Iranian domestic political forces in the atmosphere of revolutionary government change. Control over American officials in Iran gave political leverage to the militants and their backers and offered a device for them to enhance their power over competing forces within the state. The United States, in taking control over Iranian assets, was not responding to the hostage terrorism event by countering with a reactive, punitive measure to hurt Iran, but just carrying out existing plans drawn up *nine months before,* to protect against vulnerability in the U.S. banking system. While the hostage-taking incident provided a triggering event for this decision, it was not the reason it occurred. The potential problem of a sudden withdrawal of funds worried the banking community, who had benefited considerably by the rise of petrodollars deposited by OPEC countries and sought protection.

The hostages were released shortly after President Carter's term had expired and Ronald Reagan had been inaugurated as the next U.S. president. Whether the timing of release was due to conditions agreed by parties in the "October Surprise," which would mean that Iran was following to the letter what Republican strategists had insisted in their proposal, keep the hostages until Reagan is in power, and reflecting a deal they made with the mullahs, or if Iran was pursuing an independent course of dual purpose—to punish Carter, who had been responsible for the controversial policy permitting the Shah to travel to United States, a choice that led to hostage captivity from the start; and to demonstrate conciliation toward the fresh group of people who would be decision makers in the new American administration—may never be known. It is possible, too, that the bureaucratic process conditioning hostages' release simply churned at a pace that brought it to closure on inauguration day. In early August 1980, two Iranian officials, Rafsanjani, speaker of the Majlis, and President Bani-Sadr separately indicated that the American election would be a clear factor in timing hostage releases. Khomeini, who firmly believed Carter tried to prevent his coming to power and took efforts to bring down the Islamic regime, had stated as early as December 1979 that Carter wanted only a quick release of the hostages in order to ensure his reelection (*Christian Science Monitor,* August 14, 1980, 4). But after election day, an advisor to the militants holding the hostages declared Reagan's victory would prolong the crisis, stating, "We would have reached a solution earlier if Carter, who was already in power, had been reelected" (*New York Times*, November 6, 1980, A9).

There is evidence that the United States began selling military equipment to Iran via Israel as needed, in March 1981, two months after Reagan's inauguration (Magnuson 1983; Hersh 1991; Sick 1991). Does that fact provide sufficient evidence that an arms-for-hostage deal was worked out months before? Would the situation have been different if the Democratic administration had continued in office? Once the hostages were free and Iranian assets unfrozen, rules for trade in other areas would seem to be open, and it is apparent that both the outgoing and incoming U.S. administrations were thinking along these lines, as were the Iranians.

The negotiation outcome—what was traded—appears to be a case of successful conflict resolution. Both sides achieved their basic aims: the fifty-two Americans held hostage were freed, and billions of dollars in Iranian assets were freed. Military sales from the United States to Iran—ongoing for a decade—resumed. Financially, Iran paid extra to get a quick settlement to implement their part of the agreement by January 20. The United States had paid extra too, by some accounts several million dollars for Iran negotiators as payoff to various political factions. The Iranians, as the more powerful party in the negotiation with seemingly greater leverage and options in decision making and setting alternative reciprocal exchange terms for an agreement, played the game for the better deal, weighing the choices offered them by Americans. The United States, by contrast, in publicly declaring its major goal—to preserve the lives of the hostages—was more restricted. Did Carter made a mistake by taking on a personal, all-consuming approach to the issue? Would quiet diplomacy have worked better? Did Republican strategists go beyond the ethical bounds of politics with the arms-for-hostage exchange?

Negotiation Preconditions

The outcome of this highly publicized, intensive crisis between the United States and the Islamic Republic of Iran reaffirmed some basic highlights of research on negotiation strategy, namely that: (1) rights-based approaches do not advance a negotiation process; (2) interest-based negotiation shows promise; and (3) hard, power-based bargaining is more effective than soft concession making in moving an uncooperative party toward a negotiation mindset. Mutual willingness to settle was critical to bring about resolution, paralleling scholarly findings. Iran did not really engage in a serious negotiation process until after the hostage rescue mission attempt. Shortly following, Iran agreed to meet with the group of Republican strategists and made discreet inquires about resolving the financial part of the problem.

Did particular negotiation strategies influence the outcomes? Both interest-based bargaining and hard, power-based bargaining seem to bring results in this setting. Was this negotiation context unique? Probably not. The setting squared off a group of terrorists against authorities. Instrumental terrorism—a strategy by the weak to create a more powerful standing in order to bargaining effectively with a stronger party—proved to be an effective mode of confrontation to set settlement conditions, giving the weaker part (in absolute capability terms) credible negotiating leverage over its adversary. In this way, the smaller party's basic grievance in the dispute, indeed the source of the original problem, led to the consistent demand expressed by Iran, that the United States refrain from intervening in their country's domestic affairs. As negotiations came to a close, the tally shows the United States granted this concession in several ways: through the first of four points stated in the Algiers Accord, the United States pledged not to intervene, directly or indirectly, politically or militarily, in Iran's internal affairs; through guarantees of continuous supply of military arms from the United States to Iran (its international adversary!), which would bolster homeland armament strength and help ward off potential intruders; and through the patience and meekness it was forced to display during the long, difficult, somewhat humiliating experience it endured for 444 days to learn the lesson. In the future, one might expect to see similar negotiation settings: a strong conventional state power pitted against an instrumental terrorist group, seeking to extract a fair exchange through retribution, revenge, award, and satisfaction. Table 5.1 lists the factors in terminating this terrorist campaign and resolving the hostage crisis.

Table 5.1 Terminating Terrorism:
Factors in the U.S.-Iran Hostage Case

Mutual Hurting Stalemate—Conflict Ripeness

Two impending deadlines moved the resolution of this conflict forward: first, the date of the U.S. national elections in November, 1980, and second, the date of the inauguration of the American President on January 20, 1981. The issue of hostages held in Iran was important in the election campaign. Both the Democratic and Republican Parties were concerned about deal-making that would free them, and hence clinch the voting outcome. The Iranians operated in this context from their own deal-making perspective, deciding with which side they would form the ultimate agreement to free the hostages.

Turning Points

For the United States, the lack of negotiation progress for almost six months into the crisis prompted a change of strategy that led to the rescue mission attempt in late April, 1980. Ironically, it was this show of force that brought Iran into serious negotiation consideration—only a week later, they opened a secret channel.

Negotiation Readiness

For the United States, interest-based negotiating became acceptable after the rescue mission attempt, but not to the Carter Administration, who declined to deal with the terms Iran was suggesting, namely arms for hostages. But when approached for the same deal, the Republican Party National Campaign manager was willing to consider it. Iran was ready for serious negotiation after the rescue mission attempt and after its internal political power struggle had been settled and Khomeini was clearly in charge.

Interest-Based Bargaining

The provisions of the public agreement, the Algiers Accord, show that an exchange between Iran and the United States consisted of trading hostages' freedom for unfrozen Iranian assets. The "October Surprise" alternative explanation indicates that the exchange consisted of bartering hostage freedom for armament supplies to Iran, a badly needed commodity for them to fight the war with Iraq.

Appendices

Table B.1 U.S.-Initiated Negotiation Proposals
on the Iran Hostage Crisis

U.S. Proposal: November 6, 1979

Demand: That Iran releases all American hostages.

Proposal: After the hostages are released in compliance with international law, the U.S. will work to improve diplomatic relations.

Action: Carter writes a letter to Khomeini to be delivered in person by Ramsay Clark, former U.S. Attorney General in the Johnson Administration, known for civil and human rights activism, and William Miller, a former Foreign Service Officer fluent in Farsi, who travel to Turkey and make phone contact with Tehran officials.

> "Dear Ayatollah Khomeini,
>
> . . . In the name of the American people, I ask that you release unharmed all Americans presently detained in Iran and those held with them and allow them to leave your country safely and without delay. I ask you to recognize the compelling humanitarian reasons, firmly based in international law, for doing so. I have asked both men to meet with you and to hear from you your perspective on events in Iran and the problems which have arisen between our two countries. The people of the United States desire to have relations with Iran based on equality, mutual respect, and friendship… (signed) Jimmy Carter"

Outcome: Failure. No hostages released.

Khomeini refused to meet or talk to them announcing the basic precondition for negotiation was repatriation of the Shah. Carter's letter never delivered. Team called back to Washington Nov 15.

Initiator Style: principled   **Recipient Response:** non-compliance

Source: Saunders, 1985b.

U.S. Proposal: November 6, 1979

Demand: That Iran releases the women and Marine guard hostages.

Proposal: Iran could free some hostages who do not have the same political involvement as the regular Foreign Service Officers.

Action: Ramsay Clark phones Palestinian leaders in Beirut Lebanon to issue request.

Outcome: Success. Thirteen hostages released.

On November 9, the United States learns from top PLO leadership that Khomeini is seriously considering releasing women and African American hostages "not considered spies." On November 14, the hostage-takers state they will release this group, in solidarity with other oppressed minorities, but expect a U.S. statement on the departure of the Shah from the United States. On November 18–19, the group is freed, an Iranian gesture undertaken without the U.S. statement, but Khomeini says the remaining hostages would be on trial soon.

Initiator Style: principled   **Recipient:** compliance

Sources: Saunders, 1985b; *New York Times, 1980.*

Table B.1 (continued)

U.S. Proposal: November 12, 1979

Demand: That Iran releases all the remaining hostages.

Proposal: After hostages are released, *then* Iran's grievances and other issues will be discussed.

Action: U.S. goes to UN Secretary General Kurt Waldheim for help in conveying the demands to Iran.

Outcome: Failure. No hostages released.

Iran presents counter demands: *First,* (1) U.S. recognition of injustices in Iran under Shah; (2) U.S. acknowledgement of some responsibility for the Shah's action; (3) U.S. commitment to noninterference in Iranian affairs; and (4) U.S. recovery of some portion of the Shah's assets, *then* hostages will be released. No mention of demand for Shah's extradition.On November 13, Iran's acting foreign minister Bani Sadr threatens to withdraw Iranian funds from U.S. banks (Iran had nearly $12 billion deposited in European and American banks, especially Chase Manhattan, owned by David Rockefeller). Funds withdrawn will be deposited in banks that have friendly relations with the Islamic Republic of Iran.

Initiator Style: soft   **Recipient:** non-compliance

Source: Sauders, 1985b.

U.S. Proposal: November 14, 1979

Demand: That Iran releases all American hostages.

Proposal: If hostages are not released, Iranian assets in under U.S. control will be frozen.

Action: U.S. stops all trade with Iran (including oil) and freezes all Iranian government assets in American banks and American branches of banks located abroad. American banks permitted to offset the funds that Iran had deposited in their vaults against the monies that the banks had loaned Iran. This turned control of the frozen assets over to the banks and deprived the U.S. government of the leverage it needed to solve the hostage crisis. Carter issued Executive Order 12170, invoking for the first time, the authority of the International Emergency Economics Power Act (IEEPA), which required a presidential finding that there was "an unusual and extraordinary threat to the national security, foreign policy and economy of the United States," of sufficient magnitude to justify declaring a national emergency. The timing was critical: On November 5, the Iranian Central Bank telexed Chase Manhattan instructing them to make the forthcoming interest payment of $4.05 million due on Nov 15 from the surplus funds available in their London office. This interest was owed on a $500 million loan negotiated in January 1977 under the Shah (seven American and four foreign banks were involved). Carter's freeze announcement was made one day before the loan was due to be paid, enabling Chase Bank to declare Iran in default on interest payment, and late enough so that Iran was unable to make other arrangements to honor the interest payment. Once the $500 million loan was in default, Chase declared all loans to Iran in default and seized Iran deposits to offset these loans.

Outcome: Failure. No hostages released.

Initiator Style: hard   **Recipient:** no response

Sources: Christopher, *et al.,* 1985; Bill, 1988.

Table B.1 (continued)

U.S. Proposal: November 17, 1979

Demand: That Iran releases all American hostages

Proposal: After hostages are released, *then* an international commission to inquire into violations of human rights in Iran under the Shah will be held. American courts would be made available to the Iran government to hear its claims for return of assets illegally taken from Iran under the condition that Iran and the United States agree to abide by International Law, including the UN charter and Vienna Convention on Diplomatic Relations.

Action: Communicated to the UN Secretary General Waldheim who presents conditions to Iran.

Outcome: Failure. No response.

Initiator Style: rights   Recipient: no response

Source: Sanders, 1985b; *The New York Times,* 1980.

U.S. Proposal: November 23, 1979

Demand: That Iran releases all American hostages in a peaceful solution.

Proposal: If Iran holds a public trial or government trial of U.S. personnel in Iran it will lead to an interruption of Iranian commerce. If Iran harms any of the hostages there will be direct retaliatory action.

Action: Message is conveyed through secret secure channels to be sure it would not be misunderstood.

Outcome: Partial success. No hostages released, but no American hostages were tried nor seriously threatened with criminal proceedings thereafter.

Initiator Style: hard   Recipient: compliance

Sources: Saunders, 1985b; Buhite, 1995.

U.S. Proposal: November 29, 1979

Demands: That Iran releases all American hostages.

Proposal: Proper action from Iran could be determined by international justice standards, not U.S. demands.

Action: U.S. petitions International Court of Justice for a legal decision that Iran's action in taking and holding hostages violated International Law.

Outcome: Failure. No hostages released. On December 15, the International court of Justice says hostages should be released immediately and U.S. diplomatic property should be reinstated. On May 25, 1980, International Court reaffirms their original order.

Initiator style: rights   Recipient: no response

Source: Los Angeles Times, 1980.

Table B.1 (continued)

U.S. Proposal: December 4, 1979

Demand: That Iran releases all American hostages.

Proposal: After the hostages are released, the United States will organize a forum for Iran grievances. The form would be worked out in advance, that Iran could prepare law suits for U.S. courts to recover assets taken illegally from Iran by the Shah. The United States and Iran would agree to abide by International Law Principles, and the United States will seek resolution of all U.S.-Iran issues.

Action: U.S. presents the case to UN Security Council, a resolution passed calling upon Iran to release the hostages, for the parties to seek a peaceful settlement of the dispute, and urging the Secretary-General to lend good offices.

Outcome: Failure. No hostages released.

Iran did not attend the Security Council sessions. UN Secretary-General Kurt Waldheim visits Tehran January 1, 1980, to see the hostages and begin discussions and present the U.S. conditions. The trip is short and unsuccessful. Iranians protested the visit; students holding the hostages refused to alter their stand.

Initiator Style: soft   **Recipient:** non-compliance

Source: Saunders, 1985b.

U.S. Proposal: December 12–15, 1979

Demand: That Iran releases all American hostages.

Proposal: Iran Embassy staff in Washington will be cut.

Action: United States cuts Iran diplomatic staff in America from around 190 to 35 persons. The Shah leaves the United States bound for Panama.

Outcome: Failure. No hostages released. Repatriation of the Shah is dropped from subsequent demands.

Initiator Style: hard   **Recipient:** compliance

Source: New York Times, 1980.

Table B.1 (continued)

U.S. Proposal: December 31, 1979

Demand: That Iran releases all American hostages.

Proposal: If hostages are not released, the international community will impose sanctions against Iran.

Action: The UN Security Council passes a resolution to consider formalizing economic sanctions against Iran to adopt effective measures, pending outcome of communication with Iran, and Secretary-General Waldheim's visit to Tehran.

Outcome: Failure. No hostages released.

On January 11, Iran requests UN consideration of a commission of inquiry to help improve the atmosphere for a settlement, though the idea was not linked to hostage release. On January 13, the UN votes in favor of sanctions, including embargo on all shipments of goods to Iran except food and medicine. The United States delayed formal application of economic sanctions until April 1980, pending hostage negotiation breakthroughs.

Initiator Style: hard   Recipient: non-compliance

Sources: Buhite, 1995; *Los Angeles Times,* 1980.

U.S. Proposal: January 13, 1980

Demand: That Iran releases all American hostages.

Proposal: After hostages are released, under conditions of sympathy with Iran grievances (to be worked out in advance with a firm understanding as to how to air them); *then* the United States would facilitate legal action brought by the government of Iran in U.S. courts seeking return of the Shah's assets; the United States would lift frozen assets and facilitate normal commercial relations; U.S.-Iran discussion of Soviet threats in Afghanistan would follow; President Carter would make a public statement about Iran grievances to the American people; and the United States would recognize the Islamic Republic of Iran.

Action: Presented to the UN Secretary-General Waldheim for transmittal to Iran.

Outcome: Failure. No hostages released.

Initiator Style: soft   Recipient: no response

Sources: Saunders, 1985b.

Table B.1 (continued)

U.S. Proposal: January 23, 1980

Demand: That Iran releases all American hostages.

Proposal: The United States will regard any attempt by an outside force to gain control of the Persian Gulf region as an assault on the vital interests of the United States and repelled by any means necessary, including military force.

Action: A "rapid deployment force" will be created. (It must have led Iranian revolutionaries to ponder the possibility of military intervention, states Buhite [1995: 177].) Message delivered in State of the Union Address by President Carter.

Outcome: partial success. No hostages released, but Persian Gulf not threatened by Iran.

Initiator Style: hard   Recipient: no response

Sources: Buihite, 1995; *New York Times,* 1980.

U.S. Proposal: February 11, 1980

Demand: That Iran releases all American hostages.

Proposal: The hostages would be released after a UN Special Commission (membership would be from Venezuela, Algeria, Syria, Sri Lanka, and France) on a fact-finding mission, urging Iran to air grievances and achieve an end of the crisis; the commissioners would meet each of the hostages, they would be turned over to the Revolutionary Council of Iran as a preliminary step to their final release.

\Action: The United States requests UN Secretary-General Waldheim to establish a commission of inquiry to go to Tehran.

Outcome: Failure.

On February 20, Iran agrees to the plan; the Commission members arrive in Tehran on February 23. They are not permitted to see or meet with any of the hostages, for Khomeini declared on the eve of their arrival that only the Iranian Parliament, the Majlis, whose election was several months away, could decide the hostages' fate. On March 19, Iran says that documents in U.S. embassy should be turned to the Commission, that meeting with hostages implicated by the documents would be permitted, and if the commission declared its viewpoint in Tehran about the crimes of the United States and of the Shah, then a visit with all the hostages would be permitted. The Commission refuses to go beyond its mandate. Mission departs.

Initiator Style: soft   Recipient: partial compliance

Sources: Metz, 1987; Saunders, 1985b.

Table B.1 (continued)

U.S. Proposal: March 1980, "A Disputed Letter"

Demand: Iran-U.S relations should be improved.

Proposal: That a joint U.S.-Iranian commission should be established to settle all outstanding bilateral problems after the hostages are transferred from militants to the Iranian government. The United States will not apologize to Iran but is willing to express its concern about how past developments have affected the current state of U.S-Iranian relations, and admit to its errors; will consider normalizing relations after the hostage are freed. The common U.S. and Iranian fears of Soviet designs mean that new facts of the revolutionary government must be accepted.

Action: President Carter allegedly sends a confidential message to Ayatollah Khomeini.

Outcome: Failure. No bilateral commission established; no hostages returned.

Iran published this purported confidential message on March 29—released without commentary by Khomeini's office on the national news wire, radio and television. Iranian foreign minister Ghotbzadah said Carter's honest gesture should be considered very favorably by all parties concerned, but the United States categorically denied Carter had sent any message, insisting it was not genuine, though on March 8, Carter, speaking to reporters expressed views contained in the alleged message. Ghotbzadah warned that its denial destroys any trust that Iranians may still have for America. (Reliable sources trusted by both parties said days before the message was made public that it existed.) If the transmission occurred, it demonstrates Khomeini and Carter were in direct consultation, despite Khomeini's insistence that negotiations were impossible.

Initiator Style: principled   **Recipient:** partial compliance

Source: Washington Post, 1980.

U.S. Proposal: April 7, 1980

Demand: That Iran releases all American hostages.

Proposal: If the hostages are not released, the United States will break diplomatic relations with Iran.

Action: United States breaks diplomatic relations with Iran. All diplomatic personal and military trainees are compelled to leave. From this point forward, the government of Switzerland acts for the United States in Tehran, and the Algerian embassy in Washington acts for Iran. Formal economic sanctions begin, European and Japan are encouraged to follow. Starting May 17, a formal inventory of Iran's frozen assets and of American's claims against Iran was ordered, between $11–12 billion in assets uncovered. Visas held by Iranians were invalidated.

Outcome: failure. No hostages released.

The United States could have secured the hostages' release for breaking diplomatic relations, according to Fisher (www.pon.harvard.edu/hnp/iran/hnpsrole.shtml) who recounts that from the Iranian perspective, the break was not punishment but a benefit—an indication that America was giving up on its effort to control Iran.

Initiator Style: hard   **Recipient:** no response

Sources: Carswell and Davis,1985; Harvard Negotiation Project, 2006.

Table B.1 (continued)

U.S. Proposal: April 17, 1980

Demand: That Iran releases all American hostages.

Proposal: If hostages are not released, U.S. travel to and trade with Iran will be prohibited, military equipment purchased by Iran but not yet delivered will be available for others to buy.

Action: The U.S. financial transfers to Iran are prohibited without Treasure Department license. Imports from Iran are banned. Military equipment put up for sale.

Outcome: Failure. No hostages released.

Initiator Style: hard   **Recipient:** no response

Sources: New York Times, 1980.

U.S. Proposal: April 24, 1980

Demand: That Iran releases all American hostages.

Action: A U.S. military hostage rescue mission to Tehran begins, consisting of eight helicopters and six C-130 aircraft. The mission experienced technical troubles and was aborted; one helicopter crashed, eight U.S. soldiers are killed.

Outcome: Failure. No hostages released.

On April 25, Iran moves hostages from U.S. embassy in Tehran to different sites around the country. U.S. Secretary of State Cyrus Vance, who opposed all military options for Iran and out of town when the decision was made, resigned in protest to U.S. actions. On May 5, Cynthia Dwyer, an American in Iran, is arrested and jailed and held until after the remaining group of American hostages are released in January 1981. A second rescue attempt was planned, but testing results at the end of October, and the presidential election outcome, led to its abandonment.

Initiator Style: hard   **Recipient:** no response

Sources: New York Times, 1980; Washington Post, May 4, 1980; www.sheppardsoftware.com/ Middleeastweb/factfile/Unique-facts-MiddleEast9.htm.

Table B.1 (continued)

U.S. Proposal: May 1980

Demand: That Iran releases all American hostages

Proposal: That the United States and Iranian officials meet in secret to deal with the hostage issue.

Actions: The United States proposes to Iran a secret meeting of high level contacts.

Outcome: Success.

On May 8, Iran agrees to meet with United States officials via a linkage established through the Hashemi brothers, Iranian Americans arms dealers. One contact, Medhi Karrubi, was given to William Casey, the Republican Party presidential campaign manager, and two contacts, Medhi Karrubi and a relative of Khomeini, were given to the official U.S. government. On July 2, the relative of Khomeini and a representative of the U.S. government met in Madrid, a meeting arranged by Cyrus Hashemi, held in the Ritz Hotel. No breakthroughs. On July 27, Karrubi and Casey and others meet in Madrid at the Ritz Hotel and establish a workable plan.

Initiator Style: interests   **Recipient:** compliance

Sources: Sick, 1991.

U.S. Proposal: May 18, 1980

Demand: That Iran releases all American hostages

Proposal: A Syrian diplomat, Adib Daoudy, a member of the UN Commission that went to Iran in February, will travel to Teheran to confer with Iranian officials about whether the Commission should return and continue its work of looking at grievances against both the deposed Shah and the United States as preliminary steps to releasing the hostages.

Actions: UN Secretary-General Kurt Waldheim sends the Syrian diplomat to Teheran.

Outcome: Failure. No hostages released; Iran vetos the Commission's return

After spending nearly a month talking with Iranian officials, foreign minister Ghotzadeh said there was no more reason for either the Syrian diplomat or his Commission to return to Iran.

Initiator Style: interests   **Recipient:** noncompliance

Sources: Washington Post, May 18, 1980; *New York Times,* May 26, 1980; *Chicago Tribune,* June 17, 1980.

Table B.1 (continued)

U.S. Proposal: August 20, 1980

Demand: That Iran releases all American hostages.

Proposal: The United States recognizes the reality of the Iranian revolution and legitimacy of the Islamic Republic; the United States will proceed fairly and approach each difficult issue between the United States and Iran on a basis of mutual respect and equality; and a direct channel of communication should be opened so negotiations may proceed.

Action: U.S. Secretary of State Edmund Muskie conveys the proposal by sending a letter to the new Iranian Prime Minister, Mohammed Rajai.

Outcome: Success. Secret negotiations established in September.

Rajai read the Muskie letter aloud at a public rally in Qom, on September 8 stating "Diplomatic discussions are terms used during the satanic era. This does not mean that we will not talk." He called on the United States to repent according to the Islamic code as a precondition for any negotiations. The six stages of repentance range from confession to observing Muslim law eating habits. The United States did not reply to the request.

Initiator Style: principled   Recipient: non compliance

Source: Los Angeles Times, September 2, 1980; and September 18, 1980;

U.S. Proposal: October 16, 1980

Demand: That Iran releases all American hostages.

Proposal: Western sanctions will be dropped automatically if Iran releases the hostages. The U.S. President will meet with any Iranian official who can speak authoritatively for the government of Teheran to get a fresh start to secure the hostages' freedom.

Action: President Carter issues an open invitation to meet Iranian Prime Minister Rajai who is coming to the United States.

Outcome: Failure. No meeting held.

Rajai came to New York October 16 to present Iran's case against Iraq to the UN Security Council. The Prime Minister said he would not talk peace while Iraiqi soldiers remain on Iranian soil, and refused to meet with any U.S. official during his two-day stay or consider negotiations with the United States to provide Iran with spare parts needed in the conflict with Iraq.

Initiator style: principled   Recipient: non compliance

Source: Los Angeles Times, October 16, October 18 and October 22,1980.

Table B.1 (continued)

U.S. Proposal: October 20, 1980

Demand: That Iran releases all American hostages.

Proposal: The United States will release Iranian frozen assets and restore normal trade relations if the hostages are released. The assets would include military equipment bought and paid for before the hostage seizure—worth around $240 million.

Action: President Carter delivered his remarks during televised sessions of his election campaign.

Outcome: Partial success.

The remarks were made shortly after the Iranian Parliament house speaker, Rafsanjani said in Teheran that the conditions for hostages' release would be set within a few days. (In fact, the conditions were not issued until November 2.) Iranian assets were unfrozen when hostages were released in January, 1981. Normal relations with Iran never developed as part of the deal or thereafter.

Initiator style: interests   Recipient response: partial compliance

Sources: Los Angeles Times, October 21 and October 30, 1980. *New York Times,* October 30, 1980.

U.S. "October Surprise" Proposal: July 27–29, 1980-August 12, 1980

Demand: That Iran releases all American hostages.

Proposal: If Iran holds the hostages until after the November 1980 election and then releases them, a Republican presidential election victory will be guaranteed and the new Reagan administration promises to sell military armaments to Iran. All Iranian frozen financial assets would be freed and confiscated military equipment returned. Arms sales could be given through a third country (Israel). Iran must give assurance that the hostages would be well treated until the moment of their release, and freed as a gift to the new administration. In return, the Republicans would be most grateful for the gesture and would "give Iran its strength back."

Action: Several secret meeting in Madrid and in Paris between Iran officials (Medhi Karrubi and Hassan Karrubi, Cyrus and Jamhid Hashemi) and U.S. Republican leaders (William Casey, probably Donald Greg—of Reagan-Bush campaign staff).

Outcome: Success.

The Iranians and Americans agree that the hostages would be removed from prisoner status and treated as guests; Iran would "go through the protocol" with the Carter Administration, prolonging negotiations to be sure the release came after the inauguration but hostage would only be freed as "gesture of goodwill" to the U.S. government on the day of Reagan's inauguration. Details worked out a few days later with the Hashemi brothers and an Israeli arms dealer. In August, Iran receives about $150 million of arms shipments through Israel —four deliveries before Reagan's inauguration on January 20, 1981. On August 16 and 18: Iran Majlis Speaker Rafsanjani and Ayatollah Beheshti both made statements at press conferences in Tehran declaring that the American hostages were not of primary importance to Iran. Iran wants $52 million from the United States before the inauguration to pay off radical leaders; money was deposited in a bank in December by Israeli agent Ben-Menashe.

Initiator Style: interests   Recipient: compliance

Sources: Sick, 1991; Ben-Menashe, 1992; Bani-Sadr, 1991; *Christian Science Monitor*, August 14, 1980.

Table B.1 (continued)

U.S. "October Surprise" Proposal: October 15–19, 1980

Demand: That Iran releases all American hostages.

Proposal: The Iranians hold all hostages until Republican Presidential Candidate Ronald Reagan's Inauguration day, January 20, 1981, and then release them, not before, and arms sales from the United States to Iran will continue.

Action: The U.S. Republicans, Iranians, and Israelis meet in Paris (sixteen Iranians, six Israelis, and twelve Americans) to finalize the deal. About $40 million was made available to the Iranians by the U.S. side—either to buy arms, or go into their personal bank accounts and guarantee of arms sales, unfreezing of Iran money in U.S. banks. Reagan was elected U.S. president on November 4, 1980.

Bani-Sadr (1991: 36) writes, "In late October 1980, everyone was openly discussing the agreement with the Americans on the Reagan team."

Outcome: Success.

Initiator Style: interests   **Recipient:** compliance

Sources: Sick, 1991. Bani-Sadr, 1991.

U.S. "October Surprise" Proposal: Mid-January 1981

Demand: That Iran releases all American hostages.

Proposal: If the hostages are not released by January 20, the arms supply deal is off.

Action: The message was conveyed in a secret meeting between U.S. Republicans and Iranian officials

Outcome: Success.

The hostage release agreement, Algiers Accord is signed on January 19 by U.S. officials and the Algerians who are representing Iranian government. All fifty-two hostages are released within thirty minutes after Republican Ronald Reagan is inaugurated as U.S. President, and they are flown from Iran to Algiers.

Initiator Style: hard   **Recipient:** compliance

Sources: Sick, 1991; Bani-Sadr, 1991.

Table B.1 (continued)

U.S. "October Surprise" Proposal: January 23, 1981

Demand: That Iran release Cynthia Dwyer, an American arrested after the aborted hostage rescue mission and still held in prison in Iran.

Proposal: If Dwyer is not released, the arms supply deal is off.

Action: The new administration communicates the demand through secret channels to Iranian officials

Outcome: Success.

On February 10, Iran releases Dwyer; On February 17, the Reagan administration announces it will fulfill all terms of the Algiers accord in March. Iran begins major purchases of military equipment from Israel, who agree to supply Iran with $200 million of military equipment. Throughout 1981, U.S. acquiescence in Israeli arms shipments to Iran was an open secret. In 1982, the Israeli ambassador to the U.S. Moshe Arens, states Israel coordinated its arms to Iran at the highest levels in the U.S. government. In 1983, Iran seeks TOW missiles to stop waves of Iraqi-operated Soviet tanks crossing the border into Iran (12,000 are delivered up to 1987 according to Ben-Menashe (1992:110-117). *Time* reports that extensive supplies of U.S. weapons are flowing to Iran, despite the ban.

Initiator Style: interests   Recipient: compliance

Sources: Sick, 1991; *Time*, 1983; Ben-Menashe, 1992.

Table B.2 Iran-Initiated Negotiation Proposals on the Iran Hostage Crisis

Iran Proposal: November 12, 1979

Demands: That the U.S. recognize the injustices in Iran under the Shah; that the U.S. acknowledge some responsibility for the Shah's actions; that the U.S. commit to non-interference in Iranian affairs; and that the U.S. recover some portion of the Shah's assets and return them to Iran.

Proposal: If the U.S. meets these conditions, the hostages will be released.

Action: Repatriation of the Shah is not mentioned as a condition for hostage release. Acting Foreign Minister, Abol Hassan Beni Sadr threatens to withdraw Iranian funds from U.S. banks (nearly $12 billion was deposited in European and American banks, especially at Chase Manhattan, owned by David Rockefeller) and deposit in banks that have friendly relations with the Islamic Republic of Iran.

Outcome: Partial success.

U.S. agrees to recognizes the injustices in Iran under the Shah, and commits to non-interference in Iran domestic affairs, but on November 14, freezes all Iranian assets held in the U.S. including deposits in American banks.

Initiator Style: rights   **Recipient:** partial compliance

Sources: Buhite, 1995; Saunders, 1985b.

Iran Proposal: December 31, 1979

Demand: That Iranian public grievances be aired to the international community.

Proposal: That the UN consider a commission of inquiry to help improve the atmosphere for a settlement with the U.S. The hostages could be released after the commission finishes its works.

Action: Proposal is offered by Iran officials to UN Secretary-General Kurt Waldheim during his visit to Teheran.

Outcome: Success.

A commission of inquiry composed of five officials: one each from the following countries: Algeria, France, Sri Lanka, Syria, Venezuela visited Teheran in late February-early March, 1980.

Initiator Style: interests   **Recipient:** compliance

Source: Saunders, 1985b.

Table B.2 (continued)

Iran Proposal: February 11, 1980

Demand: That the documents from the U.S. Embassy in Iran are turned over to the UN commission.

Proposal: That the commission members would be permitted to meet with those hostages implicated by the documents, and if the commission declared its viewpoint in Teheran about the crimes of the United States and of the Shah, then a visit with all of the hostages would be permitted.

Action: Proposal presented by Iran to the UN.

Outcome: Failure.

The Commission refused to go beyond its initial mandate, and departs Teheran.

Initiator Style: principled   **Recipient:** no compliance

Source: The New York Times, 1980.

Iran Proposal: April 1, 1980

Demand: That the U.S. recognize the role of the Iranian parliament in the hostage crisis.

Proposal: If the U.S. recognizes the role of Iranian parliament in the hostage crisis and refrains from propaganda, provocation or claims against Iran, then the hostages can be transferred from rebel-held student control to governmental control in Iran.

Action: President Bani-Sadr sends a message to the U.S. outlining Iran's conditions for transferring the hostages to government control and appealed for postponement of sanctions.

Outcome: Failure.

Pres Carter appears on U.S. television stating he would delay impositions of sanctions until this development could be assessed but the militants relinquished responsibility of the hostages to the Teheran government only on November 4, 1980, the transfer of jurisdiction approved by Khomeini. Sanctions are applied later in April against Iran.

Initiator Style: rights   **Recipient:** partial compliance

Sources: Washington Post, April 1, 1980. Los Angeles Times, November 4, 1980.

Table B.2 (continued)

Iran Proposal: April 29, 1980

Demand: That the U.S. release all frozen Iranian assets.

Proposal: Iran seeks channels leading to discussion of releasing its estimated $6 billion in financial assets. The negotiations must be secret; Iran will deny it if they are made public, and Iran would not put up any fresh funds.

Action: The message is communicated through West German connections in Tehran and feelers sent to Citibank, Bank of America, and Morgan Guarantee at same time.

Outcome: Success.

Negotiations start on May 15. The U.S.-owned Citibank meets with Iranians and presents several conditions: that no separate Citibank deal is to be created; that the U.S. government would be completely informed; and that no financial settlement without release of the hostages can occur. In June 1980, Iran declares it is prepared to arbitrate all financial claims.

Initiator Style: soft   Recipient: compliance

Sources: Carswell and David, 1985; J. Hoffman, 1985.

Iran Proposal: May 1, 1980

Demands: That the U.S. refrain from interference in Iran internal affairs; that the U.S. withdraw military forces from the Persian Gulf; that the U.S. return the Shah's money; that debts and claims against Iran be cancelled.

Proposal: If these conditions are met, *then* hostages will be released, along with an exchange for arms supplies. The demand for an official American apology to Iran is dropped.

Action: One of the hostages, Colonel Charles Scott, who was fluent in Persian is visited in his cell by Mohammed Ali Khamene'i, 1979 deputy Minister of Defense involved in negotiations to restore the flow of U.S. military spare parts to Iran, (later Khomeini's personal representative to the Supreme Defense Council, top coordinating body for Iranian security policy and then President of Iran for 8 years) Scott is only American in Iran familiar with the military supply system. Iran needed access to the computerized inventory system that the U.S. was preparing for them before the Revolution.

Outcome: Success.

Khamene'i said: "If we were to release *you*, how long would it be before you could begin to supply us again with spare parts for our military forces?" The response was that if Iran would release all hostages, then normal relations might be restored and military supplies might be available.

Initiator Style: rights   Recipient: partial compliance

Sources: Sick, 1991; *Washington Post,* October 20, 1980; Bowden, 2006.

Table B.2 (continued)

Iran Proposal: June 1, 1980

Demands: That the U.S. oppressors are condemned and that all (includes specifically the hostage situation) disputes between Iran and the United States should be settled by peaceful means as soon as possible.

Proposal: The world governments should support justice and good faith not oppressors and the U.S. should publicly apologize to Iran, unfreeze Iranian assets, and end all trade sanctions before

any progress can be made toward the release of the American hostages.

Action: Iran opens an international conference, "Crimes of America," 107 delegations from some 50 countries (Ramsey Clark and nine more Americans) with a tirade against the U.S.

Outcome: Failure.

Initiator Style: hard   **Recipient:** non-compliance

Sources: Los Angeles Times, June 2 and 6, 1980. *Chicago Tribune,* June 10, 1980.

Table B.2 (continued)

Iran Proposal: September 9, 1980

Demands: That the U.S. unfreeze and return all Iranian assets; that the U.S. agree to a binding commitment of no military or political intervention in Iranian affairs; that the U.S. return the Shah 's assets; and that the U.S. cancel all claims against Iran.

Proposal: The hostages could be released prior to the U.S. November presidential elections on these conditions. America could consider providing military equipment in lieu of nonmilitary Iranian assets that have been attached to U.S. courts.

Actions: A secret message sent from the West German government to the U.S. that Sadegh Tabatabai (former press attaché to Iranian Embassy in Bonn under the Shah, former deputy prime minister under Bazargan, and brother-in-law of Khomeini's son) wants to meet urgently with a senior American official. Khomeini publicly issues the statement of conditions on September 12, read by an announcer on the official radio.

Outcome: Success.

The Iranian demand for a U.S. apology was dropped, and there was no mention of any hostage trial. The Carter administration had refused to issue any apology to Iran and had strongly warned the Iranians not to put U.S. hostages on trial. On September 16-18, U.S. deputy Secretary of State, Warren Christopher met with Tabatabai in Bonn, stating that when hostages are released, the America will unblock and return Iran assets at Federal Reserve in New York (about $2 billion), unblock Iran's assets at foreign branches of U.S. banks (about $5.5 billion) and prohibit removal of the Shah's assets from the U.S. pending outcome of any litigation—producing draft executive orders to emphasize the U.S. was ready to proceed. Iran has also paid $300 million for military supplies currently being held in the U.S.—about $50 million non-lethal, no sensitive items –tires, trucks, routine spares; $100 million of "gray area" equipment; about $150 million of bombs, missiles, sensitive technology, and software. This matter was not negotiated as the U.S. did not want to give the impression of rewarding Iran for hostage-taking, nor of siding with Iran in the conflict with Iraq. America rejected the proposition. About $50 million would be returned once hostages were released. The parties had agreed to meet the following week, but they never did. Iraq invaded Iran on September 22, and the channel closed. October 8 Tabatabai meets with Iranian president Bani-Sadr, indicating he had met with Christopher (both Christopher and Bani-Sadr are perplexed about these meetings). October 9, Iran requests an inventory of all its assets held in the U.S.

Outcome: Success.

Initiator Style: rights   **Recipient:** partial compliance

Sources: Sick, 1991; Ban-Sadr, 1991. Carswell and Davis, 1985; *Washington Post,* September 13, 1980, *Chicago Tribune,* November 4, 1980. *The New York Times,* January 28, 1981.

Table B.2 (continued)

Iran Proposal: November 2, 1980

Demands: That the U.S. unfreeze Iranian assets; that the U.S. agree to a binding commitment of no military or political intervention in Iranian affairs; that the U.S. return the Shah 's assets; and that the U.S. cancel all claims against Iran.

Proposal: If these conditions are met, the hostages will be released.

Actions: The Iranian Parliament, the Majlis, approves these conditions, set by Khomeini in September and the message is conveyed to the U.S. via the Algerian intermediary.

Outcome: Success. The hostages are released through this proposal.

On November 11 U.S. replies to the Iranian proposal: agrees to a general statement on nonintervention; would make available about $5.5 billion for immediate release after hostages are freed (the remainder would be more complicated); rejects cancellation of U.S. claims, for it would be regarded as a payment of ransom but if Iran agrees, claimants would be allowed to submit essentially the same claims to an international arbitral tribunal and to pay awards made by the tribunal; rejects returning the Shah's wealth—it would have to be the U.S. courts. All hostages must be released at the same time.

Initiator Style: rights   Recipient: partial compliance

Sources: Owen, 1985. *Los Angeles Times,* November 4, 1980. *Washington Post,* November 2, 1980.

Iran Proposal: December 19, 1980

Demands: That the U.S. deposit approximately $14 billion in frozen assets plus an additional $10 billion cash guarantee (to insure that the Shah's wealth would be returned to Iran) in Algerian central bank.

Proposal: Iran will release hostages after this money is transferred.

Action: On January 3, the U.S. replies it will place $8 billion, but provide no $10 billion cash guarantee and sets January 16 as deadline for agreement. On January 7, Iran replies that $ 9.5 billion of frozen assets must be freed. No mention of cash guarantee on Shah's wealth.

Outcome: Mixed.

Issues remain: amount of money in frozen assets to be released, and how to bring Iran loans current—making overdue payments. Bani-Sadr claims this demand was just to stall time.

Initiator Style: interests   Recipient: partial compliance

Sources: Owen, 1985; *The New York Times,* January 28, 1981. Bani-Sadr, 1991.

Table B.2 (continued)

Iran Proposal: January 15, 1981

Demand:	That the U.S. provides $8.1 billion of unfrozen assets at the time of hostage release.
Proposal:	Iran will bring all loans current by paying them off entirely in cash ($3.4 billion) and guarantee payment of the rest thus eliminating the issue, and use approximately $4.8 billion to pay off all of Iran's obligations to U.S. banks.
Action:	On January 18, Iran and the U.S. agree to a final figure, $7.995 billion (down from $8.1 billion due to the fall in gold prices since October) in unfrozen assets: as soon as the Bank of England certifies to the Algerian central bank that it had cash, gold and securities in this total amount, Iran shall immediately bring about the safe departure of the 52 U.S. nationals detained in Iraq.
Outcome:	Success.
	On January 19, a unified document of agreement is signed in the form of a declaration (a decision made by Warren Christopher) to be issued by the government of Algeria and to which U.S. and Iran would adhere. (Iran refused to sign an agreement with "the Great Satan.")

Initiator Style: soft   **Recipient:** compliance

Sources: Owen, 1985; *The New York Times,* January 28, 1981.

CHAPTER SIX

The U.S.-Beirut Kidnapping Crisis 1984–1991

Anti-American terrorism in Lebanon followed in the wake of the dramatic Teheran hostage-taking incident that marred Jimmy Carter's presidential term. It was shaped by two milestones of lasting impression. First, the massive suicide bombing attack against U.S. Marine barracks in Beirut in October 1983. Alleged to be the largest, nonnuclear blast ever detonated until that time, the attack killed 241 soldiers (Hammel 1985, 303). The Americans had been deployed at the invitation of the Lebanese government to bring stability; they were neutral peacekeepers, not partisan warriors. Most were sleeping when the surprise attack hit early on a Sunday morning. In response to the tragedy, President Ronald Reagan decided to withdraw all of the approximately three thousand remaining troops. The last soldier left Lebanon on March 31, 1984. Afterward, terrorists adopted another tactic: kidnapping. Individual American residents in Beirut—many of them academics or members of the clergy, and in one case, a CIA embassy official—were grabbed openly in daylight near their homes or places of employment and dispersed to secret hideouts. The U.S. government, under pressure to secure their release, engaged in an illegal (and, many thought, unethical) negotiated solution: an arms-for-hostage exchange. In what came to be known as the Iran-Contra affair, the second significant event associated with anti-American terrorism in Lebanon developed out of a secret bargain that surfaced in November 1986, leading to high-level political scandal in the United States—an extensive Congressional investigation and indictment of key decision makers.

Lamenting this sorry state, terrorist expert Bruce Hoffman (1989) noted: "The legacy of one presidency destroyed by its inability to free American diplomats held hostage in Teheran and another tarnished by its futile attempt to trade arms for hostages in Lebanon is a constant reminder of America's failure to loosen terrorism's grip." How is it possible to loosen the grip? The situation in Lebanon during the final quarter of the twentieth century provides a lens to examine some modern-day features of global terrorism and its strategic bargaining complexity. Does foreign intervention breed terrorism? Yes. But does it follow that foreign troop withdrawal eliminates the terrorism problem? No. The terrorists simply shift tactics and targets and continue their campaigns. Is it wise to negotiate with terrorists? The answer is mixed. By the Lebanese illustration, a few hostages were freed—a mutual, interest-based agreement offered a way to resolve the terrorism problem—but the arms-for-hostage deal violated ethical and legal norms and ultimately produced minimal results.

Nearly one hundred foreign nationals living in Lebanon were taken hostage one by one between 1982 and 1988 and kept for power leverage in bargained exchange. Among them were British, Italian, French, Russian, German, Swiss, Irish, Norwegian, Saudi Arabian, and Egyptian citizens, among others. Eighteen Americans were kidnapped. They were captured in roadside traffic, abducted at their workplace, or even kidnapped on their residential property around Beirut and kept in slavelike, tortuous confinement for months, sometimes years, as bargaining chips in conflict resolution settlement. Kidnapping has deep roots in the Middle East, stemming from desert diplomacy, according to Alani (2004, 5). The objective is to apply pressure on the target to meet financial or political demands. In antiquity, hostages were rarely killed, but it was not unusual to keep them for a long period of time. What distinguishes abduction from kidnapping from hostage seizure? Clutterbuck (1987, 4) defines abduction as "forcible and illegal carrying off or detention of a person for any purpose, criminal, political or domestic"; kidnapping refers to abduction of a hostage to an unknown location for the purpose of financial or political gain; hostage-seizure means victims are held in a known location for political concessions. In all cases, these terrorist acts are tactics of intimidation directed at one's opponents in order to advance an agenda and achieve a desired end.

The act against hostage-taking, defined by international law, is "Any person who seizes or detains and threatens to kill, to injure, or to continue to detain another person in order to compel a third party, namely a State, an international intergovernmental organization, a natural or juridical person, or a group of person, to do or abstain from doing any acts as an explicit or implicit condition for the release of the hostage" and was adopted by International Convention in December 1979. A decade later, neither Lebanon, nor Iran, nor Syria had signed it.

The terrorism campaign of hostage taking in Lebanon was a strategic design undertaken by a group of Shia Muslims that had recently emerged on the local political landscape, but it was largely directed by Iranian forces. The terrorism tactics—opening with a set of targeted bombings against foreign government property (embassies and military installations) followed by organized kidnappings—worked to the benefit of both parties due in large measure to Iran's particular grievance against the United States that developed after the Teheran hostages were freed, and the special chaotic situation of Lebanon that allowed disenfranchised Shia to organize as political activists and apply their strategy of violence very creatively to achieve their goal to become a legitimate player in the national government system. Of the eighteen American men held hostage, each kidnapped separately and used as a bargaining chip swapped as political capital for monetary rewards, different groups claimed responsibility for the abductions: Islamic Jihad, the Revolutionary Justice Organization, Organization for the Oppressed on Earth. There were as many as eight organizations overall that allegedly participated in the terrorism campaign. But in truth there was only one group responsible, Iran-sponsored Hezbollah. The aliases were intended to suggest either widespread opposition to the West or to disguise the identities of the guilty parties (Jacobsen 1993, 249–250; Ranstorp 1997, 64). Imad Mughniya, the Hezbollah leader in charge of most kidnaps, who was killed by a car bomb in Damascus in February 2008, had embarked on a reign of terror in Lebanon and racked up numerous violent acts against persons and property.[1] The various names of groups introduced by Hezbollah were merely covers for their operational wing. While some abductions of foreigners were initiated to advance individual interests of certain Hezbollah clans, all acts of hostage-taking also coincided with the collective interest of the organization as a whole. Mughniya's group conducted several terrorist acts: the April 1983 bombing of the U.S. Embassy in Beirut that claimed sixty-three lives, including a half-dozen CIA agents—among them the agency's national intelligence officer for the Near East (Baer, 2002, 67) and Agency for International Development (AID) officers; the U.S. Marine barracks suicide bombing that claimed 241 lives, and the simultaneous bombing of French paratroopers that claimed fifty-eight lives in October 1983; and the aircraft hijacking of TWA flight 847 in June 1985, where selected (American) passengers were held hostage for several weeks, including Robert Stethem, an American navy diver, who was murdered. The Hezbollah group was responsible for more American deaths than any other terrorist organization until al Qaeda struck the U.S. embassies in Africa in 1998 and the World Trade Center in New York on September 11, 2001 (Kraft, 2008, 2).

Although the number of U.S. citizens kidnapped in Lebanon was not large—it pales against recent figures for Iraq (since the war began in 2003, several hundred locals and ample numbers of well-publicized abductions of foreigners have occurred) or reports from Colombia and Venezuela—it was an affront to America. The kidnaps were undertaken for symbolic value, a means of demonstrating the power of terrorists and the impotence of U.S. authorities, in essence, extortion intended to bring about concrete changes in official policy to benefit the terrorist organization and its backers. Conflict resolution emerged out of complex negotiation settlements. The pathway to reach this end was fraught with confusion and missteps. Numerous tips and intermediary assistance were offered by individuals who claimed they had good contacts with the hostage holders. But as Kraft (2008, 4) says, "They invariably turned out to be con men trying to get money from the families or the U.S. government. Some of the leads took a considerable effort to check out and became part of what a Middle East expert in the counterterrorism office dubbed the 'sleaze bag file.'" Mughal (2005, 6) reported that more than $400,000 was spent chasing false leads: an Iranian posed as a Saud prince with good intelligence connections and got $15,000; an Armenian claimed he knew the secret location of the hostages, got $100,000, and disappeared in Syria; Lebanese informers received $100,000. Various mediators made cameo appearances to move negotiations along but had little or no impact: Terry Waite, envoy of the Archdiocese of Canterbury; the Algerians; the Swiss; and U.S. political activist, Jesse Jackson.

Three hostages (by most accounts) were eventually freed through Iran-Contra negotiated deals. Two escaped and two were apparently unexpectedly released in April 1990, according to a public announcement, by the goodwill of their captors, although in these cases their fate may have been tied to the arms-for-hostage bargained agreement. Three died in captivity. The largest number of kidnapped victims, following years of incarceration, found freedom with the help of third-party involvement through mediation and negotiation, rounding off the barter material in a complex negotiated financial deal that concluded at the end of 1991 and was crafted through the good offices of the United Nations secretary-general, especially the work of Giandomenico Picco. None of the kidnappers has ever been arrested or tried. There have been no indictments (Voss, 2004, 455).

"Hostages are a politician's nightmare," Byman (2004, 1) states; a kidnapped victim pleading for life may appear in a televised broadcast imploring government officials make a deal with terrorists to spare a threatened execution. These spectacles can consume national media reports; the victim's family pressures the government for a bargained exchange to guarantee a safe release; and "the politicians' opponents, while careful not to endorse the terrorists' demands, seize on the tragedy to portray the government's policy as misguided, inept, and callous."

If governments refuse to negotiate for hostage releases, and terrorists choose to kill their prey (videos of decapitation procedures are sometimes posted on the Internet), the value of the bargaining chip may disappear as a lesson for terrorists that such deal making will not work to their advantage. Yet, while holding firm, the government makes sacrifice of a particular life, and the policy may not alleviate threats of abduction or future executions of its citizens.

America and Iran had recently sparred over the hostage crisis in Tehran. The Algiers Accord of January 1981 freed the hostages; their release was exchanged for freeing Iranian assets under U.S. control that had been frozen right after the embassy barricade. Roberts Owen (1985, 299–301), a U.S. government official who participated in final negotiations, says complex maneuvers by both the United States and Iran in their financial dealings—seizure of American properties in Iran and contracts with U.S. companies cancelled, and the executive freeze order of Iran assets under U.S. control—made it politically impossible for officials of the Iranian government to release hostages without obtaining some commitment from America for a corresponding release of Iranian assets under U.S. control, and simultaneously made it impossible for the United States to release these assets unilaterally, without negotiation. He also declared "delinkage had become impossible." From the American perspective, release of hostages was the top priority, and had U.S. claimants against Iran been abandoned in the context of the hostage crisis, that act might have been regarded as payment for ransom for their release, a condition the American administration found unacceptable.

Neither the negotiation process nor the negotiated end reached in the Algiers Accord was perfectly satisfactory to either side. And among the loose threads that remained to be settled in the Claims Tribunal established in the agreement, some of the points of dispute seemed to resurface in the hostage-taking and release patterns involving the Beirut abductions.

The negotiating process that led to resolution of the Beirut hostage terrorism was complicated, in addition, by the cultural differences between the United States and Iran in the manner of dealing with conflict and dissention, a factor that had a major impact in the interchange leading to agreement. The American approach in foreign policy practice is increasingly derived from the tenets of Alternative Dispute Resolution (ADR), a nonadversarial conflict resolution approach, which comes from the notion that disharmony is seen as something that needs to be controlled and even in cases of injustices, coercive harmony can be used to stifle dissent. The United States considers flexibility to be appropriate to resolve differences. By contrast, Iranians are adverse to compromise, seeing it as weakness and loss of honor; compromise with evil is impossible, even blasphemous. Parties can be estranged for years until third-party mediation brings conflict resolution (Beeman, 2005, 5). Within this framework of differences, solution to the terrorism problem did not come easily. UN negotiator Picco (1999, 71, 286) experienced negative effects from both sides in his mediation efforts: Iranian reluctance to change positions and a willingness "to revisit what seemed to be settled ground, compounded difficulties in forming an agreement," as well as U.S. "flexibility," when told in 1992, a few months after the last American hostage was freed, that there would no longer be any "good will to beget good will," which was a complete reversal from the U.S.'s position in 1989.

Background

A Lebanese government crisis that escalated into street violence led to U.S. military intervention in July 1958. Fourteen thousand military troops—some 8,000 from the army and nearly 6,000 marines—were sent to Lebanon to shore up the pro-Western regime. By the end of the summer, things looked stable; the last units left in October. Shulimson's (1958) Marine Corps report noted that just four solders died during the three-month occupation, three of them in accidents. Analyzing the situation afterward, two contradictory assessments emerged. One was of "dumb relief that the United States had been able to extricate itself so painlessly from a mess," and the other was by sending in marines the United States had blocked the natural and inevitable development of a revolution within Lebanon (Randal 1983, 162). At the time, Lebanon stood apart from social structure and political conditions prevalent in other Middle East countries by virtue of its combined Christian-Sunni Muslim rule and openness to Western ways. Following the Arab-Israeli 1967 war, when Israel took control over the West Bank of Jordan, the Golan Heights of Syria, and Gaza and the Sinai that belonged to Egypt, and major Arab countries broke diplomatic relations with Washington, things changed. A number of displaced Palestinians eventually moved into southern Lebanon, especially after the Jordanian civil war in 1970. American interest in Lebanon focused on the Palestinians who lived there, particularly their use of terrorism in aircraft hijackings and attacks on Israeli citizens. The U.S. Embassy in Beirut developed an important regional intelligence network, a factor not insignificant to understanding the age of the 1980s with the unfolding anti-American terrorist campaign and the negotiated arms-for-hostage responses to it.

Lebanon has experienced several decades of domestic unrest and international violence, dating from 1974 when civil war began. From conventional combat between factional forces and frequent terrorist activity by small groups of varying allegiance, a number of countries have been drawn into the conflict. Two of Lebanon's neighbors intervened: Israel (a U.S. ally) entered the fray in 1978, left, and in 1982 returned and remained for almost two decades; and Syria (an ally of Iran), an occupier since 1976 (originally invited by Lebanese forces during the civil war), stationed between 30,000 to 40,000 troops in the country until the twentieth century's end. Cobban (1999, 23) remarked that "of all the shadow contests between these players [Israel and Syria] the confrontation in Lebanon was by far the bloodiest." Iran, an important regional player, provided substantial military training and financial support for Hezbollah, the Islamic Shiite group. The United States, Britain, Italy, and France participated in the multinational protection peacekeeping force brought in after the 1982 Israeli invasion.

The Israel invasion, sending troops into Lebanon to fight Palestinian forces, trapped the Palestine Liberation Organization (PLO) in Beirut where the group was held under siege for ten weeks in the summer of 1982, until Philip Habib, an American special negotiator, brokered an agreement to separate the parties peacefully. Under its terms, the PLO, and its leader, Yasir Arafat, departed from Lebanon under the watchful eye of the invited Multinational Peacekeeping Force that included U.S. troops. The exodus occurred without incident; around ten thousand Palestinians were evacuated by September 1 1982 (Collelo 1989, 205). About a week later, the eight hundred American marines and their Western force compatriots left too, their job finished. Afterward, serious, violent activity resumed. Within days, the recently elected Lebanese President Bashir Gemayyil was assassinated by a Syrian agent; Lebanese Christian militiamen, with the permission of Israeli troops, entered two refugee camps searching for PLO forces left behind, massacred nearly eight hundred Palestinian men, women, and children.

The Multinational Force, in the spirit of peacekeeper neutrality, was invited by the Lebanese government to return. This time the force's task was to help bring stability to the country by restoring the authority of the central government, and separating remaining Israeli troops from the people of Lebanon. U.S. Marines came ashore again on September 29, 1982. Their fate on this visit would differ sharply from previous experience. The Lebanese government had assured Habib in writing that various factions would refrain from hostilities against the marines (Collelo 1989, 207), but within six months Shia militant groups had launched their anti-American terrorist campaign. The first big hit was the mass explosion in April 1983 in the U.S. Embassy in Beirut. More than sixty people were killed.

During the civil war in Lebanon that began in the mid-1970s, the central government disintegrated, allowing private militias to multiply. The conflict empowered local Shia Muslims, heretofore an insignificant factor in national politics when, in 1982, Iran, newly reborn as the first Islamic fundamentalist state, sent approximately 650 Revolutionary Guards (Pasdaran) to assist them, setting up a guerilla training camp in the Syrian-controlled Bekaa Valley (Collelo 1989, 209). These groups, controlled by Iran, became central in the terrorist campaign against America: they carried out the large-scale attack against the U.S. Marines and were responsible for abducting U.S. citizens on the streets of Beirut and holding these hostages for years.

The U.S. Congress, in September 1983, sanctioned a continued American military presence in Lebanon for an eighteen-month period, promising defense assistance and economic aid (Schiff and Ya'ari 1984, 293). An additional two thousand marines were dispatched to Beirut (PBS Frontline, 2003). Harwood (2003) claims a secret National Command Authority Order issued on September 11 allowed U.S. engagement in offensive acts of war in direct military operations and in support of another belligerent. Marines engaged firepower in support of Lebanese army forces in the mountains east of Beirut on September 19. After that incident, hostile acts against the United States increased, and marines began taking more casualties in the lead up to the large-scale suicide bombing attack on their sleeping quarters in October 1983. The Defense Department Investigation Commission report (1983, 42) stated that the U.S. force "in the eyes of the factional militias, had become pro-Israel, pro-Phalange, and anti-Muslim," concluding that some causal linkage existed between marines' actions in September and the terrorist bombing on October 23. (Harik [2004], cites a December 1982 event, showing U.S. military partisanship that was linked to a subsequent terrorist act, namely the American embassy car bombing in April 1983.)

Alongside unrest in Lebanon, the emergence of Iran's Shia Islamic Republic, caused concern among regional states. Iraq, a secular-run, Sunni-ruled, Moslem neighbor, decided to launch an invasion into Iran in September 1980, picking a low point in expected combat response from the superior, but disarrayed, Iranian forces that had been heavily supported by a huge arsenal of sophisticated American weaponry. Both Saudi Arabia and Kuwait viewed Iran's situation as threatening to their monarchical regimes and decided to sign a secret agreement to raise oil outputs in order to contribute sales revenues to Iraq's war effort. Iran launched air raids on Kuwait borders for alleged involvement in the Iraqi military effort (Hiro 1991, 77). In December 1983, multiple bomb explosions in Kuwait at the U.S. and French embassies, the airport, and the compound of an American residential complex led to complications in the Lebanese conflict. A Hezbollah terrorist team on behalf of Iran had carried out the attacks; several were caught and taken prisoner, including the brother-in-law of Imad Mughniya, the chief Hezbollah leader in Lebanon. Later known as the "Kuwait 17," their release from prison became a consistent demand of kidnappers for the release of Western hostages in Lebanon. The government of Kuwait refused, however, to free them, and the U.S. government declined to pressure Kuwait to make a deal. (They somehow managed to escape during the 1990–1991 Gulf crisis. This issue was essentially an aside in the central negotiations to free Beirut hostages as were later demands to release Israeli-held Muslim prisoners.) The Iran–Iraq War continued for eight years, extracting a heavy toll in human life. By various estimates, up to 1 million people died.

Lebanon throughout the 1980s was in anarchy, labeled as "an epicenter of terrorist activity" (Collelo 1989, 226) where assassinations were not infrequent and car bombings were reported almost on a daily basis. Suicide bombings, too, came of age, heralding the focused future in global terrorism activities. The spate of attacks carried out in 1983 and 1984 (in addition to the U.S. Embassy and marine barracks attacks, other targets included the French military contingent base, the Israeli Defense Force headquarters, and the new U.S. Embassy building used to replace the one destroyed earlier) was an impressive demonstration of terrorist "power of the weak" force. As the frequency of suicide attacks increased, their impact waned, argues Collelo (1989, 228), which is why Lebanese groups abandoned the tactic to concentrate on a more effective technique: hostage taking.

The violent events cataloguing anti-American terrorist incidents in Lebanon and those related to Iranian policy are listed in Table 6.1. Terrorism threat assessment should be based on the number of events, rather than the number of victims harmed in individual acts of violence, since that figure provides real evidence of a campaign strategy, as O'Leary (2006) points out. A terrorist organization is a threat to its target in relation to its number and frequency of attacks against the target, rather than casualty levels achieved because a terrorist group cannot predict in advance the degree of human suffering.

One of the most significant hostage abduction events was the kidnapping of William Buckley, U.S. CIA station chief in Beirut, in March 1984. Eager that Buckley not be tortured to release state secrets, three weeks later, President Reagan signed National Security Decision Directive 138, outlining plans to get the American hostages (Cockburn 1987). Once Buckley had been taken hostage, the CIA devoted considerable energy and resources to get him released, including repositioning a military satellite over West Beirut that was normally stationed over the Soviet Union, telephone monitoring of the Iranian embassies in Beirut and Damascus, interception of Syrian communications, making plans for a rescue mission, and attempting to infiltrate Hezbollah (Hewitt 1991, 98–99). Nothing worked. It was U.S. frustration, perhaps, that led decision makers to participate in negotiations with Iran in the arms-for-hostage trade. Buckley was tortured in an attempt by his captors to reveal U.S. intelligence information. He died about fourteen months after being taken prisoner—an unfortunate situation for his captors, who had sacrificed a bargain commodity and were chastised for allowing it to happen (Sutherland 1996, 137–138; Anderson 1999; Baer, 2002, 79–92, 100). Delaying public announcement of his demise for three months, Hezbollah kidnappers claimed he was killed in retaliation for an Israeli PLO bombing incident.

U.S. State Department official Michael Kraft (2008, 3) described the efforts to release the American hostages in Beirut as "complicated by media hype about them, publicity campaigns on their behalf, and a lack of understanding among some hostage

Table 6.1 Anti-American Terrorist Events of Iran-Lebanon Linkage, November 1979–November 1991*

Date		Event
1979	Nov 4	Hostage Barricade. 66 U.S. citizens at American Embassy in Iran taken hostage, 52 held 444 days. Released January 20, 1981, in exchange for U.S. arms and financial assets returned to Iran
1982	July 19	Kidnapping. U.S. citizen David Dodge, Acting President, American University of Beirut taken hostage, imprisoned in Iran
1983	Mar 16	Attack on U.S. Marines (by hand grenade) in Beirut. 5 wounded
	Apr 18	Bombing of U.S. Embassy in Beirut. 63 killed, 120 wounded
	Oct 23	Suicide Bombing of U.S. Marine Corp Barracks in Beirut; 241 killed, 146 wounded
	Dec 12	Bombing of U.S. Embassy and American Residential compound in Kuwait (plus French embassy, airport and other targets); 6 killed, 80 wounded
1984	Jan 18	Assassination. U.S. citizen Malcolm Kerr, President of American University in Beirut
	Feb 10	Kidnapping. U.S. citizen Frank Regier, Chair, Electrical Engineering Department, American University of Beirut, taken hostage, imprisoned in Lebanon
	Mar 7	Kidnapping. U.S. citizen, Jeremy Levin, CNN reporter, taken hostage, imprisoned in Lebanon
	Mar 16	Kidnapping. U.S. citizen, William Buckley, CIA Station Chief, U.S. Embassy in Beirut, taken hostage, imprisoned in Lebanon
	May 8	Kidnapping. U.S. citizen Benjamin Weir, clergyman in Beirut, taken hostage imprisoned in Lebanon
	Sept 20	Suicide Bombing of U.S. Embassy Annex outside Beirut; 24 killed, 21 wounded
	Dec 3	Kidnapping. U.S. citizen, Peter Kilburn, Librarian, American University of Beirut, taken hostage, imprisoned in Lebanon
	Dec 3	Hijacking. Kuwait Airways Flight 221 enroute from Kuwait to Pakistan 162 aboard including 6 Americans. 2 killed (US AID workers)
1985	Jan 5	Kidnapping. U.S. citizen Lawrence Martin Jenco, clergyman in Beirut, taken hostage imprisoned in Lebanon
	Mar 16	Kidnapping. U.S. citizen Terry Anderson, Associated Press reporter stationed in Beirut, taken hostage imprisoned in Lebanon
	May 28	Kidnapping. U.S. citizen David Jacobsen, Hospital Administrator, American University of Beirut, taken hostage, imprisoned in Lebanon
	June 9	Kidnapping. U.S. citizen Thomas Sutherland, Dean of Agriculture School, American University of Beirut, taken hostage, imprisoned in Lebanon
	June 14	Hijacking. U.S. Aircraft TWA flight en route from Rome to Athens. 8 crewmembers and 145 passengers. 32 Americans held hostage for 17 days 1 killed (U.S. Navy)**
1986	Sept 9	Kidnapping. U.S. citizen Frank Reed, Principal, Lebanon International School in Beirut taken hostage, imprisoned in Lebanon
	Sept 12	Kidnapping. U.S. citizen Joseph Cicippio, Comptroller, American University of Beirut, taken hostage, imprisoned in Lebanon

(continues)

Table 6.1 (continued)

Date		Event
	Oct 21	Kidnapping. U.S. citizen Edward Tracy, salesman and writer in Beirut, taken hostage, imprisoned in Lebanon
1987	Jan 24	Kidnapping. U.S. citizen Alann Steen, Professor of Journalism, Beirut University College, taken hostage, imprisoned in Lebanon
	Jan 24	Kidnapping. U.S. citizen Robert Polhill, Professor of Business, Beirut University College, taken hostage, imprisoned in Lebanon
	Jan 24	Kidnapping. U.S. citizen Jesse Turner, Professor of Mathematics, Beirut University College, taken hostage, imprisoned in Lebanon
	June 17	Kidnapping. U.S. citizen Charles Glass, ABC news reporter in Beirut, taken hostage, imprisoned in Lebanon
1988	Feb 17	Kidnapping. U.S. citizen Lt. Col. William Higgins (Marines), U.S. chief of the United Nations Truce Supervision Organization (UNTSO), a peacekeeping observer mission set up in 1948.
	Dec 12	Bombing. U.S. aircraft, Pan Am Flight 103 over Lockerbie, Scotland, 270 killed
1989	Mar 10	Bombing of USS *Vincennes* captain's wife's car in San Diego. She escaped. (The captain had ordered Iran aircraft shot down in July 1988; 290 killed.)
1991	Nov 7	Bombing at American University of Beirut College Hall and Clock Tower, the main administration building, symbol of the institution. Completely demolished. 0 killed, 4 wounded.

*U.S. Ambassador to Lebanon, Francis Meloy and Embassy Economic Counselor, Robert Waring were kidnapped by a Palestinian faction (PFLP) on June 16, 1976 and killed on their way to meet President-elect Elias Sarkis. The assassinations, though connected with the Lebanese civil war, are not linked to Hezbollah or Iran.

**Passengers with Jewish names were taken to secret sites in the Shia part of Lebanon and ultimately rescued by a U.S. delta force unit (Faure, 2003: 478).

Sources: Mark, 1992, pp. 13-30; Jacobsen, 1993, pp. 23, 96; Sutherland, 1996, pp. 356, 424; PBS Frontline, 2001. Buhite, 1995, pp. 223-229; Jewish Virtual Library (www.us-israel.org/jsource/Terrorism/usvictims.html).

advocates of the motivations of the terrorists." Hezbollah captors tried to manipulate victims' families, offering hope by occasionally releasing photos or letters. In a highly charged, emotional, and sympathetic environment, the families put pressure on President Reagan to take more concerted action. Peggy Saye, the sister of Terry Anderson, the last hostage to be released in December 1991, was a leader in the public campaign effort. Was it by design that his captors held him longest due to his publicity value? The issue of "publicity value" was of concern for two reasons. For the United States, greater media exposure increased the market worth of the hostages in the minds of the terrorists; simultaneously it applied pressure on the government to make deals for their release. The result may have prolonged the hostages' suffering, led to unwise trading for their freedom, and encouraged more hostage abductions.

Proposals for Agreement

Anti-American terrorism in Lebanon was largely resolved through two separate sets of reciprocal exchange terms in negotiated agreements. In the early phase of settlement attempt, the United States supplied armament materiel to Iran to secure hostage releases—an arms for hostage exchange; in the second phase, hostages were freed when the United States sent money to reconcile claims due Iran—financial payment for hostage exchange.

Arms for Hostage Exchange

American power and stature in the Middle East was falling, in part due to the Marine suicide bombing attack in 1983 and continued hostage-taking terrorist incidents that occurred immediately afterward.[2] In the mind of American leaders were questions of how to regain U.S. foreign policy prestige in the Middle East. This meant freeing Beirut hostages, a problem that had to be considered in a broader light linked to U.S.-Iran relations. Iran, engaged in a tough struggling war with neighboring Iraq, badly wanted additional military weapons in order to continue fighting. The price of reestablishing cooperation would be tied to joint needs between the parties. Signal and back channel communications led them to begin arranging an exchange: U.S. citizens held in Beirut would be released, said Iran, if America could arrange the sale of armaments—currently prohibited by U.S. Law—to Iran. The barter plan was neither unique nor unusual; it was one of the topics (if not the price designation) brought into play with Iran under terms to release the larger group of hostages held in Teheran. The origins of the entire scheme for releasing the Beirut hostages trace back to late 1984 (*Tower Commission Report* 1987, 23–25). A sign that the deal would be consummated is illustrated by the "escape" of hostage Jeremy Levine in February 1985, who discovered one day that his chains were unshackled, realizing it was a deliberate act by his captors to encourage his leave-taking. This was intended to provide evidence that Iran had presented their "bona fides" and wanted a serious deal.

On August 6, 1985, at one of the first meetings of U.S. officials to discuss the plan to sell arms to Iran in exchange for American hostages, an explicit proposal, one supported by President Reagan—the release of five Hezbollah-held hostages in return for the sale of four thousand TOWS (portable antitank missiles) to Iran by Israel—was accepted as a straightforward swap by Vice President George H. W. Bush, CIA Director William Casey, and Attorney General Edwin Meese, but opposed by Secretary of State George Shultz and Secretary of Defense Casper Weinberger (Mughal, 2005, 8–9). There were six transaction arms sales from the United States to Iran that in total cost around $30 million. Some of these trades were managed through a third party, Israel, that help camouflage the international transport of money and goods. The United States delivered the first set of one hundred TOW missiles in August. A second transaction, 408 TOW missiles, was delivered under the same routing on September 14. A Beirut hostage, Benjamin Weir, was released September 15, 1985. The third transaction, eighteen HAWK missiles (ground-launched, antiaircraft missiles) were delivered November 25, but due to their obsolescence, Iran cancelled the deal and refused to pay for them. The shipment was returned. No deal, no hostage exchanges. In the fourth sale, one thousand TOW missiles arrived in Iran on February 17 and 27, 1986. Although a hostage release had been agreed upon, the plan fell through. No hostage was freed (*Tower Commission Report* 1987, 41). Instead, the Iranians indicated they wanted a high-level dialogue covering issues other than hostages. The U.S. position was to meet provided the hostages were released during or before the talks (42). Transaction five resulted in the replenishment of 508 TOW missiles delivered to Israel on May 16 and 19. Again, no hostage release followed. A small American delegation led by former U.S. National Security Special Assistant Robert McFarlane secretly traveled to Tehran on May 25 (accompanied by Oliver North, they brought an autographed Bible, and a cake in the shape of a Bible as peace offerings), carrying a planeload of HAWK missile spare parts. McFarland demanded the release of all hostages, and when no releases occurred, he and his party departed (but not before the pallet of HAWK spares had been removed from their aircraft by the Iranians). The United States, in turn, ordered the plane carrying the remaining HAWK shipment to turn back in midflight when hostages were not released. On June 20, the president decided no further meetings with the Iranians should occur until the hostages were released. A U.S. representative met his Iranian contact in London on July 21, 1986, to discuss the promised release of hostages in exchange for the HAWK spares that remained undelivered from the May mission to Tehran. July 26, less than a week later, another hostage, Father Lawrence Martin Jenco, was freed. The additional HAWK parts were subsequently delivered to Iran on August 3.

Overall, the disappointing results of the trade from the U.S. perspective—only a few hostages had been freed—pushed the Americans to open a second contact channel with Iran. In autumn 1986 meetings, the United States laid out a proposal for the provision of weapons in exchange for all remaining U.S. hostages. The Iranians presented a six-point counterproposal that promised the release of one hostage following receipt of additional HAWK parts, making clear they could not secure the release of all the hostages. Iran proposed exchanging five hundred TOWs for the release of two hostages. The U.S. side agreed. Subsequently, the president authorized the shipment of five hundred TOWs on October 29, which arrived in Iran on October 30 and 31. David Jacobsen was the last Beirut hostage to be freed under this trade; the concluding bargaining chip in the entire arms-for-hostages episode was released November 2.

The next day, on November 3, 1986, *Al Shiraa* (The Sail), a pro-Syrian and Beirut-based magazine, disclosed that America had sold arms to Iran in secret and that a U.S. group of negotiators had visited Teheran earlier in the year to meet Iranian officials. Iranian premier, Hashemi Rafsanjani went public, confirming the visit. After a period of initial denials by U.S. decision makers, questions of policy and also violations of law came to the surface, particularly when it was discovered profits of the armament sales were diverted to aid the Contra forces in Nicaragua, a move explicitly prohibited by recent acts of Congress. Attorney General Edwin Meese ordered an investigation. Why was the program leaked to the public? At least three stories emerged: one blames the Iranians in a dispute over ideological differences and internal corruption payments; one blames the Israelis for a similar internal corruption scam; the third argument blames the Syrians who were pressured by the Soviet Union to make it public. The Tower Commission (1987, 51) and Cave (1994) report the arms-for-hostage deal was leaked by dissident Islamic Iranian sources to embarrass Rafsanjani for the skimpy payoff they received in the final transaction, the one conducted through the "second channel" (it was lower: $8,000, rather than $10,000 per TOW). The Israeli source story is similar. Ben-Menashe (1992) reports the second opening of Israeli involvement in the U.S. arms exchange, following the first that began shortly after Reagan took office in January 1981, carried a different price structure and payoff margin. A third account says the KGB, aware that U.S.-Iran arms sale profits were being sent to support Nicaraguan Contras and countering USSR-backed Sandinista forces, tipped off the Syrians. Syrian agents, using terrorist coercion threats, forced the news magazine editor to print the story (Jacobsen 1993, 239–240).

The entire $30 million in sales—with profits to Iranians, Israelis, and Americans did not improve U.S.-Iran relations. Few hostages were released. Eight remained in custody for several years awaiting their freedom; they were released piecemeal fashion over a twenty-month period starting in mid-1990; the last one gaining freedom on December 4, 1991. The Iran-Contra affair chided the U.S. administration for legal violations and public scrutiny inhibited further government-based efforts to resolve the hostage crisis. The president's Special Review Board (Tower Commission 1987, 1), a three-member appointed panel with John Tower, Edmund Muskie, and Brent Scowcroft assigned to investigate the problem, concluded that, "The secret arms transfers appeared to run directly counter to declared U.S. policies. The United States had announced a policy of neutrality in the six-year Iran-Iraq War and had proclaimed an embargo on arms sales to Iran. It had worked actively to isolate Iran and other regimes known to give aid and comfort to terrorists. It had declared that it would not pay ransom to hostage-takers."

A number of U.S. officials were eventually indicted for their participation in the Iran-Contra affair, resulting from intensive investigations that started during the Reagan administration and continued when George H. W. Bush came into office. But at the end of the Bush administration, on Christmas Eve, December 24, 1992, presidential pardons were issued for all those who had been convicted, effectively bringing the investigation to a close.

The Reagan administration publicly adopted a tough line against terrorism, adamantly opposing any concessions to terrorists in exchange for the release of hostages—whether by paying ransom, releasing prisoners, or changing policies—most likely not imagining their future troubles with Iranian-based terrorism. In July 1982, in the midst of intense factional fighting in Lebanon, the United States became aware of evidence suggesting that Iran was supporting terrorist groups, including groups engaged in hostage-taking in Lebanon when David Dodge, acting president of the American University of Beirut, had been kidnapped, and through intelligence sources, discovered imprisoned in Tehran (Baer, 2002, 74; PBS Frontline, 2002). More importantly, the official report released at the end of 1983 investigating the marine barracks attack confirmed Iran's complicity in it. On January 20, 1984, U.S. Secretary of State, George Shultz, added Iran to the list of states sponsoring international terrorism. The sale of arms to countries on the list was prohibited. Growing evidence suggests the Reagan campaign, during the 1980 election period, had secret contacts with the Iranian regime where a trade plan involving arms-for-hostages had been agreed: hostages would be held until President Reagan's inauguration and arms shipped to Iran soon thereafter (Sick 1991). Waas and Unger (2002) reported that weapons and related supplies worth several billion dollars flowed to Iran each year during the early 1980s. After Iran was placed on the state-sponsored-terrorism list, an arms–hostage clandestine deal was again in the works. This time, the focus would be on hostages held in Lebanon.

Who originated the negotiated plan to exchange people for missiles? At one point, General Scowcroft, a Tower Commission panelist, asked Michael Ledeen, a National Security Council staffer, "Do you have any notion how this thing got transformed from a research project into an action program over a very short period of time and who made the transformation?" Ledeen responded: "The Iranians came forward. . . . These ideas did not come either from the Government of the United States or the Government of Israel or arms merchants" (*Tower Commission Report* 1987, 127). The U.S. Presidential covert action finding of January 17, 1986, specified that the United States would sell TOWs to Iran but would cease further arms transfers if all the hostages were not released after delivery of the first one thousand TOWs. Still, the United States continued the program in spite of the policy clause to discontinue it (41). Oliver North, a member of the National Security Council staff who emerged as one of the most important driving forces behind the arms-for-hostages initiative, prepared a number of operational plans for achieving the release of all the hostages. Each plan involved a direct link between the release of hostages and the sale of arms.

Given the manner in which the Iran initiative was conceived and conducted, there is no mystery in why it failed, only in why it continued, particularly when promise after promise was broken by the Iranian side, the U.S. Congressional Committee (1987, 277) concluded in its investigation report, adding that by the end of the initiative, the administration "had yielded to virtually every demand the Iranians ever put on the table." Wanis-St. John (2006) summarizes the perils of back channel negotiations; had his work appeared twenty-five years earlier, perhaps the following might have been avoided: (1) at least four hostages were to be released in September 1985 after 504 TOWS were shipped, but only one was; (2) all of the hostages were to be released after the HAWK missiles were sent, but none was; (3) all of the hostages were to be released when the United States completed the delivery of HAWK parts in 1986, but only one was; and (5) Iran was to release one hostage and exert efforts to release another after five hundred more TOWS were shipped in October 1986, but only one was, and Iran demanded more weapons before making efforts to release another. Interestingly, in meetings held that month, Iran made it clear they wanted the relationship with the United States to extend beyond its merchant, trading character into broader foreign policy matters. But once the arms-for-hostage trade was made public and the plan had to be abandoned, they turned to a new avenue for trading commodities, never abandoning their merchantlike approach: the hostages would only get their freedom through an exchange.

Financial Payment and Hostage Release

The negotiating terms for Iran shifted. Instead of demanding arms shipments, Iran wanted to settle outstanding financial issues with the United States, originating with America's decisions to protect itself and punish Iran, set in motion in November 1979. How much money did America owe Iran? When would payment be forthcoming? The final eight hostages were set free by a series of Iran-U.S. Claims Tribunal awards granted to Iran and coordinated with mediation efforts through the UN secretary-general's office. These awards were never considered ransom but payment due to the customer for purchases made long before the hostages were abducted. Interestingly, two hostages, in memoirs of their ordeal, suggest the U.S.-Iran conflict of the 1980s and its linkage to the Beirut hostages, could have been solved earlier if America had simply paid back Iran what it was due. Sutherland (1996, 340) described how, in 1991, the still-detained hostages viewed the situation after becoming aware of it: "Our objective conclusion was that impounding all these funds was neither legal nor fair. It had really stung the Iranians as a matter of principle. The United States was deliberately taunting the Iranians for their humiliating actions in taking embassy personnel hostage. The more we thought about all these international shenanigans, the more it resembled grade school politics." Jacobsen (1993, 291–292), another hostage, argues that the "big bucks involved and the failure after more than eleven years to reach an agreement most definitely affected the status of the hostages. . . . Restoration of what legitimately belongs to a country could hardly be classified as ransom." Even the U.S. attorney assigned to the Tribunal, Abraham Sofaer (1999, 193), has commented, "I once had the privilege of arguing before the entire tribunal a very important case involving the Iranian goods, armaments that were in the United States to which Iran had title. We refused to return those armaments, and we refused to pay for them, an extraordinary set of positions for a major nation to take. The fact is we delayed that case as we have successfully delayed every case that the Iranians have tried to push."

When George H. W. Bush came to office in January 1989, pressed into the middle of his presidential inaugural address was this statement: "There are Americans who are held against their will in foreign lands, and Americans who are unaccounted for. Assistance can be shown here, and will be long remembered. Good will begets good will. Good faith can be a spiral that endlessly moves on." It was a signal directed at Iran, indicating the United States was prepared to work to resolve the Beirut hostage issue. U.S. Tribunal representative Sofaer (1999, 196–197) says negotiating with Iran became a big issue for the administration but the appearance of trading hostages under any conditions became so sensitive he issued a memo, saying that "if we negotiate our cases and we settle them, and if they [Iran] feels good about that, and they start releasing hostages, why should we object to that? Are we suppose to say the only we will negotiate with you don't release our hostages?" But the United States had been stung: on the domestic front, the Iran-Contra investigation proved embarrassing; internationally, the United States had come up short in its negotiated bargains with Iran—while making good its promises, the Iranians had not always reciprocated, and very few hostages had been released. Negotiating with terrorists was sticky.

Through Tribunal deliberations, the United States and Iran turned to small claims settlement in November 1989. By May 1990, the United States had agreed to pay $50 million (Sofaer 1999, 197). Hostages Reed and Polhill (incidentally, both were married to Arab Muslim women) were released at the end of April 1990. The next year, at a meeting in February 1991, the United States agreed to pay Iran $278 million in compensation for seized Iranian military equipment, but the payment was delayed, it was said, by Iran's refusal in several subsequent negotiation rounds (in March, June, the end of July, and early October) to accept the United States demand that some of the money be used to replenish an Iranian account from which U.S. claims are paid. Finally, on November 29, 1991, Iran notified the United States "fairly abruptly" that it would accept the U.S position, clearing the way for the award (Oberdorfer 1992). The final six hostages, two each held by three separate groups of Hezbollah (Hoffman 1989) were freed between October and December: the Revolutionary Justice Organization released Tracy on August 12 and Ciccipo on December 2; The Islamic Holy War for the Liberation of Palestine released Turner on October 21 and Steen on December 3. The Islamic Holy War released Sutherland on November 18 and Anderson on December 4. The latter group originally held CIA chief Buckley and also Weir and Jenco (the two clergymen) and Jacobsen (a hospital administrator) released years earlier in the arms-for-hostage exchange.

With respect to UN involvement, Perez de Cuellar, the secretary-general, began in earnest in March 1991 to seek a solution to the hostage issue. Deputy Picco was responsible for the details, including secret meetings with Hezbollah terrorists. Iranians showed great interest, for the secretary-general was responsible for issuing a report on the Iran-Iraq War by December 10, indicating which party had been the aggressor. If Iraq were declared to be so, the Iranians would be due war reparations; if they themselves were guilty, they would have to pay. On December 9, after the release of the last British hostage in Beirut, the UN issued a formal finding stated that Iraq was responsible for starting the war. While the UN denied these actions were hostage-related, many U.S. officials believed otherwise. In the final composite agreement, by December 1991 all Western hostages were released, the U.S. government had returned around $300 million to Iran and provided compensation to families of victims of the Iranian Airbus shot by USS *Vincennes* in July 1988; Iran paid up to $2 million to Hezbollah of Lebanon for each of the eight hostages released (Oberdorfer 1992). Since the Tribunal started work, about four thousand cases have been resolved; the overwhelming majority in favor of U.S. claimants (Katzman, 2000, 5). A press report in 1998 (Opall) said that if the United States were found liable in claims submitted by Iran, that American might have to pay at least $10 billion.

Analysis

What were the goals of each party, the United States and Iran, that action signals and talked-out bargaining were designed to achieve? The United States, as a superpower, wanted continued presence and influence in Middle East politics. Iran, a richly endowed rising Islamic power wanted the United States to extract itself from Middle East politics and withdraw from the region. Second, Iran wanted its money owed by the United States returned; the United States, however, was determined to reduce the actual amount due and delay payment through policies and legal maneuvering, in part, as punishment for the terrorism against it. Iran-instigated hostage-taking became a leverage instrument at this level, as did U.S sanction decisions taken against Iran.

Table C.1 (displayed at the end of this chapter) shows "U.S. Punitive Acts against Iran," and data in Table 6.2 chronicles the fate of American hostages and U.S. assets returned to Iran, in a related chain of activity. Altogether, this picture shows nested sets of intense two-party bargaining in the complex conflict and allegiances involving America, Iran, Syria, Israel, and Lebanese Shia militant groups, and reveals how Iran controlled the timing and flow of negotiated deals that resolved the terrorism campaign. They set the terms.

After gaining freedom in November 1986 as barter in an arms-for-hostage exchange, David Jacobsen began in earnest to think about ways to help his fellow prisoners, offering solutions to the U.S. government. Sometime after the end of the Gulf war, in the spring of 1991, he came to believe "that the real reason for the kidnappings was still secret. Something was missing." He began to wonder if the American delay in returning the last of Iranian assets, frozen in the United States since 1979, was the missing link in the puzzle. A highly placed contact with deep Iran-Lebanese connections, confirmed his suspicions (Jacobsen 1993, 309–314). He asked the U.S. Department of State to provide a brief accounting of the billions in frozen Iranian assets and their disbursement, noticing a correlation between returned assets and hostage releases. With Iran-U.S. Claims Tribunal award data, from 1984 onward, he tracked the chronological relationship between repayment to Iran and the abduction or release of American hostages. These data, updated with corrections augmented by additional pieces of relevant information account for the fate of most of the eighteen hostages. Jacobsen's (1993, 315–316) argument about hostage exchange suggests the United States government, angry over the Marine Barrack attack and U.S. Embassy bombings in Beirut in 1983, was not in any hurry to return the Iranian asserts called for in the Algiers Accord signed in January 1981. He is

Table 6.2 Chronology of the Fate of American Hostages in Lebanon and Delivery of U.S. Payments Owed to Iran

Date	Action	Date	Action
1984		Dec 23	Iran pays $10,000,000 for Pan Am bombing (PFLP carried out the job)
Jan 18	Malcolm Kerr assassinated		
Jan 25	$218,666.31 + interest returned		
Feb 10	Frank Regier kidnapped		
Mar 7	Jeremy Levin kidnapped	**1989**	
Mar 16	William Buckley kidnapped	May 25	$28,500 returned
Apr 15	Frank Regier freed	Nov 7	$567,000,000 returned
May 8	Benjamin Weir kidnapped	Nov 22	$55,999 returned
June 8	$7,933,951.31 returned	Dec 6	$7,800,000 returned
Dec 3	Peter Kilburn kidnapped*	Dec 8	$400,000 returned
		Dec 19	4,368,750 Rials returned
1985		Dec 26	$3,000,000 returned
Jan 8	Martin Jenco kidnapped		
Feb 14	Jeremy Levin freed	**1990**	
Mar 16	Terry Anderson kidnapped	Jan 24	$125,000 returned
May 28	David Jacobsen kidnapped	Jan 29	$700,000 returned
June 9	Thomas Sutherland kidnapped	Feb 21	$96,000 returned
Aug 30	100 TOW missile shipment	Apr 22	Robert Polhill freed
Sept 14	408 TOW missile shipment	Apr 30	Frank Reed freed
Sept 15	Benjamin Weir freed		
		1991	
1986		Feb 14	$278,000,000 returned; Iran refuses to accept it
Feb 17	1,000 TOW missile shipment		
May 25	508 TOW+HAWK parts shipment	Mar 28	$278,000,000 returned; Iran refuses to accept it (2nd attempt)
July 26	Martin Jenco freed		
Sept 9	Frank Reed kidnapped	June 5	$278,000,000 returned; Iran refuses to accept it (3rd attempt)
Sept 12	Joe Cicippio kidnapped		
Oct 21	Edward Tracy kidnapped	July 29	$278,000,000 returned; Iran refuses to accept it (4th attempt)
Oct 30	500 TOW missile shipment		
Nov 2	David Jacobsen freed	Aug 12	Edward Tracy freed
		Oct 7	$278,000,000 returned; Iran refuses to accept it (5th attempt)
1987			
Jan 24	Robert Polhill kidnapped	Oct 21	Jesse Turner freed
Jan 24	Alann Steen kidnapped	Nov 14	Iran declared innocent in Pan Am bombing***
Jan 24	Jesse Turner kidnapped		
May 4	$63,000,000 returned	Nov 18	Tom Sutherland freed
May n.d.	$454,000,000 returned	Nov 29	$278,000,000 returned: Iran accepts terms****
Nov 30	$140,060.17 returned		
		Dec 2	Joe Cicippio freed
1988		Dec 3	Alann Steen freed
Feb 17	William Higgins kidnapped	Dec 4	Terry Anderson freed
Apr n.d.	$37,900,000 returned		
May 18	$325,000 returned	**1992**	
Jul 3	U.S. shoots Iran Air flight 655; 290 dead**	Feb 19	$134,128.65 returned
Dec 21	Pan Am Air Flight 103 bombing; 270 dead		

*Hostage Kilburn was purchased for execution by Libya three days after the April 14 U.S. air strike against Libya that killed Kaddafi's daughter. Reportedly, Kaddafi approached Hezbollah, purchased 3 hostages (including two British citizens) for a total of $3 million. All three were shot in the back of the head.

**Reported in Developments Concerning the National Emergency with Respect to Iran, May 16, 1996, the survivors of each victim of the Iran Air shoot down will be paid $300,000 (for wage-earning victims) or $150,000 (for non-wage-earning victims), under terms decided during the Clinton Administration.

***Until mid-1990, the U.S. implicated Iran in the 1988 Lockerbie aircraft bombing, with evidence to back their assertion. (A March 1991 U.S. Air Force Report also accused Iran of the attack.) The U.S. decided to shift its position, accusing Libya of the disaster. Libya did not release the two suspects until 1999. A trial was held in 2000, one of them was declared guilty. By August, 2003 a deal had been struck for awards: a $4 million payment to each victim's family once UN sanctions were formally lifted (additional award if U.S. lifted sanctions and removed Libya from the state-sponsored terrorism list) Libya was taken off the U.S. state-sponsored terrorism list in May, 2006.

****The payment was delayed after the U.S. had agreed in February by Iran's refusal in four more rounds of negotiations to accept the U.S. demand that some of the money be used to replenish an Iranian account from which U.S. claims are made. Iran notified the U.S. "fairly abruptly" that it would accept the U.S. position, according to Edwin Williamson, Department of State legal advisor. The money returned was in payment for military equipment Iran had purchased while under the Shah. It is listed in Table C.1 under December 1979 U.S. actions.

Sources: Antokol and Nudell, 1990, 102; Jacobsen, 1993; Oberdorfer, 1992; Rainwater, 1997; Goodenough, 1999; Scharf, 2001; Gerson and Adler, 2001; *New York Times,* passim.; *Washington Post,* November 7, 1989.

curious why no media investigation, in its full analysis of the Iran–Contra affair, had missed this probable cause behind the kidnappings. In August 1992, he says, the Department of State claimed that all of the accounts with Iran had been closed and money dispersed, yet the dispute continued, since Iran was claiming entitlement to interest on the billions of dollars that had been frozen—a position the United States opposed. Jacobsen concludes that the "interest dispute" could be motivation for more anti-American terrorism. From Table 6.2, it appears that Jacobsen is partially correct in the hostage-asset exchanges, but other exchanges were occurring, too. Picco (2005) presents an alternative argument, suggesting the initial purpose behind the Beirut kidnappings was directly connected with the imprisonment of seventeen Lebanese in Kuwait in 1983; the kidnappers sought a swap. When releasing the Lebanese became unfeasible, other *quid pro quo* plans were created, including the arms-for-hostage agreement. When that fell apart, the release of the American hostages shifted to a new plan, namely hostage freedom in exchange for financial claims due Iran.

The types of terrorist messages and negotiated bargains in the U.S.-Iranian conflict, one largely played in the Lebanon theatre, can be identified. Iran followed two strategies. First, there were fatality-driven, non–bargain-chip terrorist acts: several dramatic acts of terrorist violence were directed against symbolic targets—the U.S. Embassy bombings, the marine barrack attack, and assassination of the American University of Beirut (AUB) president committed between April 1983 and January 1984, the quid pro violent reaction to the Iran Airbus shoot down in July 1988 that killed 290 travelers, and the contract-for-hire Pan Am 103 in-flight bomb explosion six months later, in which 270 people died—events that reset the balance of power between conflict disputants to Iran's advantage. Second, non-fatality-driven, explicit bargain-chip terrorist acts: the common pattern of hostage-for-goods exchange—both military armaments (the Iran-Contra 1985–1986 deals) and owed-assets from U.S. accounts (1989–1991 paid settlements) fall into this category. Together, these activities explain the fate of thirteen of the eighteen United States kidnapped victims. Libya's $3 million purchase of an American hostage (plus two British compatriots) accounts for another case. The remainder no doubt involved a negotiated bargain, but do not show direct link to particular ending points marked here. David Dodge was freed by his Iranian captors in July 1983, one year after being abducted, once it was clear the United States was not linked to the kidnapping of four Iranian diplomats on the highway in Lebanon in 1982, and only after U.S intelligence had discovered his whereabouts in Iran and appealed to Syria to intervene to free him (Baer, 2002). Glass, kidnapped along with the son of the Lebanese defense minister, was free after two months (his Lebanese traveling partners were kept just a week), apparently again with Syrian assistance. The abduction may have been related to internal Lebanese politics, disconnected from the U.S.-Iran conflict. Two hostages, Buckley and Higgins, both high-ranking U.S. government officials, were eliminated in the exchange proceedings and lost as bargaining chips when they died. Although their captors claim they had been executed, evidence indicates that Buckley most likely died from torture injuries, while Higgins was probably inadvertently asphyxiated during car trunk transport (Jacobsen 1993, 179). Bodies of all three dead hostages were released in the final 1991 UN-brokered deal. Kilburn had been shot by a Libyan purchase-for-murder. The other two autopsied bodies show no signs of alleged execution.

Why did Iran shift tactics from bombings, including suicide bombings, to hostage-taking in its anti-American campaign? Early terrorism against U.S. targets in Lebanon applied to meet a particular objective consisted of a strategy to kill people, hence the use of explosives, including suicide bombing attacks and assassination. As Pape (2005) argues, suicide terrorist bombing campaigns against foreign occupiers are strategically geared to create massive fear and force the occupier to physically withdraw. Although his analysis is limited to suicide attacks and campaigns, the logic fits Iran's strategy. Iran wanted the Americans out of the Middle East—this was the first principle listed in the Algiers Accord—and that meant out of Lebanon, a necessary first step before it could begin to address the asset return problem with the United States. Forcing America to withdraw its military presence and scale back its diplomatic mission would help level the playing field between the two sides and put Iran on a more equal footing, making it less disadvantaged in its lower power position that in turn might produce more favorable outcomes.

Later, hostage-taking terrorism, designed not to kill victims but to enhance terrorists' bargaining power, became popular as a way to meet demands. Kidnappers usually demand ransom. The Iran regime was not seeking ransom in its pure sense, but payment on U.S. debt. In May 1984, officials at the American University of Beirut, according to Sutherland (1996, 36), an eventual hostage who had been a university administrator, learned of the hostage-taking strategy prior to its execution and reported it to faculty members in the following message:

Hezbollah will execute kidnapping operations at American University of Beirut and the U.S. Embassy. The targets will have American identities. Have prepared 100 people for the operation, from which 20 are inside the university ... Hezbollah is watching all movements and are [sic] waiting for Zero hour. The plan is prepared and its execution is soon ... First axis is from inside AUB. The second axis is from the Corniche. The third axis is from a civilian building which overlooks the new embassy. ...

The timing of the plan is important. The last marine departed Lebanon March 31, 1984. Iran was suffering: placed on the U.S. list of states sponsoring terrorism at the end of January, its trade was interrupted. A lot of its assets were still tied up in the United States; the Algiers Accord claims tribunal was handling U.S. cases first. It was in the middle of a major war with its neighbor. It was stretched financially and militarily (the country resorted to child conscription, sending thousands of young boys into battle). It was ostracized from the international community. The UN had taken nearly a week to condemn Iraqi aggression against Iran when war broke out in September 1980, yet Iraq's invasion of Kuwait brought immediate and sharp reaction from the assembly.

Evidence of a plan of hostage barter that Iran consciously followed, can be found in several important messages: the first issued in July 1988, another in October 1989, and a third in March 1990, after the end of the Gulf War (Mark 1992, 19–22; *New York Times*, November 7–8, 1989). The first two statements, both from Iranian Majlis speaker Rafsanjani, said Iran would intercede with the captors holding U.S. hostages in Lebanon if the United States would release Iranian assets frozen during the hostage crisis of 1979–1981. Shortly after the second public message, on November 6, 1989, the United States agreed to return to Iran about half a billion dollars it had held to pay claims of U.S. banks. It was a joint agreement by the U.S. and Iran within the special claims tribunal, but without independent tribunal involvement. The later statement, planted in *Al-Sharq al Awsat* the London-based Arabic language newspaper, reported that Iran's conditions for assisting in a hostage release were: (1) drop Iran from the list of terrorist countries; (2) persuade Iraq to withdraw from Iranian territory; and (3) release the frozen Iranian assets in the United States. Throughout 1989 and until the end of February 1990, the United States was returning substantial sums of money back to Iran, just prior to the March statement. In April 1990, two hostages were sent home (publicly, it was said, by "good will" implying the absence of any exchange, which was false).

In February 1991, the United States agreed to a major reimbursement award for Iran: payment for the nearly $300 million worth of military equipment bought more than twelve years earlier, which set the stage for the gradual releasing of the final six hostages. In retrospect, it appears that Iran was holding off this exchange until it was cleared of any involvement in the 1988 Pan Am 103 bombing—a plan that worked out to its liking when the United States and Britain announced on November 14, that Libya was the guilty party (though, by many accounts [Simon, 2001, 7], the evidence was slim; Iran and Syrian complicity was far more substantial, and Iran may have initiated this act as retaliation for the shooting of an Iranian civilian airliner by the USS *Vincenness* the previous July). Khadafi waited nine years to hand over the two Libyan nationals for trial, a factor that suggests behind-the-scenes bargaining that may have involved numerous parties, including the U.S. and Iran. The decision to point at Libya freed Iran from owing the United States any reparation money for its documented act of violence.

In January 1992 it was announced that Iran paid the captors of Western hostages in Lebanon between $1–2 million for each of the ten hostages (six American, three British, one Irish) released since early August 1991, a charge Iran officials deny, accusing Israel, a sore loser that did not get the return of Israeli captives or their remains, of planting the story. The payments, traced by U.S. intelligence to various bank transfers, were in addition to regular financing that Teheran had provided for years to Hezbollah. Two German hostages were not freed, pending negotiations with Germany to release two Lebanese brothers of the Hamadi family in Hezbollah, convicted and imprisoned for shooting the American military officer, Robert Stethem, during the June 1985 TWA aircraft hijacking. They subsequently gained their freedom, and the last held Hamadi prisoner was exchanged in December 2005 for a German hostage abducted in Iraq (Goodenough, 2005). As for five French hostages held in Iran, France agreed to pay $1.8 billion to Teheran in 1991; in addition, a $3 million ransom was paid for the release of its citizens, a scandal that emerged in the February 2002 elections (Karoui, 2002).

Iran, rather than the Lebanese terrorists, was in complete control of all hostage releases, a view shared by Picco, the UN mediator in the process. The entire set of strategies played by Iran seems to fit Sofaer's (1999, 194) assessment about Iranian behavior at the Claims Tribunal: they did not know how to advocate their positions well. "The Iranians feel tremendously disadvantaged in the Tribunal because they don't know how to litigate and they are not willing to pay the money to retain good lawyers to take over the task of handling their litigation." Sofaer's remarks, presented at a conference held at New York University Law School in 1996, were echoed in comments by Thomas Shack (Sofaer 1999, 209–210), stressing that Iran, unlike the United States, was not a nation of lawyers. Rather, they had few personnel trained in Western adjudication or international arbitration processes, and the revolution removed people familiar with the history of contracts and history of negotiations between the two contending sides. Perhaps that explains, to some extent, why they chose an alternative negotiation strategy where they might be strong enough to influence outcomes in their favor: a sparring based on terrorism might weaken the other side; fighting based on verbal barbs, would intimidate them. It seemed to work.

As for the U.S. strategy, it also worked. Most of the hostages were freed. Lucrative weapons sales lined the pockets of arms merchants. Financial repayment to Iran had been delayed, benefiting American banks and business. Tribunal processes brought settlement relief in many cases. UN mediation intercession meant the United States never had to confront Iran directly or to admit America negotiated with terrorists, after the Iran-Contra scandal. The American government was not forced to deal with terrorist thugs—actual kidnappers and hostage holders—or with the terrorist mastermind leadership of the new Islamic Republic of Iran. The U.S. Congress, reflecting on this episode, passed a law in 1996 that permitted for the first time, lawsuits against foreign countries specifically designated as "state sponsors of terrorism." In the fall of 2000, this body passed legislation to enable certain U.S. citizen victims of terrorism to collect on judgments they had obtained in civil lawsuits. It meant that terrorist acts sponsored by the Islamic Republic of Iran could carry substantial restitution payment to Beirut hostages and members of their immediate families.[3]

The techniques of terrorism witnessed in Lebanon in the 1980s—large-scale suicide bombings against military troops, major attacks on Western embassies, kidnapping—spread to other places in the 1990s and beyond. The diffusion of terrorism originating from Lebanese borders showed its mark in suicide bombings in Saudi Arabia and Egypt, Spain and Indonesia; Somalia, Rwanda, and Bosnia experienced attacks on foreign peacekeeping forces; and in 1998, the American embassy explosions in Kenya and Tanzania launched the serious mission of al Qaeda, the singular most feared terrorist organization of the early twenty-first century. Suicide bombing, a continuing problem for Israel, was introduced into the Palestinian conflict in the 1990s; and with the war in Iraq came a nest of kidnappers, preying on security gaps and hoping to extract financial gain and, often, to influence the political process. Beyond death and destruction the particular tool of attack tells us the terrorists' goals: bombings and assassinations, part of a fatality-driven non-bargain-chip repertoire, with one intended end—getting the intruder to leave—do not leave room for negotiating; hostage-taking, hijacking, and kidnapping constitute a non-fatality-driven, bargain-chip strategy that points to an interest in bargaining. In a terrorism campaign, the violence technique matters, giving an indication of negotiation prospects.

Negotiation Preconditions

The American tale of negotiating Beirut hostages' liberation perfectly illustrates how incentives can be structured for each side, what reciprocity means, and also the impact of the entire negotiation episode in both prolonging and ending a terrorist campaign. Among the lessons taken from this experience, a few points stand out with respect to negotiating with terrorists. First, terrorists think strategically. Acts of violence and moves in negotiation processes are goal directed, focused on concrete issues, not abstractions or vague desires. Terrorists set the terms and the pace of negotiations. Second, terrorists select alternative techniques of violence for different purposes. Fatality-driven events (bombing and assassination) mean no negotiations, and non-fatality-driven events (skyjacking, hostage barricade, kidnaps) signal negotiation willingness or eagerness. And third, terrorists follow reciprocity in negotiations. Attack begets attack, good will begets good will, illustrated with the quid pro quo exchange of airliner blowups, Libya's hostage purchase, and armaments and debt repayment exchanged for hostage releases.

Where is the other side's advantage? It lies in reciprocity moves, recognition of nonnegotiable conditions, and conflict prevention measures. The latter is most important, although few methods, according to Lum, Kennedy, and Sherley (2006) have been systematically evaluated for their effectiveness. Negotiation requires problem-solving skills, strategic analysis, imagination, and intuition. Analyzing the Vietnam War, Walker (2004) found the American use of Rapoport's (1960) "fight" model—exchange of deeds to bring harm to one another—and its reciprocity approach was effective in resolving conflicts with a bully player who employed exploitation and bluff strategies. The episodes of U.S.-Iran negotiations conform primarily to the "fight" model with occasional movement into a "game" perspective—strategic interaction–based moves. Throughout this period, conflict resolution goals by each side seem to have been quite consistent: to bring harm to the other side. In this sense, negotiating with terrorists is neither the means for communicating broad overtures of peace or for achieving understanding between parties; rather, for both sides, it will remain power-based bargaining carried out through interest-based intention. Table 6.3 lists factors in terminating the terrorist campaigns with specific application to the Beirut kidnapping problem.

Table 6.3 Terminating Terrorism: Factors in the U.S.-Beirut Kidnapping Case

Mutual Hurting Stalemate—Conflict Ripeness
There seemed to be no progress in securing hostages' release. Neither party could find acceptable plans. Things were stuck. There was one major deadline operating that pushed negotiation forward: the end of the UN Secretary-General's term of office in December, 1991. He had promised to deal fairly with Iran, in the final report on the Iraq-Iran conflict that began in September, 1980 and ended in May, 1988, that he would issue prior to leaving his post. It was important that Iran not be labeled the conflict aggressor—which was a possibility given its reputation within the international community—to leave the way open for war reparations. Because the UN Secretary-General's office was mediating resolution of the dispute, Iran was eager to cooperate.

Turning Points
Turning point events in this conflict are one-sided: all of them affected Iran. The U.S. had no parallel moments. A seismic shift in the international system seemed to have an impact on the conflict. When the Cold War ended in 1989 and the Gulf War against Saddam Hussein and Iraq started January, 1991, Hezbollah prisoners held in Kuwait jails escaped to freedom, and the value of holding the hostages also changed as the Middle East political terrain shifted. The announcement that the UN Secretary General would prepare the final report on the Iran-Iraq war before leaving office also constituted a turning point.

Negotiation Readiness
By early 1991, Iran was still owed nearly $300 million in financial claims from the United States, but had refused an award of $278 million offered to them in mid-February. They refused the award again in March, May, June, July, and October. The reason? Iran had been assumed to be the party responsible for the bombing of the Pan Am flight over Lockerbie in December, 1988 that killed 270 people. On November 14, Iran was declared innocent of the bombing and Libya was implicated as responsible for the tragedy. Four days later, one of the remaining hostages was released and a week later Iran accepted the terms of the $278 million.

Interest-Based Bargaining
The barter system was based on two separate plans, both created by Iran: an arms-for hostage exchange, a system that operated in the mid-1980s, and a financial repayment-for-hostage exchange, a plan inaugurated in 1987 that continued until the last hostage got his freedom on December 4, 1991.

Appendix

Table C.1 U.S. Punitive Acts against Iran: October 1977–July 1988

1977 October 28

• Creation of the International Emergency Economics Power Act (IEEPA)

The rapid rise in the price of oil in the 1970s and the extensive deposits of petrodollars by the wealthy nations of OPEC in U.S. banks created concern in the banking community about potential effects of a sudden withdrawal of these funds. This issue had surfaced when lawyers from Iran met with US bank officials to argue that four major loans to Iran in 1977–78 by Chase Manhattan syndicate banks had been questionably obtained. The Iranian constitution stated "no state loans at home or abroad may be raised without the knowledge and approval of the National Consultative Assembly." This was violated in the Shah-Chase Manhattan dealings. Still, the banks went through with the loans. (Bill 1988: 346-348). The IEEPA act gave the U.S. President the right to declare national emergency in the case of an unusual and extraordinary threat coming from outside the United States that affected the security of the U.S., and power to stop any withdrawal of foreign assets from the U.S.

1979 February

• Department of the Treasure considers freezing Iranian assets held under U.S. control

The alternative came under consideration several weeks after the Shah and his family left Iran in mid-January. The strategy, widely known, had its origins in the 1977 Iran-U.S. bank loan decisions. With the new government in Tehran, it was possible that loans to the Shah could be declared illegal; the government could repudiate them, which would expose Chase Manhattan bank to legal suits for fiduciary responsibility failure. Freezing Iran's U.S.-held assets would get around this problem.

1979 May 2

Foreign Minister Ibrahim Yazdi announces that Iran had requested the U.S. freeze the assets of the Pahlavi Foundation and agree not to allow the Shah, who had taken large amounts of personal wealth out of the country, to enter the United States.

1979 October 22

The Shah enters the United States. The Department of State announces the decision had been made on humanitarian grounds. The Iranian government officially protested this decision on October 26, 30, 31 and November 1, and raised it directly with National Security Assistant, Zbigniew Brzezinski at a meeting in Algiers on November 1.

1979 November 13

• Ban on importing oil from Iran

In response to the hostage crisis of November 4 with the seizure of the U.S. Embassy in Tehran along with 66 (later reduced to 52) diplomatic personal who were held hostage.

1979 November 14

• Freeze of Iranian governmental assets in American banks and their branches abroad, estimated between $8–12 billion (forcing Iran to default on its loan interest payments due Nov. 15)
• Executive Order 12170, by President Carter invoked IEEPA for the first time (applied quickly after learning Iran intended to remove all of its deposits from U.S. banks)

Table C.1 (continued)

1979 December

- Ban on exports to Iran, except food, medicine, and medical supplies
- Ban on new extension of credit to Iran
- Ban on new service contracts for Iran
- Ban on sending military equipment to Iran

Iran has paid $300 million for military supplies currently being held in the U.S. About $50 million non-lethal, no sensitive items—tires, trucks, routine spares; $100 million of "Gray area" equipment; about $150 million or bombs, missiles, sensitive technology, and software (Sick, 1991: 98-99).

1980 April 7

- Breaking diplomatic relations with Iran
- Expulsion of Iranian diplomats
- Restrictions for Iranians seeking U.S. visas
- Announcement of a census of all Iranian assets and claims against Iran under U.S. control. (A signal that these assets could satisfy U.S. claims if future events made it necessary

1980 April 17

- Ban on imports from Iran
- Discontinuation of remittances to people living in Iran, except for family members
- Revocation of operating licenses for all nonblank Iranian entities in the U.S.
- Ban on travel to Iran

1980 April 24

- U.S. aircraft and helicopters land in Iranian desert in the south to rescue the American hostages (mission failed; two aircraft collide, 8 soldiers are killed.)

1981 January 19

- The Algiers Accord signed.

The negotiated outcome of the U.S. Iran Hostages crisis, returned 52 U.S. hostages held in Tehran in exchange for unfrozen Iranian government assets of $7.955 billion held under U.S. control. Iran must pay $3.67 billion for principle and interest due U.S. bank loans and keep $1.42 billion in escrow as security against payment on disputed claims, with $500 million maintained in the account. The remainder, $2.88 billion would be paid directly to Iran.

An International Arbitral Tribunal, the Iran-United States Claims Tribunal, was established to decide claims of nationals of the either country and counter claims including property rights, expropriations. It will consist of nine members, consisting of 1/3 appointed from each government, and the group of six shall appoint the remaining third. The tribunal will conduct its business using the arbitration rules of the United Nations Commission on International Trade Law. All decisions and awards of the Tribunal are to be final and binding.

The U.S. agreed to revokes trade sanctions directed against Iran since November 14, 1979. The issue of returning the arms supplies Iran had paid $300 million for was not part of the agreement. (Ten years later, in 1991, the material was still in storage in the U.S. Iran had not received the goods nor compensation for the $300 million it had spent [Sick, 1991: 190, 265]. In February 1991, the U.S. agreed to pay Iran $278 million. Iran delays acceptance of the terms until November 14.)

Table C.1 (continued)

1983 December 27

- U.S. Report on Beirut Marine Bombing Investigation strongly hints Iran issues complicity

President Reagan in a press conference said "…this terrorism isn't just some fanatical individual who gets an idea and goes out on his own. there is evidence enough—even if you couldn't go into court with it—that it has at least a kind of tacit encouragement from various political groups and even from some states." The Department of Defense Commission report suggested Iranian connections to the bombing: "Iran operatives in Lebanon are in the business of killing Americans," but did not directly accuse Iran of sponsoring the attack. The report noted the official Defense Department definition of terrorism, which was limited to "revolutionary organizations" and excluded government sponsorship. The Commission concluded that the Defense Department now "needs to recognize the importance of state-sponsored terrorism and must take appropriate measures to deal with it."

1984 January 19

- U.S. Declares Iran a state sponsor of terrorism

Based on evidence of Iran's involvement in the bombing of U.S. Marine barracks in Lebanon, Secretary of State George Schulz designates Iran a state sponsor of terrorism. Any country on the list is prohibited from receiving U.S. foreign assistance and credits, including programs of the Export-Import Bank, the Peace Corps, or assistance authorized by the Agricultural Trade and Development Act.

1984 September 28

- U.S. denies license applications of exports to Iran, including aircraft, helicopters, and related items on national security export control list

1986 August 27

- U.S. Arms Export Control Act prohibits sending military arms to countries on the state-sponsored terrorism list

Department of Defense also ordered to deny contracts of $100,000 or more to firms that were owned or controlled by Iran, and tax credits were denied to U.S. businesses paying taxes to Terrorism List countries.

1987 October 29

- Ban on imported Iranian goods and services

In retaliation for Iranian attacks—mining, small boat assaults—on U.S.-flagged tankers in the Persian Gulf, the Iranian exports to the U.S. drop to zero from $1.6 billion in 1987

1988 July 3

- Shoot down of Iran Air (Airbus) Flight 655 by USS *Vincennes*, an American Naval Cruiser stationed in the Persian Gulf. 290 killed. United States officially declared it an accident.

Sources: "U.S. Iran Relations," passim; Bill, 1988, 343-348; Carswell and Davis, 1985, 175–234; Sick, 1991, 98–99, 190, 265; Department of State www.state/gov/s/ct/14151, Katzman, 2000, 6–8; Institute of International Economics (www.iie.com/research/topics/sanctions/iran); Simon, 2001, 7; Fayazmanesh, 2003, 222; *New York Times*, passim.

CHAPTER SEVEN

The U.S.–al Qaeda Suicide Bombing Crisis, 1998–Present

Global terrorism catapulted onto the world stage in September 2001 with dramatic attacks in the United States. Al Qaeda forces, in a carefully synchronized plan, skyjacked four passenger-loaded, domestic-based commercial jets, transformed the aircraft into guided missiles, and crashing into targets of American power—the World Trade Center in New York City and the Pentagon in Washington, DC—killed nearly three thousand people. A defining event of the twenty-first century, it altered fundamental features of political dynamics in the world. In the new environment, a major security threat to the United States comes not from a sovereign nation but a nonstate entity—al Qaeda—a nimble, shadowy organization: a group with interests beyond nation–state boundaries; a group espousing a particular ideology of Islamic holy war—jihad; a small minority of several thousand members, identified mainly, if not exclusively, by disruptive, debilitating mass violence directed against noncombatants. These jihadists seek to overthrow existing governments in Muslim states and replace them with nondemocratic theocracies. They strike at America, the so-called far enemy, benefactor to what they regard as ill-conceived, corrupt regimes, to pressure the "near enemy," their immediate target. Former U.S. Secretary of Defense Donald Rumsfeld, in testimony to the 9/11 Commission (2004, 126) called terrorism "the great equalizer," operating as a "force multiplier;" a single attack can alter behavior of great nations.

Although al Qaeda had been engaged in terrorist attacks since the early 1990s, the organization achieved international notoriety with its simultaneous suicide bombings of the U.S. embassies in Kenya and Tanzania, in August 1998. The attacks killed more than two hundred individuals, injuring around five thousand, most of them local residents. Twelve Americans died. In her remarks at the August 7, 2008, anniversary commemoration, then U.S. Secretary of State Condoleezza Rice said,

> On that dark day ten years ago, the bombings of our embassies seemed merely to be the senseless violence of evil men, an organization called al-Qaida [sic]. When seen from today, however, ten years later—after the bombing of the World Trade Center in 1993, the attack on Khobar towers in 1996, the attack on the USS Cole in 2000, and of

course, the terror of September 11th—we now see those bombings of our embassies in Nairobi and Dar es Salaam in a new light. We see them as they were—as the opening of a new "twilight struggle" between hope and fear, peace and hatred, freedom and tyranny.... [W]e remain confident, committed and unwavering, and ... will not cower to those who seek to do harm to our people and attack our ideals. (www.state.gov/secretary/rm/2008/08/107997.htm)

In the decade following the embassy bombings, more than eighteen thousand U.S. and local staff members overseas were moved to safer diplomatic quarters. Sixty capital construction projects (new embassies, consulates, and office annexes) costing more than $4 billion have been completed, and more than $1 billion was spent on security upgrades—walls, gates, access controls (www.state/go/r/pa/prs/ps/2008/aug/107989.htm).

In terms of terrorist tactics, suicide bombings represent a form of greater lethality and, hence, a greater threat than previous anti-American terrorism episodes. Techniques used in those events—aircraft hijacks, hostage-taking, and kidnapping— seemed to support the operating cliché that perpetrators wanted a lot of people watching, not a lot of people dead. This is no longer true. Instead, mass casualty goals are incorporated into these modern missions. Attention grabbing remains important because terrorists seek to promote a cause. In today's world, escalated, dramatic demonstrations of violence may be needed to reach the headlines. It is often claimed that techniques adopted by terrorists are regularly copied between groups; the assertion that skyjacking is a contagious phenomena has long been accepted (Holden 2003, 1). Suicide attack plans are also mimicked; they have become more frequent, more acceptable, and indeed, in some circles, honorable.[1] How might this manifestation of anti-American terrorism terminate?

The first U.S. strategy—fight to win—was adopted in the wake of 9/11 in the War on Terrorism, a plan lending strong support for military intervention to resolve the conflict in America's favor through its aggressive "4-D" points—defeat terrorists and their organizations; deny sponsorship, support, and sanctuary to terrorists; diminish the underlying conditions terrorists seek to exploit; and defend U.S. citizens and interests at home and abroad. The war in Afghanistan and the war in Iraq exemplify this overall strategy. Al Qaeda, too, has followed a contending, strategic course as evidenced by a series of uncovered, complicated plots to attack various Western targets, direct hits in some cases, and growing involvement in battles in Iraq.

A taskforce assembled to defeat the jihadists, chaired by Richard Clarke, U.S. national coordinator for security and counterterrorism at the time of the 2001 attacks, identified four important components to ensure defeating al Qaeda: capturing or killing hard-core terrorists who are intent on murder and martyrdom; reducing America's vulnerability to terrorist attack at home and abroad; improving relations with specific nations in the Islamic world to reduce support for the jihadists; and developing government services and capabilities to bring about these objectives (Clarke et al. 2004, 3). Key recommendations in the study include engaging the battle of ideas, providing assistance to Islamic states for development, diffusing sources of Muslim anti-American hatred, improving intelligence and law enforcement, eliminating terror financing, augmenting homeland security, appropriating funds to diversify energy resources away from oil dependence, and implementing tailored strategies for key countries. The threat is not terrorism as such, but jihadi terrorists, specifically al Qaeda (5–7, 18), and several countries are particularly susceptible to the al Qaeda threat: Saudi Arabia, with the largest oil reserve; Egypt, with the largest Arab population; and Pakistan, an Islamic state with nuclear weapons. In all three, state-sanctioned anti-Americanism thrives; pro-jihadi sentiment is widespread, and a popular, democratic vote could possibly lead to an al-Qaeda-sympathetic government. In these societies, the complex issue that confronts the United States is how to bring about a balance of increased participation, political openness, and expansion of civil society to enhance regime stability.

To confront global jihad, Byman (2007) echoes these points in recommending a five-pronged U.S. strategy that includes a strong homeland defense, good intelligence, ideological warfare, police and military control, and democratic reforms in Islamic states, urging a selective, focused approach to push counterinsurgency operations and enhancement of target state capabilities. Gunaratna (2007) highlights the ideological factor, insisting that al Qaeda's worldview poses a significant, strategic threat. The group detests America's presence in the Middle East, condemns U.S. support for Israel and neglect of Palestinians' plight, condemns U.S. aid to pro-Western governments in Muslim nations, and blames the United States for all ills. Its goal is to establish Islamic rule and law, carrying out armed struggle to achieve these ends. Because al Qaeda couches its ideology in religious terms, it is not easily moved by promises of material gain; what motivates its followers is belief in the struggle, not power, wealth, or fame, states Gunaratna (2007, 7). Hence, an effective counterideology built around political will to address grievances and aspirations is needed. Has U.S. counterterrorism policy worked?

The Call to Global Islamic Resistance, a sixteen-hundred-page manifesto prepared by an al Qaeda leading theorist, Abu Musab al-Suri (Mustafa Setmariam Nasar), published in 2005 and available on many jihadist Web sites (Lacey, 2008), identifies the war on terrorism as the key reason for the movement's disarray after 9/11. Analyzing the consequences of the 2001 attacks, al Suri states that jihadism sustained the heaviest blow and that every Muslim in every part of the world was affected negatively as a result of this war on terrorism. Referring to a statement by Defense Secretary Rumsfeld, that American military had killed or captured more than three thousand terrorists, al Suri declares this figure accurate, but perhaps too low, concluding that the jihadist movement was utterly destroyed due to the U.S.-led War on Terrorism. He compels supporters to participate in a regenerated effort, and by later U.S. State Department accounts, al Qaeda has breathed new life and once more become a formidable force. Nonetheless, this analysis gives a solid indication of the positive effects of the U.S. strategy in the Global War on Terrorism—at least over the short term.

The second strategy—withdraw from the conflict arena—advocated by general critics of the Global War on Terrorism and committed isolationists, is a sharp contrast with the first; by implication some believe it means yielding to terrorists' demands. It gained attention as a widely circulated argument, emphasizing negative consequences that follow from activist, U.S. interventionary pursuits. American foreign policy, though intended to protect national interests, may actually weaken rather than strengthen security by producing blowback—unintended hostile reactions, according to Johnson (2000, 2004). In a twist of testing the second approach, a major study by Pape (2003, 2005) indicates positive results accrue from using terrorist violence: an assessment of suicide terrorism damages in extended campaigns worldwide provides some evidence, not overwhelming but important enough to take notice, that shows intervening powers, rather than achieving their goals, have been forced to concede to terrorists' demands to withdraw from occupied territory. Sustained intervention in the end becomes a recipe for failure. Sustained terrorism may be a strategy of success: it works, at least occasionally. While contributing to the policy debate, these findings are not received as conclusive evidence of the need for fundamental overhaul or redirection in U.S. global posture.

The third alternative—mutual problem-solving—is barely discussed in serious terms; it is not high priority. Indeed, negotiating with the enemy is distantly peripheral in the current global war on terrorism, although the issue has brought some debate. Rubin and Gerschowitz (2006, 1) argue that combating terrorism effectively means looking at al Qaeda's success, rather than its goals, stating that defeat will not come about through diplomacy, but through strategies "more forceful and less compromising," which will make terrorist acts too costly to implement. Terrorists cannot be treated as negotiating partners, for such an approach will not curb violence, they assert, citing the Taliban that "embraced engagement to entrench," and the Palestinians who "embraced engagement to rearm." Negotiation rewards violence and the policy always backfires. Furthermore, engagement won't moderate terrorists, for that approach ignores the significance of ideology—where terrorists hold firm. A top aide to Britain's leader Tony Blair, Jonathan Powell, who served as chief of staff from 1995 to 2007 and was instrumental in negotiating a settlement in Northern Ireland, disagrees. He believes it is important to keep a line of communication open, even with one's most bitter enemies, stating that with respect to al Qaeda, "At some stage you're going to have to come to a political solution as well as a security solution. And that means you need the ability to talk" *(The Guardian,* March 15, 2008). Of course there are differences between talking and negotiating. President George W. Bush, speaking to Israel's parliament on that nations sixtieth anniversary, criticized those who consider negotiation with terrorists, stating "Some seem to believe we should negotiate with terrorists and radicals as if some ingenious argument will persuade them they have been wrong all along . . . we have an obligation to call this what it is—the false comfort of appeasement, which has been repeatedly discredited by history" *(New York Times,* May 16, 2008).

When faced with conflict, fighting has the edge over negotiating as the first response. As Benjamin (2008a, 1) states, "Our human brain chemistry lubricates the preference for warfare and the use of force, while negotiation, by contrast, requires a willed, determined, and conscious effort." Other anti-American terrorist campaigns operated under contending strategies for some time before serious negotiated settlement came into focus, but these outcomes became realistic modes of conflict management. In the evolving dynamics of each terrorism episode, four preconditions were necessary in order to reach this process.

Negotiation with an enemy—being eager to talk to terrorists in the U.S.–al Qaeda conflict—strikes many as illogical, for the adversary is regarded as unreasonable; negotiation can only work with reasonable parties. Attempts to open communication with this type of enemy runs the risk of "selling out" and brings accusations of weakness and appeasement—compromising one's principles in a stretch to find common ground. Benjamin (2008, 2, 5) states it well:

> Negotiation is a dirty business because principles are typically in competition with the realities of available resources, the surrounding politics, timing, and the personalities involved. Negotiators cannot forget principles entirely, nor can they afford to be too obsessed with them and are necessarily tempered by pragmatism. Concessions are obligatory and sometimes the resulting agreement can appear to be perilously close to outright appeasement. . . . [But] it is important not to allow the process to be reduced to an ineffectual, esoteric activity that cannot be taken out of the hothouse and survive on the mean streets of the real world.

Pragmatic solutions unconstrained by preconceived judgments or enemy images ought to guide conflict resolution efforts in the United States, states Ben-Ami (2006), Israeli foreign minister under Ehud Barak who urges his country to negotiate with Hamas, its terrorist Palestinian opponent.

Shortly after the 9/11 attacks, Harvard Professor Robert Mnookin (2001) addressed the topic "Negotiating in the Face of Terrorism" at an open campus meeting. While describing himself as a "negotiation imperialist" prepared in most cases to promote conflict resolution through a process of dialogue and understanding, he cautioned that negotiation has limits; it is not always the appropriate strategic reaction. Analyzing President Bush's ultimatum to the Afghan Taliban on September 20, their response, and the follow-up U.S. decision to intervene in October launching the war in Afghanistan, he constructed a cost-benefit argument on the negotiation option, defending the president's strategy. As Mnookin (2001) describes it: Bush issued an ultimatum—the Taliban must turn over bin Laden and his associates and close the terrorist training camps; the Taliban consistently denied bin Laden was responsible for the 9/11 attacks and demanded the U.S. supply proof, later stating Islamic Sharia law forbids handing over a Muslim to infidels. They refused to comply with U.S. demands, but at the same time they invited discussion and negotiation. Should America have accepted their offer to negotiate? No, because it was unclear whether the Taliban had the political will or the capability to close the camps and hand over bin Laden to U.S. forces; previous negotiations with them (after the 1998 embassy bombings in Kenya and Tanzania) on precisely these points had not been productive; and the Taliban had been warned by the U.S. State Department that they would be held responsible for any terrorist act undertaken by al Qaeda. Mnookin surmised there was little chance that negotiating would lead to an outcome that served U.S. vital interests, namely, eliminating the threat of terrorism, which meant destroying al Qaeda, incapacitating bin Laden, and eliminating Afghan support for Islamic terrorist groups.

An assessment of U.S.–al Qaeda conflict in the immediate aftermath of the 9/11 attacks shows that the conflict was not ripe for resolution: the set of four negotiation preconditions were not in place. Some evidence of a hurting stalemate was evident— Afghanistan was under international economic sanctions, and the Taliban regime was denied diplomatic recognition by all countries except three—Saudi Arabia, Pakistan, and the United Arab Emirates; and America had been suffering from jihadi terrorism since the 1990s, culminating in the massive suicide bombings in September 2001—but both sides expected their situation could be improved through conflict resolution mechanisms other than negotiated solution, that is, they would not need to depend on one another to bring about a desired end. Turning points, negative events affecting each side of the conflict separately to motivate them both toward settlement, did not exist—while the United States had been wounded severely, Afghanistan felt empowered, on an emotional high, by the successful attack against their enemy. Negotiation readiness was lacking—it was not at all clear to the United States that the Taliban had the capacity or the will to control terrorism within its borders. Trust, commitment, and good faith efforts in problem solving did not fit the profile of American leaders' perceptions of the Taliban regime. Finally, in this context, acceptable formulae for interest-based bargaining for reciprocal exchange were premature.

In the enduring years, the United States has captured a number of al Qaeda operatives, engaged in wars in Afghanistan and in Iraq, withdrawn U.S. military troops from Saudi Arabia, and created the Department of Homeland Security to defend and deter America against terrorist attacks, spending billions of dollars in an effort to bolster national defense. Still, the State Department, in annually updated reports on terrorism (issued the following April), continue to show trends, indicating the al Qaeda network remains the greatest terrorist threat to the United States. By the end of 2007, pre-9/11 operational capabilities had been restored, its leadership (now attributed primarily to Ayman Zawahiri over bin Laden) was conducting training and operational planning, plots of attacks were routinely uncovered in the Western world, and the terrorist group continued "to cultivate stronger operational connections that radiated outward from Pakistan to affiliates throughout the Middle East, North Africa, and Europe" (U.S. State Department *Country Reports on Terrorism,* Strategic Assessment, 2008, 1). Have the facts on the ground changed sufficiently to render a different assessment of negotiated settlement prospects in this conflict? In the next sections, following a description of the conflict, this question will be considered in the context of settlement preconditions: whether and how they might apply and what features do not fit.

Background

The roots of al Qaeda trace back to at least three different sources and related events: Soviet Union intervention in the civil war in Afghanistan and Islamic call to arms to defend against USSR forces in the 1980s; American intervention to counter Iraqi aggression against Kuwait and sustained troop stationing in Saudi Arabia in the 1990s; and the Egyptian Islamic movement—a development starting with the Muslim Brotherhood in the early twentieth century, to the later teachings of Sayyid Qutb, who pioneered modern jihad ideology, to sponsorship of President Anwar Sadat's assassination in 1981 and vetted government punishments that followed.

Soviet Intervention

The monarch of Afghanistan was overthrown in 1973 by a military coup led by Daoud Khan, with the cooperation of some elements of the Afghan Communist party who established the republic of Afghanistan with strong ties to its adjacent neighbor, the USSR. In 1978, Daoud Khan was killed in another coup, and a new regime proclaimed independence from Soviet influence, declaring its policies to be based on Islamic principles and Afghan nationalism. The Soviet Union intervention on December 24, 1979, was designed to bolster the faltering communist rule. The Mujahadeen guerilla movement, precursor to al Qaeda, formed in opposition, pledging a holy war. Islamic soldiers and sympathizers from around the Arab world, especially Egypt and Saudi Arabia, were recruited and drawn into the cause (many young men faced unemployment at home and fighting in Afghanistan offered an enticing alternative), including Osama bin Laden, a multimillionaire Saudi, raised in the fundamental Wahabi Muslim tradition of his country, committed to Islamic purity, who had studied management at King Abdu-Aziz University in Jeddah. He joined the movement not as a military combatant, but as a recruiter; and because of his father's vast construction business in Saudi Arabia, he was able to develop the infrastructure of paramilitary training camps. He eventually formed close relationships with Egyptian Islamists—voluntary recruits and forced exiled professionals, including the Cairo physician and longtime Islamic activist, Ayman Zawahiri (originally asked by a Muslim Brother to travel to the region to help relief efforts; one of three doctors working with Afghan refugees in Peshawar, Pakistan), who had been indicted and imprisoned as accomplices to Sadat's 1981 assassination. The Egyptian dissidents together with Osama bin Laden and others hoped to establish a political order based on strict Koranic teachings in Arab countries to replace Western secular influence and control. By early 1980, the guerillas, supported by covert arms shipments from the

United States, Britain, and China (smuggled through Pakistan) in a united fight to defeat the Soviet invaders and USSR-backed Afghan army, had gained control over rural areas, while Soviet troops held urban centers. Many Afghan citizens—nearly 3 million—fled from the war into neighboring Pakistan; another 1.5 million sought refuge in Iran. The conflict continued until 1988. When the war ended, the United States, Pakistan, Afghanistan, and the Soviet Union signed peace accords in Geneva, guaranteeing Afghan independence and the withdrawal of one hundred thousand Soviet troops.

In the decade that followed the Soviet invasion, Saudi public and private funds, along with covert American training and military support, backed the Mujahedeen war. The Pakistani army provided logistical support, and religious schools located at the foot of the Khyber Pass guaranteed a flow of Islamic missionaries and devout fighters for the battle against the "godless" USSR. As the Soviets were withdrawing, Osama bin Laden founded al Qaeda, "the base," which consisted of a cluster of military-ideological camps and a roster of committed Islamists. As Williams (2002, 94–95) describes it, the Soviet withdrawal from Afghanistan was a heady victory for Saudi Arabians, Egyptians, Algerians, and other Arab Mujahedeen who had fought them. As a result of defeating the USSR, the Mujahedeen thought they could do anything. After the USSR retreat, the Mujahedeen continued their resistance against Soviet-backed, Afghan communist president Najibullah, who was ousted from power in 1992 and publicly executed in 1997. In the latter half of the 1990s, a newly formed Islamic militia, the Taliban, that sought to put Islamic law rigidly in place, seized control. It cracked down on crime, outlawed cultivation of poppies for the opium trade, and stopped education and employment opportunities for women. The regime—recognized by just three states, including Saudi Arabia and Pakistan—imposed harsh rule, engaged in numerous human rights abuses, and isolated itself from the rest of the world.

The years of conflict in Afghanistan had resulted in defeat for the USSR and contributed to the eventual downfall of the Soviet Union, thus ending the Cold War. The beginning of the new age marked a time of uncertainty as well as expanded opportunities for various countries that were previously restricted by the international power structure and norms of behavior operating under the U.S.-USSR-dominated world and reluctant to take bold actions in foreign policy.

American Intervention

In the summer of 1990, the Organization of Petroleum Exporting Countries (OPEC) decided to reduce the price of oil, but Saddam Hussein argued against this policy, for he needed the money to restore the economic conditions of Iraq; unemployment was high, and soldiers would need to be demobilized from the eight-year war service against Iran. He began to deploy troops along the Kuwaiti border in July. On August 2, 1990, about one hundred fifty thousand Iraqi troops invaded Kuwait, quickly occupying the entire country and installing a puppet government. The United States reacted by developing a military presence in the region. According to former U.S. National Security Advisor Anthony Lake (1999, 207), this was "ostensibly to deter further Iraqi aggression against Saudi Arabia and, later, to expel Iraq from Kuwait." Saudi Arabia held the key to this objective. Defense Secretary Richard Cheney traveled to the kingdom to brief King Fahd on the buildup of Iraqi armor on Kuwait's southern border with Saudi Arabia and to consult on possible joint efforts. As Lake (1999, 208) reports, the purpose and outcome of this meeting is subject to different interpretations. "For some analysts, Cheney appears to have exaggerated the Iraqi threat to Saudi Arabia and misled the King into an alliance that the United States alone wanted. For others, the intelligence reports revealed an ominous buildup of armor, troops, and supplies and—although intent cannot be discerned from aerial photographs—the Iraqi threat was sufficient to draw the United States and Saudi Arabia into a mutually beneficial relationship. There is no hard evidence—even in captured Iraqi documents subsequently released to the public—that Iraq was planning to invade Saudi Arabia." Others say that King Fahd had already decided to invite American troops prior to the Secretary of Defense's visit. President George H. W. Bush had resolved to send twenty thousand American troops to Saudi Arabia, providing the Saudis agreed. They granted approval four days after the Kuwait invasion—on August 6. By November 1990, more than 200,000 American troops were stationed on Saudi soil, a figure which grew to more than 500,000 by the start of the war, with a total coalition force of 795,000. Operation Desert Storm began January 16, 1991; its mission was to restore and protect worldwide access to Middle East oil resources, to free Kuwait from occupying Iraqi forces, and to stabilize security in Saudi Arabia.

By the end of February 1991, Kuwait was liberated. Iraq sustained between twenty thousand and thirty-five thousand casualties. Coalition losses were minimal—less than two hundred, and the majority were Americans. Saddam Hussein remained in power for more than a decade. For the first time in the twentieth century, non-Muslim, Western military forces launched an offensive against an Arab country from Saudi Arabia, the land of the two most sacred shrines of Islam. Despite the legitimization of the offensive by some Muslim religious authorities, other Muslim clergy and activists considered the Saudi act blasphemous. The war produced a popular reaction that was neither uniform across the Arab world nor consistent from the beginning to the end of the crisis, writes Faour (1993, 3) For example, in Arab states that allowed people to express their feelings freely, demonstrators supporting Iraq marched in the streets, while in the states that participated in the Gulf War, popular reaction was closer to passivity. External forces can have a significant impact on the process of social transformation within states. In Arab countries, the record of external intervention for the purpose of promoting nation-building civil society or supporting democracy groups is not good. When the United States intervened militarily in Kuwait and economically and politically in other Arab countries, it served to strengthen oligarchies and dictatorships at the expense of prodemocracy movements. Given the overwhelming power of the centralized Arab state over various aspects of people's lives, the authoritarian nature of political leadership, the strength of kinship and sectarian ties, the absence of a civil society, the ambivalence of the majority of Muslim Arabs toward Western democracy, and the lack of continuous, strong, external support for democracy, there seems little chance for Western democracy to develop and prosper in the Arab world, at least in the short run, predicted Faour (1993, 53) soon after the Gulf War ended. The redirection or refashioning of existing conditions and attitudes brought about by the war—for instance, the growth of Islamism and the essential authoritarianism of most Arab regimes—have perpetuated, or even accentuated, potentially inflammatory forces. Most Arab governments seem reluctant to offer their people more than token gestures of democracy, even though demands for real democratic reforms have grown. The diminishing legitimacy of many regimes in the eyes of their people is further endangered by the continuing growth of Islamism as the ideology of popular dissent. Throughout the 1990s and beyond, the continued presence of several thousand American military forces became an irritant for Saudi rulers—widely perceived as corrupt, extravagant, wasteful, and ineffective in governing—facing strong anti-American sentiment among a growing, restive population.

Bin Laden was part of that opposition. He had returned to Saudi Arabia after the experience in Afghanistan and began importing arms from Yemen, allegedly to mount a rebellion against King Fahd. The major turning point in his work came when Iraq invaded Kuwait: he proposed to launch a jihad against Saddam Hussein and his soldiers but was turned down by Saudi authorities who sought U.S. aid instead—a decision he found highly objectionable for it meant that nonbelievers (i.e., non-Muslim, American soldiers) would be stationed in the birthplace of Islam. Was the purpose of mustering a grand coalition against Iraq to push American national interests, in particular to secure safe and continued flow of oil? Protecting the territorial integrity of Kuwait seemed hypocritical. Under American pressure in 1991, Saudi Arabian authorities expelled bin Laden from his home country, revoked his passport, and froze his assets. He moved to Sudan. In the spring of 1996, Washington succeeded in pressuring Sudan to deny him safe haven and as a last resort, he sought refuge with the Taliban—an Islamic fundamentalist group that originated among the dislocated and deprived children of the Afghan refugees trained in the religious schools of Pakistan financed by private Saudi funding—who had taken control of Kabul in 1996, in exchange for his financial and logistical support. From this base, bin Laden built a worldwide network of terrorism and terrorist training camps.

Egyptian Islamic Movement

The Muslim Brotherhood, an Islamic group founded in Egypt in 1928 as a reaction to the growing influence of Western culture in the Middle East—the breakup of the Ottoman Empire by European victors, British control over Egypt, and changes Turkey introduced in the 1920s, promoting secularism, had led to the adoption of the Western alphabet, abandonment of traditional dress, revision in educational curricula—was meant to remind Arabs of their heritage, and urge them to return to the Koranic scripture for guidance, privileging ancient authority over modern interpretations of Islam, and forbidding non-Muslim practices and customs. Hassan al Banna, the founding leader, was assassinated in 1949 (several months after the Brotherhood had killed the Egyptian prime minister), and when Gamal Abdul Nasser became Egyptian premier following the 1952 military coup, the movement—viewed as a primary threat to the secular, nationalist regime—was targeted in order to eliminate government opposition. Thousands of members were arrested and jailed; some, including its prominent thinker, Sayyid Qutb, were executed. Qutb's widely circulated book, *Milestones,* outlined an ideological battle of authority between god and manmade laws, calling on Muslim people to unite in militant confrontation against corrupt, apostate Islamic regimes as a sacred duty—jihad. From his experience of spending several years in the United States after World War II, Qutb came to the conclusion that America was decadent; people were materialist, greedy, and lacking in spiritual morals. Fearing his native land would succumb to these practices, he put his ideology to use, urging institutionalization of sharia law and attempted to establish secret jihadi organizations to carry out his ideas (Lacey 2008, 69). Regarded as a dangerous revolutionary for proselytizing against modernity, he was put to death by the Nasser regime in 1966. Members of the Brotherhood drew away and others went underground. But the spirit of the movement spread as Egyptian teachers, engineers, and doctors in great numbers became expatriate workers in neighboring Arab countries. Saudi Arabia, whose Wahabi brand of the Muslim faith largely fell in line with the jihadi philosophy, gave the brethren's leaders asylum (Posner 2005, 35).

Most al Qaeda members are drawn from Egypt, followed by Saudi Arabia (Bukay 2008, 245). Joining an Islamic group in Cairo at age fifteen, Ayman Zawahiri (2001) in "Knights under the Prophet's Banner," a treatise on al Qaeda, describes how Qutb's words inspired Muslim youth throughout the Arab world. When Sadat came to power in 1970, repressive measures against the Muslim Brotherhood and Islamic jihad in Egypt were lifted. Saudi Arabia launched a global campaign to counter communism and atheism, and Sadat, in need of assistance to curb communist influences at Egyptian universities, supported the idea. The movement began to grow. By the end of the 1970s, most student leaders were jihadists (Schanzer 2004, 33). At the same time, political transformation in the Egyptian state—moving from the Soviet into American sphere of influence—led to greatly expanded, unprecedented ties with the United States and massive foreign assistance, following the Camp David Accords with Israel that had been brokered by President Carter at the end of the 1970s.[2] Jihadists realized the new regime was no different than the one before it and conspired to assassinate the Egyptian president (they had attempted to kill Nasser as well) and shot him dead during a military parade in October 1981. When asked to explain the cause of their animosity, Khalid al Islambuli, a captured jihadi leader charged with the crime, said it was because Sadat failed to rule in accordance with sharia law, he insulted the scholars of Islam, and he made peace with Israel. Mass arrests, executions, imprisonment, and torture followed for many Egyptian Islamists, including Zawahiri who declared, "The brutal treadmill of torture broke bones, stripped out skins, shocked nerves, and killed souls. Its methods were lowly" (Zawahiri, in Mansfield,

2006, 73). Following prison release, some Egyptian jihadi strategists left the country to fight in Afghanistan, Zawahiri among them, who became a top al Qaeda leader. The FBI has had a $25 million reward for information leading to his capture.

U.S.–al Qaeda Conflict

The war in Afghanistan with Soviet Union intervention was winding down and al Qaeda was in formation: Zawahiri and bin Laden eventually joined forces in creating a global jihadi movement. On August 23, 1996, bin Laden issued a "Declaration of War against the Americans Occupying the Land of the Two Holy Mosques," and formed the World Islamic Front for Jihad Against Jews and Crusaders in February 1997. In November, two al Qaeda members were convicted of conspiracy in the World Trade Center bombing of 1993, each sentenced to 240 years in prison. Three months later, on February 23, 1998, bin Laden and his associates declared war against the United States in "Jihad Against Jews and Crusaders," instructing Muslims to kill Americans, including civilians, wherever they could be found. Al Qaeda decided to attack giant structures representing the superpower's economic and military might. In August 1998, American embassies in Kenya and Tanzania were bombed; the attacks killed more than two hundred people. In response, U.S. cruise missiles struck a terrorist training complex in Afghanistan that was believed to have been financed by Osama bin Laden. According to Williams (2002, 96), shortly thereafter, the Taliban rejected President Clinton's offer to grant the new Afghanistan regime international recognition and millions in foreign aid in exchange for the release of bin Laden into U.S. custody. The UN Security Council Taliban/al Qaeda Sanctions Committee passed two resolutions, in 1999 and 2000, demanding Taliban cease their support for terrorism and hand over bin Laden for trial.

The major al Qaeda attack against America was carried out September 11, 2001—fifteen of the nineteen attackers were Saudi nationals. Following the 9/11 attacks, the U.S. Congress passed unanimous resolutions, authorizing the use of military force. On October 7, 2001, U.S. and British forces launched air strikes against targets in Afghanistan. On November 13, the Northern Alliance, fighting alongside the U.S. forces, entered Kabul, and the Taliban fled. Some were captured, but most leaders escaped. On December 22, 2001, a provisional government with Hamit Karzai as chairman, began running the country. On March 2, 2002, Operation Anaconda started, the largest land campaign of the war, which included two thousand allied forces, led by nine hundred U.S. Special Forces. The Taliban were defeated, refugees living in Pakistan were returning to Afghanistan, sanctions were lifted, and a new government based on semidemocratic principles was formed. International peacekeeping forces arrived in the capital; at peak around five thousand. The United States pledged more than $300 million worth of humanitarian assistance to rebuild the country. U.S. soldiers continued to occupy the country. Fighting between warlord-controlled groups did not cease. Battles with the defeated Taliban did not end. Taliban militants grew stronger; Osama bin Laden was not captured. Counterterrorism measures have been set up to protect Americans via the "homeland security" concept, with substantial public expenditure and a series of complex screening techniques designed to deter the enemy, yet the fear of terrorism is ever present.

What is al Qaeda—a social movement that is becoming an umbrella name for radical Islam—trying to accomplish? Basically, it has two objectives: to remove Western influence and to install Islamic governance in Muslim states. The preferred technique to pursue these goals is armed struggle, presumably because other methods won't work. A Spanish analyst, Gustavo de Aristegui (Wright 2004) and Gunaratna (2007) believe the network is composed of four parts. The original body, al Qaeda central (that committed the 9/11 attacks), uses its own resources and specially trained recruits. Operationally weak, its ideology message remains strong. Second, the ad hoc set of al Qaeda–created (with financing, training, and weapons) franchise organizations of some thirty groups spread over the Third World. Next, ideologically affiliated homegrown terrorist cells, self-financed and operationally independent but inspired by the al Qaeda message; and, finally, other global jihad groups, violent and nonviolent, ideologically aligned in some ways, but critical of bin Laden and al Qaeda's tactics. It is true that al Qaeda's capacity to draw disparate groups together and coordinate their ideology and practice through collaboration and exchange to broaden the reach from local to national to regional has expanded to fashion global terrorism. Engel (2001) and Raufer (2003) claim al Qaeda was crafted deliberately as bin Laden sought to become aligned with local militant groups with country-specific grievances in order to increase global reach and influence. Jones, Smith, and Weeding (2003, 444, 452) provide a perfect example of the network: In the 1990s, bin Laden reportedly promised some $60 million to the *Iranian* Revolutionary Guard to train *Egyptian* fighters in *Afghanistan* who would be transferred to theatres of Islamic resistance in places like *Bosnia*. Two *British* Muslim suicide bombers responsible for an attack in *Israel* for Hezbollah were apparently recruited from the wide al Qaeda–linked circuit.

The founding charter of al Qaeda, prepared by Abdullah Azzam, a Palestinian scholar-activist devoted to the Afghanistan cause and bin Laden's former professor in Saudi Arabia, modeled an Islamic society; it did not necessarily promote violence, although Azzam's main slogan was "jihad and the rifle. No negotiations, no conferences, no dialogue" (quoted in Bukay 2008, 257). Azzam was a victim of terrorism, killed in a car bombing, and subsequently Zawahiri, battle-hardened by his experience in Egyptian prison, became the organization's chief theoretician. Armed struggle through terrorism moved to the forefront (Gunaratna 2007, 4). Al Qaeda's goals are to provoke conflict by increasing the destabilization within Muslim countries, especially Egypt, epicenter of the Arab-Muslim world, and Saudi Arabia, self-proclaimed guardian of the holy places of Islam. Pakistan, Jordan, Morocco, and Yemen are also identified as regions qualified for liberation. No plan for Islamic governance is offered beyond instituting sharia law. The group's goals seem anarchistic and, according to some experts, nihilistic, motivated only by attack success and body count instead of political change. Are the new Islamic fundamentalists interested in transforming their corrupt societies into democracies? Do they care about providing jobs, education, or social benefits to their followers or creating harmony between the various ethnic groups that inhabit Muslim countries? The groups depend on single charismatic leaders, believing that the character, piety, and purity of their leader rather than political abilities, education, or experience will provide a sufficient basis for establishing a new society, says Rashid (2002, 3). The new jihadi groups are obsessed with implementing Islamic law, not because it presents an enlightened code of justice, but because it offers a means to regulate personal behavior, giving the leader an absolute, yet legitimate basis of rule within the society.

The al Qaeda organization's doctrine is simple and clear: the United States is a hegemonic power, and propping up Israel and corrupt, un-Islamic regimes (Egypt, Saudi Arabia, the Arab Gulf States, Pakistan, and elsewhere) that would not exist but for American backing. The American idea of global stability is to ensure the longevity of these governments. But from al Qaeda's perspective, there is hope, for the weakness of the United States is that it cannot tolerate casualties inflicted by attacks against it and will back away when challenged—it withdrew from Lebanon after the 1983 suicide bombing at the marine barracks that resulted in 240 deaths and withdrew from Somalia after a local battle led to the death of eighteen U.S. Army Rangers and Delta Force commandos in 1993. Therefore, the strategy of terrorism against U.S. intervention works. Yet, challenges remain. Al Qaeda had three primary objectives at the start: ousting the Americans from Saudi soil, bringing down the Saudi Arabian government, and establishing a political system in the country that adheres more strictly to the Wahabi interpretation of Islam. In February of 2003, the Saudi regime decided that all U.S. troops should be withdrawn from its territory, an operation that was completed the following September, thus ending more than fifty years of American military presence in the kingdom. The decision was meant to neutralize the chief complaint of radical Islamic groups, including al Qaeda. Though the U.S. soldiers have left, thousands of U.S. citizens remain, working in various industries within the country. The terrorist attack on May 12, 2003, in Saudi Arabia, occurring after the official pullout announcement, may have been intended to drive even these people out. More than twenty were killed. Since the pull back of U.S. troops, directed hits against American expatriates and other Westerners, Saudis, and other Arabs living in the kingdom have occurred. In 2007 and 2008, the Saudi security forces arrested hundreds of terrorist suspects.

Al Qaeda has managed to link grievances of local citizens to global issues in an anti-Western movement. The United States is at once everywhere in the world: the culture and general influence are pervasive, even though no centralized effort has been made to control, or directly manage it. Al Qaeda strives to be everywhere in the world—it is everywhere that members of the transnational group live and plot, yet nowhere in the sense of having a low-profile, decentralized organization. The al Qaeda militant leaders, many Western educated, often have scientific backgrounds, part of the cadre of middle-class leaders in many societies. These individuals are cultural outcasts both in their countries of origin and in their host countries and except for Saudi Arabians, few have attended religious school, a *madressa*. They left their home countries for education and training in the war: they left Europe or the United States to fight for Islam in Afghanistan, not in their country of origin. They had been fighting mostly outside or on the periphery of the Middle East: their terrorism includes attacks in New York, London, Bosnia, Somalia, Pakistan, and the Philippines—and only more recently in Egypt and Saudi Arabia. It was Western foreigners, not local inhabitants or the rulers who were targeted in those two Arab states. According to Roy (2003, 71), what most agitates militants are side effects from their own Westernization, suggesting that they are caught between two cultures, traditional and modern, and as a result they are frustrated, which explains their aggression. An equally plausible alternative explanation is that Arab regimes, while tolerating and even encouraging anti-American attitudes, through powerful moves have effectively repressed homegrown Islamic jihadi oppositional movements and instilled harsh punishment for those in violation, forcing the struggle outward rather than inward.

The omniscient presence of America, a recognized but reluctantly accepted necessity for protecting government elites, has become a stable image throughout regimes in the Arab world. While the image reflects benevolence, it also harbors negative aspects: the United States is perceived as a bully ready to use all means, including overwhelming force, against those who resist it. The wide array of roles that America plays in the world ensures that criticisms of local regimes will be redirected against the United States. Al Qaeda ideology fills a need for people who feel frustrated, humiliated, and in despair.

Conventional wisdom among U.S. policymakers about governance in the Arab world, particularly in the oil-rich monarchies, says Gauss (1994, 3) is based upon two general assumptions. First, that tribal social structures and Islam define the base: political participation is not a serious issue; political loyalty is given and withdrawn on the basis of religious criteria; and personalized rule by tribally based elite families is culturally suited to the region. The second is that these regimes are weak and fragile—the social and economic upheavals of the oil boom have upset the old political order, threatening its survival. Monarchies cannot defend themselves against the demands brought about by the Iranian Revolution and the rise of Islamic opposition movements. Thus, these traditional regimes, culturally distinct from the West, need Western help to maintain themselves—military and political support against external forces. American commitment to the defense of these states is their ultimate protection against outside attack. That commitment was frequently played down in public, but the old reasons leaders were wary about open military ties with external parties have not disappeared. Foreign military bases and presences in the Middle East have historically been lightning rods for domestic opposition to ruling regimes, calling into question the independence of the host country and the nationalist credentials of its rulers. As Gauss (1994, 187) notes, Saudi Arabia's reluctance to sign a formal defense agreement with Washington indicates that those lessons still carry weight. Another important, yet guarded political arrangement is the U.S.-Egyptian bilateral relationship that has deepened and broadened since 1979, following the Camp David

Agreement between Israel and Egypt brokered by American power. Egypt remains one of the United States' most important Arab allies and has been one of the top recipients of U.S. aid for about three decades. While the U.S.-Egyptian relationship has grown, it has not flourished; higher-level officials understand its importance, but few in the country are willing to proclaim its centrality, states Alterman (2003). Egyptians feel resentment toward the United States as an outside power in the Middle East, fear U.S. cultural hegemony, and question American intentions. Public opinion in Egypt appears deeply unsympathetic to a relationship that government officials widely consider crucial. Some Egyptians cast blame on the United States for much of what has gone wrong in Egypt, arguing that if the U.S. government really wanted to accomplish its publicly declared objectives of improvement and progress, America only needs to galvanize its own power to make things happen.

The 9/11 Commission Report, prepared by Thomas Kean and Lee Hamilton, issued in July 2004, sidestepping charges of American empire-building in the Middle East, chose instead to define U.S.–al Qaeda conflict as a globally central ideological dispute; the al Qaeda enemy, with its hostile belief system to Western thinking, would be impossible to confront with negotiation or compromise, that is, it cannot be dealt with through reasoning but only through isolation and destruction. What might help, the commission recommended, is mounting an offensive to deal with Third World grievances, using tools of intelligence and financial and diplomatic capabilities, perhaps intellectual mobilization to give an international platform to modern Muslims and to introduce them to Western ideals.

Among anti-American terrorist attacks, most incidents to date have taken place beyond the shores of the United States. In the post–Cold War period, only a small number of international-sponsored terrorist attacks—seven incidents in all—happened on home soil (see Table 7.1). All of the terrorist attacks carry heavy symbolic meaning and provide a closer look at terrorism in America and its connection to U.S. presence abroad. The intervention-terrorism linkage between at least three of the events is unmistakable: from the November 1990 attack in New York when Rabbi Kahane of the Jewish Defense League was assassinated, an incident that occurred around the time that U.S. military force presence in Saudi Arabia was significantly expanded in preparation for the invasion into Iraq two months later, to the World Trade Center bombings in 1993 and 2001. These acts of violence are tied in some way to al Qaeda. Less obvious, but still important, is the shooting of CIA employees in 1993, and the Oklahoma bombing in 1995, which also revealed shades of al Qaeda ties. The overall picture points in one direction: al Qaeda acted against the United States for its interventionary activity in Middle East politics.

Proposals for Agreement

No official, formal open plans for a negotiated settlement in the U.S.–al Qaeda conflict are available or publicly discussed. Instead, speculations abound to explain

Table 7.1 Notable Terrorism Attacks in the United States, 1990–2001

Date	Event
1990 November 5	
Assassination:	Rabbi Meir Kahane, founder of Jewish Defense League, in New York
Responsible:	El Sayyid Nossair (Egyptian), arrived in the U.S. in 1981, became a citizen in 1989
Outcome:	Nossair imprisoned (acquitted for murder, convicted for related crime). He was linked to individuals imprisoned for 1993 World Trade Bombing
1993 January 25	
Shootings:	CIA employees outside Langley Headquarters in Washington, D.C., 2 killed, 3 injured.
Responsible:	Amir Aimal Kansi, Pakistani (Baluchi), who arrived in U.S. March 1991
Outcome:	Kansi fled the U.S. the next day, was extradited from Pakistan in June 1997, tried, executed by lethal injection in November 2002. Terrorist attacks on Americans in Karachi, Pakistan, in March 1995 and November 1997 were reportedly in retaliation for Pakistan's extradition to the U.S. and sentencing, were arranged by Khalid Sheikh Muhammad, 9/11 World Trade Bombing mastermind. (Gunaratna, 2002, xxi)
1993 February 26	
Bombing:	World Trade Center, New York, 7 killed, 1,042 injured
Responsible:	Abouhalima (Egyptian), Salameh (Palestinian), Elgabrowny (Egyptian, Ayyad (Palestinian), Ajaj (Palestinian), al Qaysi (Palestinian), Yasin (Iraqi), Ismail (Palestinian), and Ramzi Yousef (Pakistani)
Outcome:	Ramzi Yousef (extradited to U.S. from Pakistan, tried, convicted and imprisoned) is the nephew of Khalid Sheikh Muhammad, 9/11 mastermind; others imprisoned and two still fugitives.
1995 April 19*	
Bombing:	Alfred Murrah Federal Building, Oklahoma City, 168 killed, 600 injured
Responsible:	Timothy McVeigh and Terry Nichols, U.S. citizens
Outcome:	McVeigh executed by lethal injection June 2001; Nichols imprisoned. Ramzi Yousef, 1993 World Trade bombing mastermind, and Abdul Hakim Murad (Pakistani), imprisoned in U.S. met with Nichols in Cebu City, the Philippines, December 1994 to instruct him in making and handling of bombs. Informants testify they met Nichols with Yousef. Records show Nichols visited the Philippines several times and married a Filipino woman. Post attack Murad told prison guards that a branch of Al Qaeda was responsible for the attack. He later made the claim in writing (Williams, 2002,145-146).
1997 February 23	
Shootings:	Tourists fired on at the top of the Empire State Building in New York. 1 killed, 5 injured (all non-U.S. citizens)
Responsible:	Ali Hassan Abu Kamal (Palestinian), killed himself at the scene.

(continues)

Table 7.1 (continued)

Date	Event
Outcome:	Kamal left 2 suicide notes—English and Arabic—blaming the U.S. for using Israel as an instrument against Palestine, also named enemy individuals from Gaza, Egypt, and Ukraine.

2001 September 11

Bombings:	Aircraft flown as missiles into the World Trade Center, New York; the Pentagon, Washington, D.C.; and downed in Pennsylvania, nearly 3,000 people killed
Responsible:	al Qaeda, including 19 hijackers (15 are Saudis), their leader, Osama bin Laden (Saudi Arabia) and planning mastermind, Khalid Sheikh Muhammad (Pakistani)
Outcome:	U.S. intervention in Afghanistan on October 7 attacked al Qaeda training camps, killing and capturing many individuals. Bin Laden was indicted; he remains at large. Khalid Sheikh Muhammad, 9/11 mastermind, was captured in Pakistan in March 2003 and imprisoned in the U.S.

2001 October 4

Biological Attack:	Letters of Anthrax powder mailed to members of U.S. Congress, television and print media personalities; 5 ordinary citizens killed, 18 injured
Responsible:	Possibly Bruce Ivins (American), U.S. government scientist
Outcome:	Ivins indicted in August 2008; he committed suicide shortly thereafter.

*Considerable dispute about international participation in the Oklahoma City bombing continues. Conspiracies aside, there is no official, final U.S. declaration that this attack was exclusively the work of domestic American forces. See Davis (2004).

Sources: Davis, 2004; Gunaratna, 2002; Mickolus, 1993; Mickolus and Simmons, 1997, 2002; National Consortium for the Study of Terrorism and Responses to Terrorism (START), http://www.start.umd.edu/start/; Rubin et al., 2003; U.S. Department of State, Patterns of Global Terrorism, 1995, 1996, 1997, 1998, 1999, 2000, 2001, 2002, 2003; U.S. Government Information, http://usgovinfo.about.com/od/defenseandsecurity/a/randon911.htm?p=1; Williams, 2002.

why the conflict persists and what overarching policy issues should be addressed to bring it to an end. These perspectives, in large measure, draw together multiple pieces of Middle East political intrigue to fashion an account of hostility and violence, often pointing to a villain, and to recommend broad strokes of policy in need of revision in order to terminate terrorism. For example, two common themes suggested for U.S. foreign policy overhaul are U.S.-Israel relations and U.S.-Arab relations.

U.S.-Israel Relations

A basic premise attributing the causes of anti-American terrorism to is the United States' close ties with Israel. In one particular story of intrigue, Nash (1998, 287) alleges that the anti-Israeli Palestinian terrorist group, the Popular Front for the

Liberation of Palestine (PFLP) is the mastermind of al Qaeda terrorism. According to Nash (1998, 286), in his mountain retreat at Zhawar Kili near the Pakistan border, bin Laden had a sophisticated communications system—faxes, video by satellite, and Internet access—that served as the staging area for ordering the bombings of the U.S. embassies in Africa in the summer of 1998. In retaliation, on August 20, 1998, President Clinton ordered U.S. warships in the Arabian Sea to unleash Tomahawk missiles, which targeted bin Laden's camp at Zhawar Kili. The camp was targeted was to disrupt a conference of top-level Islamic terrorists who were to meet on that day, including members of the Islamic jihad and among those scheduled to attend were representatives of PFLP. Although seen as the director of the August 1998 bombings, some suggested that bin Laden's posturing and threats and willingness to give interviews and to be photographed in his Afghanistan hideout, made him too much of a public figure to be the real master behind the bombings—he was simply another high-profile PFLP front man. By the 1990s, the PFLP "had a strutting, arrogant Saudi millionaire, bin Laden, to do their bidding," states Nash (287). Two months before the attacks in Nairobi and Dar es Salaam (June 19 and June 21, 1998), two bomb attacks in Beirut were made by PFLP terrorists, a car bomb killing two persons and, two days later, rocket-propelled grenades that exploded near the U.S. embassy, which brought about no injuries. The attacks were symbolic demonstrations against the United States to compel America to further pressure Israel into giving up West Bank territory. But the Israeli government, despite U.S. pressure, resolved not to give up territory until the Palestinians cracked down on terrorism. The PFLP thus ordered bin Laden's attacks in Africa, returning to the city of Nairobi where the PFLP had exploded a bomb on December 31, 1980, destroying the Zionist-owned Norfolk Hotel, and killing at least sixteen to twenty people and injuring many more. The 1980 Nairobi bombing conducted by the PFLP was in retaliation for the successful raid by Israeli commandos in Entebbe in 1976 when Israeli hostages were rescued from a hijacked Air France flight. Nairobi (and Tanzania) were staging areas for the raid. In that explosion, and the August 1998 attacks, Nash (1998, 289) asserts, the PFLP left its calling card, traces of Semtex, "an explosive manufactured in Czechoslovakia and used consistently by the PFLP in its terrorist bombings." The conclusion is that al Qaeda is merely a front for advancing the Palestinian cause, and that the U.S.-Israel alliance explains the reasons for anti-American terrorism.

U.S.-Arab Relations

Another basic premise connects the causes of anti-American terrorism to the U.S.'s close ties with oil-rich states, especially Saudi Arabia, which ranks first with almost one-quarter of the world's known reserves. Oil was discovered in 1938 by Americans. The Arabian-American Oil Company (ARAMCO) formed thereafter.[3] A U.S.–Saudi Arabian joint Economic Commission (JECOR) was established to train Saudis in all aspects of modernization. Operating for more than twenty-five years, on the U.S. side it included representatives from the Departments of State, Treasury, and

Commerce; its projects ranged from updating the Saudi Navy to establishing customs regulations, to building national parks, to arranging for Saudi medical students to train in the United States (Lippman 2003, 167–178). Commission activities came to an end in 2000. The U.S.-Iranian relationship under the Shah resembled the U.S.-Saudi relationship in some ways, especially close economic ties and America's support for an unpopular regime. With the revolution in Iran, the Shah was forced out, and a major terrorism event—the U.S. hostage crisis—provided a model that would bring fundamentalists into power. Could this model apply to Saudi Arabia to bring about regime change? Revolutionary forces in Iran divided into two camps: moderates and clerical hardliners. In November 1979, the clerical camp stormed the U.S. Embassy in Iran, as U.S. National Security Advisor Zbigniew Brzezinski was meeting in Algiers with the Iranian Prime Minister Mehdi Bazargan, who represented the moderate camp and desired cordial relations with Washington. By taking the Americans hostage, the clerical camp toppled the moderate camp and the Americans simultaneously and also drove them apart from each other. Drawing from the U.S.-Iran example, al Qaeda has sought to eliminate foreign occupation of Muslim lands by demonstrating through their acts of violence that close U.S. relations with corrupt Arab regimes will cause terrorism. The 9/11 events increased tensions between Washington and Riyadh, and the protracted U.S. wars in Afghanistan and Iraq have driven deep into the structure of the American-Saudi alliance and U.S.-Arab relations generally. The conclusion is that al Qaeda sees the road to success through the Iranian revolution model and that the U.S.-Arab country alliances explain the reasons for anti-American terrorism.

Analysis

Threats issued by al Qaeda against America began in the early 1990s and continue. Al Qaeda engages in terrorism to fight various forms of U.S. intervention—economic, political, military, and America engages in intervention to fight against terrorism. The presumption is that terrorism will stop when intervention stops and/or that intervention will stop when terrorism stops. Eland (1998) documents many examples of terrorist attacks against the United States in retaliation for American intervention. Pape (2005) shows that terrorism stops when government forces withdraw from an occupied area. What has to stop first? From the intervener's perspective, first comes regional stability, then withdrawal. From the terrorists' perspective, first comes withdrawal, then terrorism ceases (at least against U.S. targeting, but maybe not against the regime). The issue for the intervener is what price to pay to protect the existing regime. The operating equation is this: greater stakes mean higher tolerable costs. The conflict resolution strategy chosen by both parties is to fight. Al Qaeda fights intervention with terrorism. The United States fights terrorism with intervention.

   Conflict strategies by the United States and al Qaeda detailed in policy papers urge parties to isolate their respective enemy. The American position, outlined in the

"National Strategy for Combating Terrorism," published in February 2003, is based on the assumption that the 9/11 attacks constituted acts of war, that the enemy is terrorism, declaring enemy defeat as a primary priority. The United States will not wait for terrorists to act, but will employ an offensive strategy using law enforcement powers, intelligence, and military force; the overall objective is to eliminate terrorism as a threat to the American way of life was the basis of the global war on terrorism. Shortly after it was announced, George W. Bush's administration activated the policy. The essence of the strategy, containment, to be achieved by isolating and then destroying the enemy, continues in the Obama administration, although various parts of GWOT were abandoned.

The jihadists' policy seems to operate under a similar premise, namely isolating and weakening the enemy, U.S. global power and influence, in order to achieve victory for its cause. A document prepared in September 2003 by the "Media Committee for the Victory of the Iraqi People (Mujahidin Services Center), discovered on a Web site after the Madrid bombings in March 2004 called "Global Islamic Media," deals with the question of strategy to oust occupation forces from Iraq. The proposal stated that to increase the impact of the jihadi campaign, action should be undertaken to limit the number of American allies participating in the Iraqi conflict, forcing greater expense burden on the United States. If one or two allies could be forced out, it will cause others to follow. The document provides a detailed analysis of domestic conditions in three countries contributing coalition troops to the U.S.-led war in Iraq—Britain, Poland, and Spain—with a view to identifying the weakest link, that is, which of the domino pieces might fall first. Spain is the country identified as most vulnerable to attack because of widespread public opposition; only the government supported the country's participation in the Iraqi war. A few weeks before the Spanish elections, commuter train bombings in Madrid linked to al Qaeda caused nearly 200 deaths and around 1,600 people were injured. The result was the government was defeated in the elections, and Spain withdrew its forces from Iraq. Further evidence of this strategy is the abduction of truck drivers, bringing essential goods and materials into Iraq. More than seventy people from a variety of countries have been held. Kidnapping incidents increased following the decision by President Arroyo of the Philippines to accelerate the withdrawal of her nation's token contingent of troops in July 2004 in order to spare the life of a Filipino hostage. An Egyptian diplomat was held captive briefly by militants in order to deter his country from sending security experts to help the new Iraqi government was released unharmed after censure from Arab world leaders from militant excesses including beheadings. Each side has opted for a strategy of containment as top preference. For America, it means taking the fight to its geographic, cultural source, the Arab–Islamic Middle East, in order to drain the swamp and prevent attacks on the U.S. homeland. For Islamist militants, including al Qaeda, it means expanding operations by punishing U.S. allies, thereby forcing greater isolation and burden on America to contain its action.

Negotiation is generally ruled out, although in April 2004 bin Laden, broadcasting on the Al Arabiya satellite channel, tried to open this game for a three month period when he proposed reconciliation to be achieved by a European committee to study Islamic issues. European leaders rejected the proposal, seeing desperation in the ploy (Wright 2004, 52). No mediating entity of universal persuasion and effectiveness is likely to be identified. Promises and rewards given in financial payment or freedom of movement, enticements that help settlement in many instances, including seemingly intractable conflict, are unsuitable.

Is negotiation acceptable or feasible for the United States? In an early Democratic presidential debate on July 23, 2007, candidates Hillary Clinton and Barack Obama sparred when asked whether, in the spirit of bold leadership, they would be willing to meet separately, without conditions, at the start of their administration, with the leaders of Iran, Syria, Venezuela, Cuba, or North Korea in order to bridge the gap that divides America from these countries. Obama spoke first; he favored the idea, stating, "... the notion that somehow not talking to countries is punishment to them, which has been the guiding diplomatic principle of this administration is ridiculous. . . . One of the first things that I would do in terms of moving a diplomatic effort in the region forward is to send a signal that we need to talk to Iran and Syria, because they're going to have responsibilities if Iraq collapses."

Clinton gave a more measured response, "I will not promise to meet with the leaders of these countries during my first year. I will promise a very vigorous diplomatic effort because I think it is not that you promise a meeting at that high a level before you know what the intensions are. I don't want to be sued for propaganda purposes. I don't want to make a situation even worse. But I certainly agree that we need to get back to diplomacy. . . . "

The real questions about dealing with America's enemies to resolve conflict are whether and how we should negotiate with terrorists. While U.S. politicians support diplomacy, most hedge and urge caution before moving ahead on this issue. Public opinion, largely untested, has not crystallized, although straightforward, sharp arguments against negotiating appear on Internet posts. One blogger (http://www. iris.org.il/blog/categories/10-Global-Jihad) states frankly that "there are only two ways to stop the terrorism: Surrender and live under the domination of Islam, or soundly defeat the Islamic jihad. You can't talk to it. You can't buy it off. You can't understand it. You can't win it over with compassion. You can't reason with it. You can't negotiate with it. You can't bargain with it. You can't appease it away."

To counter this perspective, Kent (2006), while admitting a policy based on no negotiations with terrorists makes good politics because it enhances the appearance of strength and resolve of national leaders, traces out its serious consequences for bargaining solutions that might end conflict:

> This decision to take negotiation off the table has serious consequences. Terrorists now know, in advance, that negotiation is not a possible outcome from their activities. If there is no option for negotiating then what is the point in terrorism that has demands. If you are going to risk your life to hijack an aircraft in order to bargain, there is no point if your opponents will never bargain with you. Terrorist strategy adapts to these

new conditions. Terrorism with no hope of negotiation becomes more violent as the spectacle supersedes the hostage negotiation as a way to further the cause. Terrorists who accept that there can be no escape must be willing to die, and as such, are far more dangerous. While once a hostage was taken to bargain, now the same hostage is murdered as horrific theatre on the Internet. Aircraft full of passengers are no longer used as bargaining chips, they are flown into buildings.

A more nuanced discussion about negotiating with terrorists aired on National Public Radio's (NPR) "Talk of the Nation," March 22, 2007, shortly after an abducted Italian journalist, through efforts of his government, was released in exchange for five Taliban terrorists being held prisoner by the Afghan government. The Italian position risked the chance to save a life and succeeded. Washington and London criticized the deal. The Dutch said these exchanges, in the long run, would serve to eliminate journalists—it sends a defeating message. Indeed, those remarks were prescient. About five months later, in August, another hostage exchange deal with Taliban terrorists came to light when nineteen South Korean missionaries, abducted six weeks earlier, were released after Seoul reaffirmed a pledge to withdraw its troops from Afghanistan by the end of 2007 and to prevent Christian missionaries from working there in the future; an original demand for prisoner exchange was dropped. Through mediation by the International Committee of the Red Cross, South Korea's government held face-to-face negotiations with the militants to work out the settlement plan. The Taliban had already killed two South Korean hostages and released two others a month before and were now sitting with diplomats discussing conflict resolution, a fact that could possibly elevate their political legitimacy and enhance their credibility as a bargaining partner in governmental-level talks.

Former UN negotiator, Gianni Picco, who was largely responsible for the deal that freed the Beirut hostages captured by Hezbollah in the 1980s in exchange for U.S.-owed financial payments to Iran, a guest on the same NPR program of March 2007 offered his opinion on exchanges of this nature: the issue is not "the question of negotiating with the kidnappers" but understanding first who the terrorists are. Do they take hostages for sport or prowess, to demonstrate power to their supporters? If so, negotiation is irrelevant. Or do they take hostages because they want something back or because they want to give them back—are they signaling a message to talk to us on the other side? His parting advice was "We have to try to understand who the kidnappers are, because that determines the strategy and what you can hope to do, let alone what you can do."

With respect to the war in Iraq, this lesson bears some resemblance to the Iraq Study Group (2006) that concluded in their report that there is no military solution to the conflict; the choice is not about total victory and utter defeat—the only way out is via negotiation. "Violence cannot end unless dialogue begins, and the dialogue must involve those who wield power, not simply those who hold political office." The report urges authorities in Baghdad and Washington to sit together with their opponents and talk about every issue as part of the national reconciliation process.

One recommendation states that "The question of the future U.S. force presence must be on the table for discussion as the national reconciliation dialogue takes place. Its inclusion will increase the likelihood of participation by insurgents and militia leaders, and thereby increase the possibilities for success."

As reported in some press outlets, these negotiation openings already exist. Behind-the-scenes contacts between American military officers, CIA officials, and representatives of the U.S. embassy in Baghdad with various resistance leaders have been ongoing. *Newsweek* reported in February 2006 on secret meetings between senior representatives of the national insurgency and members of the United States military forces, showing that insurgency forces are open to negotiating an end to their struggle with the United States. The discussion was not authorized officially; it's been strictly back-channel communication. Publicly, U.S. administration officials have steadfastly refused to negotiate with enemy fighters. Wayne White, leading the State Department's intelligence unit in Iraq until 2005, indicated that some armed groups are tired of fighting and want to make a deal. U.S. Congressional Representative James McDermott (D-Washington) has said it is time to open formal talks with the resistance in Iraq: "We fought our way in, but we've got to talk our way out." Although the outlines of any negotiated settlement are vague, the talk about talks and informal forays of coded and unlicensed dialogue are hints that negotiation willingness, an eventuality if belligerents are set on ending their differences by peaceful means, may be factored into the mix of strategic plans that parties consider seriously. Former U.S. Senator Chuck Hagel (R-Nebraska), a member of the Senate Foreign Relations Committee, in a July 2007 editorial published in the *Financial Times* proposed an international mediator, under the auspices of the UN Security Council should be appointed to move the Iraq conflict away from violence. The initiative would need to be complemented by other elements of a new, regional strategy pursued by the United States in the Middle East, including a comprehensive security framework that involves engaging Syria and Iran and renewed commitment to push political reconciliation in the Israeli-Palestinian conflict.

In the past, terrorism problems were ultimately resolved at official government-to-government levels, even though the United States never physically sat at the table with its state adversary: the 1973 hijacking accord with Cuba was facilitated through Swiss channels on the U.S. side and the Czechoslovakian government that stepped in to represent the Cubans; the 1981 Algiers Accord that freed Teheran hostages took its name from the detail role assigned to Algerian attorneys who as a third party worked separately with the United States and Iran (the Islamic Republic of Iran refused to negotiate directly with "The Great Satan"); the 1991 agreement that released Beirut hostages was crafted by Picco, a UN official who communicated with each of the parties (Iran, Hezbollah, Israel, and the United States) in a series of bilateral meetings. The group as a whole never convened. The basic issue facing the United States now is how to resolve an anti-American terrorist campaign; it goes far beyond resolving a particular incident of kidnapping or hostage abduction through a swap. Whatever developments might be underway, the larger terrorist campaign perspective or rethinking conditions under which to negotiate in particular terrorist incidents, or how the process might unfold in the near future, they are far from public consciousness.

Negotiation Preconditions

In this conflict, few signs exist that the parties have moved from their basic conflict strategy (fight to win) into one of the alternatives (withdraw from the conflict arena or engage in mutual problem solving), a signal that the dispute is not yet in "advanced" stages. Some battle fatigue exists for the United States in the Afghan war and the war in Iraq. An ideological characterization of the conflict remains popular: the war between America and al Qaeda is a clash of civilizations—the Islamists versus the West—each side wants total control over the Muslim world. A focus at this level deters thinking about conflict termination particulars—leaving little room for making issues concrete, fractionalizing them into smaller, manageable, and solvable pieces—and prolongs conflict. Homeland security for target hardening to prevent future terrorist attacks is heavily financed and the major focus in controlling the terrorism problem. There has been no attack in the United States since 9/11 by foreign terrorists.

Target hardening and homeland defense consciousness serve a useful role in obstructing plans for attacks and frustrates the planners, two conditions that can move conflict in a stalemated direction for the terrorists. No host state has stepped in officially to represent and ultimately take control over terrorist's interests or to become identified as a liaison or intermediary. None is in a position to do so. While it is possible that the fight-to-win strategy might lead to a successful outcome for the United States—eliminating or severely reducing the terrorist threat posed by Islamic fundamentalism—it is not probable given the historic record: after nearly a decade-long sustained effort to combat it, the threat of terrorism against U.S. interests in certain parts of the world remains strong. Signs of obvious American victory, such as deposing the fundamentalist-ruling Taliban during the war in Afghanistan in 2001, and toppling Saddam Hussein and his Baathist regime during the war in Iraq in 2003, did not produce stability but instead, in both cases, led to greater division, reenergized opposition, and increasing violence, including al Qaeda–sponsored expanded operations within these countries. But it is not likely that al Qaeda forces will prevail. Their strength is too weak and diversified.

An eventual stalemate between the U.S.-supported Islamic regimes and al Qaeda forces could develop. If it does, and if it reaches a level of intolerance for all sides, it will be marked by concerted movement toward conflict termination in line with a pattern that unfolded in earlier anti-American terrorist campaigns. Any moves indicating willingness by all sides to engage in negotiations would seem to suggest that each party perceives itself to be in an ultimate bargaining position—a powerful force negotiating from strength, rather than a weak player whose sole job is to make concessions—and each party perceives the moment is ripe to extract maximum benefits for itself. This calculus requires more strategic thinking on the part of the terrorist side, for ultimately they are weaker and have engaged in a lot of disruptive activity to move into a space where they are able to bargain and hope to get useful concessions in return. Is it possible to see this pattern as it develops? How much and what kind of jolt would it take to bring global terrorism conflict into line? Thinking about the problem in local settings, that is, how Islamic fundamentalist terrorism factors into individual situations within specific countries, is probably more useful than working from the global perspective—which makes the problem seem everywhere and nowhere at the same time—an overwhelming obstacle to overcome. A bilateral, country-by-country approach is more apt. To some extent, this policy orientation is already in motion.

The current campaign of anti-American terrorism is not global; it centers on issues in the Islamic world, and within that vast region it is largely confined to a few specific states: a couple of important Arab countries—Egypt (intellectual center of Islamic thought, largest populated Arab state, neighbor to Israel), Iraq, and Saudi Arabia (both rich in oil resources); and a couple of important U.S. Cold War legacy countries that transitioned into terrorist havens—Afghanistan (USSR intervention and U.S. Mujahedeen support in the 1980s, and al Qaeda training camps, elevated its significance) and Pakistan (its adjacency to Communist China and massive long-term U.S. military support worked to support containment policy during the Cold War; its mountainous tribal-controlled border with Afghanistan secretly housed al Qaeda leaders, including bin Laden and Zawahiri).

The United States is engaged in open warfare in two of these countries (Iraq and Afghanistan), demonstrating a coercive fight-to-win conflict resolution strategy; it is pursuing a complicated combative and influence policy in one state (Pakistan) and applying pressure for reforms in two others (Egypt and Saudi Arabia) designed to alter policies of the current ruling regimes that increase their openness to political participation, enhance transparency to encourage greater rule of law and less corruption, and reduce the atmosphere of tolerated anti-Americanism within the societies, demonstrating a carrot-and-stick approach. Owing to al Qaeda's leadership origins—bin Laden of Saudi heritage, and Zawahiri, an Egyptian, plus the significant representation of Saudi Arabia and Egypt in its membership—what kinds of efforts have developed in these societies to resolve anti-American terrorism?

The main threat from Saudi Arabia has been the level of financing and internal, even official, support for al Qaeda, suggesting a U.S. ally promoted anti-American terrorism. Posner (2005, 3–8) relates the story of an al Qaeda terrorist, who under a complicated interrogation procedure in April 2002 revealed that his bosses were three Saudi Princes, including the son of the governor of Riyadh, and provided their contact information. Three months after CIA officials passed on these charges to the Saudi regime to determine their authenticity, all three princes were dead, each of them under mysterious circumstances. As Posner (10–11) points out, the 9/11 Commission did not investigate the issue, and while acknowledging the kingdom was a problematic ally in the fight against terrorism, their report concluded that no evidence was found indicating senior Saudi officials individually funded al Qaeda. But a Council on Foreign Relations study drew the opposite conclusion about Saudi government complicity. The United States withdrew its military forces from that country in late 2003. In November 2005, a U.S.-Saudi Strategic Dialogue was inaugurated by Secretary of State Condoleezza Rice and Foreign Minister Saud al-Faisal (reporting to President Bush and King Abdullah) to focus on various problems managed through six working groups, including one each on military cooperation and counterterrorism, designed to coordinate interests of the two countries (U.S. Department of State 2007 Country Reports on Terrorism, www.state.gov/s/ct/rls/crt/2007/104112.htm). America continues to urge Saudi officials to enact and implement counterterrorism laws. A number of terrorism financiers—more than thirty, the government announced—were arrested in 2007; in some cases their assets were seized or frozen, and travel bans imposed. In October 2007, the country's Grand Mufti issued a fatwa (religious decree), forbidding Saudi youth to join jihadi groups outside the country, and two months later authorities arrested members of an al Qaeda cell who allegedly were plotting to assassinate the Grand Mufti (Wright 2008, 13). A counseling program to re-educate and rehabilitate imprisoned terrorist sympathizers was launched by the Saudi Arabian Interior Ministry. It consists of four subcommittees: religious, psychological and social, security, and media. The religious subcommittee, composed of about 150 clerics and scholars, is the largest (Boucek 2009, 217). Members of this group directly engage in dialogue with prisoners about jihadi propaganda, and with a benevolent attitude, rather than a punitive one, work to de-radicalize their extremist views about Islam. Boucek (212) calls this approach "a unique Saudi solution to a Saudi problem."

The main threat from Egypt has been the creation and dissemination of jihadi ideology. Egyptian officials have severely opposed homegrown Islamic movements, dating to policies against the Muslim Brotherhood and al Qaeda from the start, arresting thousands of political opponents and imprisoning them—where torture is not uncommon, says Wright (2008)—which often deepened their commitment to the cause. One of its celebrated prisoners, Sayyed Imam al-Sharif, known as Dr. Fadl—once a compatriot of Zawahiri (they were fellow medical students and Islamist group members) who now renounces him for pursuing nonviolence—put behind bars in 2005, was responsible for the philosophical and religious underpinnings for conducting militant jihad. He wrote seminal texts providing the intellectual basis for al Qaeda used to indoctrinate new recruits to holy war around the world. In November 2007, he issued another publication—serialized in two major Arab newspapers—recanting and reversing his previous arguments. He states that jihadists have committed grave violations of Islamic law—murderous acts and wrongful destruction of property—and forbids Muslims from engaging in any acts of violence in foreign countries where they live, or taking up arms against ruling regimes in the Islamic world, stressing that attacks on civilians, at any time, even in war, are prohibited (Rashwan 2008, 88). Reflecting on 9/11, Dr. Fadl asks, "What good is it if you destroy one of your enemy's buildings, and he destroys one of your countries? What good is it if you kill one of his people, and he kills a thousand of yours? (Quoted in Wright 2008, 10). The split in global jihadism appeared with Zawahiri's response to Dr. Fadl's philosophical shift denouncing terrorism, publicly released in a video and a two-hundred-page "letter" posted on the Internet in March 2008. It may point to the demise of al Qaeda's terrorism strategy, although reverberations may take some time. Brachman (2008) notes the Western media's lack of coverage of such "a major ideological victory against global Jihadism [sic]" is because few appreciate Dr. Fadl's significance to the al Qaeda organization, suggesting the split could be amplified to weaken its jihadi message.

The situation in Pakistan is more volatile. The country has experienced hundreds of terrorist attacks, more than two thousand between 2004 and 2009. A leading candidate for the presidency, Benazir Bhutto was assassinated in December 2007 just weeks before national elections. The mountainous border dividing the country from Afghanistan—a haven for anti-American terrorists—is under the control of militant tribes, and from there, the country launches attacks on U.S. forces in the ongoing war next door. In support of the U.S. Global War on Terrorism, former president Musharraf used his army in the region in a way that many Pakistanis thought was heavy-handed, losing hundreds of troops in the fighting. In opposition to U. S. strategy, the government has conducted negotiations with the umbrella jihadi group, the Taliban Movement of Pakistan. Agreements have come to naught, security has not increased, and America consistently discourages such talks. Pakistan's minister to Afghanistan, kidnapped in February 2008 by the militants, was finally freed in May. Was his release part of an impending peace deal or a case of law enforcement action? Interpretations vary depending on whether one views the Pakistani government or the militants in charge in events.

In the autumn of 2009, a series of attacks against top security installations in Pakistan by an alliance of the Taliban, al Qaeda, and other militant groups (once nurtured by the government) seemed directed at bringing down the Pakistani state. Jihadi groups formally banned by former president Musharraf after 9/11 when the country joined the United States in the global campaign against terrorism, have retained domestic political constituencies and also ties to former military officials. In October, the United States signed a $7.5 billion aid package for Pakistan over a five-year period, with some tension over conditions of the gift: the Americans wanted Pakistan to control terrorists; Pakistan viewed the demand as an infringement on its sovereignty. Around the same time, the Pakistani army began an offensive against militants along the Afghanistan tribal border. But was the mission to disperse the militants or destroy them, as America preferred (Perlez 2009)? A growing perception in Pakistan is to blame the United States for the country's instability. This was underscored when a car bomb exploded in a Peshawar market near the end of October, killing more than one hundred people—mainly women and children—within hours of U.S. Secretary of State Hillary Rodham Clinton's arrival in Pakistan. Speaking to the issue, she pledged support for the fight against Islamic militants; the Pakistani Foreign Minister, Shah Mahmood Qureshi, standing alongside her, said the country's resolve and determination would not be shaken; the violence would not break the government's will to fight.

The vastly different developments within these three countries provide strong indication that managing the U.S.–al Qaeda threat at the national level in bilateral relations with individual states is more appropriate than collectivizing the terrorism problem into a global phenomena. If a piecemeal approach is in order, it is likely that anti-American terrorism issues will be resolved one country at a time. The changes in Pakistan into expanded violence and greater instability seem to point in one direction: greater emphasis on coercive, combative, fighting strategies. By contrast, the movements in Saudi Arabia and Egypt suggest some quiet actions that may help to stop the threat of violence against the United States here and abroad to terminate anti-American terrorism. These changes may not bring an end to Islamic fundamentalist movements or force anyone's surrender—resolving the clash of civilization issues would take a lifetime of dialogues—but they may bring about some understood, or unwritten, or secret arrangement through negotiated settlement that stops terrorism against the United States. Outright victory over al Qaeda terrorism seems a remote possibility at this stage in the conflict.

How do negotiation preconditions size up for the U.S.–al Qaeda terrorism conflict within each of these three conflict environments—Saudi Arabia, Egypt, and Pakistan? There is little evidence a mutual hurting stalemate exists in Saudi Arabia or Egypt; the terrorism conflict is being reduced in both countries by government strategies of resistance (target hardening, law enforcement, intelligence), thus there is no progression toward resolution along the negotiation framework because the target government strategy seems to be working. But some indications point to a developing stalemate in Pakistan through the linkage with the war in Afghanistan, and with that, increasing attention is being given to negotiation possibilities—as would be expected from applying the framework of this study.

Saudi Arabian officials decided in 2003 that U.S. troops stationed since the Gulf War in 1990–1991 should be withdrawn. By agreement, the process was announced in April and completed by the end of August. Although Pape (2005) showed that troop withdrawal reduces terrorism, in this case the opposite happened: beginning in May 2003, terrorism attacks in the kingdom proliferated, from Western residential compound bombings in Riyadh, to the killings of individual Westerners who resided in the country. Shootouts and raids by Saudi security forces ensued; a number of al Qaeda arrests followed. The Saudi government began an extensive investigation on terror financing and money laundering. A U.S.-Saudi task force was organized for intelligence sharing and joint operations in the fight against terrorism. The era of instability lasted nearly four years, until February 2007 when four French nationals were murdered. The government also launched a rehabilitation program for terrorists and a media campaign to educate young Saudis in Islam to prevent them from becoming drawn to extremist doctrines. For most of 2007 and onward, Saudi Arabia has been relatively free of terrorist attacks (but not threats), bringing the problem under control for the present time.

Terrorism in Egypt was a particularly severe problem in the 1990s with numerous attacks on political leaders and the tourism industry—a mainstay in the country's economy. But from November 1997, when terrorists killed sixty-two tourists in Luxor, no attacks occurred until nearly seven years later, in October 2004, when Red Sea villages filled with Israeli visitors were bombed, killing thirty-four people. In 2005, 2008, and 2009, there were three dramatic terrorist attacks (one in Sharm el-Sheikh, one in the Egyptian desert, and another in Cairo), though no frequency pattern of terrorism events developed from them. Egyptian law enforcement and security crackdown has been extensive, and since 9/11 the situation in the country has differed from that of other Arab states. For example, Egypt has *released* more than twenty thousand members of The Islamic Group detained in prison, in part because in the late 1990s, the group declared its intention to cease violence and reassess its politics (Rashwan 2009, 121). A recently released strategy statement published by installments in Egyptian newspapers by Dr. Fadl a reformed jihadi strategist (and former associate of al Qaeda leader, Zawahiri), who is now advocating nonviolence, became an important aspect in the revision, as did extended internal dialogue among the members of the movement, an essential development toward accepting a nonviolent approach to politics (Rashwan 2009, 129). For now, as the Egyptian and U.S. governments maintain strong relations and information sharing, the terrorism problem in Egypt, far from a stalemate, shows sign of governmental control.

The Pakistan situation is quite different. In 1992, America issued a warning that continued support to Islamic militants in Kashmir and the Sikh insurgents in India could put the country on the state-sponsored-terrorist list, noting the Inter-Services Intelligence Agency (ISI) involvement (Hussain 2007, 26). By 1994, the ISI was back in Afghanistan (after the extensive CIA-ISI covert operation during the 1980s to oust the Russians military presence), sponsoring the emerging Taliban Islamic movement. The role of the ISI increased tremendously after the Taliban seized Kabul in September 1996 and moved to establish its control over the rest of the country (Hussain 2007, 29). Pakistan's aim was to secure Afghanistan as a key ally for its geographic position, hoping it would provide the country strategic depth against India, its hostile and more powerful neighbor. On September 11, 2001, the chief of the ISI, Lieutenant General Mahmood Ahmed, in Washington for routine consultations, was summoned to an emergency meeting with Richard Armitage, the U.S. Deputy Secretary of State, the day after the attacks and presented a list of nonnegotiable demands: that Pakistan stop al Qaeda operations on its border with Afghanistan; provide immediate flight and landing rights for U.S. planes, access to naval and air bases and borders, and intelligence and immigration information; curb all domestic support for anti-American terrorism; cut off fuel supply to the Taliban and stop Pakistani volunteers going into Afghanistan to join the Taliban; and break diplomatic relations with the Taliban and help the United States destroy the al Qaeda network (Woodward 2003, 59).

Pakistan was one of only three countries (Saudi Arabia and the United Arab Emirates were the others) that formally recognized the Afghan Islamic government and was the only country maintaining diplomatic relations with Kabul. After spending the previous seven years helping the Taliban consolidate its rule—including military, political, and financial support—Pakistan was now asked to help the United States dislodge them (Hussain 2007, 37). War came to Pakistan after the U.S. intervention to Afghanistan in October, as al Qaeda fighters fleeing the U.S. bombardment crossed over the extended, unguarded mountain trails and disappeared into the lawless tribal areas. Pakistani soldiers posted in the region "looked the other way as foreign fighters crossed over to the Pakistani side and many in the ISI arranged safe passage for the fugitives," states Hussain (121). Pakistan was not willing to launch military operations against al Qaeda while its troops were massed along the Indian border due to tensions over Kashmir. Daniel Pearl's kidnapping in early 2002 was the first violent response of the al Qaeda–linked Pakistani militant groups to the American attack on Afghanistan. In a statement of demands for his release, the terrorists wanted Taliban prisoners released, and U.S. F-16 fighter planes delivered immediately to Pakistan (the delay in delivery was due to U.S. sanctions related to Islamabad's nuclear weapons program) (124).

During 2002 and 2003, Karachi turned into a terror capital; Islamic militants carried out more than half a dozen attacks in the city, targeting western nationals and U.S. assets. In mid-March 2004, Pakistani security forces launched an offensive against militants in Waziristan, located along the Afghan border, but in three years of fighting, the military campaign had produced mainly negative results—high casualties, and a truce marking a temporary halt in the hunt for foreign militants in the tribal areas (151, 186). By 2005, al Qaeda appeared to be increasingly involved in the mounting Afghan insurgency and vitally involved in the Taliban's transformation from a "frontal fighting force/government, to a modern guerrilla terrorism movement (Williams 2008, 50, 56). The U.S. National Intelligence Estimate, released in July 2007, declared that the greatest threat to the American homeland emanates from al Qaeda's central leadership based in the tribal areas of Northwest Pakistan. In November, an explosion of the Marriott Hotel in Islamabad killed sixty people; in December, just weeks before national elections, former Prime Minister Benazir Bhutto was killed in a suicide bombing in Rawalpindi. Terrorist attack frequency by the Taliban and al Qaeda increased significantly in 2008 and 2009.

Pakistani security services have cooperated with the United States to fight terrorism. Hundreds of suspected al Qaeda operatives have been killed or captured by Pakistan authorities since 9/11, including Khaled Sheikh Muhammad, mastermind of the dramatic attacks, according to the U.S. State Department's *Country Reports on Terrorism 2008*. America has engaged Pakistan in a broad range of counterterrorism efforts; the United States has provided extensive financial support, more than $10 billion in assistance since 2001, channeled primarily through the Pakistani military according to Cohen and Chollet (2007, 9). Yet Washington seems to have relatively little leverage to influence events in Pakistan. And Pakistan controls neither al Qaeda forces nor the Taliban. According to the Failed States Index (a project jointly created by the Fund for Peace and *Foreign Policy* to assess national economic, social, and political stability), from 2006 through 2009 (results are released in July each year) Pakistan ranked in the top ten failed states among 177 countries each year (except for 2007 when it was twelfth). The situation in Afghanistan is similar—that country, too, ranks in the top ten among failed states. This may explain why terrorism is rising in both states and why neither government is able to take control to reduce the violence. State failure, that is, economic crisis, corruption, limited application of the rule of law, and low capacity for effective governance regardless of the magnitude of U.S. support funneled in to assist the ruling regimes, allows contenders for power to engage in terrorism. Overall, these conditions have created a stalemate in the conflicts of terrorism in both Pakistan and Afghanistan.

As the framework for terminating drawn-out conflicts of terrorism posits, consideration of negotiated solutions come into focus only after a stalemate is entrenched. Since April 2007, Western sources have given more and more public attention to negotiating with the Taliban and with al Qaeda. For example, in Germany, after Social Democrat leader Kurt Beck suggested that all parties should be invited to Berlin for negotiations, *Der Spiegel* explored reactions to the proposal, arguing that negotiating is simply a means to achieve a political end, negotiated settlements are humane and sensible, and that governments cannot win insurgency conflict with purely military means (http://kotare.typepad.com/thestrategist/2007/04/never_negotiate.html). In May 2008, the Police Chief of Northern Ireland suggested Britain could open talks with al Qaeda, since in his thirty years spent tackling the IRA, security work and arrests were not enough; he knew of no terror campaign that had not ended with negotiations. The idea was promptly dismissed by the UK Foreign Office, but a year later, in July 2009, British Foreign Secretary David Milband proposed that NATO allies should change strategy in Afghanistan to include talks with elements of the Taliban. In October 2008, the outgoing Bush administration announced it was reconsidering fundamental aspects of its strategy in the war in Afghanistan and that momentum for peace talks with the Taliban was building after Pakistani and Afghan leaders had declared an urgent need for negotiations. Rubin and Rashid, in their *Foreign Affairs* (November–December 2008) essay, outlined a strategy for dialogue and negotiation with terrorist forces. In January 2009, it was reported that Barack Obama was working with Arab intermediaries to establish an unofficial dialogue with al Qaeda prior to his election as U.S. president, and al Qaeda had offered a truce in exchange for American military withdrawal from Afghanistan (Geostrategy-Direct.com). In March 2009, the Council on Foreign Relations published an online report, "Six Experts on Negotiating with Taliban." In July 2009, the United States Institute of Peace organized a program, "Negotiating with the Taliban: Reconciliation in Afghanistan and Pakistan?" to a sold-out audience. Why the sudden interest in this strategy to terminate the conflict? What accounts for the shift in strategy? As one columnist states somewhat sarcastically, "In 2001, negotiating with the Taliban wasn't an option; now, seven years later, it is viewed as a 'way to reduce violence'" (Friedman 2008). Similarly, Peters (2009, 238) writes,

"Suddenly it has become the rage to offer talks to the Taliban," but cautions that Mullah Omar, the Taliban leader, has rejected peace talks.

The framework in this study stipulates that a stalemate causes rethinking in decision making and conflict strategy. It is an essential prerequisite. But progression toward conflict termination requires other elements, namely turning points, negotiation readiness, and interest-based bargaining proposals. Elements of readiness and reciprocal exchange ideas for settlement are already floating. Have turning points been carved out on each side, indicating a movement toward willingness to consider negotiation? The signs of feared escalation of the conflict on each side have not yet developed to a crisis level. Signs of structural, strategic, or tactical changes affecting the conflict arena are not looming overhead. Only one point is notable: the change in U.S. leadership brought about by the new administration assuming control in January 2009. In the past, new faces meant new starts: serious openings in terrorism termination processes.

Table 7.2, indicates progression on the four factors that play a role in terminating drawn-out conflicts of terrorism. By these signs, conflict settlement is not on the immediate horizon, although "signal strength" on some markers for change in American government policy orientation from framing to gaming, and behind-the-scenes movement by the U.S. and allied governments at various levels in various ways is growing. But the interactive nature of a settlement to end terrorism requires all sides to buy into a negotiated settlement. This last resort and generally unpalatable situation is not a unilateral choice. So what will bring the Taliban and al Qaeda—the forces of opposition violence along the Afghan-Pakistani border—to the table for serious talks on reducing terrorism? How would the United States participate? Internal power-sharing governance within Afghanistan (for the Taliban) and within Pakistan (for the ISI and al Qaeda) would have to be agreed beforehand. That arrangement would require firm commitment by all sides to abide by its terms. After that, these parties would be in a position to renegotiate their relations with the United States in state-to-state contact. In other words, the Taliban and al Qaeda as perpetrators of terrorism need to be incorporated into a governance structure—as equals or as weak subordinates—so their influence is brought under control through official channels. The ominous signs of state failure in the two societies render this possibility remote at a national level. But local deals in confined small regions within the territories of each state are possible. That's a more realistic way to start.

The formula presented in these pages stipulates that "power of the weak" needs to perceive a hurting stalemate and to calculate the point in their growing power where they are likely to gain no more and will benefit from bargained concessions. They have benefited from previous agreements by violating their obligations, factors considered by "forces of the strong" to foresee dangers in a negotiation strategy. Nonetheless, in this environment, turning points in structural, strategic, or tactical change that affect *both sides* would likely bring the parties to the table. Is this factor controllable? Yes and no. *Strategic* turning points from outside the immediate conflict environment (whereby each side imagined sharp escalations in violence) brought the parties to negotiate an end to skyjack terrorism. A *tactical* turning point by the United States in the Iran hostage terrorism (the aborted rescue mission) was critical in drawing disputants into serious bargaining. *Structural* change of the international system and the U.S.-led victorious Gulf War, constituted an important turning point for opening talks with Beirut kidnappers. One can speculate how alternative scenarios might have an impact on the current conflict (U.S. withdrawal from Iraq; withdrawal of troops, or significant force surge in Afghanistan; serious, open talks with Iran; viable nuclear threats from Pakistan). In the end, the four-part framework, consisting of a mutual hurting stalement-conflict ripeness, turning points, negotiation readiness and interest-based bargaining offers focal points for understanding conflict resolution processes, and a monitoring tool to help track developments toward terminating "global" terrorism, a phenomenon somewhat localized today by the threat of al Qaeda forces in the tribal areas of northwest Pakistan and Afghanistan, a result of extensive, American-led strategies of resistance and reform. Table 7.2 illustrates a simple assessment of the current problem.

Table 7.2 Terminating Terrorism:
Factors in the U.S.-al Qaeda Suicide Bombing Case

Mutual Hurting Stalemate—Conflict Ripeness
The frequency of al Qaeda attacks against U.S. government targets has declined since
September 11, 2001. Enhanced combat in Afghanistan and tribal areas of northwest
Pakistan has intensified, with no single-sided victory, and the frequency of terrorist attacks
against government and western interests in Pakistan has increased sharply. Signs of a
mutual hurting stalemate are developing.

Turning Points
The only specific turning point in al Qaeda's assessment of the future would have been
the attacks against its headquarters in Autumn 2002, when the hierarchical leadership
was decimated. No turning points mark the U.S. government's assessment of the future,
although the January 2009 inauguration of a new U.S. president could be a marker as
different administrations come to power with fresh ideas. Decisive blows against al Qaeda
forces or decisive blows against the U.S. (or great fear that they would be unleashed in the
near future) might provide turning points.

Negotiation Readiness
The new U.S. president, Barack Obama, indicated in campaign interviews he would be
in favor of a negotiation strategy. Osama bin Laden previously put forth a time-sensitive,
limited negotiating idea to the European Union. More discussion within the West looks
favorably on negotiations. But if settlement is a realistic option, first, a matter of certain
state-to-state bilateral relationships, i.e. official links between the United States and
its allied country where al Qaeda and Taliban influence is widespread (Pakistan and
Afghanistan); and second, most importantly, the nature of control the government of each
state actually wields over these forces, must be established. Such signs of readiness are
remote.

Interest-Based Bargaining
Barter conditions, as in all previously resolved cases of anti-American terrorism, would
likely remain beyond the public's knowledge until well after the fact.

Conclusion

Terminating Terrorism: Assessment Guidelines

The Argument

What explains why the politics of some terrorism conflicts move target country policies from strategies of resistance—offensive violent moves, vulnerable target hardening, and explicit government policy not to negotiate with terrorists—into problem-solving settlement with the adversary? What is the nature of the transition process to get to that point?

Conflict Resolution research (Zartman 1989, 2000; Pruitt 1997, 2002; Druckman 2001) shows that parties who are experiencing a mutual hurting stalemate in conflicts they are eager to solve (and have the capacity to do so), where both sides recognize the political capital commitment extended to enhance their bargaining power vis-à-vis one another, and where each has confronted a turning point event that pushed their interactive trajectory toward cooperating with their adversary, are more willing to consider nonviolent problem-solving in difficult situations.

Bargaining power analysis (Bachrach and Lawler 1981, 1986) projects that weaker sides are more likely to enter into negotiations with their strong opponents when they believe they have reached a maximum level of power achievable from their relative position and as a result stand to gain some concessions from their opponent. Strong parties may be more or less forced into negotiations if they face a power dependence situation with their adversary, that is, the weaker side has acquired special relational power over them that puts the two sides more in balance, and hence they become more equal than their actual asymmetric capabilities show. Power balancing toward the middle increases the likelihood of negotiation onset.

Prospect theory (Kahneman and Tversky 1979; Farnham 1994) stipulates that individual choice is a product of viewing problems from different angles: one's relative position in status and wealth along with other markers of power rank determine whether parties will be risk acceptant or risk adverse in making decisions, depending respectively on whether they stand to lose what they have or to gain something new in a transaction. People are willing to take risks to avoid an outcome framed as a loss, risks they refuse to take if the outcome is presented as a gain. In negotiating an end to terrorist conflict, if parties perceive that they stand to lose at the point where a mutual hurting stalemate combined with willingness and readiness to settle intersect, they will probably pay more to invest in decisions that prevent that outcome. This dynamic helps impel them into a problem-solving orientation.

Cognitive framing and strategic gaming, two decision-making perspectives, help provide an understanding of the transition process that moves terrorism termination into nonviolent settlement. The target of terrorist violence considers the "framing" of the enemy and its acts and the "framing" of the conflict and its threat by editing, coding, and simplifying images and response sets. With respect to cognitive understanding, *metaphors of terrorism* applied by a targeted government at particular times and the referent remedies associated with them change through progressive phases and developments in terrorist episodes. Belligerents' perceptions and structural interpretation of the *conflict game* carried during terrorism periods, in turn, provide a basis for understanding strategic choices and help account for shifting moves. Both perspectives are important because together cost-benefit evaluations derive from this two-level understanding and account for changes in interaction that lead to conflict termination. The cognitive-strategic frames—interpretation of enemy moves and game labeling—in the minds of government decision makers are key signals. In this framework, the cognitive and strategic approaches are not integrated into a single, holistic form, but operated in sequence: one element influencing changes in the other as the conflict persists.

Case-Study Evidence

What transpired in previous anti-American terrorism conflicts to move them into negotiated settlement? At least four factors seem to be critical in moving the process in this direction. First, the conflict has reached a stalemate where neither side is able to advance its goals any further (terrorists no longer gain political capital or achieve political demands through their actions, and targets are no longer able to expand defensible arenas for protection). Second, each of the parties has a mutual interest-based reciprocal exchange in mind to show seriousness and bargaining power in reaching a settlement (this might include promises on future policy as well as material resource bartering). Third, each side has experienced a "turning point" (events originating within or beyond the immediate conflict environment that contribute significantly to uncertainty, feeding fears and insecurity with respect to the perceived future, striking an urgency for a party to consider reaching a solution to arrest the process). Fourth, negotiation readiness. These conditions largely explain the termination outcome conditions.

Cuba Skyjacking Crisis

In the terrorism campaign of skyjacking, factors of a mutual hurting stalemate included, on the U.S. side, Americas' inability to convince Fidel Castro to sign an extradition treaty on bilateral terms, or to sign multilateral, international conventions that had developed in recent years that would serve as a deterrent to would-be hijackers who might seek refuge in neighboring Cuba. Thus, threats of skyjacks continued. For Cuba, the continued surprise landings of U.S. passenger-loaded aircraft in Havana eventually became a nuisance—time consuming and no longer the attention-grabbing propaganda Fidel Castro had exploited over several years. With respect to turning points, from the U.S. perspective, when Palestinian copycat skyjackers in the Middle East began taking over American, European, and Israeli planes, the level of national security threat in the region intensified; urgent Congressional hearings were set up in September 1970 to consider ways to avoid an impending disaster. Castro's turning point—when Cuba decided to negotiate with the United States to resolve the crisis—occurred after a few American criminals, in the final leg of their prison escape plan, fatally shot ticket agents during their attempted plane hijack to Havana in November 1972. No longer was the situation bounded in political propaganda; outright murder was happening. Together, when the pool of individuals engaged in hijackings expanded to include a prominent, political propaganda-seeking group in an already unstable place in another part of the world, and also when common gangsters decided to use the technique to escape capture, both sides reevaluated their strategies. The onset of negotiations was the turning point leading to final agreement. In this situation, negotiating capacity and readiness had also advanced, as America had spent considerable resources to establish a reliable passenger-screening device installed at selected U.S. airports to detect concealed weapons travelers might be carrying. These metal detectors improved on the aircraft marshal's program to deter instances of terrorism, reducing America's power dependency on Cuba to reduce incentives for skyjacking planes and ordering them to Havana. For negotiation readiness and capacity to deliver within in the Cuban side, Castro was in full control of the hijack situation from the start; he tolerated no internal dissent, so he faced no complex three-way arrangement in getting control over the terrorists who eventually sought refuge in his land. He was in charge from the start. In imagining a reciprocal exchange plan for mutual gains, the United States sought a one-way transfer where airline hijackers from the United States would be returned to America by Cuban authorities or punished if they stayed (extradite or punish). Cuba, for its part, wanted the arrangement applied two ways, and sought to extend hijacked vehicles to include ships, as Cuban refugees living in Miami were known to pirate Cuba's fishing vessels and force them to U.S. shores. The eventual agreement included air and ship transport in a bilateral, two way, extradite-or-punish law enforcement deal.

Teheran Hostage-Taking Crisis

In the case of Teheran hostages, the United States reached a hurting stalemate when no policy initiative succeeded in freeing the fifty-two individuals incarcerated in Iran. President Carter was frustrated and felt paralyzed in his predicament: the greatest country on earth could not influence Iran to let these citizens go home. Iran reached a stalemate when, after holding the group of hostages for months, the critical element underlying the original reason for their abduction—that America return the Shah, their deposed, former leader—changed when the Shah died in Egypt. Turning points toward negotiation came in this terrorism episode from two directions: for the U.S. side, a national election campaign was underway, and both Democrats and Republicans knew that the hostage' fate by voting day in early November would determine the winner: if freed, Carter would win; if not, Reagan would win. For Iran, a different moment defined the turning point, making Iranians receptive to a negotiated settlement: the U.S. rescue mission attempt to free American hostages carried out in April 1980. Although it failed, the threat of further military efforts to get the hostages was a wakeup call in Iran; within days afterward, secret contact with West German officials to work on the financial aspects of an eventual agreement were set in motion. When the turning points converged, both Iran and America shifted their negotiating style from one based on power, rights, and justice to an interest-based approach. A solution followed shortly thereafter: Americans held hostage were released in exchange for freeing up Iran's frozen assets, and it is also likely that subsequent arms sales from the United States to Iran were part of the deal. Reciprocal exchange consisted of two identified commodities for trade. As to negotiation readiness, there are two perspectives to mention: first, that inside the United States an acceptance to consider an arms-for-hostage exchange by some important group had to develop (the Republicans rather than the Democrats were willing) and second, that inside Iran, the clerical and secular forces vying for regime control had to be brought into a singular plan with apportioned benefits (conflict between Bani Sadr versus Khomeini needed closure).

Beirut Kidnapping Crisis

Individuals held in Beirut kidnappings gained their freedom in a more complicated form—Iran needed to settle before the UN secretary-general issued his report on the Iran-Iraq War and left office. In this case, a deadline, rather than a strong mutual hurting stalemate, event led to agreement and involved principally the matter of setting fair reciprocal exchanges and financial pricing levels that were tied closely to U.S-Iran contracts established during the time of the Shah. The deadline marked the incentive to deal with the stalemate for parties in this conflict. For the United States, the stalemate consisted of President Reagan's extreme frustration over America's inability to free these hostages, a factor that grew particularly intense after terrorists had captured an important CIA officer of the Middle East region. For Iran, the stalemate problem developed out of the Algiers accord that had freed the hostages of Teheran—in the arbitration court to settle claims of both parties, Iranians were suffering, and the United States owed millions of dollars due to deals negotiated under the Shah's regime. Neither side was satisfied with the arrangement. The turning points came via a structural, global system shift: the kidnaps happened in the 1980s, under a different world, before the Gulf War when Iraq invaded Kuwait and things changed. The original plan then was to exchange arms for hostages, but public revelation of the Iran-Contra affair had effectively brought that arrangement to a halt. In the new setting, there were no possibilities for using the reciprocal exchange plan of the past; the issue was how to introduce signals to the other side, showing interest in negotiated settlement. On this, both the U.S. president and Iran leaders had inserted statements of accommodation to the other side in public speeches, so when the UN secretary-general's office made the decision to work out a solution, the parties were prepared to do so. Negotiation readiness came to mean that the United States would be willing and able to pay back significant cash funds to Iran; and that for Iran, deals had been worked out with the original terrorists, the Hezbollah group of Lebanon, for a cut of the proceeds, and a legitimate place in the Lebanese government.

Estimating Terrorism Termination Via Negotiation

Basic features in a framework for terrorism termination were identified to show progression in a transition of conflict processes toward settlement: conflict strategy, framing and gaming decision models, conflict scope, negotiation preconditions, and bargaining strategy; each accompanied with a template of guidelines applicable to a particular conflict to assess current conditions and project progression to ending a terrorist campaign. They are reproduced in Table 8.1 with a column for estimating rough "signal strength" of U.S. policy. More sophisticated, detailed applications could be developed to calibrate conflict movement, but at this stage a basic estimate is all that is necessary.

Using this template, it seems that the al Qaeda conflict will not be settled soon via a negotiation process, based on estimated signal strength from American policy on the selected items. The United States is fighting to victory in its conflict strategy; it is still in the "framing" not "gaming" orientation phase of the conflict, and considers the dispute ideological and broad; negotiation preconditions are minimal—no mutual hurting stalemate, no turning point events, limited negotiation readiness, and no floated barter formula.

A mutual hurting stalemate in the U.S.–al Qaeda terrorism conflict has not developed. Although the conflict has lasted more than a decade, with significant and costly target defense expansion, and al Qaeda attacks against the United States in some noncombat zones (that is, excluding Iraq and Afghanistan) have declined—for example, Egypt and Saudi Arabia—the conflict shows little sign of a mutual hurting stalemate, for the parties continue fighting in Pakistan and elsewhere to increase the probability of an outcome in their favor. Neither impending deadlines nor fears of great disasters seem to have taken hold. Optimistically, the signal strength of this factor in U.S. policy is about in the middle—certainly not at a high level, nor low. The first step on the road to settlement occurs when parties have reached a mutual

Table 8.1 Terrorism Termination:
A Framework for Estimating Progression toward Negotiated Settlement

Factor		Signal Strength
Decision-Making Logic: level of commitment and focus of conflict participants self-images		
Conflict Onset		
Terrorists self-image	Victim - Cognitive Frame Perspective	high-medium-low
Government self-image	Victim - Cognitive Frame Perspective	high-medium-low
Conflict Mid-Point		
Terrorists self-image	Fighter - Strategic Game Perspective	high-medium-low
Government self-image	Victim - Strategic Game Perspective	high-medium-low
Conflict Late Stage		
Terrorists self-image	Fighter - Strategic Game Perspective	high-medium-low
Government self-image	Fighter - Strategic Game Perspective	high-medium-low
Conflict Termination		
Terrorist self-image	Negotiator - Strategic Game Perspective	high-medium-low
Government self-image	Negotiator - Strategic Game Perspective	high-medium-low
Conflict Strategy: level of commitment and focus of conflict participant preferences		
Terrorists		
first preference	Fight to Win: government yields to its demands	high-medium-low
second preference	Fight to Gain Power: coercive dependency with government	high-medium-low
third preference	Negotiate: if gains threatened, get government concessions	high-medium-low
Government		
first preference	Fight to Win: terrorist threat minimized or eliminated	high-medium-low
second preference:	Fight to Maintain Power: prevent bargaining situation	high-medium-low
third preference	Negotiate: if losses intolerable, grant some concessions	high-medium-low
Conflict Scope: level of commitment and focus of the target government		
Terrorism is difficult to resolve when conceptualized as:		
a pervasive problem of global sweep		high-medium-low
an ideology based on hatred and violence		high-medium-low
a clash of civilization over irreconcilable values		high-medium-low
Terrorism is easier to resolve when conceptualized as:		
confined actions in limited settings		high-medium-low
a political directed strategy		high-medium-low
asymmetric warfare		high-medium-low
Negotiation Preconditions: degree of development for conflict participants		
Mutual Hurting Stalemate		high-medium-low
Turning Point Events on both sides		high-medium-low
Negotiation Readiness on both sides		high-medium-low
Reciprocal Exchange Formula		high-medium-low
Bargaining Strategy: level of commitment and focus of conflict participant behavior		
Positional Bargaining—power and rights-based arguments		high-medium-low
Principled Bargaining—mutual interests arguments		high-medium-low

hurting stalemate—neither side is able to reach its objectives, to achieve victory in the conflict. But that fact alone, with "high signal strength" would not be sufficient for them to consider serious settlement talks without the support of the other precondition elements.

Turning points, whether brought about through structural, strategic, or tactical changes is the second factor affecting party decisions to agree to negotiate to end their conflict. Structural change—shifts in the international system constellation of power balance and rules of the game—forces parties to recalculate the costs and benefits of continuing conflict. Strategic change is an alteration in the normal, routine conflict behavior pattern developed between belligerents—when one party makes an unexpected, dramatic move or if an outside event forces conflict dynamics to shift. Tactical change concerns triggers, thresholds, shocks, or deadlines—fears of impending disaster in some way—in the perceptions of the players. To move toward negotiated settlement, *both* sides must be affected by some turning point events, although the process may not be simultaneous—one party may reach a turning point far in advance of its opponent, but this situation is not conducive to negotiation. Many candidates for turning points events could be considered—each dramatic terrorist attack, more lethal than ones coming before it, might signal conflict dynamic changes toward a process of termination. This has not happened. Specific crackdowns on terrorist activity in the front line Middle Eastern countries could indicate turning point events, but such indications are hard to assess short of access to good intelligence. While critical, turning points within a mutual hurting stalemate context will not be sufficient to bring parties to the negotiating table. Why? Because hostile parties need to figure out whom to talk to, and decide whether the opponent can be trusted and is in a position to deliver on promises and contractual arrangement of any agreement.

Negotiation readiness—the capacity and willingness of parties to consider settlement—is a key feature in the overall framework for settlement consideration in conflicts of terrorism. Each side has to reach a point where they believe it possible to communicate with one another and discuss ways to end the conflict. In cases of anti-American terrorism rarely did belligerents hold direct talks. Rather, they usually were able to find an interlocutor, a mediator, someone with authority and respect from everyone in the conflict who would be sure that any serious talk could produce a serious agreement, and that the agreement would be implemented quickly and appropriately. In the case of Cuban skyjacking, negotiations were managed through diplomatic representatives on each side: the Swiss acting for the Americans and the Czechs acting for Cuba throughout the exchanges the led to the hijacking accord in 1973. The role of Algeria was important in settling the Iran hostage crisis. As Iran refused to deal with the U.S. government—"the Great Satan"—directly, Algerian diplomats (at the suggestion of America) became the conduit through which messages and demands were communicated. Solving the Beirut hostage problem fell to the UN office of the secretary-general; Giandomenico Picco mediated a solution through a series of bilateral talks with each of the parties—Hezbollah, Iran, Israel, and the United States.

In addition, for the U.S. side, assessing readiness meant seeing the opponent as a rational actor who had applied techniques of terrorism to reach a political goal, a change from previous images of the enemy as an evil, irrational, unpredictable entity. It also means believing that the other side has the capacity to take control over terrorist operations: to stop such violence and to punish perpetrators. In a self-assessment, readiness for America meant it has reduced the power dependency value that the terrorist side tried to wield, either by putting up defensive measures to ward off attacks (as installing metal detectors in the case of the Cuban skyjacking crisis) or gathering bargaining chips to be exchanged in a negotiated deal (as freezing Iranian assets in the case of the Teheran hostage crisis). For the terrorist side, it means they are motivated to settle, believing a better deal (or some deal) is possible to achieve through this venue, enabling them to reach objectives that until now had been unattainable. In essence, this means their position is likely to be deteriorating, and their power base eroding due to the success of defensive measures. Negotiating readiness for parties to discuss their issues and reach an agreement seems remote, however, in the U.S.–al Qaeda conflict. In Saudi Arabia, enactment of strict punishment for terrorists is gaining ground, partially as a result of the special, high-level U.S.-Saudi commission that has operated since 2007. In Egypt, severe punishment for terrorists and "prison reform" effects, as indicated by the about face of a leading theorist, Dr. Fadl, who now embraces nonviolence, may lead to an eventual, open, bilateral agreement with the United States to suppress terrorism. The Pakistani army has been fighting directly with al Qaeda forces

A reciprocal exchange barter emerges once other preconditions—a mutual hurting stalemate, turning points affecting each side, and negotiation readiness all around have been met. Departing from a resolution formula that stresses rights-based thinking, or imposing one's will by virtue of force and influence, discovering reciprocal exchange terms—a combination of benefits and concessions for each party that preserves some values important to each side and provides face-saving to disputants—is important in defining the interest-based mutual gains solutions essential to reaching an agreement. Terrorists usually stick to their original demands and seek an exchange that is somehow built around them. To a large extent, it remains up to the target government to structure the barter commodities, but "market pricing" for trade is strictly a matter of negotiation. In the Hijacking Accord with Cuba, a two-way extradite-or-punish arrangement was important: hijackers going in either direction in their intended travels would be subject to the law, as was the inclusion of two types transportation vehicles—in addition to aircraft (a problem for U.S. terrorism), sea traffic (a problem for Cuba when pirates took over fishing vessels demanding they head for Florida shores) would be under jurisdiction of the law. In the Teheran and Beirut hostage cases, the barter terms were identical: the first level was an arms-for-hostage deal (although it was only admitted by all parties working to resolve problems in Lebanon, and stopped when it came to light), and the second level was trading hostages in return for financial claims payment (where the United States agreed to settle back debts to Iran from deals negotiated during the Shah's rule years earlier). There are no really clear signs of a major barter exchange in the U.S.–al Qaeda conflict.

Summary

Terrorism termination agreements emerging from negotiated settlement in previous anti-American campaigns glossed over the root causes of party differences and failed to repair or make anew the antagonists' relationship in a broad sense. Still, they were not inconsequential. Tangible improvements with respect to restored security levels resulted from them. To reach this stage, several specific prenegotiation conditions needed to develop on each side: a hurting stalemate, turning point events, negotiation readiness, and a "softening up" process. These milestones provided clear indications of conflict "ripeness for resolution," yielding sufficient cause for the parties to advance into a phase of considered negotiated settlement. Together, they constitute an important set of dynamics to understand how terrorism episodes terminate. Evaluating each of these elements in the current anti-American, al Qaeda–sponsored terrorism campaign, however, indicates the prenegotiation phase is in its infancy. The terrorism campaign is still underway but has not reached a mutually hurting stalemate point or any step beyond. Perhaps it never will. If so, resistance strategies will be sufficient to overcome its threat and hence eliminate the need for conflict reframing. But in a world of grievance and ample opportunity to initiate violence, a hurting stalemate might develop eventually, and if that occurs, some negotiation effort may result. What is the probability of its occurrence? Apart from the consistent historical pattern leading to anti-American terrorist campaign conflict resolution through negotiation, although, admittedly drawn from a very small number of cases, the record shows how the U.S. government generally responds when facing terrorism.

What can we extract from the case studies of anti-American terrorism that may shed light on the current terrorist campaign? A case study, due to the importance placed on contextual focus, allows new conceptualizations, plausibility probes, and theory-building exercises through its exploratory format, providing specific evidence for the "instance of" or "counter to" generalized substantive themes or accepted hypotheses. Its usefulness rests on a detailed understanding of events above wider application of propositional results in the search for operating causal mechanisms. Selection bias in case study research is an oft-mentioned danger for scholars who employ this strategy. The benefits of examining an individual case is that it encourages process analysis, pattern matching, and causal narrative as research tools for capturing nuanced relationships—forms of understanding that open possibilities for generating information that may be useful in a larger setting for application. Yet, there is no telling whether hypothesized connections constitute the set of causal factors, even though it may help serve as a method that can contribute to understanding outcomes, for digging into details helps identify plausible factors of explanation (Collier and Mahoney 1996, 73–74).

In the case studies of anti–American terrorism termination, several questions were highlighted: (1) How does negotiation start? The U.S.-Cuba hijacking conflict specifies clearly the conditions of onset: a stalemate and turning points; (2) What negotiation strategies lead to satisfactory outcomes? The U.S.-Teheran hostage incident specifies that an interest-based approach works; (3) How does negotiated bartering work? The Beirut kidnapping releases demonstrate the complex interconnected arrangements of reciprocal exchange.

The forgoing analysis outlines ideas for thinking about ways to resolve the terrorism problem, reversing the emphasis from the causes of terrorism outbreak to the causes of terrorism cessation. Terrorism is not inevitable; given the world environment, it can be avoided. Emphasizing the instrumental perspective, the strategic motivation that drives activities of terrorist groups adapted at late stages of conflict by the targeted government, may be more useful in imagining conditions for a negotiated settlement. As Malhotra (2009) argued in *Foreign Affairs*, the role of negotiation in confronting extremism and managing international conflict is critical, and if a country refuses to negotiate when it is clearly in a position of strength, when will it ever negotiate? Although terrorism is seen as a global issue, only in the context of a bilateral setting, involving specific disputants—for example, the United States and the Taliban, the United States and Iran, the United States and Iraqi insurgents, and the United States and Pakistan (with al Qaeda representation)—will it be possible to consider realistic solutions through deep discussions that could lead to terrorism termination.

Notes

Notes for Chapter Three

1. In China-U.S. talks in 1955 over the release of American citizens held since the revolution, the United States repeated the view that to "bargain" over the Americans would be dubious morally and legally, states Raymond Cohen (1997, 64). China's concern was to extract an agreement establishing China's equality of status and to get other U.S. concessions. They viewed the hostage issue in strictly political exchange terms. The American negotiator was instructed to free citizens without haggling over a price. The opening position was a call for the redress of a moral wrong. It is hard to conduct negotiations with these sharp differences.

2. O'Kane (2006) argues that declaring ripeness as a necessary condition for conflict resolution simply gives an excuse for the failure to resolve a conflict or for not attempting to resolve a conflict. It becomes a justification for inaction. Conflict ripeness lacks a predictive capacity but is useful for understanding developments toward negotiations.

Notes for Chapter Four

1. Landes (1978) analyzes the role of deterrence (measured by rates of apprehension, likelihood of incarceration, and severity of sanctions) to explain skyjacking, concluding that mandatory pre-board screening of passengers and carryon luggage had a far greater impact in reducing the number of hijack incidents than did the treaty. He also notes that the number of offenders attempting to reach Cuba had fallen sharply between 1969 and 1972, attributing this pattern to random activity, unrelated to specific identifiable causes. The change may have been linked to U.S.-Cuba negotiation efforts, their clandestine policies, or possibly both. Since Landes does not incorporate these factors the impact of pre-board screening measures against the negotiated agreement may be overestimated. The purpose here is not to reach precise measurement of either effect, however, but to understand negotiation proceedings and its relationship to terrorism.

2. U.S. diplomacy during the crisis focused on Khrushchev—judging the USSR had caused the problem—not Castro, the Cuban leader, who expected an American invasion and had ordered his air defense forces to start shooting at U.S. planes entering Cuban airspace. Khrushchev instructed Castro to rescind the order. He also received a message from the Cuban premier stating a U.S. attack was almost inevitable; if it happened, Castro hoped the Soviets would consider eliminating such a danger, referring to the use of nuclear weapons, with full knowledge that Cuba would be decimated entirely. Khrushchev was unnerved by

such recklessness. Castro was not relieved at the resolution of the crisis—he was enraged, states Zelikow (2000, 8), analyzing official documents of the era. From Castro's perspective, the conflict was a U.S.-Cuban affair, not a superpower conflict, in spite of the conventional narrative of the situation (Laffey and Weldes 2008). The favorable outcome for the United States, according to Dominguez (2000, 1) was in part due to Soviet diplomacy in managing and controlling its unhappy Cuban ally.

3. The memoirs of both President Richard Nixon (1978, 485–489) and his Secretary of State Henry Kissinger (1999, 771) report another potential Cuban Missile Crisis occurred in September 1970, when the United States became suddenly aware that the Soviets were building a base suitable for servicing nuclear missile-carrying submarines in Cienfuegos, a Cuban port. According to Nixon's account, he demanded "a report on a crash basis on What CIA can do to support *any* [*sic*] kind of action which will irritate Castro," and instructed Kissinger to communicate to USSR emissaries that the 1962 understandings on Cuba had been violated but the United States did not want public confrontation on the matter. The president outlined in detail, these understandings: "that the USSR will not establish, utilize, or permit the establishment of any facility in Cuba that can be employed to support or repair Soviet naval ships capable of carrying offensive weapons, i.e., submarines or surface ships with nuclear-capable, surface-to-surface missiles." In October, TASS, the Soviet government news agency, issued a statement that no submarine base existed, a message interpreted by Nixon that the crisis was over, solved through "strong but quiet diplomacy."

4. Other Conventions related to aviation terrorism were created years after the U.S.-Cuban bilateral accord: the 1979 Convention Against the Taking of Hostages; the 1988 Protocol for the Suppression of Unlawful Acts of Violence at Airports Servicing International Civil Aviation; the 1991 Convention on the Marketing of Plastic Explosives for the Purpose of Detection; the 1997 Convention for the Suppression of Terrorist Bombings; the 1999 Convention for the Suppression of the Financing of Terrorism, and for this reason are not discussed here (www. emergency-management.net/terror_convent.htm).

5. Castro, addressing a rally on April 19, 1976, threatened to call off the anti-hijacking agreement if Cuban refugee groups based in the United States continued attacking Cuban fishing boats. Six months later, on October 16, he renounced the agreement because of what he described as American complicity in the crash of a sabotaged Cuban airliner a week earlier. The DC-8 aircraft enroute from Venezuela to Trinidad and Tobago exploded after takeoff from its intermediate stop in Barbados, killing seventy-three passengers and crew members. Two men with alleged ties to the United States, who boarded the plane in Caracas and got off in Barbados, were convicted. After nearly three decades of silence, one of them implicated a third man, Luis Posada Carriles, a former CIA operative, currently in U.S. custody after sneaking into the country in 2005, who seeks asylum in matters related to the 1976 crash. The Venezuelan government filed an extradition request in Washington, DC, in June 2005. (Corral and Chardy, July 24, 2005).

Notes for Chapter Six

1. Harik (2004, 171–175) raises the issue whether Mughniya was actually a member of Hezbollah, stating that while considerable circumstantial evidence links him to the organization and that American intelligence was convinced he was part of the group and responsible for a number of anti-American terrorist acts, the full proof of these allegations has never been

publicly revealed. On this basis, she questions the U.S. decision to designate Hezbollah as a foreign terrorist group.

2. The Soviet Union, America's superpower rival was not plagued by these problems, having overcome Lebanese terrorism after just a single incident. Three of four minor Soviet diplomats kidnapped in Beirut on September 30, 1985, were released after only one month in captivity (the fourth was murdered shortly after being abducted). The speedy release came about in the following way: the KGB allegedly reacted to the terrorist event by kidnapping in turn, a relative of a high-ranking Hezbollah official and, after killing him, mutilated his body and sent the package to his family with a warning. Shoumikhin (2004, 5) interpreted this to mean that "Moscow spoke the language of the terrorists." Then the USSR officially stated it would hold responsible not just the terrorists, but also anyone "who could have stopped the criminal action but did not do everything possible to this effect," for this was an "evil deed for which there can be no forgiveness" (quoted in Zakaria 1989). Syrian, Palestinian, and Shiite militias helped round up at least seventy-five individuals for interrogation. The Syrian chief of military intelligence came to Beirut to manage the search. On October 30, 1985, the hostages were freed.

3. The amount for compensatory damage for an individual hostage was standardized at $10,000 per day in captivity, and money would be borrowed from the U.S. Treasury as credit against frozen Iranian assets still held in the United States, unless Iran was willing to pay directly (Martinez and Newberger 2002, 5). A total of $23.2 million in diplomatic property plus $400 million in a Department of Defense account were remaining Iranian assets held in the United States in 2001 (Katzman 2002, 36). Many Beirut hostages sued. The law firm, Crowell and Moring of Washington, DC, has handled a large number of their cases: Anderson, Sutherland, Polhill, Kilburn, Regier, Weir, and Dodge. In 2003, favorable judgments were issued in cases that had been considered. Others are currently pending (www.crowell.com/content/Expertise/VictimsofTerrorism). Moreover, a ruling by U.S. district Judge Royce Lamberth, on May 30, 2003, said the suicide bombing carried out against the marines in Lebanon in 1983 was sponsored by Iran, giving wounded plaintiffs (and their families) a right to obtain compensatory damages. In April 2009, the Obama administration asked a federal judge to throw out a lawsuit against Iran filed by Americans held hostage at the U.S. Embassy in Teheran from 1979 to 1981, arguing that the Algiers Accords precluded lawsuits against Iran.

Notes for Chapter Seven

1. Luft (2002, 2–4) describes a suicide attack as a strategic weapon, a poor man's "smart bomb" that can miraculously balance technological prowess and conventional military dominance of a state: in the Israeli-Palestinian dispute, for example, traditional Palestinian Fatah forces were launching hundreds of attacks but killing very few people but Hamas and Islamic jihad were showing results—their kill ratio was considerably higher, and the strongest impact came from suicide attacks that killed and wounded many. Thus, in 2001, fearing a loss of popular support if the Islamists' methods were more effective than the traditional approach, leaders decided to follow suit, carrying out their first operation. In this process, Palestinians have elevated the suicide bomber to the highest throne of courage and devotion to the national cause, factors important in recruitment and support for its terrorists' tactics. Al Qaeda ideology as well strongly emphasizes the heroic features of martyrdom and supreme spiritual commitment to encourage members to risk their lives.

2. Posner (2005, 165–166) claims Saudi Arabia exerted tremendous influence on Egypt in the 1970s—the Kingdom provided billions of dollars in annual aid to help the economy. When President Jimmy Carter brokered the Camp David peace accords he sought Saudi support, thinking that the 1978 controversial sale of sixty F-15 fighter jets to Saudi Arabia would moderate Saudi policy toward Israel. The Saudis refused to support an Egyptian-Israel peace agreement, and at the pan-Arab summit in December 1978 offered $3.5 billion to Sadat to renounce the accords. In March 1979, they cut diplomatic relations with Egypt, instituted a trade embargo, and cut off aid.

3. In the 1970s, Saudi Arabia nationalized the company, keeping on U.S. citizens as managers. A plan of rapid modernization and buildup of military weaponry was inaugurated at the end of that decade. The most important and controversial American sale to Saudi Arabia was the sixty F-15 Eagle fighters, part of a Middle East "plane package" in 1978. The sale acquired symbolic significance, becoming a test for what has been perceived as a special relationship between the United States and Saudi Arabia for since that time, the Saudis have been a good customer for U.S. arms sales; a large part of foreign military sales comes in the form of construction, logistical facilities and training, for example, modernizing the Saudi National Guard. All of these developments were a direct result of the growth in global demand for oil; the selling price was $1.39 a barrel in January 1970, $8.32 in January 1974, and $32 in January 1981 (Lippman 2003, 160). The government embarked on a nation-wide construction program, building schools, roads, hospitals, airports, power plants, military facilities, ports, and telecommunication networks. In 1980 alone, American companies received many of the $14 billion contracts for these projects. Aramco became the general contractor for what its company treasurer called "the single largest industrial project in the world ever undertaken" (162).

References

Adair, Wendi L. 2005. "The Negotiation Dance: Time, Culture, and Behavioral Sequences in Negotiation." *Organization Science* 16, no 1 (January–February): 31–51.

"Aircraft Hijacking." 1970. *Hearings before the Committee on Foreign Affairs House of Representatives.* 91st Cong., 2nd session, September 17, 22, 23, and 30. Washington, DC: Government Printing Office.

Al Suri, Abu Musab (Mustafa Setmariam Nasar). 2008. *The Call to Global Islamic Resistance.* Condensed version and translation. In Jim Lacey, ed., *A Terrorist's Call to Global Jihad: Deciphering Abu Musab Al-Suri's Islamic Jihad Manifesto.* Annapolis, MD: Naval Institute Press.

Alani, Mustafa. 2004. "Political Kidnapping: An Operational Methodology." Dubai, United Arab Emirates: Gulf Research Center.

Albright, Madeleine. 2007. *The Mighty and the Almighty: Reflects on America, God, and World Affairs.* New York: HarperCollins.

Alexander, Yonah, ed. 2002. *Combating Terrorism: Strategies of Ten Countries.* Ann Arbor: University of Michigan Press.

Alexander, Yonah, Marjorie Ann Browne, and Allan S. Nanes, eds. 1979. *Control of Terrorism: International Documents.* New York: Crane Russak.

Allred, Keith. 2000. "Anger and Retaliation in Conflict: The Role of Attribution." In Morton Deutsch and Peter T. Coleman, eds., *The Handbook of Conflict Resolution: Theory and Practice.* San Francisco: Jossey-Bass, 236–255.

Allred, Keith G., J. S. Mallozzi, F. Matsui, and C. P. Raia. 1997. "The Influence of Anger and Compassion on Negotiation Performance." *Organizational Behavior and Human Decision Processes* 70: 175–187.

Alterman, Jon B. 2003. "The United States and Egypt: Building the Partnership" *Middle East Notes* (August).

Amuzegar, Jahangir. 1997. "Iran's Economy and the U.S. Sanctions." *Middle East Journal* 51, no. 2 (Spring): 185–199.

Anderson, Jack. 1999. *Peace, War, and Politics.* New York: Forge.

Antokol, Norman, and Mayer Nudell. 1990. *No One a Neutral: Political Hostage-Taking in the Modern World.* Medina, OH: Alpha.

Archibugi, Daniele, and Iris Young. 2002. "Toward a Global Rule of Law." *Dissent* 49 (Spring): 27–32.

Armstrong, Tony. 1993. *Breaking the Ice: Rapprochement between East and West Germany, the United States and China, and Israel and Egypt.* Washington. DC: U.S. Institute of Peace.

Arnold, Terrell E. 1987. "The King Is Hostage." *National Review,* April 10.

Arquilla, John, David Ronfeldt, and Michele Zanini. 1999. "Networks, Netwar, and

Information-Age Terrorism," In Ian O. Lesser et al., eds., *Countering the New Terrorism*. Santa Monica, CA: RAND, 39–84.

Arreguín-Toft, Ivan. 2001. "How the Weak Win Wars: A Theory of Asymmetric Conflict." *International Security* 26, no. 1: 93–128.

———. 2005. *How the Weak Win Wars: A Theory of Asymmetric Conflict*. Cambridge: Cambridge University Press.

Arrow, Kenneth, Robert Mnookin, and Amos Tversky. 1995. *Barriers to Conflict Resolution*. New York: Norton.

Atkinson, Scott E., Todd Sandler, and John Tschirhart. 1987. "Terrorism in a Bargaining Framework." *Journal of Law and Economics* 30, no. 1 (April): 1–21.

Axelrod, Robert. 1980. "Effective Choice in the Prisoner's Dilemma." *Journal of Conflict Research* 24, no. 1: 3–25.

Bacharach, Samuel B., and Edward J. Lawler. 1981. *Bargaining: Power, Tactics, and Outcomes*. San Francisco: Jossey-Bass.

———. 1986. "Power Dependence and Power Paradoxes in Bargaining." *Negotiation Journal*: 167–174.

Baer, Robert. 2002a. *See No Evil: The True Story of a Ground Soldier in the CIA's War on Terrorism*. New York: Crown.

———. 2002b. *PBS Frontline* Interview. www.pbs.org/wgbh/pages/frontline/shows/tehran/interviews/baer. Accessed April 7, 2006.

Baldwin, David A. 1976. "Bargaining with Airline Hijackers." I. William Zartman, ed., *The 50% Solution: How to Bargain Successfully with Hijackers, Strikers, Bosses, Oil Magnates, Arabs, Russians, and Other Worthy Opponents in this Modern World*. New Haven, Conn.: Yale University Press. 404–429.

———. 1998. "Exchange Theory and International Relations." *International Negotiation* 3, no. 2: 121–149.

Bani-Sadr, Abol Hassan. 1991. *My Turn to Speak: Iran, the Revolution and Secret Deal with the U.S.* McLean, VA: Brassey.

Bapat, Navin A. 2005. "Insurgency and the Opening of Peace Processes." *Journal of Peace Research* 42, no. 6: 699–717.

———. 2006. "State Bargaining with Transnational Terrorist Groups." *International Studies Quarterly* 50: 213–229.

Barker, Jonathan. n.d. *The No-Nonsense Guide to Terrorism*. London: Verso.

Barnet, Richard J. 1968. *Intervention and Revolution: America's Confrontation with Insurgent Movements around the World*. New York: World.

Barnett, Michael, and Raymond Duvall. 2005. "Power in International Politics." *International Organization* 59 (Winter): 39–75.

Baron, R. A. 1977. *Human Aggression*. New York: Plenum.

Barry, Bruce, Ingrid Smithey Fulmer, and Nathan Goates. 2006. "Bargaining with Feeling Emotionality in and around Negotiation." Leigh L. Thompson, ed., *Negotiation Theory and Research*. New York: Psychology Press, 99–127.

Barston, R. P. 1988. *Modern Diplomacy*. London: Longman.

Bartos, Otomar J. 1967. "How Predictable Are Negotiations?" *Journal of Conflict Resolution* 11, no. 4 (December): 481–496.

Bazerman, Max H., and Margaret A. Neale. 1991. "Negotiator Rationality and Negotiator Cognition: The Interactive Roles of Prescriptive and Descriptive Research." In H. Peyton Young, ed., *Negotiation Analysis*. Ann Arbor: University of Michigan Press, 109–130.

BBC News. 2004. "Remembering the Iran Hostage Crisis." November 4. http://newsvote. bbc.co.uk/mpapps/pagetools/print/news.bbc.co.uk/1/hi/world/middle_east/3978523. stm. Accessed July 30, 2008.

Bearak, Barry. "Hijackers—They're Still Flying High." *Los Angeles Times,* August 4, 1983. www. latinamericanstudies.org/hijackers/flying-high.htm. Accessed July 19, 2005.

Beeman, William O. 2005. *The "Great Satan" vs. the "Mad Mullahs."* Westport, CT: Praeger.

Beg, Shazadi, and Laila Bokhari. 2009. "Pakistan: In Search of a Disengagement Strategy." In Tore Bjørgo and John Horgan, eds., *Leaving Terrorism Behind: Individual and Collective Disengagement.* London: Routledge, 224–242.

Ben-Ami, Shlomo. 2006. *Scars of War, Wounds of Peace: The Israeli-Arab Tragedy.* New York: Oxford University Press.

Benjamin, Robert. 2008a. "Of War and Negotiation: Part 3, The Allure of War: If You Want Peace, Study War." *Mediate.com.* www.mediate.com/articles/benjamin40.cfm Accessed April 24, 2008.

———. 2008b. "The Dirty, Risky Business of Negotiation: Ideology and the Risk of Appeasement." *Mediate.com.* www.mediate.com/pfriendly.cfm?id=3923. Accessed June 11, 2008.

Benford, Robert D., and David A. Snow. 2000. "Framing Processes and Social Movements: An Overview and Assessment." *Annual Review of Sociology* 26: 611–639.

Ben-Menashe, Ari. 1992. *Profits of War: Inside the Secret U.S.-Israeli Arms Network.* New York: Sheridan Square Press.

Ben-Yehuda, Hemda, and Meirav Mishali-Ram. 2006. "Ethnic Actors and International Crises: Theory and Findings, 1918–2001." *International Interactions* 32: 49–78.

Bercovitch, Jacob, and Allison Houston. 2000. "Why Do They Do It Like This? An Analysis of the Factors Influencing Mediation Behavior in International Conflicts." *Journal of Conflict Resolution* 44, no. 2 (April): 170–202.

Berezin, Mabel. 2002. "Secure States: Towards a Political Sociology of Emotion." In Jack Barbalet, ed., *Emotions and Sociology.* Oxford, UK: Blackwell.

Berger, Dan. 2006. *Outlaws of America: The Weather Underground and the Politics of Solidarity.* Petrolia, CA: Counterpunch/AK Press.

Betts, Richard. 1998. "The New Threat of Mass Destruction." *Foreign Affairs* 77 (January– February).

Bill, James A. 1988. *The Eagle and the Lion: The Tragedy of American-Iranian Relations.* New Haven, CT: Yale University Press.

Bjørgo, Tore, and John Horgan, eds. 2009. *Leaving Terrorism Behind: Individual and Collective Disengagement.* London: Routledge.

Bjørn Stærk Blog, July 26, 2004. www.bearstrong.net.

Blainey, Geoffrey. 1973. *The Causes of War.* New York: Free Press.

———. 1988. *The Causes of War.* 3rd ed. New York: Free Press.

Bloom, Mia. 2005. *Dying to Kill: The Allure of Suicide Terror.* New York: Columbia University Press.

Blum, William. 2004. *Killing Hope: U.S. Military and CIA Interventions since World War II.* Monroe, ME: Common Courage.

———. 2005. "Cuba: 1959–1980: The Unforgivable Revolution." http://members.aol.com/ bblum6/cuba.htm. Accessed September 25, 2005.

Bonanate, Luigi. 1979. "Some Unanticipated Consequences of Terrorism." *Journal of Peace Research* 16, no. 3: 197–211.

Boot, Max. 2003. "The End of Appeasement: Bush's Opportunity to Redeem America's Past Failure in the Middle East." Council on Foreign Relations Publications online *Weekly Standard*, February 10. www.cfr.org/publications. Accessed April 7, 2006.

Boucek, Christopher. 2009. "Extremist Re-Education and Rehabilitation in Saudi Arabia." In Tore Bjørgo and John Horgan, eds., *Leaving Terrorism Behind: Individual and Collective Disengagement*. London: Routledge, 212–223.

Bowden, Mark. 2006. *Guests of the Ayatollah: The First Battle in America's War with Militant Islam*. New York: Atlantic Monthly Press.

Brachman, Jarrett. 2008. "Abu Yahya's Six Easy Steps for Defeating al-Qaeda." *Perspectives on Terrorism* 1, no. 5.

Brady, Linda P. 1991. *The Politics of Negotiation: America's Dealings with Allies, Adversaries, and Friends*. Chapel Hill, NC: University of North Carolina Press.

Braithwaite, Alex, and Quan Li. 2007. "Transnational Terrorism Hot Spots: Identification and Impact Evaluation." *Conflict Management and Peace Science* 24: 281–296.

Brams, Steven J., and Donald Wittman. 1981. "Nonmyopic Equilibria in 2 x 2 Games." *Conflict Management and Peace Science* 6: 39–62.

Brannan, David W., Philip F. Esler, and N.T. Anders Strondberg. 2001. "Talking to 'Terrorists': Towards an Independent Analytical Framework for the Study of Violent Substate Activism." *Studies in Conflict and Terrorism* 24, no. 1 (January–March): 3–24.

Braungart, R., and M. Braungart. 1992. "From Protest to Terrorism: The Case of SDS and the Weathermen." *International Social Movement Research* 4: 45–78.

Bremer, Stuart. 2004. "Resolving Conflicts: Conditions Favoring Negotiated Compromise in Militarized Interstate Disputes." In Zeev Maoz, Alex Mintz, T. Clifton Morgan, Glenn Palmer, and Richard J. Stoll, eds. *Multiple Paths to Knowledge in International Relations: Methodology in the Study of Conflict Management and Conflict Resolution*. Lanham, MD: Lexington, 193–214

Brett, Jeanne M. 2001. *Negotiating Globally: How to Negotiate Deals, Resolve Disputes, and Make Decisions across Cultural Boundaries*. San Francisco: Jossey-Bass.

Bridis, Ted. 2002. "Terror Was a Rare Topic." *Denver Post*, June 29, 22.

Bronson, Rachel. 2006. *Thicker Than Oil: America's Uneasy Partnership with Saudi Arabia*. New York: Oxford University Press.

Brooks, David. 2002. "A Man on a Gray Horse." *Atlantic Monthly* (September.24–25).

Brooks, Stephen G., and William Wohlforth. 2002. "American Primacy in Perspective." *Foreign Affairs* 54 (July–August): 20–33.

Brown, Seyom. 1987. *The Causes and Prevention of War*. New York: St. Martin's.

Buchanan, Patrick J. 1999. *A Republic, Not an Empire: Reclaiming America's Destiny*. Washington, DC: Regnery.

———. 2006a. "On Talking with Terrorists." August 5. www.antiwar.com. Accessed February 28, 2008.

———. 2006b. "On Talking with Terrorists." August 4. www.townhall.com. Accessed June 3, 2008.

Buhite, Russell D. 1995. *Lives at Risk: Hostages and Victims in American Foreign Policy*. Wilmington, DE: Scholarly Resources.

Bukay, David. 2008. *From Muhammad to Bin Laden: Religious and Ideological Sources of the Homicide Bomber Phenomenon*. New Brunswick, NJ: Transaction.

Bull, Hedley, ed. 1984. *Intervention in World Politics*. New York: Oxford University Press.

Bunge, Mario. 1963. *Causality: The Place of the Causal Principle in Modern Science.* New York: Meridian/World.

Burgess, Heidi, and Guy Burgess. 1996. "Constructive Confrontation: A Transformative Approach to Intractable Conflicts." *Mediation Quarterly* 13: 305–322.

Burnside, Craig, and David Dollar. 2000. "Aid, Policies, and Growth." *American Economic Review* 90, no. 3 (September): 847–868.

"Bush Assails 'Appeasement,' Touching Off Storm." 2008. *The New York Times* (May 16). http://www.cnsews.com/ViewPolitics.asp?Page=Politics/archive/200805. Accessed May 15, 2008.

Byman, Daniel. 2004. "Why We Can't Help Margaret Hassan: No Matter How Tempting, Governments Shouldn't Negotiate with Hostage-Takers." *Slate.* http://www.slate.com/id/2108861. Accessed June 27, 2008.

———. 2006. "The Decision to Begin Talks with Terrorists: Lessons for Policymakers." *Studies in Conflict and Terrorism* 29: 403–414.

———. 2007. *The Five-Front War: The Better Way to Fight Global Jihad.* New York: Wiley.

Calahan, H. A. 1944. *What Makes a War End?* New York: Vanguard.

Carnevale, Peter J. 2007. "Creativity in the Outcomes of Conflict." In Morton Deutsch and Peter T. Coleman, eds., *Handbook of Conflict Resolution.* 2nd ed. San Francisco: Jossey-Bass.

Carr, Caleb. 2002. *A History of Warfare against Civilians.* New York: Random House.

Carroll, Berenice A. 1970. "War Termination and Conflict Theory: Value Premises, Theories, and Policies" *Annals of the American Academy of Political and Social Science* 392 (November): 14–29.

Carswell, Robert, and Richard J. Davis. 1985a. "Crafting the Financial Settlement." In Warren Christopher, et al., eds., *American Hostages in Iran: The Conduct of a Crisis.* New Haven, CT: Yale University Press, 201–234.

———. 1985b. "The Economic and Financial Pressures: Freeze and Sanctions." In Warren Christopher et al., eds., *American Hostages in Iran: The Conduct of a Crisis.* New Haven, CT: Yale University Press, 173–200.

Caruso, Raul. 2006. "Conflict and Conflict Management with Interdependent Instruments and Asymmetric Stakes (The Good-Cop and Bad-Cop Game)." *Peace, Economics, Peace Science, and Public Policy* 12, no. 1: 1–53.

Cauley, Jon, and Eric Iksoon Im. 1988. "Intervention Policy Analysis of Skyjackings and Other Terrorist Incidents." *American Economic Review* 78, no. 2 (May): 27–31.

Cave, George. 1994. "Why Secret 1986 U.S.-Iran 'Arms for Hostages' Negotiations Failed." *Washington Report on Middle East Affairs* (September–October): 8, 89.

Chan, Steve. 2003. "Explaining War Termination: A Boolean Analysis of Causes." *Journal of Peace Research* 40 no. 1: 49–66.

Chang, Noh-Soon. 1995. "Determinants for Negotiated Settlements in Militarized Disputes: A Perspective on Democratization in Northeast Asia." *Journal of East Asian Affairs* 9 (Summer–Fall): 462–479.

Chayes, Antonia Handler, and Abram Chayes. 1999. *Planning for Intervention: International Cooperation in Conflict Management.* The Hague, the Netherlands: Kluwer Law International.

Chomsky, Noam. 1986. *Pirates and Emperors: International Terrorism in the Real World.* Brattleboro, VT: Amana.

Christopher, Warren, Harold H. Saunders, Gary Sick, Robert Carswell, Richard J. Davis, John Hoffman Jr., and Robert Owen. 1985. *American Hostages in Iran: The Conduct of a Crisis.* New Haven, CT: Yale University Press.

Clark, Derek J., and Kai A. Konrad. 2007. "Asymmetric Conflict: Weakest Link against Best Shot." *Journal of Conflict Resolution* 51, no 3 (June): 457–469.

Clark, Robert P. 1990. *Negotiating with ETA: Obstacles to Peace in the Basque Country, 1975–1988.* Reno: University of Nevada Press.

Clarke, Richard A., Glenn P. Aga, Roger W. Cressy, Stephen E. Flynn, Blake W. Mobley, Eric Rosenbach, Steven Simon, William F. Wechsler, and Lee S. Wolosky. 2004. *Defeating the Jihadists: A Blueprint for Action.* New York: Century Foundation.

Clauset, Arron, Maxwell Young, and Kristan Skrede Gleditch. 2007. "On the Frequency of Severe Terrorist Events." *Journal of Conflict Resolution* 52, no. 1 (February): 58–87.

Clutterbuck, Richard. 1977. *Guerrillas and Terrorists.* London: Faber and Faber.

———. 1987. *Kidnap, Hijack, and Extortion: The Response.* New York: St. Martin's.

Cobban, Helena. 1999. *The Israeli-Syrian Peace Talks: 1991–96 and Beyond.* Washington, DC: U.S. Institute of Peace.

Cockburn, Leslie. 1987. *Out of Control: The Story of the Reagan Administration's Secret War in Nicaragua, the Illegal Arms Pipeline, and the Contra Drug Connection.* New York: Atlantic Monthly Press.

Cohen, Craig, and Derek Chollet. 2007. "When $10 Billion Is Not Enough: Rethinking U.S. Strategy toward Pakistan." *Washington Quarterly* 30, no. 2 (Spring): 7–19.

Cohen, Raymond. 1997. *Negotiating across Cultures.* Rev. ed. Washington, DC: U.S. Institute of Peace.

Cohen, S. P. et al. 1977. "Evolving Intergroup Techniques for Conflict Resolution." *Journal of Social Issues* 33: 165–188.

Coker, Christopher. 2002. *Globalization and Insecurity in the Twenty-first Century: NATO and the Management of Risk.* Adelphi Paper No. 345. London: International Institute for Strategic Studies.

Colander, David. 2005. "The Future of Economics: The Appropriately Educated in Pursuit of the Knowable." *Cambridge Journal of Economics* 29: 927–941.

Coleman, Loren. 2004. *The Copy-Cat Effect: How the Media and Popular Culture Trigger the Mayhem in Tomorrow's Headlines.* New York: Paraview/Pocket.

Coleman, Peter T. 1997. "Redefining Ripeness: A Social-Psychological Perspective." *Power and Conflict* 3: 81–103.

———. 2000a. "Intractable Conflict." In Morton Deutsch and Peter T. Coleman, eds., *The Handbook of Conflict Resolution: Theory and Practice.* San Francisco: Jossey-Bass, 428–450.

———. 2000b. "Power and Conflict." In Morton Deutsch and Peter T. Coleman, eds., *The Handbook of Conflict Resolution: Theory and Practice.* San Francisco: Jossey-Bass, 108–130.

Collelo, Thomas. 1989. *Lebanon: A Country Study.* Washington, DC: U.S. Headquarters, Department of the Army.

Collier, David, and James Mahoney. 1996. "Insights and Pitfalls: Selection Bias in Qualitative Research." *World Politics* 49, no. 1: 56–91.

Collier, Paul, and Anke Hoeffler. 2001. "Greed and Grievance in Civil War." World Bank Policy Research Working Paper No. 2355. Available at econ.worldbank.org/files/12205_greedgrievance_23oct.pdf. Accessed January 15, 2004.

Congressional Record. 1991. "Partisan Politics and the Myth of the October Surprise." Extension of Remarks. http://www.fas.org/irp/congress/1991_cr/h911104-october.htm. Accessed July 24, 2008.

Copeland, Thomas. 2003. "Is the 'New Terrorism' Really New? An Analysis of the New Paradigm for Terrorism." Available at www.oss.net. Accessed March 26, 2008.

Cordesman, Anthony H., and Nawaf Obaid. 2004. "Saudi Internal Security: A Risk Assessment." Working Paper. Washington, DC: Center for Strategic and International Studies.

Corral, Oscar, and Alfonso Chardy. 2005. "Man Convicted in Bombing Wants Suspect Extradited." *Reno Gazette-Journal,* July 24.

Corsi, Jerome R. 1981. "Terrorism as a Desperate Game: Fear, Bargaining, and Communication in the Terrorist Event." *Journal of Conflict Resolution* 25, no. 1 (March): 47–85.

Cortright, David, and George A. Lopez, eds. 2007. *Uniting against Terror: Cooperative Nonmilitary Responses to the Global Terrorist Threat.* Cambridge: Massachusetts Institute of Technology Press.

Coser, Lewis A. 1961. "The Termination of Conflict." *Journal of Conflict Resolution* 5, no. 4 (December): 347–353.

Cottam, Richard. 1988. *Iran and the United States: A Cold War Case Study.* Pittsburgh, PA: University of Pittsburgh Press.

Crenshaw, Martha. 1981. "The Causes of Terrorism." *Comparative Politics* 13, no. 4 (July): 379–399.

———. 1990. "The Logic of Terrorism: Terrorist Behavior as a Product of Strategic Choice." In Walter Reich, ed., *Origins of Terrorism: Psychologies, Ideologies, Theologies, States of Mind.* New York: Cambridge University Press, 7–24.

———. 1999. "How Terrorism Ends." U.S. Institute of Peace Special Report. Washington, DC: U.S. Institute of Peace.

———. 2001. "Why America? The Globalization of Civil War." *Current History* (December): 425–432.

Cronin, Audrey Kurth. 2002a. "Behind the Curve: Globalization and International Terrorism." *International Security* 27, no. 3 (Winter): 30–58.

———. 2002b. "Rethinking Sovereignty: American Strategy in the Age of Terrorism." *Survival* 44 (Summer): 119–139.

———. 2006. "How Al-Qaida Ends." *International Security* 31, no. 1 (Summer): 7–48.

———. 2007. "Ending Terrorism: Lessons for Defeating al Qaeda." Adelphi Papers No. 394. London: International Institute for Strategic Studies.

Cronin, Audrey Kurth, and James M. Ludes, eds. 2004. *Attacking Terrorism: Elements of a Grand Strategy.* Washington, DC: Georgetown University Press.

Crowell and Moring LLP. www.crowell.com/content/Expertise/VictimsofTerrorism/High. Accessed April 5, 2006.

David, Steven R. 1995. "The Necessity for American Military Intervention in the Post–Cold War World." In Aspen Strategy Group, ed., *The United States and the Use of Force In the Post Cold War Era.* Queenstown, MD: Aspen Institute, 39–70.

Davis, Jayna. 2004. *The Third Terrorist: The Middle East Connection to the Oklahoma City Bombing.* Nashville, TN: Thomas Nelson.

Davis, Mike. 2007. *Buda's Wagon: A Brief History of the Car Bomb.* London: Verso.

De Dreu, Carsten K. W., Bianca Beersma, Wolfgang Steinel, and Gerber A. VanKleef. 2007. "The Psychology of Negotiation." In A. W. Kruglanski and E. T. Higgins, eds. *Handbook of Basic Principles in Social Psychology.* 2nd edition. New York: Guiford, 608–629.

Dempsey, Judy. 2002. "Raid on Agency in Bosnia Points to al Qaeda Link." *Financial Times Online.* February 21.

Dershowitz, Alan. 2002. *Why Terrorism Works: Understanding the Threat, Responding to the Challenge.* New Haven, CT: Yale University Press.

Deutsch, Morton. 1973. *The Resolution of Conflict.* New Haven, CT: Yale University Press.

————. 1985. *Distributive Justice: A Social Psychological Perspective.* New Haven, CT: Yale University Press.

————. 2000. "Commentary on 'Civil Political Discourse in a Democracy.'" *Peace and Conflict: Journal of Peace Psychology* 6, no. 4: 319–323.

Deutsch, Morton, and Peter T. Coleman, eds. 2000. *The Handbook of Conflict Resolution: Theory and Practice.* San Francisco: Jossey-Bass.

Dillion, Dana R. 2004. "Arroyo's Policies Disappoint." *Asian Wall Street Journal,* October 7.

Dion, Douglas. 1998. "Evidence and Inference in the Comparative Case Study." *Comparative Politics* 30, no. 2 (January): 127–145.

Dobbins, James. 2007. "Who Lost Iraq?" *Foreign Affairs* 86, no. 5 (September–October): 61–74.

Docherty, Jayne Seminare. 2005. *Strategic Negotiation: Negotiating during Turbulent Times.* Intercourse, PA: Good Books.

Dollard, J., L. Doob, N. Miller, O. H. Mowrer, and R. R. Sears. 1939. *Frustration and Aggression.* New Haven, CT: Yale University Press.

Dolnik, Adam. 2003. "Contrasting Dynamics of Crisis Negotiations: Barricade vs. Kidnapping Incidents." *International Negotiation* 8: 495–526.

Dolnik, Adam, and Keith M. Fitzgerald. 2008. *Negotiating Hostage Crises with the New Terrorists.* Westport, CT: Praeger Security International.

Dominguez, Jorge I. 2000. "The @#$%& Missile Crisis: (Or What Was 'Cuban' about U.S. Decisions during the Cuban Missile Crisis?)" *Diplomatic History* 24, no. 2 (Spring): 1–9.

Donohue, William A., and Paul J. Taylor. 2003. "Testing the Role Effect in Terrorist Negotiations." *International Negotiation* 8: 527–547.

Doob, Leonard. 1974. "The Analysis and Resolution of International Disputes." *Journal of Psychology* 86, no. 2: 313–326.

Doran, Michael. 2002. "The Pragmatic Fanaticism of al Qaeda: An Anatomy of Extremism in Middle Eastern Politics." *Political Science Quarterly* 117 (Summer): 177–190.

Druckman, Daniel. 1986. "Stages, Turning Points, and Crisis." *Journal of Conflict Resolution* 30, no. 2 (June): 327–360.

————. 1997. "Negotiating in the International Context." In I. William Zartman and J. Lewis Rasmussen, eds., *Peacemaking in International Conflict: Methods and Techniques.* Washington, DC: U.S. Institute of Peace, 81–124.

————. 2001. "Turning Points in International Negotiation." *Journal of Conflict Resolution* 45, no. 4 (August): 519–544.

————. 2005. "Conflict Escalation and Negotiation: A Turning-Points Analysis." In I. William Zartman and Guy Olivier Faure, eds., *Escalation and Negotiation in International Conflicts.* New York: Cambridge University Press. 185–212.

Druckman, James N. 2004. "Political Preference Formation: Competition, Deliberation, and the (Ir)relevance of Framing Effects." *American Political Science Review* 98, no 4 (November): 671–686.

Dukitt, J. H. 1992. *The Social Psychology of Prejudice.* New York: Praeger.

Dupont, Christophe, and Guy-Oliver Faure. 2002. "The Negotiation Process." In Victor A. Kremenyuk, ed., *International Negotiation: Analysis, Approaches, Issues.* 2nd ed. San Francisco: Jossey-Bass, 39–63.

Duyvesteyn, Isabelle. 2004. "How New Is the New Terrorism?" *Studies in Conflict and Terrorism* 27: 439–454.

Easterly, William, Ross Levine, and David Roodman. 2004. "Aid, Policies, and Growth: Comment." *American Economic Review* 94, no. 3 (June): 774–780.

Eban, Abba. 1998. *Diplomacy for the Next Century.* New Haven, CT: Yale University Press.

Edwards, John. 2007. "Reengaging with the World." *Foreign Affairs* 86, no 5 (September–October): 19–37.

Eland, Ivan. 1998. "Does U.S. Intervention Overseas Breed Terrorism? The Historical Record." *Foreign Policy Briefings,* December 17. Washington, DC: CATO Institute.

———. N.d. "Excessive U.S. Military Action Overseas Breeds Anti-U.S. Terrorism." Unpublished Paper, CATO Institute.

Elster, Jon. 2004. "Kidnappings in Civil Wars." Paper presented at the Workshop on Techniques of Violence, Oslo, Norway, August 20–21.

Enders, Walter, and Todd Sandler. 1993. "The Effectiveness of Anti-Terrorism Policies: Vector-Autoregression-Intervention Analysis." *American Political Science Review* 87: 829–844.

———. 2000. "Is Transnational Terrorism Becoming More Threatening?" *Journal of Conflict Resolution* 44, no. 3 (June): 307–332.

Enders, Walter, Todd Sandler, and John Cauley. 1990. "UN Conventions, Technology, and Retaliation in the Fight against Terrorism: An Economic Evaluation." *Terrorism and Political Violence* 2, no. 1 (March): 83–105.

Engel, Richard. 2001. "Inside Al Qaeda: A Window into the World of Militant Islam and the Afghan Alumni." *Janes' International Security.* September 28. www.ujanes.com/security/international_security/news/misc/janes010928_1_html.

Escalante, Fabian. 2004. *The Cuba Project: CIA Covert Operations 1959–62.* Melbourne, Australia: Ocean Press.

Evans, Ernest. 1979. *Calling a Truce to Terror: The American Response to International Terrorism.* Westport, CT: Greenwood.

Etzioni, Amitai. 2004. *From Empire to Community: A New Approach to International Relations.* New York: Palgrave Macmillan.

Fallows, James. 2006. "Declaring Victory." *Atlantic* 298: 60–73.

Faour, Muhammad. 1993. *The Arab World after Desert Storm.* Washington, DC: U.S. Institute of Peace.

Farnham, Barbara, ed. 1994. *Avoiding Losses/Taking Risk: Prospect Theory and International Conflict.* Ann Arbor: University of Michigan Press.

Faure, Guy Oliver. 2003a. *How People Negotiate: Resolving Disputes in Different Cultures.* Dordrecht, The Netherlands: Kluwer Academic.

———. 2003b. "Negotiating with Terrorists: The Hostage Case." *International Negotiation* 8: 469–494.

Fayazmanesh, Sasan. 2003. "The Politics of the U.S. Economic Sanctions against Iran." *Review of Radical Political Economics* 35, no. 3 (Summer): 221–240.

Fearon, James D. 1995. "Rationalist Explanations for War." *International Organization* 49, no. 3: 379–414.

Fearon, James D., and David D. Laitin. 2003. "Ethnicity, Insurgency, and Civil War." *American Political Science Review* 97: 75–90.

Ferris, Gerald R., Robert Zinko, Robyn L. Brouer, M. Ronald Buckley, and Michael G. Harvey. 2007. "Strategic Bullying as a Supplementary, Balanced Perspective on Destructive Leadership." *Leadership Quarterly* 18: 195–206.

Feste, Karen A. 2003. *Intervention: Shaping the Global Order.* Westport, CT: Greenwood.

Filson, Darren, and Suzanne Werner. 2002. "A Bargaining Model of War and Peace: Anticipating the Onset, Duration, and Outcome of War." *American Journal of Political Science* 46, no. 4 (October): 819–838.

————. 2007. "The Dynamics of Bargaining and War." *International Interactions* 33: 31–50.

Fischer, Michael M. J. 1980. *Iran: From Religious Dispute to Revolution.* Cambridge, MA: Harvard University Press.

Fisher, Erik A., and Steven W. Sharp. 2004. *The Art of Managing Everyday Conflict.* Westport, CT: Praeger.

Fisher, Roger. 1964. "Fractionating Conflict." In Roger Fisher, ed., *International Conflict and Behavioral Science: The Craigville Papers.* New York: Basic Books, 91–109.

Fisher, Roger, and William Ury. 1981. *Getting to Yes: Negotiating Agreement without Giving In.* New York: Houghton Mifflin.

Fisher, Roger, William Ury, with Bruce Patton. 1991. *Getting to Yes: Negotiating Agreement without Giving In.* Second edition. New York: Penguin.

Fiske, Alan Page. 1991. *Structures of Social Life.* New York: Free Press.

Flavin, William. 2003. "Planning for Conflict Termination and Post-Conflict Success." *Parameters* (Autumn): 95–112.

Foley, Conor. 2006. "Talking to Terrorists." *Guardian,* September 12. http://commentisfree. guardian.co.uk/conor_foley/2006/09/why_not_talk_to_the_terrorist. Accessed May 15, 2008.

Follett, Mary P. 1940. "Constructive Conflict." In H. C. Metcalf and L. Urwich, eds., *Dynamic Administration: The Collective Papers of Mary Parker Follett.* New York: Harper and Row.

Fontaine, Roger W. 1975. *On Negotiating with Cuba.* Washington, DC: American Enterprise Institute.

Forde, Steven. 2004. "Thucydides on Ripeness and Conflict Resolution." *International Studies Quarterly* 48: 17–195.

Fortna, Virginia Page. 2003. "Scraps of Paper? Agreements and the Durability of Peace." *International Organization* 57 (Spring): 337–372.

————. 2004. *Peace Time: Cease-Fire Agreements and the Durability of Peace.* Princeton, NJ: Princeton University Press.

Fox, William T. R. 1970. "The Causes of Peace and Conditions of War." *Annals of the American Academy of Political and Social Science* 392 (November): 1–13.

Freeman, Joanne B. 2001. *Chronicle of Higher Education* (September 28): *Chronicle Review,* B6.

Frieden, Jeffrey A., and David A. Lake. 2005. "International Relations as a Social Science: Rigor and Relevance." *Annals of the American Academy of Political and Social Science* 600 (July): 136–156.

Friedland, Nehemia, and Ariel Merari. 1992. "Hostage Events: Descriptive Profile and Analysis of Outcomes." *Journal of Applied Social Psychology* 22, no. 2: 134–156.

Friedman, Brandon. 2008. "Lurching toward Negotiations with the Taliban." October 9. http:// www.vetvoice.com/showDiary.do?diaryID=2016&view=print. Accessed July 30, 2009.

Fromkin, David. 1975. "The Strategy of Terrorism." *Foreign Affairs* 53 (July): 683–698.

Frum, David, and Richard Perle. 2003. *An End to Evil: How to Win the War on Terror.* New York: Random House.

Fry, Earl H. 2007. "The Decline of the American Superpower." *The Forum: A Journal of Applied Research in Contemporary Politics* 5, no. 2: Article 3.

Fuller, Graham E. 2004. "Terrorism: Sources and Cures." In Adam Garfinkle, ed., *A Practical Guilde to Winning the War on Terrorism.* Stanford, CA: Hoover Institution Press, 19–25.

Fund for Peace. "Failed State Index." http://www.fundforpeace.org/web/index.phhp?option.

Gaddis, John Lewis. 2001. "And Now This: Lessons from the Old Era for the New One." In

Strobe Talbott, Strobe and Nayan Chanda, eds., *The Age of Terror: America and the World after September 11*. New York: Basic Books, 3–21.

Garfinkle, Adam. 2004. *A Practical Guide to Winning the War on Terrorism*. Stanford, CA: Hoover Institution Press.

Gates, Robert. 1997. *From the Shadows*. New York: Simon and Shuster.

Gauss, F. Gregory. 1994. *Oil Monarchies: Domestic and Security Challenges in the Arab Gulf States*. New York: Council on Foreign Relations.

George, Alexander, D. K. Hall, and W. Simons. 1972. *The Limits of Coercive Diplomacy*. Boston: Little, Brown.

Gerges, Fawaz A. 2005. *The Far Enemy: Why Jihad Went Global*. New York: Cambridge University Press.

Gerring, John. 2004. "What Is a Case Study and What Is It Good for?" *American Political Science Review* 98, no. 2 (May): 341–354.

Gerson, Allan, and Jerry Adler. 2001. *The Price of Terror: One Bomb. One Plane. 270 Lives. The History-Making Struggle for Justice after Pan-Am 103*. New York: HarperCollins.

Gilbert, Martin. 2002. "Superman Versus Lex Luther: British Anti-Americanism since September 11." *World Policy Journal* 19 (Summer): 88–92.

Giuliani, Rudolph. 2007. "Toward a Realistic Peace." *Foreign Affairs* 86, no. 5 (September–October): 1–18.

Gladwell, Malcolm. 2002. *The Tipping Point: How Little Things Can Make a Big Difference*. Boston: Little, Brown.

Goldfarb, Jeffrey C. 2002. "Losing Our Best Allies in the War on Terror." *New York Times*, August 8, op-ed. http://www.nytimes.com/2002/08/20/opinion/20GOLD.html?todaysheadlines.

Gongol, Brian. "When to Negotiate with Terrorists, Hijackers, and Kidnappers." www.gongol. com/research/negotiationwithterrorists. Accessed February 24, 2006.

Gonos, George. 1977. "'Situation' versus 'Frame': The 'Interactionist' and the 'Structuralist' Analyses of Everyday Life." *American Sociological Review* 42, no. 6 (December): 854–867.

Goodenough, Patrick. 1999. "Was Iran behind Lockerbie?" Conservative News Service. April 6. www.conservativenews.net/InDepth/archive/199904/IND199. Accessed April 19, 2006.

———. 2005. "German Trade-Off Suspected in Release of Terrorist Killer." *CNS News. Com*. December 22. www.cnsnews.com/ViewForeignBureaus.asp. Accessed April 4, 2006.

Goodwin, Richard N. 1961a. "Memorandum from the President's Assistant Special Counsel (Goodwin) to President Kennedy." U.S. Department of State. Office of the Historian. Foreign Relations of the United States 1961–1963. Vol. 10. Cuba. Document 256 (August 22).

———. 1961b. "Memorandum from the President's Assistant Special Counsel (Goodwin) to President Kennedy." U.S. Department of State. Office of the Historian. Foreign Relations of the United States 1961–1963. Vol. 10. Cuba. Document 258 (September 1).

Gower, Barry. 1997. *Scientific Method: An Historical and Philosophical Introduction*. London: Routledge.

Gray, B. 1997. "Framing and Reframing of Intractable Environmental Disputes." In R. J. Lewicki, R. J. Bies, and B. Sheppard, eds., *Research on Negotiation in Organization*. Vol. 6. Greenwich, CT: Jai Press. 163–188.

———. 2003. "Framing of Environmental Disputes." In R. J. Lewicki, B. Gray, and M. Elliott, eds. *Making Sense of Intractable Environmental Disputes*. Washington, DC: Island.

Greenhalgh, Leonard. 1987. "In Theory: Relationships in Negotiation." *Negotiation Journal* (July): 235–243.

————. 2001. *Managing Strategic Relationships: The Key to Business Success.* New York: Free Press.

Greenstein, Jonathan S. 2008. "Terrorism as a Rent Generator for the State." *New Society Journal.* http://newsocietyjournal.com/2008/01/29/terrorism-as-a-rent-generator-for-the-state. Accessed February 26, 2008.

Grieg, J. Michael. 2001. "Moments of Opportunity: Recognizing Conditions of Ripeness for International Mediation between Enduring Rivals." *Journal of Conflict Resolution* 45, no. 6 (December): 691–718.

Grieg, J. Michael, and Paul F. Diehl. 2006. "Softening Up: Making Conflicts More Amenable to Diplomacy." *International Interactions* 32: 355–384.

Guerrero, Laura K., and Angela G. LaValley. 2006. "Conflict, Emotion, and Communication." In John G. Oetzel and Stella Ting-Toomey, eds., *The Sage Handbook of Conflict Communication: Integrating Theory, Research, and Practice.* Thousand Oaks, CA: Sage, 69–96.

Gunaratna, Rohan. 2002. *Inside Al Qaeda: Global Network of Terror.* New York: Berkeley.

————. 2007. "Strategic Counter-Terrorism: Getting Ahead of Terrorism Part II: The Ideological Response." Tufts University Jebsen Center for Counter-Terrorism Studies Research-Briefing Series 2, no. 2 (November).

————. 2008. "Strategic Counter-Terrorism: Getting Ahead of Terrorism Part III Mass Media Response to Terrorism." Tufts University Jebsen Center for Counter-Terrorism Studies Research-Briefing Series 3, no. 1 (January).

Gurr, Ted. 1970. *Why Men Rebel.* Princeton, NJ: Princeton University Press.

Gwertzman, Bernard. 1981. "How Hostage Pact Was Forged: Turning Point in September." *New York Times,* January 28.

Haass, Richard N. 1990. *Conflict Unending: The United States and Regional Disputes.* New Haven, CT: Yale University Press.

————. 1995. "Military Intervention: A Taxonomy of Challenges and Responses." In Aspen Strategy Group, ed., *The United States and the Use of Force in the Post–Cold War Era.* Queenstown, MD: Aspen Institute, 1–18.

Habeeb, William Mark. 1988. *Power and Tactics in International Negotiation: How Weak Nations Bargain with Strong Nations.* Baltimore: Johns Hopkins University Press.

Hagel, Chuck. 2007. "A Less American Face for Mediation in Iraq." *Financial Times,* July 3. http://hagel.senate.gov/index.cfm. Accessed August 28, 2007.

Hammel, Eric. 1985. *The Root: The Marines in Beirut, August 1982–February 1984.* New York: Harcourt Brace Jovanovich.

Hammond, Kenneth R. 2000. *Judgment under Stress.* New York: Oxford University Press.

Hamner, W. C., and G. A. Yukl. 1977. "The Effectiveness of Bargaining Strategy and Pressure to Reach Agreement in a Stalemated Negotiation." In Daniel Druckman, ed., *Negotiations: Social-Psychological Perspectives.* Beverly Hills, CA: Sage.

Hampson, Fen Osler. 2006. "The Risks of Peace: Implications for International Mediation." *Negotiation Journal* (January): 13–30.

Hancock, Landon. E. 2001. "To Act or Wait: A Two-Stage View of Ripeness." *International Studies Perspectives* 2: 195–205.

Harik, Judith Palmer. 2004. *Hezbollah: The Changing Face of Terrorism.* London: Tauris.

Harnett, D. C. et al. 1973. "Personality, Bargaining Style, and Payoff in International Bargaining." *Sociometry* 36: 325–345.

Harsanyi, John C. 1965. "Bargaining and Conflict Situations in the Light of a New Approach." *American Economic Review* 55: 447–457.

Hartman, Phillip. 2002. "The War on Terrorism: Phase Two or Phase Ridiculous?" *Intervention Magazine Online.* June 28. http://www.interventionmag.com.

Harvard Negotiation Project. 2006. "The Iranian Hostage Conflict." http://www.pon.harvard.edu/hnp/iran/iranmain.shtml. Accessed June 10, 2008.

Harwood, Charles Judson. 2003. "Beirut 1983–1984: Judicial Theft?" http://homepage.ntlworld.com/jksonc/Beirut–1980s.html. Accessed February 5, 2005.

Hayes, Richard E. 2002. "Negotiating with Terrorists." Victor A. Kremenyuk, ed., *International Negotiation: Analysis, Approaches, Issues.* 2nd ed. San Francisco: Jossey-Bass.

Hayes, Richard E., Stacey R. Kaminski, and Steven M. Beres. 2003. "Negotiating the Non-Negotiable: Dealing with Absolute Terrorists." *International Negotiation* 8: 451–467.

Hayes, Richard E. et al. 2006. "Negotiating Large-Scale Terrorist Initiated Hostage Events." Paper presented at the International Institute for Applied Systems Analysis, Vienna, June 9–10.

Heise, David R. 1975. *Causal Analysis.* New York: Wiley.

Henrikson, Alan K. 1991. "Mental Maps." In Michael J. Hogan and Thomas G. Paterson, eds., *Explaining the History of American Foreign Relations.* New York: Cambridge University Press, 177–192.

Hersh, Seymour M. 1991. "The Iran Pipeline: A Hidden Chapter/A Special Report; U.S. Said to Have Allowed Israel to Sell Arms to Iran." *New York Times,* December 8.

———. 2006. "The Iran Plans: Would President Bush Go to War to Stop Teheran from Getting the Bomb?" *New Yorker* (April 17): 30–38.

Hertzberg, Hendrik. 2007. "Sparring Partners (The Talk of the Town) (Hillary Clinton and Barack Obama)." *New Yorker* (August 20): 23.

Hewitt, Gavin. 1991. *Terry Waite and Ollie North: The Untold Story of the Kidnapping and the Release.* Boston: Little, Brown.

"Hijacking Accord between the United States and Cuba." 1973. *Hearings before the Sub-Committee on InterAmerican Affairs of the Committee on Foreign Affairs House of Representatives.* 93rd Cong., 1st session. Washington, DC: Government Printing Office. February 20.

Hill, Charles. 2001. "A Herculean Task: The Myth and Reality of Arab Terrorism." In Strobe Talbott and Nayan Chanda, eds., *The Age of Terror: America and the World after September 11.* New York: Basic Books, 83–111.

Hiro, Dilip. 1991. *The Longest War: The Iran-Iraq Military Conflict.* New York: Routledge.

Hoffman, Abbie, and Jonathan Silvers. 1988. "An Election Held Hostage." *Playboy* (October).

Hoffman, Bruce. 1989a. "U.S. Policy Options in the Hostage Crisis in Lebanon." RAND Corporation Report P-7585. Santa Monica, CA: RAND.

———. 1989b. "World Taken Hostages." *Los Angeles Herald Examiner,* August 6.

———. 1998. *Inside Terrorism.* New York: Columbia University Press.

———. 1999. "Terrorism Trends and Prospects." In Ian O. Lesser, Bruce Hoffman, John Arguilla, David Ronfeldt, and Michele Zanini, eds., *Countering the New Terrorism.* Santa Monica, CA: RAND, 7–38.

Hoffman, John E. 1985. "The Bankers' Channel." In Warren Christopher et al., *American Hostages in Iran: The Conduct of a Crisis.* New Haven, CT: Yale University Press, 235–280.

Hoffmann, Stanley. 2001. "Why Don't They Like Us?" *American Prospect 12, 20* (November 19). 18–21.

———. 2002. "Clash of Globalizations." *Foreign Affairs* 81 (July–August): 104–115.

Holden, Robert T. 2003. "The Contagiousness of Aircraft Hijacking." http://pegasus.cc.ucf.edu~surette/hacking.html. Accessed February 15, 2005.

Hollis, Martin, and Steve Smith. 1994. "Two Stories about Structure and Agency." *Review of International Studies* 20, no. 3: 241–251.

Holmes, Mary. 2004. "Introduction: The Importance of Being Angry: Anger in Political Life." *European Journal of Social Theory* 7, no. 2: 123–132.

Holsti, Ole R. 1967. "Cognitive Dynamics and Images of the Enemy." In John C. Farrell and Asa P. Smith, eds., *Image and Reality in World Politics.* New York: Columbia University Press, 16–39.

Holzinger, Katharina. 2004. "Bargaining through Arguing: An Empirical Analysis Based on Speech Act Theory." *Political Comunication* 21: 195–222.

Honegger, Barbara. 1989. *October Surprise.* New York: Tudor.

Hopmann, P. Terrence. 1995. "Two Paradigms of Negotiation: Bargaining and Problem Solving." *Annals of the American Academy of Political and Social Science* 542 (November): 24–47.

———. 2001. "Bargaining and Problem Solving: Two Perspectives on International Negotiation." In Chester A. Crocker, Fen Osler Hampson, and Pamela Aal, eds., *Turbulent Peace: The Challenges of Managing International Conflict.* Washington, DC: U.S. Institute of Peace, 445–468.

Houghton, David Patrick. 2001. *U.S. Foreign Policy and the Iran Hostage Crisis.* Cambridge: Cambridge University Press.

Howard, Nigel. 1999. *Confrontation Analysis: How to Win Operations Other than War.* Washington, DC: U.S. Department of Defense.

Hubbard, David G. 1971. *The Skyjacker: His Flights of Fantasy.* New York: Macmillan.

Hughes, M. 1990. "Terror and Negotiation." *Terrorism and Political Violence* 2, no. 1: 72–82.

Human Rights Watch. 2008. "Egypt: Jailing 800 Activists Casts Doubt on Elections." http:// hrw.org/english/docs/2008/03/30/egypt18397_txt.htm. Accessed August 18, 2008.

Huntington, Samuel. 1998. *The Clash of Civilizations and the Remaking of World Order.* New York: Simon and Schuster.

Hussain, Zahid. 2007. *Frontline Pakistan: The Struggle with Militant Islam.* New York: Columbia University Press.

Iklé, Fred Charles. 1964. *How Nations Negotiate.* New York: Harper and Row.

Iklé, Fred Charles. and Nathan Leites. 1962. "Political Negotiation as a Process of Modifying Utilities." *Journal of Conflict Resolution* 6, no. 1 (March): 19–28.

Institute of International Economics. 2005. "Case Studies in Sanctions and Terrorism." Case 84–1, *U.S. v. Iran* (1984–: Terrorism, Proliferation). www.iie.com/research/topics/sanctions/ iran.htm. Accessed February 5, 2006.

"Iran Hostage Crisis." http://sheppardsoftward.com/Middleeastweb/factfile/Unique-facts-MiddleEast 9.htm. Accessed July 22, 2008.

Irmer, Cynthia, and Daniel Druckman. 2009. "Explaining Negotiation Outcomes: Process or Context?" *Negotiation and Conflict Management Research* 2, no. 3 (August): 209–235.

Jackson, Richard. 2000. "Successful Negotiation in Violent Conflict." *Journal of Peace Research* 37, no. 3: 323–343.

Jacobsen, David. 1993. *My Life as a Hostage: The Nightmare in Beirut.* New York: Shapolsky.

Jehn, Karen, and Keith Weigelt. 1999. "Chinese Thought, Game Theory, and Strategic International Negotiations." *International Negotiation* 4: 79–93.

Jensen, Lloyd. 1963. "Soviet-American Bargaining Behavior in the Postwar Disarmament Negotiations." *Journal of Conflict Resolution* 7, no. 3: 522–541.

Jervis, Robert. 1999. "Introduction." In Demetrios James Caraley, ed., *The New American*

Interventionism: Essays from Political Science Quarterly. New York: Columbia University Press, 1–7.

Joffe, Josef. 2002. "One Year On: A September 11 Anniversary Symposium: Of Hubs, Spokes, and Public Goods." *National Interest* 69 (Fall): 17–20.

Johnson, Chalmers. 2000. *Blowback: The Cost and Consequences of American Empire*. New York: Holt.

———. 2004. *The Sorrows of Empire: Militarism, Secrecy, and the End of the Republic*. New York: Holt.

Johnson, David W., and Roger T. Johnson. 2000. "Civil Political Discourse in a Democracy: The Contributions of Psychology." *Peace and Conflict: Journal of Peace Psychology* 6, no. 4 (May): 291–317.

Johnson, Dominic D. P., and Dominic Tierney. 2006. *Failing to Win: Perceptions of Victory and Defeat in International Politics*. Cambridge, MA: Harvard University Press.

Jones, D. M., M. L. R. Smith, and M. Weeding. 2003. "Looking for the Pattern: Al Qaeda in Southeast Asia—the Genealogy of a Terror Network." *Studies in Conflict and Terrorism* 26 (November–December): 443–457.

Jones, Seth G., and Martin C. Libicki. 2008. *How Terrorist Groups End: Lessons for Countering al Qa'ida*. Santa Monica, CA: RAND.

Jordan, Hamilton. 1982. *Crisis: the Last Days of the Carter Presidency*. New York: Putnam.

Joyner, Nancy Douglas. 1974. *Aerial Hijacking as an International Crime*. Dobbs Ferry, NY: Oceana.

Judt, Tony. 2008. *Reappraisals: Reflections on the Forgotten Twentieth Century*. New York: Penguin.

Kahneman, Daniel, and Amos Tversky. 1979. "Prospect Theory: An Analysis of Decisions under Risk." *Econometrica* 47: 263–292.

———. 1983. "Choice, Values, and Frames." *American Psychologist* 39, no. 4 (April): 341–350.

———. 1995. "Conflict Resolution: A Cognitive Perspective." In Kenneth J. Arrow, ed., *Barriers to Conflict Resolution*. New York: Norton.

Kahneman, Daniel and Amos Tversky, eds. 2000. *Choice, Values, and Frames*. New York: Cambridge University Press.

Kalyvas, Stathis N. 2001. "'New' and 'Old' Civil Wars: A Valid Distinction?" *World Politics* 54 (October): 99–118.

Karmon, Ely. 2002. "The Risk of Terrorism against Oil and Gas Pipelines in Central Asia." www.ict.org.il/articles/articledet.cfm?articleid=426. Accessed April 26, 2006.

Karoui, Hichem. 2002. "Iskandar Safa and the French Hostage Scandal." *Middle East Intelligence Bulletin* 4, no. 2 (February).

Katzman, Kenneth. 2000. "Iran: U.S. Policy and Options." CRS Report for Congress. January 14. Washington, DC: Congressional Research Service.

———. 2002. "Terrorism: New Eastern Groups and State Sponsors, 2002." CRS Report for Congress. February 13. Washington, D.C.: Congressional Research Service.

———. 2006. "Iran: U.S. Concerns and Policy Responses." CRS Report for Congress. April 6. Washington, DC: Congressional Research Service.

Kaufman, Stuart. J. 2006. "Symbolic Politics or Rational Choice? Testing Theories of Extreme Ethnic Violence." *International Security* 30, no. 4 (Spring): 45–86.

Kean, Thomas H., and Lee H. Hamilton, *The 9/11 Report: The National Commission on Terrorist Attacks Upon the United States*. New York: St. Martin's.

Keen, Sam. 1986. *Faces of the Enemy: Reflections of the Hostile Imagination*. New York: Harper and Row.

Kelman, Herbert C. 1997. "Social-Psychological Dimensions of International Conflict." In I. William Zartman and Lewis Rasmusen, eds., *Peacemaking in International Conflict: Methods and Techniques*. Washington, DC: U.S. Institute of Peace.

Kennedy, D. B. 2006. "A Précis of Suicide Terrorism." *Journal of Homeland Security and Emergency Management* 3: 1–7.

Kent, Mike. 2006. "Talking to Terrorists?" *On-Line Opinion: Australia's e-journal of Social and Political Debate*. January 6. http://www.onlineopinion.com. Accessed August 20, 2007.

Kiel, L. Douglas, and Euel W. Elliott. 1997. *Chaos Theory in the Social Sciences*. Ann Arbor: University of Michigan Press.

Killen, Andreas. 2005. "The First Hijackers." *New York Times Sunday Magazine*. (January 16) 22–24.

Kim, Chae-Han. 2005. "Reciprocity in Asymmetry: When Does Reciprocity Work?" *International Interactions* 31: 1–14.

Kim, Peter H., Robin L. Pinkley, and Alison R. Fragale. 2005. "Power Dynamics in Negotiation." *Academy of Management Review* 30: 799–822.

Kim, Sung Hee. 2005. "The Role of Vengeance in Conflict Escalation." In I. William Zartman and Guy O. Faure, eds., *Escalation and Negotiation in International Conflicts*. New York: Cambridge University Press, 141–160.

Kissinger, Henry. 1999. *Years of Renewal*. New York: Simon and Schuster.

Kleiboer, Marieke. 1994. "Ripeness of Conflict: A Fruitful Notion?" *Journal of Peace Research* 31, no. 1: 109–116.

———. 1996. "Understanding Success and Failure of International Mediation." *Journal of Conflict Resolution* 40, no. 2 (June): 360–389.

Kolb, Deborah M., and Judith Williams. 2001. "Breakthrough Bargaining." *Harvard Business Review* 6080 (February): 87–107.

Kraft, Michael. 2008. "Imad Mughniyeh: How He Held America Hostage." *Counter-Terrorism Blog*. February 14. http://counterterrorismblog.org/2008/02/imad_mughniyeh_how_he_held_ame.php. Accessed July 30, 2008.

Kremenyuk, Victor A. 2002. "The Emerging System of International Negotiation." In Victor A. Kremenyuk, ed., *International Negotiation: Analysis, Approaches, Issues*. 2nd ed. San Francisco: Jossey-Bass, 22–38.

Kriesberg, Louis. 2003. *Constructive Conflicts: From Escalation to Resolution*. 2nd ed. Lanham, MD: Rowman and Littlefield.

Kruglanski, Arie W., and Shira Fishman. 2006. "The Psychology of Terrorism: 'Syndrome' versus 'Tool' Perspective." *Terrorism and Political Violence* 18: 193–215.

Kupchan, Charles A. 2002. "One Year On: A September 11 Anniversary Symposium: Misreading September 11th." *National Interest* 69 (Fall): 26–30.

Kuvaas, Bård, and Marcus Selart. 2004. "Effects of Attribute Framing on Cognitive Processing and Evaluation." *Organizational Behavior and Human Decision Processes* 95, no. 2: 198–207.

Kydd, Andrew, and Barbara Walter. 2006. "The Strategies of Terrorism." *International Security* 31, no 1 (Summer): 49–80.

Labévière, Richard. 2000. *Dollars for Terror: The United States and Islam*. Translated by Martin DeMers. New York: Algora.

Lacey, Jim, ed. 2008. *A Terrorist's Call to Global Jihad: Deciphering Abu Musab Al-Suri's Islamic Jihad Manifesto*. Annapolis, MD: Naval Institute Press.

Laffey, Mark, and Jutta Weldes. 2008. "Decolonizing the Cuban Missile Crisis." *International Studies Quarterly* 52, no. 3 (August): 555–577.

Lakoff, George. 2008. *The Political Mind*. New York: Viking.

Landes, William. 1978. "An Economic Study of U.S. Aircraft Hijackings, 1961–1976." *Journal of Law and Economics* 21, no. 1 (April): 1–31.

Lapan, Harvey E., and Todd Sandler. 1988. "To Bargain or Not to Bargain: That Is the Question." *American Economic Review* 78, no 2 (May): 16–21.

Laqueur, Walter. 1987. *The Age of Terrorism*. Boston: Little, Brown.

Laue, James H. 1991. "Contributions of the Emerging Field of Conflict Resolution." In W. Scott Thompson and Kenneth M. Jenson, eds., *Approaches to Peace: An Intellectual Map*. Washington, DC: U.S. Institute of Peace.

"Lebanon—Party of God." 2003. *PBS Frontline*. May. www.pbs.org/frontlineworld/stories/lebanon. Accessed April 16, 2006.

Ledeen, Michael. 2002. *The War against the Terror Masters: Why It Happened. Where We Are Now. How We'll Win*. New York: St. Martin's.

Lehrer, Jonah. 2009. *How We Decide*. New York: Houghton Mifflin Harcourt.

Leng, Russell J., and Stephen G. Walker. 1982. "Comparing Two Studies of Crisis Bargaining." *Journal of Conflict Resolution* 26, no. 4 (December): 571–591.

Lepgold, Joseph, and Alan C. Lamborn. 2001. "Locating Bridges: Connecting Research Agendas on Cognition and Strategic Choice." *International Studies Review* 3, no. 3: 3–29.

Lesser, Ian O. 1999a. "Countering the New Terrorism: Implications for Strategy." In I. O. Lesser et al., eds., *Countering the New Terrorism*. Santa Monica, CA: RAND, 85–144.

———. 1999b. "Introduction." In I. O. Lesser et al., eds., *Countering the New Terrorism*. Santa Monica, CA: RAND, 1–6.

Lesser, Ian O., Bruce Hoffman, John Arquilla, David Ronfeldt, and Michele Zanini, eds. 1999. *Countering the New Terrorism*. Santa Monica, CA: RAND.

Levinson, J. C., M. S. A. Smith, and O. R. Wilson. 1999. *Guerrilla Negotiating: Unconventional Weapons and Tatics to Get What You Want*. New York: Wiley.

Levy, Jack. 1994. "Prospect Theory and International Relations: Theoretical Applications and Analytical Problems." In Barbara Farnham, ed., *Avoiding Losses / Taking Risks: Prospect Theory and International Conflict*. Ann Arbor: University of Michigan Press, 119–146.

Lewicki, Roy J., David M. Saunders, and Bruce Barry. 2006. *Negotiation*. 5th ed. New York: McGraw-Hill.

Lewis, Bernard. 2002. *What Went Wrong? Western Impact and Middle East Response*. New York: Oxford University Press.

Lewis, David. 2003. "Interview with David Lewis: Negotiating with Hezbollah." *PBS Frontline*. June. www.pbs.org/frontlineworld/stories/lebanon. Accessed April 6, 2006.

Lewis, Neil A. 1991. "A Book Asserts Reagan Slowed Hostage Release." *New York Times,* November 8.

Lexington Institute. 2003. "Cuba Policy Report." July 23. www.lexingtoninstitute.org/cuba/newsletter/030724newsletter. Accessed July 21, 2005.

Li, Quan, and Drew Schaub. 2003. "Economic Globalization and Transnational Terrorist Incidents: A Pooled Time-Series Cross-Sectional Analysis." Paper presented at the Annual Meeting of the International Studies Association, February, Portland, Oregon.

Lichfield, Gideon. 2007. "Explaining the Terrorists." *Foreign Affairs* 86, no 5 (September–October): 191–192.

Licklider, Roy. 1995. "The Consequences of Negotiated Settlement in Civil Wars, 1945–1993." *American Political Science Review* 89, no. 3 (September): 681–690.

Lieberfeld, Daniel. 1999. *Talking with the Enemy: Negotiation and Threat Perception in South Africa and Israel / Palestine*. Westport, CT: Praeger.

Lipsky, Michael. 1968. "Protest as a Political Resource." *American Political Science Review* 62, no. 4 (December): 1144–1158.

Lockhart, Charles.1977. "Problems in the Management and Resolution of International Conflicts." *World Politics* 29, no. 3 (April): 370–403.

Lowenfeld, A. F. 1972. *Aviation Law: Cases and Materials.* Albany, NY: Bender.

Luft, Gal. 2002. "The Palestinian H-Bomb: Terror's Winning Strategy." *Foreign Affairs* 81 (July–August): 2–7.

Lum, C., L. W. Kennedy, and A. J. Sherley. 2006. "The Effectiveness of Counter-Terrorism Strategies: A Campbell Systematic Review." New Brunswick, NJ: Rutgers University School of Criminal Justice and Center for the Study of Public Security.

Lyman, Peter. 2004. "The Domestication of Anger: The Use and Abuse of Anger in Politics." *European Journal of Social Theory* 7, no. 2: 133–147.

Mack, Andrew. 1975. "Why Big Nations Lose Small Wars: The Politics of Asymmetric Conflict." *World Politics* 27, no. 2: 175–200.

Magnuson, Ed. 1983. "Arms for the Ayatullah." *Time.* http://www.time.com/time/magazine/article/0,9171,953997,00.html. Accessed July 24, 2008.

Mahieu, Silvie. 2007. "When Should Mediators Interrupt a Civil War? The Best Timing for a Ceasefire." *International Negotiation* 12, no. 2: 207–228.

Malhotra, Deepak. 2009. "Without Conditions." *Foreign Affairs* 88, 5 (September-October). 84–90.

Mansfield, Laura. 2006. *His Own Words: A Translation of the Writings of Dr. Ayman Al Zawahiri.* TLG publications.

Maoz, Zeev. 1983. "Resolve, Capabilities, and the Outcomes of Interstate Disputes, 1816–1976." *Journal of Conflict Resolution* 27, no. 2 (June): 195–229.

March, James, and Johan P. Olsen. 1998. "The Institutional Dynamics of International Political Orders." *International Organization* 52: 943–969.

Mark, Clyde R. 1992. "Lebanon: U.S. Hostages, An Overview and Chronology, February 10, 1984–December 27, 1991." CRS Report for Congress. April 7.

Marsella, Anthony. 2004. "Reflections on International Terrorism: Issues, Concepts and Directions." In Fathali Moghaddam and Anthony Marcella, eds., *Understanding Terrorism: Psychological Roots, Consequences, and Interventions.* Washington, DC: American Psychological Association.

Martinez, Michael L., and Stuart H. Newberger. 2002. "Combating State-Sponsored Terrorism with Civil Lawsuits: *Anderson v. Islamic Republic of Iran* and Other Cases." *Victim Advocate: The Journal of the National Crime Victim Bar Association* 3, no. 4 (Spring–Summer): 5–8.

Mason, T. David. 2007. *Sustaining the Peace after Civil War.* Carlisle, PA: U.S. Army War College.

Mason, T. David, Joseph P. Wingarten Jr., and Patrick J. Fett. 1999. "Win, Lose, or Draw: Predicting the Outcomes of Civil Wars." *Political Research Quarterly* 52, no. 2 (June): 239–268.

Mayer, Bernard. 2000. *The Dynamics of Conflict Resolution: A Practitioner's Guide.* San Francisco: Jossey-Bass.

———. 2004. "Beyond Neutrality." July. www.mediate.com/articles/mayerB1.cfm?nl=57. Accessed August 17, 2004.

McCauley, Clark. 2002. "Psychological Issues in Understanding Terrorism and the Response to Terrorism." In Chris E. Stout, ed., *The Psychology of Terrorism,* vol. 3: *Theoretical Understandings and Perspectives.* Westport, CT: Praeger, 3–29.

McDermott, Rose. 1994. "Prospect Theory in International Relations: The Iranian Hostage

Rescue Mission." In Barbara Farnham, ed., *Avoiding Losses/Taking Risks: Prospect Theory and International Conflict*. Ann Arbor: University of Michigan Press, 73–100.

McGrath, Mary Jo. 2007. *School Bullying: Tools for Avoiding Harm and Liability*. Thousand Oaks, CA: Corwin.

McInerny, D. Q. 2005. *Being Logical: A Guide to Good Thinking*. New York: Random House.

McWhinney, Edward. 1987. *Aerial Piracy and International Terrorism: The Illegal Diversion of Aircraft and International Law*. Second edition. Boston: Martinus Nijhoff.

Mead, Walter Russell. 2004. *Power, Terror, Peace, and War: America's Grand Strategy in a World at Risk*. New York: Knopf.

Meany, John. 2008. *Should We Ever Negotiate with Terrorists?* Oxford, UK: Heinemann Library, Harcourt Education.

Mearsheimer, John J. 2002. "One Year On: A September 11 Anniversary Symposium: Hearts and Minds." *National Interest* 69 (Fall): 13–16.

Mercer, Jonathan. 2005. "Rationality and Psychology in International Politics." *International Organization* 59 (Winter): 77–106.

Metz, Helen Chapin, ed. 1987. *Iran: A Country Study*. Washington, DC: Government Printing Office.

Mickolus, Edward F. 1980. *Transnational Terrorism: A Chronology of Events, 1968–1979*. Westport, CT: Greenwood.

———. 1993. *Terrorism: A Chronology of Events and a Selectively Annotated Bibliography*. Westport, CT: Greenwood.

Mickolus, Edward F., T. Sandler, and J. M. Murdock. 1989a. *International Terrorism in the 1980s: A Chronology of Events*, vol. 1: *1980–1983*. Ames: Iowa State University Press.

———. 1989b. *International Terrorism in the 1980s: A Chronology of Events*, vol. 2, *1984–1987*. Ames: Iowa State University Press.

Mickolus, Edward F., with Susan L. Simmons. 1997. *Terrorism, 1992–1995: A Chronology of Events and a Selectively Annotated Bibliography*. Westport, CT: Greenwood.

———. 2002. *Terrorism, 1996–2001: A Chronology, Volumes I and II*. Westport, CT: Greenwood.

Mill, John Stuart. 1984. *Essays on Equality, Law, and Education*. Edited by John M. Robson and Stefan Collini. Toronto: University of Toronto Press.

Miller, Abraham H. 1980. *Terrorism and Hostage Negotiations*. Boulder, CO: Westview.

Miller, Gregory D. 2007. "Confronting Terrorisms: Group Motivation and Successful State Policies." *Terrorism and Political Violence* 19: 331–350.

Miller, Reuben. 1986. "Acts of International Terrorism: Governments' Responses and Policies." *Comparative Political Studies* 19, no. 3 (October): 385–414.

Mintz, Alex. 1997. "Foreign Policy Decision Making: Bridging the Gap between the Cognitive Psychology and Rational Actor Schools." In Nehemia Geva and Alex Mintz, eds., *Decision Making on War and Peace: The Cognitive-Rational Debate*. Boulder, CO: Lynne Rienner, 1–7.

———. 2003. "The Decision to Attack Iraq: A Noncompensatory Theory of Decision-Making." In Gary Goertz and Harvey Starr, eds., *Necessary Conditions: Theory, Methodology, and Applications*. Lanham, MD: Rowman and Littlefield, 277–294.

Mintz, Alex, Nehemia Geva, and Karl Derouen Jr. 1994. "Mathematical Models of Foreign Policy Decision-Making: Compensatory vs. Noncompensatory." *Syntheses* 100, no. 3 (September): 441–460.

Mintz, Alex, Nehemia Geva, Steven Redd, and Army Carnes. 1997. "The Effect of Dynamic Vs. Static Choice Sets on Strategy and Outcome in Political Decision Making." *American Political Science Review* 91: 553–566.

Mitchell, Christopher R. 1991a. "A Willingness to Talk: Conciliatory Gestures and De-Escalation." *Negotiation Journal* 7: 405–430.

———. 1991b. "Ending Conflicts and Wars: Judgment, Rationality and Entrapment." *International Social Science Journal.* 127 (February): 35–55.

———. 2000. *Gestures of Conciliation: Factors Contributing to Successful Olive Branches.* New York: St. Martin's.

Mitchell, Luke. 2004. "A Run on Terror." *Harpers* (March): 79–81.

Mnookin, Robert H. 2001. "Afghanistan: Negotiating in the Face of Terrorism." Remarks, Program on Negotiation Open House, Harvard University, November 13.

Moghaddam, Fathali M. 2006. *From the Terrorists' Point of View: What They Experience and Why They Come to Destroy.* Westport, CT: Praeger.

Moin, Baqer. 2000. *Khomeini: Life of the Ayatollah.* New York: St. Martin's Press, Thomas Dunne Books.

Mooradian, Moorad, and Daniel Druckman. 1999. "Hurting Stalemate or Mediation? The Conflict over Nagorno-Karabakh, 1990–1995." *Journal of Peace Research* 36, no. 6 (November): 709–727.

Mor, Ben D. 2007. "The Heuristic Use of Game Theory: Insights for Conflict Resolution." *World Political Science Review* 3, no. 2: 1–26. http://www.bepress.com/wpsr/vol3/iss2/art3. Accessed July 13, 2007.

Morgan, T. Clifton. 1994. *Untying the Knot of War: A Bargaining Theory of International Crisis.* Ann Arbor: University of Michigan Press.

Morrow, James D. 1989. "Capabilities, Uncertainty, and Resolve: A Limited Information Model of Crisis Bargaining." *American Journal of Political Science* 33, no. 4 (November): 941–972.

Moshiri, Farrokh. 1991. "Iran: Islamic Revolution against Westernization." In Jack Goldstone, Ted Robert Gurr, and Farrokh Moshiri, eds., *Revolutions of the Late Twentieth Century.* Boulder, CO: Westview.

Mueller, John. 2002. "Harbinger or Aberration? A 9/11 Provocation." *The National Interest* 69 (Fall): 45–50.

———. 2005. "Terrorism and the Dynamics of Threat Exaggeration." Paper presented at the American Political Science Association Annual Meetings. Washington, DC, September 1–4.

Mughal, Muahammad Aamir. 2005. "Iran-Contra." Asia Times Online Community and News Discussion. http://forum.atimes.com/topics.asp?TOPIC_ID=2174. Accessed July 30, 2008.

Mukerjee, Bumba. 2006. "Why Political Power-Sharing Agreements Lead to Enduring Peaceful Resolution of Some Civil Wars, But Not Others." *International Studies Quarterly* 50: 479–504.

Murphy, John F. 1985. *Punishing International Terrorists: The Legal Framework for Policy Initiatives.* Totowa, NJ: Rowman and Allanheld.

Nader, Laura. 1997. "Controlling Processes: Tracing the Dynamic Components of Power." *Current Anthropology* 38, no 5 (December): 711–737.

Nash, Jay Robert. 1998. *Terrorism in the 20th Century: A Narrative Encyclopedia from the Anarchists, through the Weathermen, to the Unabomber.* New York: Evans.

Nasiri, Omar. 2006. *Inside the Jihad: My Life with al Qaeda—A Spy's Story.* New York: Basic Books.

National Consortium for the Study of Terrorism and Responses to Terrorism. http://www.start.umd.edu/start/. Accessed July 15, 2009.

Neale, Margaret A., and Max H. Bazerman. 1992. *Cognition and Rationality in Negotiation.* New York: Free Press.

Neumann, Peter R. 2007. "Negotiating with Terrorists." *Foreign Affairs* 86: 128–138.

Neumann, Peter R., and M. L. R. Smith. 2005. "Strategic Terrorism: The Framework and Its Fallacies." *Journal of Strategic Studies* 28, no. 4 (August): 571–595.

———. 2008. *Strategic Terrorism: How It Works and Why It Fails.* New York: Routledge.

Newhouse, John. 2002. "The Threats America Faces." *World Policy Journal* 19 (Summer): 21–37.

Newman, Lawrence W., and John M. Walker. 1999. *Revolutionary Days: The Iran Hostage Crisis and the Hague Claims Tribunal: A Look Back.* Tampa, FL: Juris.

Newsweek. 2006. "U.S. in Direct Talks with Sunni Insurgents." (February 6).

New York Times. 2004. *The 9/11 Report: The National Commission on Terrorist Attacks upon the United States.* New York: St. Martin's.

Nicholson, Marc E. 2003. "An Essay on Terrorism." *American Diplomacy* 8. http://0-www.ciaonet.org.bianca.penlib.du.edu/olj/ad/ad_v8_3.

Nicolaïdis, Kalypso. 1999. "Power and Negotiation: When Should Lambs Negotiate with Lions?" In Deborah M. Kolb, ed., *Negotiation Eclectics: Essays in Memory of Jeffrey Z. Rubin.* Cambridge, MA: Harvard University Press, 100–117.

Nixon, Richard M. 1971. "U.S. Foreign Policy for the 1970s: Building for Peace." Report to Congress. February 25. *Department of State Bulletin* 64 (March 22).

———. 1978. *The Memoirs of Richard Nixon.* New York: Grosset and Dunlap.

Oberdorfer, Don. 1992. "Iran Paid for Release of Hostages: Tehran Gave Captors up to $2 Million for Each, Officials Say." *Washington Post,* January 19.

O'Brien, Conor Cruise. 1986. "Thinking about Terrorism." *Atlantic Monthly* (June): 62–66.

"October Surprise." 1992. *PBS Frontline.* Aired April 7.

O'Kane, Eamonn. 2006. "When Can Conflicts be Resolved? A Critique of Ripeness." *Civil Wars* 8, 3–4 (September–December). 268–284.

O'Leary, Jeffrey. 2006. "Counterterrorism: Intelligence Gathering." http://faculty.ncwc.edu/toconnor/427/427lect17.htm. Accessed April 26, 2006.

Olweus, Dan. 1993. *Bullying at School.* London: Blackwell.

O'Neill, Brendan. 2003. "Cross-Border Terrorism: A Mess Made by the West." *Spiked* (July 24): 1–11.

Opall, Barbara. 1998. "U.S. May Owe Iran Billions in Penalties." *Defense News* (February 22–26).

Opotow, Susan. 2000. "Aggression and Violence." In Morton Deutch and Peter T. Coleman, eds., *The Handbook of Conflict Resolution: Theory and Practice.* San Francisco: Jossey-Bass, 403–427.

Ost, David. 2004. "Politics as the Mobilization of Anger: Emotions and Movements and in Power." *European Journal of Social Theory* 7, no. 2: 229–244.

Owen, Roberts B. 1985. "The Final Negotiation and Release in Algiers." In Warren Christopher et al., eds., *American Hostages in Iran: The Conduct of a Crisis.* New Haven, CT: Yale University Press, 297–324.

Pape, Robert. 2003. "The Strategic Logic of Suicide Terrorism." *American Political Science Review* 97, no. 3 (August): 343–361.

———. 2005. *Dying to Win: The Strategic Logic of Suicide Terrorism.* New York: Random House.

Parry, Robert. 1993. *Trick or Treason: The October Surprise Mystery.* New York: Sheridan Square Press.

———. 2004. *Secrecy and Privilege: Rise of the Bush Dynasty from Watergate to Iraq.* Media Consortium.

———. 2005. "Russia's Prime Minister and October Surprise." *Consortiumnews.com.* www.consortiumnews.com/1999/051399.html. Accessed February 8, 2005.

Parsi, Trita. 2008. *Treacherous Alliance: The Secret Dealings of Israel, Iran, and the U.S.* New Haven, CT: Yale University Press.

Payne, John W. 1982. "Contingent Decision Behavior." *Psychological Bulletin* 92: 382–402.

Payne, John W., James R. Bettman, and Eric J. Johnson. 1988. "Adaptive Strategy Selection in Decision-Making." *Journal of Experimental Psychology: Learning, Memory, and Cognition* 14, no. 3: 534–552.

———. 1993. *The Adaptive Decision Maker.* New York: Cambridge University Press.

Pearl, Richard, and David Frum. 2003. *An End to Evil: How to Win the War on Terror.* New York: Random House.

Pelton, R. Y., with C. Aral and W. Dulles. 1998. *Fielding's the Worlds Most Dangerous Places.* Redondo Beach, CA: Fielding.

Pen, J. 1952. "A General Theory of Bargaining." *American Economic Review* 42, no. 1: 24–42.

Perl, Raphael F. 2006. "Terrorism and National Security: Issues and Trends." Congressional Research Service Issue Brief for Congress. Washington, DC: Congressional Research Service.

Perlez, Jane. 2009. "Pakistan Attacks Show Tighter Militant Links." *New York Times.* (October 16).

Peters, Gretchen. 2009. *Seeds of Terror: How Heroin Is Bankrolling the Taliban and al Qaeda.* New York: St. Martin's.

Pfetch, Frank R. 2007. *Negotiating Political Conflicts.* New York: Palgrave MacMillan.

Pfetsch, Frank, and Alice Landau. 2000. "Symmetry and Asymmetry in International Negotiation." *International Negotiation* 5: 21–42.

Phelps, Christopher. 2001. *Chronicle of Higher Education* (September 28): *Chronicle Review,* B11.

Phillips, David. 1973. *Skyjack: The Story of Air Piracy.* London: Harrap.

Piazza, James A. 2006. "Rooted in Poverty?: Terrorism, Poor Economic Development, and Social Cleavages." *Terrorism and Political Violence* 18: 159–177.

Picco, Giandomenico. 1999. *Man without a Gun: One Diplomat's Secret Struggle to Free the Hostages, Fight Terrorism, and End a War.* New York: Random House.

———. 2005. "The Challenges of Strategic Terrorism." *Terrorism and Political Violence* 17: 11–16.

Pillar, Peter. 1983. *Negotiating Peace: War Termination as a Bargaining Process.* Princeton, NJ: Princeton University Press.

Pinkley, R. L. 1990. "Dimensions of Conflict Frame: Disputant Interpretations of Conflict." *Journal of Applied Psychology* 75: 117–126.

Pipes, Daniel. 2003. "The 'October Surprise' Theory." *Conspiracy Theories in American History: An Encyclopedia.* Santa Barbara, CA: ACB-Clio, 547–550.

———. 2006. "What Do Terrorists Want?" *New York Sun,* July 26. www.nysun.com/article/17543. Accessed February 26, 2008.

Posner, Gerald. 2005. *Secrets of the Kingdom: The Inside Story of the Saudi-U.S. Connection.* New York: Random House.

Powell, Robert. 2002. "Bargaining Theory and International Conflict." *Annual Review of Political Science* 5: 1–30.

———. 2004. "Bargaining and Learning while Fighting." *American Journal of Political Science* 48, no. 2 (April): 344–361.

Pronin, Emily, Kathleen Kennedy, and Sarah Butsch. 2006. "Bombing versus Negotiating: How Preferences from Combating Terrorism Are Affected by Perceived Terrorist Rationality." *Basic and Applied Social Psychology* 28, no. 4: 385–392.

Pruitt, Dean. 1997. "Ripeness Theory and the Oslo Talks." *International Negotiation* 2: 177–182.

———. 2005. "Escalation, Readiness for Negotiation, and Third-Party Functions." In I. W. Zartman and G. O. Faure, eds., *Escalation and Negotiation in International Conflicts.* New York: Cambridge University Press, 251–270.

———. 2007. "Readiness Theory and the Northern Ireland Conflict." *American Behavioral Scientist* 50, 11. (July) 1520–1541.

Pruitt, Dean G., and Sung Hee Kim. 2004. *Social Conflict: Escalation, Stalemate, and Settlement.* 3rd ed. New York: McGraw-Hill.

Putnam, Linda. 2006. "Definitions and Approaches to Conflict and Communication." In John G. Oetzel and Stella Ting-Toomey, eds., *The Sage Handbook of Conflict Communication: Integrating Theory, Research, and Practice.* Thousand Oaks, CA: Sage, 1–32.

Putnam, Linda, and Majia Holmer. 1992. "Framing, Reframing, and Issue Development." In Linda L. Putnam and Michael E. Roloff, eds., *Communication and Negotiation: Sage Annual Reviews of Communication Research.* Newbury Park, CA: Sage, 128–155.

Rahim, M.A. 1990. *Rahim Organizational Conflict Inventory: Professional Management.* Palo Alto, CA: Consulting Psychologists Press.

Raiffa, Howard. 1995. "Analytical Barriers." In Kenneth Arrow et al., eds., *Barriers to Conflict Resolution.* New York: Norton, 133–148.

Rainwater, Janette. 1997. "Afghanistan, 'Terrorism,' and Blowback: A Chronology." www.janwainwater.com/hdocs/afghan2p9.htm. Accessed April 19, 2006.

Raman, B. 2000. "Plane Hijacking: In Perspective." South Asia Analysis Group. www.saag.org/papers2/paper103.html. Accessed February 25, 2005.

Randal, Jonathan C. 1983. *Going All the Way: Christian Warlords, Israeli Adventurers, and the War in Lebanon.* New York: Viking.

Ranstorp, Magnus. 1997. *Hizb'allah in Lebanon: The Politics of the Western Hostage Crisis.* New York: St. Martin's.

Rapoport, Anatol. 1960. *Fights, Games, and Debates.* Ann Arbor: University of Michigan Press.
———. 1995. *The Origins of Violence: Approaches to the Study of Conflict.* New Brunswick, NJ: Transaction.

Rapoport, David C. 2004. "The Four Waves of Modern Terrorism." In Audrey K. Cronin and James M. Ludes, eds., *Attacking Terrorism: Elements of a Grand Strategy.* Washington, DC: Georgetown University Press.

Rashid, Ahmed. 2002. *Jihad: The Rise of Militant Islam in Central Asia.* New Haven, CT: Yale University Press.

Rashwan, Diaa. 2008. "Egypt's Contrite Commander." *Foreign Policy* (March–April): 88–90.
———. 2009. "The Renunciation of Violence by Egyptian Jihadi Organizations." In Tore Bjørgo and John Horgan, eds., *Leaving Terrorism Behind: Individual and Collective Disengagement.* London: Routledge, 113–132.

Rasler, Karen. 2000. "Shocks, Expectancy Revisions, and the De-escalation of Protracted Conflicts: The Israeli-Palestinian Case." *Journal of Peace Research* 37, no. 6 (November): 699–720.

Rasler, Karen, and William Thompson. 2009. "Looking for Waves of Terrorism." *Terrorism and Political Violence* 21: 28–41.

Raufer, Xavier. 2003. "Al Qaeda: A Different Diagnosis." *Studies in Conflict and Terrorism* 26, no. 6 (November): 391–398.

Reiter, Dan. 2003. "Exploring the Bargaining Model of War." *Perspectives on Politics* 1, no 1 (March): 27–43.

Reuter, Christoph. 2004. *My Life as a Weapon.* Translated by Helena Ragg-Kirkby. Princeton, NJ: Princeton University Press.

Rich, Mary K. 1991. "'My Kingdom for a Horse': The Problem of War Termination and Modern Military Strategy." Global Security Report. www. globalsecurity.org. Accessed March 1, 2005.

Richardson, Louise. 2006. *What Terrorists Want: Understanding the Enemy, Containing the Threat*. New York: Random House.

Richmond, Oliver. 1998. "Devious Objectives and the Disputants' View of International Mediation: A Theoretical Framework." *Journal of Peace Research* 35, no. 6: 670–722.

Risse, Thomas. 2000. "'Let's Argue!' Communicative Action in World Politics." *International Organization* 54: 1–39.

Roberts, Jani. 1991. "Armsgate." *The Age* (May 18).

Rodman, Peter W. 1981. "The Hostage Crisis: How Not to Negotiate." *Washington Quarterly* 4, no. 3 (Summer): 9–24.

Roloff, Michael E., and Courtney Waite Miller. 2006. "Social Cognition Approaches to Understanding Interpersonal Conflict and Communication." In John G. Oetzel and Stella Ting-Toomey, eds., *The Sage Handbook of Conflict Communication: Integrating Theory, Research, and Practice*. Thousand Oaks, CA: Sage, 97–128.

Rosenthal, A. M. 1981. "America in Captivity." *New York Times Magazine* Special Section (May 17): 33–35.

Ross, Benjamin. 2002. "In Search of Root Causes." *Dissent* 49 (Spring): 40–43.

Ross, Jeffrey Ian. 1993. "Structural Causes of Oppositional Political Terrorism: Towards a Causal Model." *Journal of Peace Research* 30, no. 3 (August): 317–329.

———. 2006. *Political Terrorism: An Interdisciplinary Approach*. New York: Peter Lang.

Ross, Jeffrey Ian, and Ted Robert Gurr. 1989. "Why Terrorism Subsides: A Comparative Study of Canada and the United States." *Comparative Politics* 21, no. 4 (July): 405–426.

Rothman, Jay, and Marie L. Olson. 2001. "From Interests to Identities: Toward a New Emphasis on Inter-Active Conflict Resolution." *Journal of Peace Research* 38, no. 3: 289–305.

Rubin, Barnett R., and Ahmed Rashid. 2008. "From Great Game to Grand Bargaining: Ending Chaos in Afghanistan and Pakistan." *Foreign Affairs* 87, no. 6 (November–December): 30–44.

Rubin, Barry, and Judith Colp Rubin, eds. 2002. *Anti-American Terrorism and the Middle East: A Documentary Reader*. New York: Oxford University Press.

Rubin, Claire, William R. Cumming, Irma K. Renda-Tanali, and Thomas Birkland. 2003. "Major Terrorism Events and Their U.S Outcomes (1988–2001)." National Hazards Research Working Paper No. 107. Boulder, CO: National Hazards Research and Applications Information Center, Institute of Behavioral Science.

Rubin, Jeffrey Z., and B. Brown. 1975. *The Social Psychology of Bargaining and Negotiation*. New York: Academic.

Rubin, J., D. Pruitt, and S. Hee Kim. 1994. *Social Conflict: Escalation, Stalemate, and Settlement*. New York: McGraw-Hill.

Rubin, Michael, and Suzanne Gerschowitz. 2006. "Political Strategies to Counterterrorism." *Middle East Forum*. July 12. http://www.meforum.org/article/974. Accessed May 15, 2008.

Rubinstein, Ariel. 1982. "Perfect Equilibrium in a Bargaining Model." *Econmetrica* 50, no. 1 (January): 97–109.

———. 1995. "On the Interpretation of Two Theoretical Models of Bargaining." In Kenneth Arrow et al., *Barriers to Conflict Resolution*. New York: Norton, 121–130.

Ryan, Paul B. 1985. *The Iranian Rescue Mission: Why It Failed*. Annapolis, MD: Naval Institute Press.

Salacuse, Jeswald W. 1999. "How Should the Lamb Negotiate with the Lion? Power in International Negotiations." In Deborah M. Kolb, ed., *Negotiation Eclectics: Essays in Memory of Jeffrey Z. Rubin*. Cambridge, MA: Harvard University Press, 87–97.

———. 2000. "Lessons for Practice." In I. William Zartman and Jeffrey Rubin, eds., *Power and Negotiation*. Ann Arbor: University of Michigan Press, 255–269.

Salem, Paul E. 1993. "In Theory: A Critique of Western Conflict Resolution from a Non-Western Perspective." *Negotiation Journal* 9 (October): 361–369.

Salin, Denise. 2003. "Ways of Explaining Workplace Bullying: A Review of Enabling, Motivating, and Precipitating Structures and Processes in the Work Environment." *Human Relations* 56, no. 10: 1213–1232.

Sambanis, Nicholas. 2004. "Using Case Studies to Expand Economic Models of Civil War." *Perspectives on Politics* 2, no. 2: 259–279.

Samii, A. William. 2002. "Tehran, Washington, and Terror: No Agreement to Differ." *Middle East Review of International Affairs* 6, no. 3 (September): 1–15.

Sandler, Todd, and Walter Enders. 2002. "An Economic Perspective on Transnational Terrorism." University of Alabama, Department of Economics, Finance and Legal Studies Working Paper Series Index. www.cha.ua.edu.

———. 2007. "Applying Analytical Methods to Study Terrorism." *International Studies Perspectives* 8: 287–302.

Sandler, Todd, and John L. Scott. 1987. "Terrorist Success in Hostage-Taking Incidents: An Empirical Study." *Journal of Conflict Resolution* 31, no. 1 (March): 35–53.

Sandler, Todd, John T. Tschirhart, and Jon Cauley. 1983. "A Theoretical Analysis of Transitional Terrorism." *American Political Science Review* 77, no. 1: 36–54.

Saunders, Harold H. 1985a. "Beginning of the End." In Warren Christopher et al., *American Hostages in Iran: The Conduct of a Crisis*. New Haven, CT: Yale University Press, 281–296.

———. 1985b. "The Crisis Begins." In Warren Christopher et al., *American Hostages in Iran: The Conduct of a Crisis*. New Haven, CT: Yale University Press, 35–71.

———. 1985c. "Diplomacy and Pressure, November 1979–May 1980." In Warren Christopher et al., *American Hostages in Iran: The Conduct of a Crisis*. New Haven, CT: Yale University Press, 72–143.

———. 1996. "Prenegotiation and Circum-negotiation: Arenas of the Peace Process." In Chester A. Crocker and Fen Osler Hampson with Pamela Aall, eds., *Managing Global Chaos: Sources and Responsibilities to International Conflict*. Washington, DC: U.S. Institute of Peace, 419–432.

Sawyer, Jack, and Harold Guetzkow. 1965. "Bargaining and Negotiation in International Relations." In Herbert Kelman, ed., *International Behavior: A Social-Psychological Analysis*. New York: Holt, Rinehart, and Winston, 466–520.

Schanzer, Jonathan. 2004. *Al Qaeda's Armies: Mid-East Affiliate Groups and the Next Generation of Terror*. New York: Specialist.

Schelling, Thomas. 1960. *The Strategy of Conflict*. Cambridge, MA: Harvard University Press.

———. 2007. *Choice and Consequence: Perspectives of an Errant Economist*. Cambridge, MA: Harvard University Press.

Schiff, Ze'ev, and Ehud Ya'ari. 1984. *Israel's Lebanon War*. New York: Simon and Schuster.

Schmid, Alex P. 1993. "The Response Problem as a Definition Problem." In Alex Schmid and Ron Crelinsten, eds., *Western Responses to Terrorism*. London: Frank Cass.

———. 2004. "Frameworks for Conceptualizing Terrorism." *Terrorism and Political Violence* 16, no. 2 (Summer): 197–221.

Schmid, Alex P., and Albert Jongman. 1988. *Political Terrorism: A New Guide to Actors, Concepts, Databases, Theories, and Literature*. New Brunswick, NJ: Transaction.

Schmitt, Gary. 2002. "One Year On: A September 11 Anniversary Symposium: A Case of Continuity." *National Interest* 69 (Fall): 11–13.

Schön, Donald A., and Martin Rein. 1994. *Frame Reflection: Toward the Resolution of Intractable Policy Controversies.* New York: Basic Books.

Schrodt, Philip, Ömür Yilmaz, and Deborah J. Gerner. 2003. "Evaluating 'Ripeness' and 'Hurting Stalemate' in Mediated International Conflicts: An Event Data Study of the Middle East, Balkans, and West Africa." Paper presented at the Annual Meeting of the International Studies Association.

Schweitzer, Maurice, and Leslie E. deChurch. 2001. "Linking Frames in Negotiations: Gains, Losses, and Conflict Frame Adoption." *International Journal of Conflict Management* 12, no. 2: 100–113.

Scott, Catherine V. 2000. "Bound for Glory: The Hostage Crisis as Captivity Narrative in Iran. *Intertnational Studies Quarterly* 44: 177–188.

Scott, John. 2001. *Power.* Cambridge, UK: Polity.

Scowcroft, Brent. 2002. "New Directions in American Foreign Policy." Remarks delivered at the U.S. Institute of Peace Conference: 9/11 a Year On: America's Challenges in a Changed World, Washington, DC, September 5.

Seawright, Jason. 2002. "Testing for Necessary and/or Sufficient Causation: Which Cases Are Relevant." *Political Analysis* 10, no. 2: 178–193.

Sebenius, James K. 2002. "International Negotiation Analysis." In Victor A. Kremenyuk, ed., *International Negotiation: Analysis, Approaches, Issues.* 2nd ed. San Francisco: Jossey-Bass, 229–255.

Sederberg, Peter. 2003. "Global Terrorism: Problems of Challenge and Response." In Charles W. Kegley Jr., ed., *The New Global Terrorism: Characteristics, Causes, Controls.* Upper Saddle River, NJ: Prentice-Hall, 267–284.

Selbourne, David. 2005. *The Losing Battle with Islam.* New York: Prometheus.

Sezgin, Erkan. 2007. "Formation of the Concept of Terrorism." In Suleyman Ozeran, Ismail Dincer Gunes, and Diab M. Al-Badayneh, eds., *Understanding Terrorism: An Analysis of Sociological and Psychological Aspects.* Amsterdam: IOS Press, 17–26.

Shafir, Eldar. 1994. "Prospect Theory and International Relations: Theoretical Applications and Analytical Problems." In Barbara Farnham, ed., *Avoiding Losses / Taking Risks: Prospect Theory and International Conflict.* Ann Arbor: University of Michigan Press, 147–158.

Sharf, Michael. 2001. "The Broader Meaning of the Lockerbie Trial and the Future of International Counter-Terrorism." *Syracuse Journal of International Law and Commerce* 29, no. 1.

Shoumikhin, Andrei. 2004. "Deterring Terrorism: Russian Views." Fairfax, VA: National Institute for Public Policy.

Shukri, Muhammad Aziz. 1991. *International Terrorism: A Legal Critique.* Brattleboro, VT: Amana.

Shulimson, Jack. 1958. "Marines in Lebanon 1958." Report to Department of the Navy/ Headquarters U.S. Marine Corps. http://www.au.af.mil/au/awc/awcgate/usmchist/ lebanon.txt. Accessed April 17, 2006.

Sick, Gary. 1991a. *October Surprise: America's Hostages in Iran and the Election of Ronald Reagan.* New York: Random House.

———. 1991b. "The Election Story of the Decade." *New York Times,* April 15.

———. 1992. "Dialogue: Should Congress Investigate the 'October Surprise'? An Official Inquiry Might Crack the Case." *New York Times,* January 15.

Silke, Andrew, ed. 2004. *Research on Terrorism: Trends, Achievements, and Failures.* London: Frank Cass.

Simon, Jeffrey D. 2001. *The Terrorist Trap: America's Experience with Terrorism.* 2nd ed. Bloomington: Indiana University Press.

Sjöstedt, Gunnar, ed. 2003. *Professional Cultures in International Negotiation: Bridge or Rift?* Lanham, MD: Lexington.

Skow, John. 1981. "The Long Ordeal of the Hostages." *Time* (January 26). http://www.time.com/time/magazine/article/0,9171,954605,00.htm. Accessed July 21, 2008.

Slantchev, Branislav L. 2003. "The Principle of Convergence in Wartime Negotiations." *American Political Science Review* 97, no. 4 (November): 621–632.

———. 2004. "How Initiators End their Wars: The Duration of Warfare and the Terms of Peace." *American Journal of Political Science.* 48, no. 4 (October) 813–829.

Smelser, Neil J. 2007. *The Faces of Terrorism: Social and Psychological Dimensions.* Princeton, NJ: Princeton University Press.

Smith, James D. D. 1995. *Stopping Wars: Defining the Obstacles to Cease Fire.* Boulder, CO: Westview.

Smith, Wayne S. 1987. *The Closest of Enemies: A Personal and Diplomatic Account of U.S.-Cuban Relations since 1957.* New York: Norton.

Snyder, Glenn H., and Paul Diesing. 1977. *Conflict among Nations: Bargaining, Decision Making, and System Structure in International Crises.* Princeton, NJ: Princeton University Press.

Sobek, David, and Alex Braithwaite. 2005. "Victim of Success: American Dominance and Terrorism." *Conflict Management and Peace Science* 22: 135–148.

Sofaer, Abraham D. 1986. "Terrorism and the Law." *Foreign Affairs* 64, no. 5 (Summer): 901–922.

———. 1999. "Government-to-Government Cases and Settlement of the Small Claims." In A. F. Lowenfeld, L. W. Newman, and J. M. Walker, eds., *Revolutionary Days: The Iran Hostage Crisis and the Hague Claims Tribunal: A Look Back.* Tampa, FL: Juris.

Spector, Bertram. 1977. "Negotiation as a Psychological Process." In I. William Zartman, ed., *The Negotiation Process.* Beverly Hills, CA: Sage.

———. 1998. "Deciding to Negotiate with Villains." *Negotiation Journal* 14: 43–60.

———. 2002. "Negotiation Readiness in the Development Context: Adding Capacity to Ripeness." In H. W. Jeong, ed., *Approaches to Peacebuilding.* New York: Palgrave.

Sprinzak, Ehud. 1990. "The Psychopolitical Formation of Extreme Left Terrorism in a Democracy: The Case of the Weathermen." In Walter Reich, ed., *Origins of Terrorism: Psychologies, Ideologies, Theologies, States of Mind.* New York: Cambridge University Press, 65–85.

Steel, Ronald. 1996. "Blowback: Terrorism and the U.S. Role in the Middle East." *New Republic* (July 28): 7–11.

Stein, Janis Gross, ed. 1989. *Getting to the Table: The Process of International Prenegotiation.* Baltimore: John Hopkins University Press.

Stevens, Carl M. 1958. "On the Theory of Negotiation." *Quarterly Journal of Economics.* 72: 77–97.

Stevens, Michael J. 2002. "The Unanticipated Consequences of Globalization: Conceptualizing Terrorism." In Chris E. Stout, ed., *The Psychology of Terrorism,* vol. 3: *Theoretical Understandings and Perspectives.* Westport, CT: Praeger, 31–55.

St. John, Peter. 1999. "The Politics of Aviation Terrorism." In Paul Wilkinson and Brian M. Jenkins, eds., *Aviation Terrorism and Security.* London: Frank Cass.

Stout, Chris E., ed. 2002. *The Psychology of Terrorism,* volume 3: *Theoretical Understandings and Perspectives.* Westport, CT: Praeger.

Strasser, Steven, ed. 2004. *The 9/11 Investigations: Staff Reports of the 9/11 Commission, Excerpts from the House-Senate Joint Inquiry Report on 9/11.* New York: Public Affairs.

Strednansky, Susan E. 1995. *The Fine Art of Conflict Termination*. Unpublished thesis, School of Advanced Airpower Studies, Air University, Maxwell Air Force Base, Alabama.

Street, Paul. 2002. "Towards a 'Decent Left'"? *Z Magazine* (July–August): 61–68.

Strong, Morgan. 2004. "Arafat and the Original 'October Surprise.'" *Consortium News*. http://www.consortiumnews.com/2004/110204.html. Accessed July 22, 2008.

Sutherland, Tom and Jean. 1996. *At Your Own Risk: An American Chronicle of Crisis and Captivity in the Middle East*. Golden, CO: Fulcrum.

Taillon, J. Paul de B. 2002. *Hijacking and Hostages: Government Responses to Terrorism*. Westport, CT: Praeger.

Talbott, Strobe and Nayan Chanda, eds. 2001. *The Age of Terror: America and the World after September 11*. New York: Basic Books.

Tarpley, Webster G., and Anton Chaitkin. 2004. *George Bush: The Unauthorized Biography*. Joshua Tree, CA: Progressive.

"Terrorist Attacks on Americans, 1979–1988." 2001. *PBS Frontline*. www.pbs.org/wgbh/pages/frontline/shows/taraget/etc/cron.html. Accessed February 5, 2005.

Testrake, John. 1987. *Triumph over Terrorism: Flight 847—A Story of Raw Courage That Shocked America and Changed Its Attitude on Terrorism*. Old Tappan, NJ: Revell.

Time. January 15, 1973.

"Top Blair Aide: We Must Talk to al-Qaida." 2008. *Guardian,* March 15. http://www.guardian.co.uk/uk/2008/mar/15/uksecurity.alqaida/print. Accessed May 12, 2008.

Tower Commission Report: The Full Text of the President's Special Review Board. 1987. New York: Random House.

Townshend, Charles. 2002. *Terrorism: A Very Short Introduction*. Oxford: Oxford University Press.

Trager, Robert F., and Dessislava P. Zahorcheva. 2005. "Deterring Terrorism: It Can Be Done." *International Security* 30, no 3 (Winter): 87–123.

Tripscha, C. B., W. A. Donohue, and D. Druckman. 2006. "Forward/Backward Contextual Frames Surrounding the Israeli-Palestinian Oslo I Accords." Paper presented at the 2006 Annual Meeting of the International Conflict Management Association, Montreal, June 25–28.

Tucker, David. 2001. "What Is New about the New Terrorism and How Dangerous Is It?" *Terrorism and Political Violence* 13, no. 3 (August): 1–14.

Tucker, Robert W. 2002. "One Year On: A September 11 Anniversary Symposium—The End of a Contradiction?" *National Interest* 69 (Fall): 5–7.

Turney-High, Harry Holbert. 1971. *Primitive War: Its Practice and Concepts*. 2nd ed. Columbia: University of South Carolina Press.

Tversky, Amos, and Daniel Kahneman. 1981. "The Framing of Decisions and the Psychology of Choice." *Science* 211, no. 4481 (January 30): 453–458.

Underdal, Arild. 2002. "The Outcomes of Negotiation." In Victor A. Kremenyuk, ed., *International Negotiation: Analysis, Approaches, Issues*. 2nd ed. San Francisco: Jossey-Bass, 110–125.

UN General Assembly Resolution 2625 (25) of October 24, 1970. UN General Assembly Official Record, 25th session, Supplement No. 28 (A/8028).

Ury, W., J. M. Brett, and S. B. Goldberg. 1988. *Getting Disputes Resolved: Designing Systems to Cut the Cost of Conflict*. San Francisco: Jossey-Bass.

U.S. Army and Marine Corps Counterinsurgency Field Manual. 2007. Chicago, IL: University of Chicago Press.

U.S. Congress. House. 1970. Committee on Foreign Affairs. *Hearings on Aircraft Hijacking*. 91st

Congress, 2nd session. September 17, 22, 23, and 30. Washington, DC: U.S. Government Printing Office.

U.S. Congress. House. 1973. Committee on Foreign Affairs. *Subcommittee on Inter-American Affairs. Hearings on the Hijacking Accord Between the United States and Cuba. 93rd Congress, 1st session.* February 20. Washington, DC: U.S. Government Printing Office.

U.S. Congress. Senate. 1992. Committee on Foreign Relations. *The "October Surprise" Allegations and the Circumstances Surrounding the Release of American Hostages Held in Iran.* Washington, DC: U.S. Government Printing Office.

U.S. Department of Defense. 1983. *Report of the Commission on Beirut International Airport Terrorist Act,* October 23, 1983. Washington, DC: U.S. Department of Defense.

———. 1997. *The Defense Science Board 1997 Summer Study Task Force on DOD Responses to Transnational Threats.* Washington, DC: U.S. Department of Defense.

U.S. Department of State. 1966. "Fact Sheet: The Cuban Adjustment Act." Public Law 89–732. November 2, 1966 as Amended. http://usembassy.state.gov/havana/wwwhact.htm. Accessed August 3, 2005.

———. 1998. "Chronology of U.S.-Cuban Relations, 1958–1998." http://havana.usint.gov/uploads/images/ypjIFsSBY-nmKb3Z2QZ7Rw/chronology5891. Accessed January 30, 2005.

———. 2006. *Foreign Relations of the United States 1961–1963,* vol. 10: *Cuba, 1961–62;* and Nixon-Ford Administration, E-1, Chapter 2, "U.S. Hijacking Agreement, 1969–1973." http://www.state/gov/r/pa/ho/frus/nixon/el/52992.htm. Accessed January 27, 2005.

———. 2007a. *Country Reports on Terrorism 2006, 2007, 2008.* Washington, DC: U.S. Department of State.

———. 2007b. "Daily Press Briefing with Tom Casey, Deputy Spokesman." July 31. www.state.gov/r/pa/prs/dpb/2007/jul/89862.htm. Accessed March 1, 2008.

———. 2008a. "Remarks at the Tenth Anniversary Commemoration of the Bombing of U.S. Embassies in Nairobi and Dar es Salaam. August 7. www.state.gov/secretary/rm/2008/08/107997.htm. Accessed August 13, 2008.

———. 2008b. "Steps Taken after 1998 Bombings in Nairobi and Dar es Salaam." August 7. www.state/gov/r/pa/prs/ps/2008/aug/107989.htm. Accessed August 13, 2008.

———. n.d. *Patterns of Global Terrorism, 1995–2003.* Washington, DC: Office of the Coordinator for Counterterrorism. www.state.gov/s/ct/rls/pgtrp.

———. n.d. "State Sponsors of Terrorism" www.state.gov/s/ct/c14151.htm. Accessed April 17, 2006.

U.S. Department of Transportation, Office of Civil Aviation Security. 1981. "U.S. and Foreign Registered Aircraft Hijackings Updated January 1, 1981." Washington, DC: Federal Aviation Administration.

———. 1986. "U.S. and Foreign Registered Aircraft Hijackings, 1931–1986." Washington, DC: Federal Aviation Administration.

"U.S. Explores Mideast Dialogue." 1973. *Christian Science Monitor,* March 3, 2.

U.S. Government Information. http://usgovinfo.about.com/od/defenseandsecurity/a/randon911.htm?p=1.

U.S. Immigration and Customs Enforcement. "ICE: Federal Air Marshal Service (FAMS) Historical Background." www.ice.gov/graphjics/fams/history/htm, 1–6. Accessed July 21, 2005.

U.S. Institute of Peace. 1999. "How Terrorism Ends." Special Report 48. http://www.usip.org/pubs/specialreports/sr990525.html. Accessed May 11, 2004.

"U.S. Iran Relations." www.acus.org/InternationalSecurity/policy_updates.htm. Accessed February 9, 2005.

Vetter, Harold J., and Gary R. Perlstein. 1991. *Perspectives on Terrorism*. Pacific Grove, CA: Brooks/Cole.

Voll, John O. 2001. *Chronicle of Higher Education* (September 28): *Chronicle Review*, B10.

Voss, Christopher T. 2004. "Crisis Negotiation: A Counter-Intuitive Method to Disrupt Terrorism." *Studies in Conflict and Terrorism* 27: 455–459.

Waas, Murray, and Craig Unger. 2002. "In the Loop: Bush's Secret Mission." *New Yorker* (November 14).

Wadley, Reed L. 2003. "Treachery and Deceit: Parallels in Tribal and Terrorist Warfare?" *Studies in Conflict and Terrorism* 26, no. 5 (September): 331–345.

Wagner, R. Harrison. 1994. "Peace, War, and the Balance of Power." *American Political Science Review* 88 (September): 593–607.

———. 2000. "Bargaining and War." *American Political Science Review* 44: 469–485.

Walker, Martin. 2002. "America's Virtual Empire." *World Policy Journal* 19 (Summer): 13–20.

Walker, Stephen G. 2004. "The Management and Resolution of International Conflict in a 'Single' Case: American and North Vietnamese Exchanges during the Vietnam War." In Zeev Maoz et al., eds., *Multiple Paths to Knowledge in International Relations: Methodology in the Study of Conflict Management and Conflict Resolution*. Lanham, MD: Lexington, 277–308.

Wall, J. A., J. B. Stark, and R. L. Standifer. 2001. "Mediation: A Current Review and Theory Development." *Journal of Conflict Resolution* 45, no. 3 (June): 370–391.

Walter, Barbara. 1997. "The Critical Barrier to Civil War Settlement." *International Organization* 51, no. 3 (Summer): 335–364.

———. 2002. *Committing to Peace: The Successful Settlement of Civil Wars*. Princeton, NJ: Princeton University Press.

———. 2003. "Re-Conceptualizing Conflict Resolution as a Three-Stage Process." *International Negotiation* 7: 299–311.

Walton, Richard E., and Robert B. McKersie. 1965. *A Behavioral Theory of Labor Negotiations*. New York: McGraw-Hill.

Walzer, Michael. 2000. *Just and Unjust Wars: A Moral Argument with Historical Illustrations*. 3rd ed. New York: Basic Books.

———. 2002. "Five Questions about Terrorism." *Dissent* 49 (Winter): 5–15.

Wanis-St. John, Anthony. 2006. "Back-Channel Negotiation: International Bargaining in the Shadows." *Negotiation Journal* 22, 2 (April). 119–144.

Washington Post. 1976. Editorial. October 19, A18.

Watkins, Harold D. 1968. "Air Transport: Federal Action in Hijackings Urged." *Aviation Week and Space Technology* (December 2): 24–25.

Waugh, William. 2002. "The Global Challenge of the New Terrorism." Paper presented at the American Political Science Association Annual Convention, Boston, Massachusetts.

Weinberg, Leonard, and Louise Richardson. 2004. "Conflict Theory and the Trajectory of Terrorist Campaigns in Western Europe." In Andrew Silke, ed., *Research on Terrorism: Trends, Achievements, and Failures*. London: Frank Cass, 138–159.

Weinberg, L., A. Pedahzur, and S. Hirsch-Hoefler. 2004. "The Challenge of Conceptualizing Terrorism." *Terrorism and Political Violence* 16, no. 4 (Winter): 777–794.

Weinberg, Steve. 1992. "The October Surprise: Enter the Press." *Columbia Journalism Review* (March–April). http://backissues.cjrarchives.org/year/92/2/october.asp. Accessed July 24, 2008.

Weiss-Wik, Stephen. 1983. "Enhancing Negotiators' Successfulness: Self-Help Books and Related Empirical Research." *Journal of Conflict Resolution* 27, no. 4 (December): 706–739.

Weitzman, Eban A., and Patricia Flynn Weitzman 2006. "The PSDM Model: Integrating Problem Solving and Decision Making in Conflict Resolution." In Morton Deutsch, Peter T. Coleman, and Eric C. Marcus, eds., *The Handbook of Conflict Resolution: Theory and Practice.* 2nd ed. San Francisco, CA: Jossey-Bass, 197–222.

Wendt, Alexander. 1999. *Social Theory of International Politics.* New York: Cambridge University Press.

Werner, Suzanne. 1995. "Should We Take This Outside? The Resolution of Crises." *Mershon International Studies Review* 39, no. 2 (October): 255–258.

———. 1998. "Negotiating the Terms of Settlement." *Journal of Conflict Resolution* 42, no. 3 (June): 321–343.

———. 1999. "The Precarious Nature of Peace: Resolving the Issues, Enforcing the Settlement, and Renegotiating the Terms." *American Journal of Political Science* 43, no. 3 (July): 912–934.

Wierzbicki, Andrzej P. 2007. "Rationality of Choice versus Rationality of Knowledge." In Rudolf Avenhaus and I. William Zartman, eds. *Diplomacy Games: Formal Models and International Negotiations.* Berlin: Springer, 69–81.

Wight, Colin. 2001. "Linking Agents and Structures to Levels of Analysis." Paper presented at the 42nd Annual Convention of the International Studies Association, Chicago, Illinois, February.

Wilkenfeld, Jonathan. 2006. "Concepts and Methods in the Study of International Crisis Management." In Michael D. Swain and Zhang Tuosheng, eds., *Managing Sino-American Crisis: Case Studies and Analysis.* Washington, DC: Carnegie Endowment for International Peace, 103–132.

Wilkerson, W.S. 2001. "Simulation, Theory, and the Frame Problem: The Interpretive Moment." *Philosophical Psychology* 14, no. 4: 141–153.

Wilkinson, Paul. 2001. *Terrorism vs. Democracy: The Liberal State Response.* London: Frank Cass.

Williams, Brian Glyn. 2008. "Talibanistan: History of a Transnational Terrorist Sanctuary." *Civil Wars* 10, no 1: 40–59.

Williams, Paul. 2002. *Al Qaeda: Brotherhood of Terror.* Upper Saddle River, NJ: Pearson.

Williamson, Kenneth. 1996. "U.S.-Canada Negotiating Situations." *International Negotiation* 1: 303–312.

Wilson, James Q. 1961. "Strategy of Protest: Problems of Negro Civic Action." *Journal of Conflict Resolution* 5, no. 3 (September): 291–303.

———. 2004. "What Makes a Terrorist? It Takes a Village—Even a Whole Culture." *City Journal.* www.city-journal.org/printable.php?id=1202. Accessed June 16, 2008.

Wilson, Margaret A. 2000. "Toward a Model of Terrorist Behavior in Hostage-Taking Incidents." *Journal of Conflict Resolution* 44, no. 4 (August): 403–424.

Wilson, S. Brian. "Who Are the *REAL* Terrorists? The *Real* Terror Network: Terrorism Facts and Propaganda." http://www.brianwillson.com/awolrealterror.html. Accessed June 20, 2007.

Wittman, Donald. 1979. "How a War Ends: A Rational Model Approach." *Journal of Conflict Resolution* 23, no. 4 (December): 743–763.

Woodward, Bob. 2003. *Bush at War.* New York: Simon and Schuster.

Woodworth, John. 2002. "How Should an Unrivalled Superpower Behave?" *Miller Center Report* 18 (Spring): 16–20.

Wright, Lawrence. 2004. "The Terror Web." *New Yorker* 80, 21 (August 2). 40–46.

————. 2006. *The Looming Tower: Al-Qaeda and the Road to 9/11.* New York: Knopf.

————. 2008. "The Rebellion within." *New Yorker 84, 16* (June 2). 37.

Wrong, Dennis H. 2005. *The Persistence of the Particular.* New Brunswick, NJ: Transaction.

Wurmser, David. 2001. "The Saudi Connection: Osama bin Laden's a Lot Closer to the Saudi Royal Family Than You Think." *Weekly Standard* (October 29).

Yang, Douglas H., ed. 1999. *Dictionary of Conflict Resolution.* San Francisco: Jossey-Bass.

Young, H. Peyton, ed. 1991. *Negotiation Analysis.* Ann Arbor: University of Michigan Press.

Young, Oran. 1968. *The Politics of Force.* Princeton, NJ: Princeton University Press.

Young, Oran, ed. 1975. *Bargaining: Formal Theories of Negotiation.* Urbana: University of Illinois Press.

Zahrani, Mostafa T. 2002. "The Coup That Changed the Middle East: Mossadeq v. the CIA in Retrospect." *World Policy Journal* 19 (Summer): 93–99.

Zakaria, Fareed. 1999. "Make Hostages' Lives the Second Goal." *Wall Street Journal.* (August 10).

Zartman, I. William. 1971. *The Politics of Trade Negotiations between Africa and the European Economic Community.* Princeton, NJ: Princeton University Press.

————. 1975. "Negotiations: Theory and Reality." *Journal of International Affairs* 9, no. 1: 69–77.

————. 1976. "Reality, Image, and Detail: The Paris Negotiations, 1969–1973." In Zartman, I. William, ed., *The 50% Solution: How to Bargain Successfully with Hijackers, Strikers, Bosses, Oil Magnates, Arabs, Russians, and Other Worthy Opponents in This Modern World.* New Haven, CT: Yale University Press.

Zartman, I. William, ed. 1976. *The 50% Solution: How to Bargain Successfully with Hijackers, Strikers, Bosses, Oil Magnates, Arabs, Russians, and Other Worthy Opponents in This Modern World.* New Haven, CT: Yale University Press, 372–398.

————. 1985. *Ripe for Resolution: Conflict and Intervention in Africa.* New York: Oxford University Press.

————. 1989. "Prenegotiation: Phases and Functions." In J. G. Stein, ed., *Getting to the Table: The Process of International Prenegotiation.* Baltimore: Johns Hopkins University Press, 3–17.

————. 1990. "Negotiating Effectively with Terrorists." In Barry Rubin, ed., *The Politics of Counterterrorism: The Ordeal of Democratic States.* Washington, DC: Foreign Policy Institute, 163–188.

————. 2000. "Ripeness: The Hurting Stalemate and Beyond." In Paul C. Stern and Daniel Druckman, eds., *International Conflict Resolution after the Cold War.* Washington, DC: National Academy Press, 225–250.

————. 2003. "Negotiating with Terrorists." *International Negotiation* 8: 443–450.

Zartman, I. William, and Maureen R. Berman. 1982. *The Practical Negotiator.* New Haven, CT: Yale University Press.

Zartman, I. William, and Guy Olivier Faure. 2005a. *Escalation and Negotiation in International Conflicts.* New York: Cambridge University Press.

————. 2005b. "The Dynamics of Escalation and Negotiation." In I. William Zartman and Guy O. Faure, eds., *Escalation and Negotiation in International Conflicts.* New York: Cambridge University Press, 3–19.

Zartman, I. William, and Victor Kremenyuk. 2005. *Peace versus Justice: Negotiating Forward-and Backward-Looking Outcomes.* Lanham, MD: Rowman and Littlefield.

Zartman, I. William, and J. Lewis Rasmussen, eds. 1997. *Peacemaking in International Conflict: Methods and Techniques.* Washington, DC: U.S. Institute of Peace.

Zartman, I. William, and Jeffrey Z. Rubin. 2000. *Power and Negotiation.* Ann Arbor: University of Michigan Press.

Zartman, I. William, and Jeffrey Z. Rubin. 2000a. "The Study of Power and the Practice of Negotiation." in I. William Zartman and Jeffrey Z. Rubin, eds., *Power and Negotiation*. Ann Arbor: University of Michigan Press, 3–28.

———. 2000b. "Symmetry and Asymmetry in Negotiation." In I. William Zartman and Jeffrey Z. Rubin, eds., *Power and Negotiation*. Ann Arbor: University of Michigan Press, 271–293.

Zawahiri, Ayman. 2001. "Knights under the Prophet's Banner." In Laura Mansfield, ed., *His Own Words: A Translation of the Writings of Dr. Ayman al Zawahiri,* 17–225.

Zeeman, E. C. 1977. *Catastrophe Theory: Selected Papers, 1972–1977.* Reading, MA: Addison-Wesley.

Ziring, Lawrence. 1984. *The Middle East Political Dictionary.* Santa Barbara, CA: ABC-Clio.

Index

About the Author

Karen Feste, professor at the Josef Korbel School of International Studies, University of Denver in Colorado, is director of its International Security graduate program and founded and directs the University's interdisciplinary M.A. Conflict Resolution Program. Her publications include *Intervention: Shaping the Global Order* (2003); *Expanding the Frontiers: Superpower Intervention in the Cold War* (1992); and *Plans for Peace: Negotiation and the Arab-Israeli Conflict* (1991). She received her Ph.D. from the University of Minnesota.